D0469919

Fifty Signs of Mental Illness

YALE UNIVERSITY PRESS **HEALTH & WELLNESS**

A Yale University Press Health & Wellness book is an authoritative, accessible source of information on a health-related topic. It may provide guidance to help you lead a healthy life, examine your treatment options for a specific condition or disease, situate a healthcare issue in the context of your life as a whole, or address questions or concerns that linger after visits to your healthcare provider.

Thomas E. Brown, Ph.D., *Attention Deficit Disorder: The Unfocused Mind in Children and Adults*

Ruth Grobstein, M.D., Ph.D., *The Breast Cancer Book: What You Need to Know to Make Informed Decisions*

James Hicks, M.D., *Fifty Signs of Mental Illness: A Guide to Understanding Mental Health*

Mary Jane Minkin, M.D., and Carol V. Wright, Ph.D., *A Woman's Guide to Menopause and Perimenopause*

Mary Jane Minkin, M.D., and Carol V. Wright, Ph.D., *A Woman's Guide to Sexual Health*

Catherine M. Poole, with DuPont Guerry IV, M.D.: *Melanoma: Prevention, Detection, and Treatment,* 2nd ed.

Barry L. Zaret, M.D., and Genell J. Subak-Sharpe, M.S., *Heart Care for Life: Developing the Program That Works Best for You*

James Whitney Hicks, M.D.

Fifty Signs of Mental Illness

A Guide to Understanding Mental Health

Yale University Press / New Haven and London

Designed by Nancy Ovedovitz and set in Sabon type by Binghamton Valley Composition. Printed in the United States of America by Vail-Ballou Press

The Library of Congress has cataloged the hardcover edition as follows:
Hicks, James Whitney.
Fifty signs of mental illness : a guide to understanding mental health / James Whitney Hicks.
p. cm.—(Yale University Press health & wellness)
Includes index.
ISBN 0-300-10657-2 (cloth : alk. paper)
1. Psychology, Pathological. 2. Mental illness. I. Title. II. Series.
RC454.H536 2005
616.89—dc22   2004021535

A catalogue record for this book is available from the British Library.

The paper in this book meets the guidelines for permanence and durability of the Committee on Production Guidelines for Book Longevity of the Council on Library Resources.

ISBN-13: 978-0-300-11694-6 (pbk. : alk. paper)
ISBN-10: 0-300-11694-2 (pbk. : alk. paper)

10   9   8   7   6   5   4   3

To Colin, *da te la vita prende ogni splendore*
To my parents for encouraging me to write, teach, and listen

Over the victim
We sing this song of madness
Distracting and destroying the mind.
　—Aeschylus, *The Furies*, c. 458 B.C.

Contents

Acknowledgments

Several friends and family members took time to make suggestions, read drafts of my manuscript, and provide valuable feedback. Thanks to Nishith and Suman Bhattacharyya, Alison Bethel and Alfredo Pastor, Colin Bethel, Jeanette Bethel, Terence Bethel, Lynn and Steve Clayton, Joe and Linda Hicks, Teri Jacobs, Louise Phillips, and Tom Wells. I especially appreciate the feedback on chapters dealing with child mental health provided by my colleague Paulina Loo, a child psychiatrist at Columbia University, College of Physicians and Surgeons, and director of the elementary school-based mental health program at Children's Hospital of New York-Presbyterian.

Elizabeth Law provided valuable guidance in the world of publishing. Thanks to my agent, Glen Hartley, and to my editors at Yale University Press: Jean E. Thomson Black, Erin Carter, and Jeffrey Schier. Thanks also to my colleagues at Yale University, Kirby Forensic Psychiatric Center, the New York State Office of Mental Health, and New York University Medical Center.

I am most indebted to the patients I have worked with in Connecticut, California, Ohio, and New York for sharing their personal, frightening, perplexing, and inspiring experiences with mental illness. I hope that this book will help others, as you have helped me, to understand.

Fifty Signs of Mental Illness

Introduction

This book will teach you what you need to know about mental illness, whether you have been diagnosed with a mental illness, have untreated problems, or care about someone who may be mentally ill. The book is organized alphabetically by symptom so that you can look up the specific symptoms that concern you. In each section you will learn how the symptom presents itself in various illnesses.

The symptoms of psychiatric illness frequently overlap and are easily misdiagnosed. For example, if you have bipolar illness, or manic depression, you will see, on average, at least three physicians over an eight-year period before you receive a correct diagnosis and proper treatment. If you feel anxious all the time, you may have depression, phobia, obsessive-compulsive disorder, panic disorder, a drug or alcohol problem, or any number of other underlying illnesses. This book will inform you about the possibilities and help you and your physician or therapist to make the correct diagnosis in your case.

In selecting topics, I have tried to use terms that are commonly used and easily recognized, even if their medical meanings are not widely known. The extensive index will help you find detailed discussions of specific illnesses, medications, and symptoms. Each topic includes multiple italicized references to other related topics. For example, when you read about *psychosis*, you will also be referred to *delusions*, *hallucinations*, and *nonsense*.

Many of us are initially reluctant to seek help from a professional. This book will help answer your questions and guide you to treatment, if treatment is needed. Moreover, each section suggests ways to cope with your specific concerns.

Everyone Experiences Mental Health Problems

Nearly one of every three of us experiences psychiatric symptoms each year. These range from the relatively minor, such as a short period of anxiety or grief during times of stress, to the severely disabling and painful. Nearly half of us have a family member or a close friend with serious mental illness. One common illness, depression, is the major cause of medical disability in the United States. Mental illness can kill: rates of suicide are as high as one in five in bipolar illness, one in six in depression, and one in ten in schizophrenia. Though poorly understood by most people, mental illness clearly rivals any other area of medicine in its widespread and serious impact on people's lives.

Fortunately, mental illness has been coming out of the closet in the past decade. The respected television journalist Mike Wallace has talked about his experiences with severe depression. The actor Margot Kidder has candidly discussed her recurrent bouts of manic psychosis and her recovery with medication. The best-selling author Stephen King has written about his struggles with alcohol and drug abuse. The Oscar-winning box office hits *A Beautiful Mind* and *Shine* dramatize the real-life stories of talented individuals who developed schizophrenia or similar mental illnesses. In 1999, the surgeon general of the United States issued a national report on mental health and illness, bringing the symptoms and treatment of psychiatric illness to the attention of physicians, public health workers, politicians, and the general public.

What Causes Mental Illness?

Scientists do not know exactly what causes mental illness. Like cancer, mental illness can strike anyone and has a variety of causes. Scientists are certain that genetic vulnerability plays a role in many mental illnesses, since the risk of becoming ill is greater if you have a close relative who suffers from depression, bipolar illness, schizophrenia, anxiety, or alcoholism, among others. However, no specific gene has yet been isolated that causes any of these illnesses. Even identical twins (who have identical genetic makeup) do not always develop the same mental illnesses.

Everyone agrees that stress plays a role in most mental illness. Even if you have a genetic vulnerability, the illness might not develop unless something disturbs your equilibrium. The loss of an important relationship—

for example, through divorce—is one of the most serious stresses to the mind. You may become sick after experiencing extraordinary dangers. On the other hand, serious illness can arise seemingly out of the blue, without any obvious stress or loss. You may have always thought of yourself as a confident and happy person until, over the course of a month or two, you find yourself feeling inexplicably hopeless and sad, confused and suspicious, or unable to sleep and concentrate.

Scientists are also uncertain about which physical changes in the brain lead to psychiatric symptoms. They have studied brain volume, hormone levels, blood flow, and other physiological data without finding conclusive answers. We know that abnormal proteins cause plaques in the brains of people who suffer from Alzheimer's dementia, but no smoking gun has been found for depression, schizophrenia, or other major illnesses. The medications that treat mental illness have complex effects on certain molecules in the brain, particularly those involved in the communication between brain cells. Scientists speculate that abnormal levels of these molecules may cause the underlying illness. This is why psychiatrists often talk about a chemical imbalance in the brain. Eventually it may be possible to connect specific genes to specific molecules to specific illnesses and, ultimately, to specific treatments. But the brain is a very complex organ, and scientists are far from achieving this goal. Scientific breakthroughs have been rare in other illnesses, such as diabetes and angina, even though the organs involved—in these cases, the pancreas and the heart—are considerably simpler than the brain.

Mental Health Problems Are Treatable

Effective treatments exist for most mental health problems. Some problems respond very well to psychotherapy, in which a skilled clinician talks to you and helps you to change your feelings, choices, and behaviors. For several decades medications have been available for successfully treating illnesses such as depression, anxiety, bipolar illness, and schizophrenia. Antidepressant medications are prescribed more widely in the United States than any other class of medication, with the exception of antibiotics. They are among the most effective of medications, with at least two-thirds of sufferers responding within weeks to the first antidepressant prescribed. Similar rates of improvement are seen in the treatment of other mental illnesses.

Why do our feelings, our thoughts, and our behaviors improve with medication? Most of us like to think of our minds as independent of our body and of the effects of medication. In fact, what we call the mind is inseparable from the physical functioning of the brain. Our ability to think, to perceive the outside world, and to experience emotions derives from the continuous cellular growth, electrical transmission, and movement of molecules within our brain. Even our memories are physically "stored" in the cellular structure of our brain. Like any other part of the body, the brain can sometimes experience stress. When that happens (and it does happen to all of us at one time or another), then either rest, the attention of friends and family, religious faith, or the passage of time—or a combination of these—can lead to recovery. On the other hand, the brain, like all other organs, can sometimes become sick to the extent that it will not get better without medical treatment.

Most of us now understand that there are medical explanations and treatments for many of our emotional pains and worries. Americans make more than twenty-six million visits to a psychiatrist each year. But most of us first turn to our primary care physicians, if we turn to anyone. Unfortunately, half of us who experience mental health problems do not seek treatment at all. And physicians often misdiagnose and undertreat the psychiatric symptoms that we bring to their attention.

Signs, Symptoms, Syndromes, and Disorders

The fifty topics that follow cover the full range of psychiatric disturbances. Most of them are what physicians refer to as signs and symptoms. A symptom is a medical complaint that you bring to the attention of your physician, such as chest pains or feeling sad. A sign is an abnormal finding by the physician, which you may or may not be aware of, such as high blood pressure or rapid speech.

A few of the fifty topics belong to a broader category, which physicians refer to as syndromes. A syndrome is a collection of signs and symptoms that typically occur together but which may be seen in several different illnesses. For example, pneumonia is a syndrome that typically includes cough, breathing difficulty, and fever but can be caused by several different germs. In this book *mania* and *psychosis* are syndromes made up of a number of signs and symptoms, most of which are also discussed as separate topics. Mania and psychosis can occur in several different illnesses, though they are most often associated with bipolar disorder and schizo-phrenia, respectively. *Depression* can refer to both a symptom and a syndrome (when sadness is combined with changes in energy, sleep, and appetite).

Psychiatrists have classified the wide range of mental disturbances into several specific disorders that are listed in the textbook *Diagnostic and Statistical Manual of Mental Disorders* (or *DSM*; see "Recommended Resources"). None of these disorders can be diagnosed exclusively on the basis of laboratory tests or other physical findings, so psychiatrists have reached a consensus, based on clinical experience and research, on the signs and symptoms that are required to make a specific diagnosis. Most of these illnesses have been well described and reliably diagnosed for decades, if not centuries. The disorders that psychiatrists diagnose and treat can be grouped into several major categories:

- Adjustment disorders (temporary emotional reactions to stress).
- Anxiety disorders (phobias, panic attacks, and disabling worries).
- Depression (which affects mood, sleep, appetite, sexual desire, and energy level).
- Bipolar disorder, formerly known as manic-depressive illness (periods of depression alternating with elevated mood and hyperactivity).
- Schizophrenia (hallucinations, delusions, and disorganized thinking).
- Obsessive-compulsive disorder (intrusive thoughts and repetitive behaviors).
- Post-traumatic stress disorders (reactions to life-threatening events).
- Personality disorders (persistent and extreme character styles that often lead to problems in relating to others).
- Drug and alcohol disorders (intoxication, addiction, and withdrawal).
- Physical complaints and worries (can reflect psychological difficulties).
- Sexual disorders (performance problems and unwanted urges and preoccupations).
- Autism, mental retardation, hyperactivity, and other learning disorders emerging in childhood.
- Dementia and delirium (memory loss and confusion, most common in the elderly).

You should keep in mind when reading this book that there is a wide range of variation in what can be considered normal. Even something as seemingly disturbed as hearing voices when no one is around may be normal in certain circumstances. We have a wide range of temperaments, cultural backgrounds, beliefs, experiences, and idiosyncrasies, and the world would be a boring place if this were not so. So when you read about personality disorders, you should be aware that shyness, impulsiveness, empathy, grandiosity, moodiness, and other traits exist on a spectrum. We all have these traits to some extent. Likewise, we all experience sadness, joy, and nervousness from time to time. We each get stressed-out, and sometimes we each make bad decisions. One goal of this book is to show the extent to which many of these experiences can be normal. You should resist the temptation to diagnosis yourself just because you once felt jealous or lost your temper, for example. Another goal of this book is to demonstrate how normal even the oddest behaviors can seem once you understand the underlying illness.

What Treatments Are Available for Mental Illness?

If you experience mental health problems, you should consult a professional at some point. Many mental health problems can worsen if left untreated, or they can occur again in the future. And there may be physical causes of your symptoms that only a physician can uncover. This book will help you to recognize your symptoms and communicate to your physician about them. It also provides valuable information about the benefits and side effects of available medications, which your physician may not discuss with you in depth. In some cases, you will learn that psychotherapy may be more appropriate than medication.

A psychiatrist is a medical doctor who specializes in the assessment and treatment of mental illnesses. Psychiatrists have an M.D. or a D.O. degree and are licensed to practice and prescribe as a physician. Fellowship training and board certification are signs of additional expertise or qualification. A psychiatrist is able to perform a medical examination, order tests, assess for signs and symptoms of mental illness, make a diagnosis, prescribe medication, perform psychotherapy, or make a referral to a qualified therapist. If you have a serious, chronic, or difficult-to-treat mental illness, then you should certainly see a psychiatrist.

General medical doctors are also able to make a psychiatric diagnosis and prescribe psychiatric medications. However, they have less experience than psychiatrists in working with mental illness. If you have mild to moderate problems with anxiety, depression, alcoholism, or nicotine addiction, then your regular doctor may be able to provide adequate treatment. A general doctor does not provide psychotherapy.

Psychologists and social workers can be licensed to provide psychotherapy. Some psychologists have a Ph.D. or Psy.D. degree and are referred to as doctors, though they are not medical doctors. They often have greater expertise than psychiatrists in providing specific types of psychotherapy and in administering psychological tests that assist in diagnosis. They can assess for signs and symptoms of mental illness and make a diagnosis. They can refer you to a psychiatrist for further medical workup or to see if you might benefit from medication. Social workers have a master's degree and can provide psychotherapy or more general counseling and support.

There are many types of psychotherapy, or talk therapy, that may help you feel better, either as a sole treatment or in combination with medication. The types of therapy that are generally most effective are those that use cognitive-behavioral techniques aimed at changing your habits and modifying attitudes that can cause or perpetuate your symptoms. These techniques are particularly helpful in the treatment of anxiety disorders. When you are in a personal crisis, you may benefit from counseling that helps you to problem-solve and improve your relationships with others. Couple therapy and family therapy focus on problems that have developed between people who care about each other. Relapse-prevention therapy is the treatment of choice for addiction, often supplemented with participation in a self-help group.

Psychodynamic therapies, which evolved out of the theories of Freud and his successors, try to explore your unconscious motivations and link your current patterns of behavior to past experiences. This may increase anxiety and other symptoms, at least initially, and has not been proven to be effective in the treatment of most serious mental illnesses. However, if your symptoms are mild, you may find a deeper exploration of your motivations and relationship patterns to be enlightening and enriching. Over time, psychodynamic therapy may help you to alter your personal patterns of behavior and long-standing ways of thinking that bother you.

All forms of psychotherapy share some basic features. You will receive information about psychological disturbances and the significance of your experiences. You will be reassured and feel more confident as a result of understanding the symptoms that have troubled you. You will have a safe and confidential relationship with a professional and be able to say things that you might not be able to share with anyone else. You will be given guidance and suggestions on how to understand and resolve your problems. You will feel glad that you took a positive step toward helping yourself feel better.

You may be able to find some of these features in a deep discussion with a parent, best friend, or religious leader. But mental health professionals are much more experienced with psychiatric symptoms and solutions and can provide you with more specific information. They can also take a fresh and objective look at your problems.

There are several types of medications for mental illness, often referred to as psychotropics. You may not need psychiatric medication in order to feel better. Whether you do depends on the type of problem you are having, the severity of your symptoms, and your willingness to devote time and energy to psychotherapy instead. Psychiatric medications are generally as effective, and often safer, than medications used for other medical conditions, like heart disease and diabetes. Medications never control your thoughts or alter your personality. Rather, they restore your ability to think clearly and to feel like yourself again. Medications and their potential side effects are described in detail, especially at the end of the chapters on *depression, anxiety, psychosis, mania, hyperactivity, memory loss, sleep problems,* and *physical complaints and pain.*

A Note About Sources of Information

The chapters that follow present specific figures for the prevalence of mental illnesses and response rates to various treatments, among other data. These numbers are derived from research studies and are easily found in most psychiatric textbooks. Much of what we know about the prevalence of mental illness in the general community derives from studies such as the Epidemiological Catchment Area Study conducted in the 1980s and the National Comorbidity Survey of the early 1990s.

If you are interested in further detailed information about mental health and illness, you may wish to refer to the comprehensive psychiatric textbooks listed in the appendix "Recommended Resources." The appendix also lists emergency hotlines, respected organizations, informative Web sites, and books about particular illnesses.

Anger

*The car in front of you slows down and edges toward the curb,
even though the light ahead is green. What is the driver up to? He
hasn't signaled to turn. You sound your horn and start to move
around him, but he hasn't pulled over enough to allow you to
pass. Meanwhile, the passenger door opens, and a woman steps
out. She turns and leans on the car and continues to talk to the
driver while the light turns red. Your vision seems to turn red as
well, and you lean on the horn harder. You roll down your window and attempt to shout at him over the blare of your horn. You
stop only when you spot a police officer down the block turning
your way.*

*You finally make it to the office, nearly half an hour late for a
meeting. As you rush in you practically throw your folders onto
the secretary's desk, nearly spilling her coffee in the process.
"Have those typed for me before lunch," you shout.*

Anger is one of the basic human emotions. When we feel threatened, harmed, obstructed, betrayed, or disrespected, our bodies
automatically prepare to fight or escape. Our heartbeats accelerate, our mouths become dry, our pupils constrict, our breaths
shorten, our speech becomes louder, and our bodies become tense.
Anger tends to escalate and be contagious. If you become angry
while speaking with someone, both of you may end up talking
louder and louder and adopting hostile postures.

Though anger is an instinctive reaction, the extent to which you
express anger depends much on your attitude. If you have a generally hostile view of the world, then you are likely to perceive
threats and feel a need to defend yourself in situations where oth-

ers would remain calm. You may tend to leap to conclusions and misinterpret the intentions of others. On the other hand, you may be deferential and too easily taken advantage of. As is the case with many other emotions, your demeanor, attitude, and emotional response reinforce each other. When you are physically tense or thinking unpleasant thoughts, you are much more likely to become angry than when you are physically relaxed and cheerful. Irritability is the term for this emotional tone that predisposes one to anger.

Psychiatrists have identified several defensive, or subconscious, ways in which we deal with anger. You may repress your anger. Some therapists believe that bottled-up anger comes to the surface in the form of *depression*. You may sublimate anger by channeling your aggressive energy into a good cause, such as fighting against political oppression. You may express your anger passively—for example, by refusing to talk or by dragging your feet on an important project. You may express your anger but displace it onto easier targets; if your boss humiliates you, for example, you may feel unable to respond until you get home, where you scream at your wife instead. When you lose your temper, it is common to rationalize your behavior, claiming, for example, that you were drunk and not yourself. You may also project your anger, accusing your target of being the hostile one. We all utilize these defense mechanisms from time to time.

Anger is of concern to psychiatrists because it can lead to hostility and violence and because it is a feature in several psychiatric conditions. If you are not generally an angry person but find you are increasingly irritable and prone to losing your temper, then you may be responding to *stress*. Anger, nervousness, and sadness are all typical responses to stress, and sometimes they occur together. For example, if you are having financial difficulties, you may find yourself becoming tearful on the way home, snapping at your kids, and having trouble sleeping. Anger is often a reaction to the unexpected loss of a loved one, or being diagnosed with a serious illness (see "Grief"). After a *traumatic* event, you may find yourself constantly on edge and prone to overreact, sometimes with angry outbursts. If you develop post-traumatic stress disorder (or PTSD), you may purposely avoid situations in which you are likely to lose your temper.

Anger and irritability can sometimes be signs of clinical *depression*, especially in those who are uncomfortable expressing sadness or emotional vulnerability. Anger also can emerge during a *manic* episode, when people fail to realize how important and brilliant you are, or when people seek to restrain or obstruct you, for example, by putting you in a hospital.

Anger is a prominent feature of several personality disorders. If you have a *paranoid* personality style, you view everyone as potentially threatening. You are quick to take offense and to respond in kind. In both paranoid and narcissistic (see "Grandiosity") personality disorders, you feel that you are superior to most people you know. You blame others for keeping you from reaching your potential. You may blame specific people, or you may express your resentment toward a whole group of people, for example, blaming immigrants for invading the job market when you lose a job. If you have a borderline personality disorder (see "Self-Esteem Problems"), you are often full of rage. You express anger at others when you feel that they have emotionally attacked, betrayed, or abandoned you. You may be angry at yourself when you feel worthless or ashamed, and you may consider *suicide* or indulge in *self-mutilation*. Sometimes, in a passive-aggressive manner, you hurt yourself in order to make others feel bad.

Anger seems to be the most genuine and characteristic emotion in *antisocial* personality disorder. If you have an antisocial personality, you tend to violate rules and the rights of others, and you feel entitled to do so. You lose your temper quickly whenever you do not get your way, and you often express anger to intimidate others. Most domestic violence (see "Jealousy") and violence against strangers is committed by individuals with antisocial personality disorders.

Even if you are not normally an angry person, you may be prone to become angry when you are drunk. Cocaine and amphetamines, like alcohol, can increase irritability and decrease common sense. When *intoxicated,* you become more provocative and willing to express your thoughts and feelings without thinking about them first. If you are prone to anger, then being drunk or high will likely bring out the worst in you.

Hate is a chronic form of anger. Hate is not a sign of mental illness on its own, but psychiatrists, sociologists, and religious leaders would probably agree that it is rarely healthy. Persistent hate usually reflects a failure to utilize more constructive coping strategies to resolve angry feelings. Hate is often combined with prejudice, such that you hate individuals solely because of their membership in a larger group. Prejudices arise out of faulty thinking, attitudes such as generalization, entitlement, resentment, and an unwillingness to consider evidence that challenges your beliefs. Nevertheless, nearly everyone seems to have the potential to develop prejudices.

How to Cope with Anger

If you suffer from frequent and disturbing angry feelings, you may benefit from anger management, a type of psychotherapy. You identify your tendency to perceive hostility in others when it is not intended, and to under-appreciate your own proneness to violence and anger. You learn the triggers to your anger so that you can avoid them or defuse them rather than reacting automatically. You learn relaxation techniques (see "Anxiety") to decrease tense and irritable feelings. You learn coping strategies and try to reduce the level of stress in your life. You practice asserting yourself without being threatening. You gain confidence in your ability to remain in control of your feelings. You may still lose your temper from time to time, but you regain control faster.

If you care about someone who has problems with anger, you should encourage him to seek treatment. You may be scared to suggest treatment to someone who is easily angered and might resent the implication that he is at fault. You might find it easier to engage his interest in couple therapy, even if you think that he is the only one who needs help. When your loved one is irritable, you should try to give him the time and space he needs to cool down. You want to communicate to him that you trust his ability to restrain his anger, rather than exacerbating the situation by yelling at him or accusing him of being out of control. Situations are more likely to get out of hand if both of you become angry. On the other hand, you should not tolerate anger, threats, or abuse, and you should calmly make this clear to your partner once he has cooled down. If you are concerned for your safety, then you should enlist the assistance of family, friends, or a domestic violence hotline before, or instead of, engaging in any confrontation.

Antisocial Behavior

Man, nobody ever cuts you a break. You're released from prison after three years, and nobody comes to pick you up. What do they expect you to do, walk home?

You look around and notice a cup of money on the sidewalk next to a beggar sleeping nearby. Hey, if that drunk's going to pass out and not watch his cup, he deserves to have it stolen. It's like he wants to give it away. No wonder he's homeless.

So you take the money, which is enough to buy some weed at the corner. You make your way to a subway station, where you decide to jump the turnstile even though you still have more than enough money to pay for a ride. You should have looked around first, because a cop is standing just around the corner. You quickly drop the joint and run.

Some people seem to believe that rules do not apply to them. They lie, cheat, steal, fight, rape, and intimidate others in order to satisfy their own desires and needs, without concern for their victims. Psychiatrists refer to these as antisocial (or, sometimes, dissocial, sociopathic, or psychopathic) behaviors. (The term asocial is sometimes confused with antisocial, but an asocial person is someone who *avoids* social situations because of shyness, disinterest, or a fear of embarrassment.)

You may engage in antisocial behavior for a variety of reasons, and many of them have nothing to do with mental illness. For example, you may steal food to feed your starving child because you have no money. You may lie about your age to get into a bar where your favorite band is performing. You may fight a bully who has been harassing you so that others will not think you are weak. You may underreport your income on your tax forms if you think you can get away with it. These are all antisocial behaviors, and, depending on the circumstances, they may be unethical or illegal, but they are also understandable. As isolated behaviors, they do not necessarily suggest a psychological problem.

On the other hand, people who have an underlying personality disorder often engage in antisocial behaviors whenever they can and not just as a last resort. If you have an antisocial personality, you believe that rules and laws were made to be broken. Since your teenage years or earlier you have repeatedly been in trouble with your parents, teachers, and the police. As an adult, your behaviors may have led to fines, arrests, and incarceration. Or you may have engaged in fraudulent business practices, which are more difficult to uncover.

Outside of your criminal activities, you are reckless and *impulsive*. You dare a friend to drive home drunk. You abandon an infant after agreeing to baby-sit. You borrow money without considering how you will repay it. Easily bored, you take chances without thinking of the consequences to yourself or others. When bad things happen, you blame others or find excuses for your own behavior. Over and over, you claim that you would straighten up and fly right if only someone would give you the chance.

Scientists believe that approximately three out of one hundred men in America (and perhaps one out of one hundred women) have an antisocial personality disorder. As you would expect, the rates are much higher in jails and prisons, where half to three-quarters of inmates have an antisocial personality disorder.

Psychopathy Refers to a Particularly Dangerous Antisocial Personality Style

In the last few decades, scientists have reintroduced the term psychopathy in an attempt to identify individuals whose antisocial personalities make them especially dangerous. The general public has come to use the term to refer to particularly ruthless and seemingly crazy criminal offenders, and psychiatrists had abandoned the term because of its imprecision and stigma. Nevertheless, the term is now being used to identify a subset of patients with antisocial personality disorder who are particularly callous, manipulative, and unable to constrain themselves.

If you have a psychopathic personality, you are a smooth talker and you intuitively recognize how to approach people in order to charm them or gain their sympathy. You are skillful at feigning emotions, and you manipulate the emotions of others, who initially find you to be sincere and engaging. But if someone confronts you or gets in your way, you quickly become *angry* or vindictive. You feel that you are the center of the world and entitled to do whatever you want. If people interfere, they deserve what they get. You beat up your girlfriend, steal from your family, and take advantage of strangers without feeling remorse. Others may view you as quick-tempered and cold-blooded.

Many individuals have an antisocial personality disorder, or engage in antisocial behaviors, without demonstrating the remorseless, conning, and entitled personality traits seen in psychopathy. Likewise, many individuals are skillful at *deception* or manipulating the emotions of others but do not engage in a wide array of antisocial behaviors. But if you have both the emotional and behavioral traits characteristic of psychopathy, then you are likely to be extremely dangerous. Many scientific studies have demonstrated that criminals with a psychopathic personality commit more violence, are more likely to attack strangers, are more likely to use firearms, and are much more likely to commit additional crimes.

At least one in ten prison inmates has a psychopathic personality disorder. No one knows how many individuals in the community at large have psychopathic traits. Because of their skill in manipulating and deceiving others, some may be able to escape arrest in spite of engaging in ongoing fraudulent and abusive behaviors. If you have a psychopathic personality, you may thrive in environments where violence, corruption, and exploitation are tolerated or encouraged, such as street gangs, organized crime, shady business dealings, civil war, terrorism, and spying.

Sadistic Traits Involve Intentional Cruelty to Others

Psychiatrists use the term sadism to describe the tendency to enjoy inducing pain, suffering, fear, or humiliation in others. If you are sadistic, you feel more powerful when you dominate others. As a youth, you may torture animals, set fires, and bully others. As an adult, you may abuse your spouse and children and seek out jobs in which you can publicly criticize, discipline, or control others. You may sexually harass or coerce others in order to control them, and you may find coercion to be sexually exciting.

Serial rapists and serial killers are usually sexually sadistic. If you suffer from sexual sadism, you have probably fantasized for years about forcing sex upon unwilling partners before you actually committed your first crime. You enjoy horror movies and true crime magazines that depict helpless victims in terror and pain. You may practice on animals, torturing them before you assault humans. You may have difficulty becoming sexually excited unless pain or coercion of another person is involved. Individuals who commit serial killings enjoy physically torturing their victim. Often they have sex with the body only after death, or masturbate later while recalling their victim's tortured expressions or brutalized body.

Many people enjoy sexual role-playing and fantasy that includes domination, humiliation, leather outfits, and props. But in the absence of psychopathic traits, such behavior is carried out among consenting partners without any ill intentions. The sexual sadist is not interested in playing. He wants to induce genuine fear, suffering, helplessness, and disfigurement. Sexual sadism probably arises from a combination of psychopathic personality traits and a *sexual preoccupation* with pain and domination.

How Does Antisocial Personality Evolve?

Antisocial behavior is very costly and harmful to society as a whole. Everyone would like to know what causes it and how to prevent it. Unfortunately, we have many theories but few conclusive answers, even to the narrower question of what causes antisocial personality disorder.

Scientists have found that antisocial personality disorder runs in families. When one identical twin is diagnosed with the disorder, the twin also has it more than half the time. Other first-degree relatives are at risk about five times more than in families in which the disorder has not been diagnosed. Most scientists believe that there is a genetic predisposition to many antisocial traits, such as *impulsiveness, anger,* need for stimulation, and difficulty relating emotionally to others. A child's temperament may be oppositional from an early age, provoking parents to inflict harsher punishments or to give in too easily to the child's demands. A therapist may later blame the parents for the child's disorder, but his antisocial traits may have been the cause, not the result, of his parents' treatment.

It is difficult to separate genetic factors from environmental factors in the development of a child. A parent with antisocial attitudes may be unable to instill a respect for the rights of others in his child, even if he does not pass on antisocial genes. Physical abuse or neglect during childhood has been associated with higher rates of antisocial personality disorder as an adult. When raised in a neglectful or abusive home, a predisposed child may learn that the world is hostile, affection is unpredictable, punishment is indiscriminate, and violence and lies are tools for survival. Antisocial personality disorder has been found to be more common among poor families, especially among children of unskilled parents, but this almost certainly reflects social circumstances (including malnutrition, inadequate schooling, impoverished opportunities, and local criminal role models) rather than genes.

Antisocial personality disorder begins to manifest itself early in life. During childhood, you may be diagnosed with oppositional defiant disorder. At school and at home, you refuse to do what you are asked to do, and you lose your temper and throw tantrums when you do not get your way. You seem to argue about everything, insisting on ice cream one day, screaming that you hate ice cream the next. You have little patience and little sympathy for the needs of other children. (All children are self-centered to some degree, but they generally learn to get along and share toys and attention.) You may disobey a rule or request simply for the sake of asserting yourself and provoking others. For example, if your father asks you to come to the table for dinner, you may run out of the room even though you are hungry and had been looking forward to sitting down to eat. Your parents and teachers find that every interaction with you is a struggle. They may become frustrated and arbitrarily give in to your tantrums or impose unnecessary restrictions. You feel like a problem child.

Many children grow out of these behaviors, but by the end of elementary school some show signs of a conduct disorder, a childhood predecessor of antisocial personality disorder. If you have conduct disorder, you repeatedly violate the rights of others. At school you provoke fights, bully other children, skip classes, smoke in the bathroom, and cheat. At home you defy your parents and fight with your siblings. In your free time, you may torture animals, set fires, drink alcohol and use drugs, commit petty crimes, and sexually harass or assault others.

Conduct problems in childhood do not always lead to an antisocial personality as an adult. Sometimes your childhood environment is unstable, or you have an underlying *learning problem,* attention-deficit *hyperactivity* disorder, *anxiety,* or *depression.* Children are not able to express themselves with the psychological sophistication of an adult, and misbehaving may be the single way in which they can express a wide range of problems.

Adolescence is also a time of surging emotions, impulsivity, and experimentation. Many normal adolescents will break rules, try drugs and alcohol, explore sexual outlets, fight with siblings, and infuriate their parents, yet most will not grow up to have an antisocial personality disorder. In fact, even most juvenile delinquents do not become criminals as adults. However, if you have already committed a wide range of antisocial acts from an early age and demonstrate increasing cruelty and manipulation in interactions with others as a teenager, then the likelihood increases that you will be diagnosed with antisocial personality disorder as an adult.

Sometimes antisocial behaviors emerge for the first time in an adult as a result of another mental illness. If you suffer a *manic* episode, for example, you may behave recklessly as a result of decreased inhibitions and grandiose feelings that you are above the law. When you recover from your illness, you may be mortified by your uncharacteristic behavior. Drug and alcohol *intoxication* can also decrease inhibitions and judgment, leading you to behave in an inappropriate manner with others, or to commit impulsive crimes that you would have avoided if you had been sober. Even when you are sober, your *cravings* for drugs or sex may lead you to engage in criminal behavior to support your habit. Studies have found that drug and alcohol addiction, much more than any other mental illness, is associated with violent behavior. Finally, some people develop an antisocial personality style for the first time as the result of a physical blow to the head. Damage to the frontal lobes of the brain in particular is associated with increased *impulsiveness,* irritability, recklessness, and disregard for the rights of others.

How to Cope with Antisocial Behavior

The primary goal of parents, educators, therapists, and social scientists in approaching antisocial personality traits should be to prevent them from developing in the first place. Once established, antisocial personality disorder does not appear to be treatable. Some mood-stabilizing medications may be useful in decreasing *impulsiveness,* but medications do not change character and values. Likewise, no form of psychotherapy has been found to cure antisocial personality. If you have an antisocial personality disorder, you have difficulty learning from your mistakes. You are more interested in short-term gains rather than long-term consequences. When therapy is helpful, it is usually because you have decided that it is in your interest to conform your behavior. *Anger* management therapy may be helpful if you are motivated.

Children and adolescents who demonstrate conduct problems should be evaluated immediately for treatable conditions. A neglectful or abusive home environment should be changed; for example, perhaps relatives who can model appropriate social behavior can be enlisted to instill values such as honesty and respect for others. Counselors can help exasperated parents learn how to deal with children who are frequently defiant.

If you have a child who is oppositional, you should establish clear limits on inappropriate behavior. A time-out, which involves the child going to a predetermined place to sit quietly for several minutes, is a useful tool for several reasons. First, it immediately defuses an emotional situation. Second, since you do not continue to talk to the child while he is in time-out, he does not receive positive attention for misbehaving. And third, he is not allowed to play instead. As part of the time-out routine, the child is first given the opportunity to go unassisted with the understanding that it will last longer if he does not; thus he learns to exercise responsibility. After a period of good behavior, the child is allowed to come out of time-out, at which time he is asked if he understands why his behavior was not appropriate and how he might have behaved instead. He is provided encouragement for answering these questions, and for those occasions when he demonstrates better behavior in the future.

Sometimes children become confused when they are punished inconsistently. You should always strive to respond in the same way to inappropriate behavior, rather than condoning it when you are in a good mood and punishing it when you are in a bad mood. That mode of parenting teaches your child to take advantage of people's moods rather than follow social expectations consistently. You should also remember that you are the parent and not back down when your child is purposefully defiant. If you give in to a tantrum, you inadvertently teach your child to be more defiant in the future.

If you are in a relationship with someone who is antisocial, you need to be realistic and consider whether it is in your interest to remain involved. If you must continue to deal with someone who has the potential to exploit, deceive, and harm you, then you should at least set clear limits on those behaviors. You should realize that giving in to his pleas, cons, or threats will not change him or your relationship for the better. You should establish which behaviors you are willing to tolerate and which behaviors you will not tolerate, and then do not relent. If, at times, you feel that your safety is endangered, you may have to consider calling the police. In such a relationship you should arrange to interact only in those settings where you feel safe, for example, when other family members are present.

Anxiety

You've always been a nervous person, but with your daughter's wedding coming up in a few months you've become a wreck. You lie in bed late at night thinking about the arrangements—and the bills. Your stomach is always queasy, and you've been popping aspirin for headaches nearly every day. You run around the house taking notes and making phone calls, but sometimes you stop in the middle of the room and can't remember what you were doing.

Today you've spent the past hour crying, because your daughter called and had the nerve to tell you that you're annoying everyone! What could she mean? You're only trying to help.

Anxiety is one of the most pervasive mental health problems. It is a prominent feature in most mental illnesses ranging from depression to alcoholism to schizophrenia. Anxiety in one form or another is the hallmark of panic disorder, obsessive-compulsive disorder, post-traumatic stress disorder, and phobias. But anxiety also occurs as a more or less chronic illness of its own in about one in twenty people. If you are constantly anxious in your daily life about typical events and responsibilities, then you may have a generalized anxiety disorder.

Anxiety is more than just nervousness. In fact, you are more likely to consult your general physician than a psychiatrist because most of your symptoms seem like *physical complaints*. Your muscles are tense, and headaches are common. You may feel a tightness in your neck, shoulder, and back muscles. Stomach complaints range from a butterfly sensation to cramps, indigestion, nausea, and diarrhea. Your blood pressure and pulse may rise, and you can feel short of breath. You may sweat excessively. You are in constant motion, unable to relax. You bounce your legs, play with your hands, and putter about without a clear goal in mind. You have difficulty focusing on tasks at hand. You worry all day and have trouble setting your concerns aside at night (see "Sleep Problems"). Your sleep is restless, and you have nightmares. During the day you are tired and irritable. You feel put-upon by others, overwhelmed by expectations. You burst into tears without warning.

Psychiatrists are unsure what causes generalized anxiety. Scientists have observed that the function of certain molecules in the brain (especially gamma-aminobutyric acid, or GABA, and serotonin receptors) is affected by medications that reduce or exacerbate anxiety. But it remains unclear why some people are more vulnerable than others. Generalized anxiety appears to be about twice as common in women as in men. Anxiety usually does not run in families, though related conditions like panic disorder and depression are more common among family members. Most people who suffer from anxiety recall being worried even as children, though the degree of anxiety fluctuates throughout life, in response to life *stresses*. Stressful events pile up, and if you have had four or more in the past year your risk of anxiety increases almost tenfold. Anxiety can be distracting and disabling, and you may be more vulnerable to *depression* or drug or alcohol abuse in response to your constant anxiety. About one fourth of those who suffer from anxiety will eventually develop a *panic* attack.

If you suffer from constant anxiety, you should see a physician and receive a full medical workup to make sure that you do not have an underlying and potentially treatable medical condition. Heart conditions, asthma, thyroid problems, and other medical illnesses can cause anxiety. It will be difficult to diagnose anxiety if you are currently using alcohol or drugs, since both *intoxication* and withdrawal can cause anxiety. In fact, if you drink more than a cup or two of coffee each day, you may be experiencing the side effects of caffeine rather than an anxiety disorder. If you feel anxiety immediately upon awakening, you may be withdrawing from alcohol, nicotine, or other drugs. Anxiety is a common feature of *depression,* and feelings of worthlessness, hopelessness, and guilt may be signs that depression is the primary problem.

If you are nervous about something specific and unusual and not about life in general, then you probably have a psychiatric condition other than a generalized anxiety disorder. If you have a phobia, for example, you may be nervous only around crowds or certain animals (see "Fears"). If you have obsessive-compulsive disorder, you may be anxious about your specific *obsessions*. For example, you may worry endlessly that you forgot to turn off the stove before leaving the house. If you have post-*traumatic* stress disorder, you may become worried in situations that remind you of terrifying experiences in your past. If you have schizophrenia (see "Psychosis"), you may be anxious because of frightening *hallucinations* or *delusional* fears. It is important to distinguish between these different conditions because they each have different treatments.

How to Cope with Anxiety

Both medication and psychotherapy can be helpful in the treatment of anxiety. In psychotherapy you will learn about anxiety and be reassured that you are not medically ill. You will be instructed to stop using drugs, alcohol, and caffeine. Your counselor will help you to work through your problems by listing your challenges and seeking step-by-step solutions. If your anxiety arises mostly from your relationship with another person, you may be invited to participate in couple therapy to learn how to communicate your needs and resolve conflicts more effectively.

You may learn relaxation exercises that will help you to relax mentally and physically. You will learn how to progressively relax your muscles all over your body, from your toes to your face. You will slow your breathing and concentrate on calming thoughts. It is difficult to become anxious when you have successfully relaxed the tone and movements of your body. In fact, similar techniques can be learned outside of therapy in meditation or yoga. Regular exercise can also have a relaxing effect.

In psychotherapy, you may also explore the underlying conflicts that lead you to be anxious. Once the sources of your anxiety have been identified, you can develop more effective methods of reducing and coping with stress when it arises. You should be aware that psychotherapy of this sort may initially increase your anxiety level as you explore deeper issues that the anxiety may mask.

If someone you care about is anxious, you can be helpful by remaining calm and soothing. Anxiety can be contagious, and you should resist the natural inclination to get as worked up as your loved one. You do not have to share her worries. You do not need to argue, which may exacerbate the situation. Instead, try to be reassuring and help her to deal with her concerns one at a time.

Anxiolytic Medications

Several medications are effective in the treatment of anxiety. The class of medications that works most rapidly is referred to by its chemical name benzodiazepine. Medications in this class include lorazepam (Ativan), diazepam (Valium), clonazepam (Klonopin), alprazolam (Xanax), and others. These medications have identical effects and side effects, and the only difference is in the dosage and onset and duration of action. They all reduce anxiety, relax muscles, and cause a vague sense of well-being. They can also cause sleepiness, which is why they are sometimes referred to as sedative or hypnotic (meaning sleep inducing) medications.

The side effects at higher doses are similar to those that you might experience when drinking alcohol. The medications can be disinhibiting, and you might say or do things that you later find embarrassing. You may become unsteady on your feet and have difficulty performing tasks that require manual skill or concentration. For this reason you should not drive or operate machinery when using these medications. If you take them in higher doses, you may feel like you have a hangover the next day. In addition, you may have trouble remembering what you did after taking the medication.

Physicians have prescribed several other medications to reduce anxiety, but these have a broader range of side effects. Along with the benzodiazepines, these medications are sometimes referred to as minor tranquilizers and include the barbiturates, such as pentobarbital (Nembutal) and amobarbital (Amytal), which are rarely used for anxiety today because they can be dangerous at higher doses. Both the benzodiazepines and barbiturates can be addicting. If you have been taking them for a long time, you will experience symptoms of withdrawal, including a return of anxiety, when you stop. Both can also cause *depression* when taken for extended periods.

Some physicians prescribe antihistamine medications, such as diphenhydramine (Benadryl) or hydroxyzine (Vistaril or Atarax), for short-term relief of anxiety. But these medications also cause sedation, dizziness, dry mouth, constipation, and clumsiness. In the elderly, they can cause confusion and falls. They are also probably not as effective.

Long-Term Treatments Exist for Anxiety

Fortunately, we now have effective anxiety treatments that are not sedating in the short term or addicting over the long term. Buspirone (Buspar) is a chemically unique medication. It has few side effects and does not cause sedation, disinhibition, confusion, or clumsiness. As is the case with many medications used in psychiatry, you have to be patient; buspirone has to be taken on a daily basis for two to six weeks before the anxiety-reducing effects become apparent. If buspirone works for you, you will begin to worry less, sleep better, and suffer fewer vague physical ailments.

Many antidepressant medications (see "Depression") have also been shown to be powerful treatments for anxiety, whether or not you also suffer from depression. The SSRIs (serotonin-specific reuptake inhibitors) are the treatment of choice in most cases, because they have fewer side effects than the older tricyclic antidepressants. The antidepressants work not only on generalized anxiety, but also on *panic* attacks and on the *obsessions* and *compulsions* that are experienced in obsessive-compulsive disorder. As with buspirone, the antidepressant medications must be taken for several weeks before they become effective. They should be prescribed at very low doses initially, since they can sometimes cause a temporary increase in anxiety, restlessness, and insomnia.

Some physicians use benzodiazepines for the short-term relief of anxiety while waiting for buspirone or the antidepressant medication to kick in. Some studies have suggested that this strategy only postpones the inevitable, since anxiety returns temporarily when the benzodiazepine is stopped. However, if you are suffering from so much anxiety that you cannot wait several weeks for medication to start working, then this strategy may be useful for you.

One over-the-counter product has been touted for its anxiolytic effects. Kava, which now comes in pill form, is derived from a pepper plant from the South Pacific, where it is consumed as a brew. Like other botanical products, it is poorly studied, and the quality is variable. Kava can cause liver and skin problems in addition to the sort of clumsiness and slurred speech seen in alcohol intoxication. Marijuana, which also induces a mellow feeling in most users, is commonly used though illegal.

It should be noted that there is a large placebo response in the treatment of anxiety. About one third of treated individuals improve even though they are taking a dummy pill, suggesting that some of the effects of medication are nonspecific. You may feel better in part because you have been reassured that the medication will help you.

Appetite Disturbances

You thought you were doing better this semester, but your report card was a disaster. You got two B's and a C. You run all the way home from school and head straight for the refrigerator freezer, where you find an unopened quart of strawberry ice cream. Your mother won't be home for a couple of hours, so you'll have time to run out and get some more, you think, as you start scooping straight out of the container and into your mouth. You've been starving all day. You had just a banana for breakfast and nothing for lunch. The ice cream feels cool and creamy. Nothing else makes you feel this good. You realize you're eating more than you need. In fact, you've nearly consumed the whole quart, and your stomach is starting to hurt. But you want to finish it off. There's no point in leaving just a few scoops at the bottom.

You take the empty container outside to the trash so no one will find it. On your way back into the house, you feel nauseated. Why did you do it? Now you just have more calories to burn off. Couldn't you have stopped after a bite or two? Your whole life is out of control. Your grades are bad, you're overweight, and you can't control your eating. You head upstairs to the bathroom, bend over the toilet, and vomit. You keep going until all of the ice cream is out of your stomach and you feel the cleansing burn of acid in your mouth. You flush, rinse your mouth, and spray air freshener around the room.

Appetite is one of the basic human drives. Our bodies let us know when we need to eat and when we have eaten too much. But in many mental illnesses, such as depression, the drive to eat can be disturbed, along with other natural functions. Psychiatrists refer to these changes in natural drives as neuro-vegetative signs of mental illness. In some mental illnesses known as eating disorders, appetite is not the problem so much as your control over how much you eat. You may eat too little in a desire to be thin, or you may find it hard to stop eating once you have eaten enough. Eating disorders seem mostly to be a modern phenomenon found almost exclusively in developed countries. The incidence of obesity is rising with the unprecedented availability of food in America today. And many people engage in unhealthy practices in an attempt to control their weight, inspired in part by our idealization of thin bodies.

Anorexia Nervosa Is an Illness of Eating Too Little

The word "anorexia" means lack of appetite. Many medical conditions—for example, viral illnesses or chemotherapy for treatment of cancer—can suppress appetite. Anorexia nervosa refers to a psychiatric condition: an unhealthy and purposeful reduction in eating with the goal of becoming thinner. To be diagnosed with anorexia nervosa you must be significantly underweight. Approximately one in two hundred women in America has anorexia nervosa at some point during her lifetime. Anorexia nervosa is rare among men, with rates about ten times lower. The illness usually has its onset during adolescence, when you are likely to first become concerned about remaining thin.

If you suffer from anorexia, you restrict how much you eat so that you will lose weight. Your restrictions may start as regular dieting, but unlike most dieters you continue to restrict when you are actually underweight. You view yourself as obese or unshapely. You look in the mirror and see pads of fat where others see only skin and bones. You think that your body is flabby and ugly. In this way, anorexia is similar to body dysmorphic disorder and other *body image problems*. In spite of the objective evidence, you feel that you can never be thin enough. You weigh yourself continually, always trying to lose more pounds.

There is actually nothing wrong with appetite in anorexia nervosa. You do feel hungry. In fact, you feel hungry and think about food all of the time, at least in the early stages of the illness. You may obsess about food, collect recipes, cook elaborate meals for others, and cut your food up and arrange it on your plate; you do anything but eat it. Only late in the illness, as you become physically ill, does your appetite disappear. In spite of feeling hungry most of the time, you exert great control over your appetite and eating.

If you have anorexia, you probably do not consider it a problem. You are convinced that you need to lose weight, and you become angry if anyone suggests otherwise. You are terrified of gaining weight. You realize that others may be concerned about you, so you try to hide your weight loss and your strategies for losing weight. You wear bulky clothing that conceals your silhouette. When you cook for others, you serve yourself little. You quietly hide bites of food in your napkin or purse. You may refuse to eat at all in front of others. I treated one patient who used to hide her food in potted plants at restaurants. Another woman went to great lengths, even while hospitalized, pretending to drink a nutritional shake while in fact pouring it into a large plastic cup concealed in her baggy sweater.

If you suffer from anorexia nervosa, you are at risk for developing other illnesses. After your body has used up its stores of fat, your muscles begin to break down to provide the fuel to keep you alive. You become cachectic, the term physicians use to refer to the resulting wasted appearance. Bones become more brittle. Your menstrual periods stop, and you experience other changes in the balance of your hormones. You have trouble staying warm. You may have stomach cramps and constipation. You can develop problems with your heart, including irregular rhythms and sudden death. The risk of dying for those who have anorexia nervosa is approximately one in twenty every decade, a rate more than ten times higher than the average morbidity rate.

If you have anorexia, it is likely that you also experience *anxiety,* irritability, *fatigue, obsessions,* and *compulsions.* Some of these symptoms may be caused by malnutrition's effect on the brain and may improve as you gain weight.

Not everyone who is thin or who diets has anorexia nervosa. In fact, most teenage girls diet. In most developed countries, at least in the past half century, thinness has been idealized. Men and women read magazines that encourage them to lose weight and develop chiseled muscles in order to appear healthy and sexually desirable. In some entertainment and sports occupations, low body fat is required. For these reasons, many people restrict their eating to be slim. Reasonable dieting can, of course, be healthy, as long as you meet your nutritional needs. Most Americans eat too much and could easily afford to diet. However, if you get into the habit of dieting in order to maintain a thin physique, your risk of over-dieting and developing anorexia nervosa increases. You can lose perspective and think of yourself as obese or unshapely when your weight is actually on the low side for someone your size.

In Bulimia, Binge Eating Is Followed by Purging

Anorexia requires tremendous control. Bulimia nervosa, which is about twice as common as anorexia, involves a loss of control over eating. If you suffer from bulimia, you have episodes in which you binge. In a short period of time, you consume a huge amount of food, much more than you need. You may eat a day's worth of calories in a single binge, and you may binge several times a day. I have treated patients who could eat a bag of cookies, a gallon of ice cream, and a chocolate bar in one sitting. You realize that you are overeating, and you feel like you are out of control. Often you feel like you cannot stop once you have started, even as your stomach begins to hurt and you begin to feel nauseated.

Not surprisingly, if you suffer from bulimia, you may have difficulty remaining thin. In order to keep your weight under control, you engage in other behaviors. You may vomit immediately after bingeing, emptying your stomach. You may restrict your eating at other times. You may use laxatives to speed the food through your digestive system before it can be absorbed. You may use appetite-suppressing stimulants. You may over-exercise. Patients I have worked with spend hours each day on exercise machines and much of the rest of their time puttering about in constant motion. Though diuretics have no effect on your body fat or intake of calories, you may use them to lose weight in the form of crucial body fluids.

If you have bulimia nervosa, you are at risk for several other psychiatric conditions. In contrast to those who suffer from anorexia nervosa, you probably feel ashamed over your binge eating, which you see as a lack of control. You are at risk of developing *depression* and *anxiety*. You are prone to other *impulsive* behaviors, including drug or alcohol abuse, *self-mutilation,* shoplifting, and *suicidal thoughts* or acts. Even though your weight can be normal, you may be in physical danger. Vomiting, laxative abuse, and diuretic abuse can cause dehydration and dangerous fluctuations in natural salts (especially sodium and potassium). This may lead to seizures, irregular heart rhythms, and sudden death. You may develop inflammation of the stomach or esophagus and tooth decay from vomiting stomach acid.

Scientists do not know what causes bulimia. As with anorexia, bulimia is more common in women and usually has its onset during teenage or early adult years, the time when girls are vulnerable to gaining weight and are under tremendous pressure to appear thin. Anorexia and bulimia overlap, with restricting, bingeing, and purging behaviors common in both illnesses. In fact, approximately one-half of patients with anorexia engage in purging and other bulimic behaviors, and one-fourth of patients with bulimia start with anorexia but then lose control of their eating. It may be more reasonable to think of these illnesses on a spectrum with various degrees of self-control in response to a desire to lose weight.

Obesity Is Usually a Metabolic, Not Psychiatric, Illness

Rates of obesity have been steadily rising, and a majority of Americans are now overweight. About one-quarter of us are clinically obese. (To determine if you are obese, calculate your Body Mass Index, or BMI. Multiply your weight in pounds by 705, divide by your height in inches, then divide by your height again. Or divide your weight in kilograms twice by your height in meters. A BMI of 30 or higher is obese.) Obesity affects our ability to be productive and enjoy life. It increases the risk of diabetes, heart disease, hypertension, stroke, breathing problems, and back pain. In addition, those who are obese may experience discrimination and self-contempt.

For most people, binge eating is not the cause of obesity. Fewer than one in ten individuals who are obese experience episodes of uncontrollable overeating. In the vast majority of cases there is no evidence of a psychiatric disturbance causing obesity. Physicians think of obesity as a chronic metabolic condition. Our bodies evolved to store extra energy in the form of fat, and most of us gain weight when we have unlimited access to food. Some of us are predisposed to be heavy, as obesity tends to run in families. As many dieters know, a tendency to gain weight is hard to change. Obese children and adolescents usually grow up to be obese adults. An obese person who diets and loses weight almost certainly gains weight again once the dieting stops.

If you take psychiatric medications you may be at greater risk of becoming obese. Many antipsychotic, mood-stabilizing, and antidepressant medications (see "Psychosis," "Mania," and "Depression," respectively) cause weight gain. Not everyone who takes these medications gains weight, but many do. Scientists suspect that these medications stimulate the appetite center in the brain, though they may also slow metabolism. If you experience significant weight gain while taking psychiatric medication, you should discuss with your physician the possibility of switching to a different medication.

Appetite and Eating Are Disturbed in Several Other Mental Illnesses

If you have *depression* you are likely to experience changes in your appetite. Some people do not feel particularly hungry even when they have hardly eaten at all. Eating can become a chore; the act of putting food in the mouth and swallowing takes too much energy, and it is an unrewarding task. These people may wish that they did not have to eat at all. In severe cases they can become malnourished or dehydrated. In other cases—what psychiatrists refer to as atypical depression—the appetite may increase, and eating becomes one of the few activities that brings comfort. These people spend much of their time in bed, and they gain weight as a result of eating more while being less active.

If you experience *mania* or *psychosis,* you may be too agitated to eat. You may become confused or end up living on the street, so that you have difficulty obtaining or preparing food. You may also become so *paranoid* that you fear your food is poisoned. I have treated several patients who stopped eating altogether because they were sure hospital staff or their family were trying to poison them. Sometimes I could convince them to eat only by serving them prepared food that had been wrapped. In some cases, a manic or psychotic patient can become catatonic, not moving, talking, or eating. It may be necessary to feed a catatonic patient through a tube until other treatments become effective.

Many people fast for religious reasons, usually during specific holy days. Religious ascetics may engage in fasting on an ongoing basis as an expression of self-denial or in an attempt to achieve purity or heightened spirituality. Some people fast as a form of political protest. In some cases, fasting for spiritual or political reasons can become habitual and appear much like anorexia nervosa. In some cases, the religious or political preoccupation motivating fasting may stem from idiosyncratic or *delusional* beliefs. I once treated a patient with schizophrenia who thought that God had instructed him to stop eating. Some people fast or purge as a fad rather than to control weight. Though such fads are periodically fashionable, there is nothing healthy about alternating fasting with partying, or "detoxifying" your body with colon irrigation.

Drug or alcohol addiction can sometimes lead to tremendous weight loss. As you spend more and more of your time and money obtaining and using drugs, you spend less of your resources on eating. If you are dependent on alcohol, you may obtain most of your calories from drinking. Your stomach becomes irritated and eroded so that you lose your appetite. You may develop *memory loss* and *movement problems* due to vitamin deficiencies. If you use cocaine or other stimulants, your appetite may be suppressed, and you burn more calories because the drugs cause you to be physically *hyperactive*. Tobacco also suppresses appetite, and many smokers gain weight when they decide to quit. Marijuana actually increases appetite and suppresses nausea, making it useful (even if illegal) in some medical conditions where people might otherwise lose weight.

Any number of medical conditions can cause a loss of appetite. If you lose your appetite at a time when you are not depressed and not taking stimulant drugs, then you should receive a thorough medical workup.

Sometimes preschool children are fussy about which foods they will eat. Generally, you should continue to serve regular healthy foods and let your child know that it is up to her whether to eat it or not. In this way, fussiness is usually eliminated. In rare instances vitamin or mineral deficiency in children can cause a condition called pica, in which a person eats dirt, paint chips, or other nonnutritive substances, presumably in an attempt to replace missing minerals.

Finally, unusual drinking patterns can occur in psychiatric conditions. Some *psychotic* patients develop a craving for water or soda and will drink dangerously large amounts if they are not carefully monitored. I have known patients who would drink water directly from the tap for minutes at a time or stick their head in the toilet bowl when other sources of water were restricted. Sometimes the desire to drink fluids is a side effect of treatment with lithium (see "Mania").

How to Cope with Appetite and Eating Disturbances

If you suspect that you have an eating disorder, you should see a psychiatrist. A psychiatrist can assess your nutritional needs, make sure that you are medically stable, and suggest a treatment program. Treatment can be provided on an outpatient basis unless you are seriously underweight or malnourished, in which case you will probably need to spend several weeks in the hospital or in a day program. In these more structured treatment settings, staff can help you to leave behind bad habits, such as discarding food, vomiting, and concealing your weight loss, while helping you to develop healthy habits, such as eating a balanced diet.

If you suffer from anorexia nervosa, you may initially resist efforts to help you to gain weight. You should remind yourself that, even though you would prefer to be in complete control of your diet and body shape, your efforts to lose weight are dangerous. Your family and treatment staff are not trying to control you or punish you for being underweight. Their efforts are intended to improve your health and, in some cases, to keep you alive. In the hospital setting you may be able to gain two to three pounds per week until you are back to a weight level that is healthy for you. In an outpatient setting, the goal will be to gain about a pound per week. As you begin to regain weight, you will begin to think more clearly, you will be less distracted with thoughts about food, and you will feel better about yourself. If you stay in treatment until your weight has returned to normal, then you have a good chance of remaining healthy. Following treatment, approximately one-third of patients with anorexia have sustained, normal weight gain. Even if you continue to have worries about food and weight, or to struggle with your desire to lose weight, you will be healthier after treatment than you were before.

If you suffer from bulimia nervosa, the goal of treatment is to help you reduce bulimic behaviors such as bingeing, purging, and using laxatives. You will also engage in therapy with the goal of coming to terms with having a healthy body, which may be heavier than you desire. About two-thirds of patients with bulimia are able to stop bingeing altogether after treatment. Only about one in ten continues to have severe symptoms of bulimia in spite of treatment.

In psychotherapy, therapists will use cognitive-behavioral therapy techniques, which involve teaching you new ways of thinking about food and your body and of practicing healthy behavior.

Medications, when used alone, are not effective in the treatment of any of the eating disorders. However, they can be helpful in combination with cognitive-behavioral therapy and nutritional programs. Antidepressant medications, especially the SSRIs (see "Depression"), may help you to refrain from obsessing about food and from bingeing and purging.

If you are overweight, you should resist the temptation to use over-the-counter weight loss products. Most of these contain amphetamine-like stimulants (see "Intoxication"), which have a number of medical and psychiatric side effects, including the potential for addiction. Even if you lose weight with the help of these products, you are likely to regain the weight quickly when you stop using them. Some weight loss may be achieved with the use of orlistat (Xenical), a resin that binds fat in your digestive tract and carries it out in your feces. In severe or dangerous cases of obesity, surgical gastric restriction (narrowing of the stomach) may be recommended.

Losing weight when you are obese is a psychological challenge, even if psychiatric illness is not the cause of your weight gain. To lose weight and then maintain your healthy body weight, you must be extraordinarily motivated. You need to be conscious of the healthiness and quantity of food that you eat. You should eat no more food than you require, and you should especially limit the quantities of fat and carbohydrates. Your doctor, a dietician, or any number of self-help books can provide guidance in these areas. You also need to exercise on a regular basis. You burn calories when you exercise, and the tone and metabolism of your muscles remain higher between periods of exercise. Regular exercise also improves mood and makes you feel better physically. Your goal should be to lose ten to fifteen percent of your weight before dieting. It is generally unrealistic to plan to lose all of your excess weight and to keep it off.

If you believe that someone you care about has an eating disorder, you should encourage her to seek help. Your loved one may resist your suggestion or even become angry at you for, in her mind, judging and controlling her. You can reframe the issue by reminding her that you care about her and want her to live a healthy life. You are not interested in controlling or punishing her, or making her fat. You are concerned that she will become dangerously thin or harm herself through bingeing, vomiting, and misusing medications. You can inform her that these behaviors are well understood by physicians and therapists and can be treated.

You may have difficulty recognizing when someone you love has an eating disorder. Most people who restrict, binge, and purge take measures to conceal their behaviors. Weight loss occurs gradually, and it may be difficult for you to define the point at which your loved one starts to appear unhealthy rather than just thin. If you come across evidence of vomiting, laxative use, and abuse of pills, or if you observe your loved one losing weight or binge eating, then you should take these signs seriously and insist on evaluation and, if need be, treatment.

Eating disorders can be particularly distressing to parents. Many parents feel that one of their most important roles is to feed their children. You may feel rejected if your daughter refuses to eat. On the other hand, you may feel embarrassed by, or worried about, a child who eats too much in spite of being overweight. It can be a challenge to avoid a power struggle with your child over her eating habits, and even the most relaxed parents may feel manipulated or ignored and become frustrated or angry. You may find it helpful to join a support group, or to participate in family therapy as part of your child's treatment program. Family therapy may help you to learn how to smooth over conflicts that may have developed around the illness. You will learn from other parents that you are not alone in the challenges that you face. You will learn more about eating disorders and what constitutes a healthy body and healthy eating.

Avoidance

Your roommate begs you to come along to a party. All you do is study, she says. You tell her you'd love to meet some new people, but you feel silly at parties.

In fact, you feel embarrassed just about anywhere. If your teacher asks your opinion in class, you blush and stare at your notes. If you manage to squeeze out an answer, he has to ask you to speak up. It's not that you don't know the answer. You're always well prepared. But what if you misunderstood? Everyone in the class would think you were an idiot. They'd wonder if you belong in that class.

And parties are much worse. You never know what to say. You don't know how to dance. Your clothes are probably completely out of style. You feel out of place. And you would just die if you were left standing alone against the wall.

Many people are naturally shy. You may have been a quiet child and inclined to hide from people you did not know. You preferred to stay in the back of the classroom, play by yourself during recess, and avoid calling attention to yourself. You may have been nervous about making friends, gravitating to other children who, like you, were quiet and undemanding. You may have felt comfortable only at home with your family. As you grew older you shied away from challenges and opportunities, preferring to stay in an environment where you felt secure, surrounded by people who already knew you. The idea of leaving town, joining the military, or attending college might seem exciting to others but caused you to have butterflies in your stomach. What would be expected of you? What if nobody liked you?

This description applies to about one in ten Americans. At the other extreme are individuals who are naturally gregarious, adventurous, and eager for attention. Our temperaments probably derive to a large extent from our genes. These traits tend to be shared by identical twins, for example, and parents notice different social styles in their children practically from birth. Some babies and infants are obviously outgoing and curious while others are timid. It is normal for many infants to fear strangers.

But temperaments can change. You can raise a shy child to feel more confident in unfamiliar circumstances, while a more spirited child can become discouraged by constant criticism or punishment. Some children become quiet, inhibited, and watchful after experiencing abuse. Children raised in institutions may be too relaxed and warm with strangers. Cultural expectations may also influence personal development: strangers may be treated with warmth or wariness, children may be encouraged to be boastful or humble, and girls may be expected to be demure rather than assertive.

For some people, lifelong shyness is so extreme and inhibiting that psychiatrists refer to it as an avoidant personality disorder. If you have an avoidant personality, your shyness derives from an intense feeling of inadequacy. You feel that you are awkward, uninteresting, incompetent, and unlikable. You avoid forming relationships with other people because you are afraid that they will not like you. You do not go to social gatherings where you imagine you might be rejected when you try to meet others. You would love to be in a close relationship with another person, but you do not know how to go about pursuing this safely, because to become intimate you must expose yourself and take chances. If you find yourself unexpectedly in the company of others, you become embarrassed and flustered. You tend to put yourself down. You avoid volunteering your services or imposing on others, afraid that you will be turned down, ridiculed, or criticized. At work you tend to be solitary, undemanding, and unambitious. You may have lifelong feelings of *anxiety*, inhibition, and *depression*.

Some people are not naturally shy, but they become increasingly nervous in social situations as they grow older. Psychiatrists identify this anxiety disorder, which tends to start during the late teenage years, as a social phobia. About two percent of people suffer from social phobia at any given time, though as many as one in ten experience some symptoms. A social phobia is an intense *fear* of being scrutinized or embarrassed in public. Unlike those who suffer from an avoidant personality disorder, you realize that you are a competent and likable person. You realize that your fears are exaggerated or unreasonable, but you become anxious anyway. You feel very uncomfortable around people you do not know. If you are asked to speak in class, give a speech, sing in church, or attend a cocktail party, you begin to stammer, blush, shake, sweat, or freeze up. You may even have a *panic* attack. You begin to avoid parties, gatherings, or job duties that involve meeting or performing in front of others. I treated one man who repeatedly turned down a job promotion because he was so afraid of having to supervise his colleagues.

Scientists do not know what causes social phobia. It does not seem to run in families. Temperamental nervousness may lead to fears of being scrutinized, which interfere with performance in a spiraling cycle of anxiety. Selective mutism in children (see "Speech Difficulties") may be an early manifestation of social phobia.

Many other psychiatric illnesses can lead you to avoid social situations. If you suffer from *panic* disorder, you may develop agoraphobia, a fear of public places. You are afraid that you may have an embarrassing panic attack in public, even though you are otherwise comfortable being around other people. If you have been *traumatized,* you may be fearful of going out in public where you might suffer a *flashback* or be reminded of events that you are trying to forget. You may also view the world as increasingly threatening and consequently feel safer by remaining at home. If you suffer from body dysmorphic disorder (see "Body Image Problems"), you may stay at home rather than expose yourself to the judgment of others whom you are certain will notice in you what you believe to be obvious physical deformities. If you have obsessive-compulsive disorder (or OCD), you may be afraid that you will have to perform *compulsive* rituals if you depart from your familiar routines.

If you are *depressed,* you may be unable to enjoy the company of others, and you lack the motivation and energy to leave home. Although you may also prefer to be alone when experiencing *grief,* mourning rituals will help you to spend time with people who care about you. Otherwise, your grief may deepen as you isolate yourself and live among memories.

Drug abuse can cause social withdrawal either as a direct effect of *intoxication* (for example, the intense lethargy caused by heroin) or because you are too busy obtaining and using drugs to spend time in other activities with friends. As you become more dependent on drugs, you may start to hang out only with other drug users and abandon your old friends and family.

Finally, social awkwardness and a disinterest in social activities and relationships are major features of several chronic psychiatric illnesses that cause people to be perceived by others as *odd*. If you have a schizoid personality disorder, you have a lifelong disinterest in forming relationships with others. You may develop solitary interests and pursue occupations that do not require you to interact with other people. If you have autism or Asperger's disorder, you have difficulty appreciating or caring about typical human emotions. Lacking an understanding of emotional cues, you may have difficulty communicating with others except in a stilted fashion. Of the dozens of patients with Asperger's disorder I have treated, only one was married, and this was an arranged marriage to a slightly retarded woman.

If you have schizophrenia, you may experience negative symptoms (see "Oddness") that lead you to misunderstand or lose interest in other people. You may be apathetic and have little to say. Social withdrawal is the most common long-term symptom of schizophrenia. Being institutionalized in an unstimulating environment also may lead to worsening social skills and increasing apathy. Decades ago many people with schizophrenia withdrew almost completely into inner worlds when they were housed on crowded "back wards" of psychiatric hospitals. Many seemed to come back to life when treated with newly available medications, discharged, and engaged in outpatient rehabilitation programs.

How to Cope with Shyness

Most shyness stems from fears of unfamiliar social situations. In avoidant personality disorder you are afraid of being criticized, rejected, or humiliated. In social phobia, you are afraid of being judged by others. In agoraphobia, you are afraid of being publicly embarrassed by losing control. Psychotherapy for each of these conditions starts with an identification of the underlying fears. Psychotherapy for avoidant personality disorder is the most challenging. It can be very difficult to change a lifelong pattern of timidity and poor *self-esteem*. You may be reluctant to trust your therapist who, after all, is a stranger who may seem to pass judgment on you. Therapy should proceed slowly so that you can learn to accept that your therapist will not grow to dislike you or abandon you after he gets to know you. You will gradually come to accept his professional feed-back as a tool for improvement rather than as wounding judgments about your character.

Cognitive-behavioral therapy is the psychotherapy of choice for social phobia, agoraphobia, and many other anxious conditions. Your therapist will help you to recognize that your fears are exaggerated, and you will realize that you do not come across as boring, silly, or foolish, and that your colleagues recognize you to be a competent worker. You will also learn that if you have a *panic* attack or flashback in public, it is not the end of the world. After this preparation, and after learning relaxation techniques (see "Anxiety"), you gradually expose yourself to the social situations that you fear. You begin to gain confidence from your success in these exercises, and you begin to enjoy the benefits of going out and spending time with friends and colleagues.

Medications can also be very helpful in the treatment of social phobia and agoraphobia. The antidepressant medications, especially the SSRIs and MAOIs (see "Depression"), have been found to be effective for these conditions as well as for several other anxiety disorders. The combination of medication and cognitive-behavioral therapy will probably lead to the most rapid and sustained improvement in your mental health.

The negative symptoms of schizophrenia, including social withdrawal, may improve with a change of medications. The newer generation of anti-psychotic medications (see "Psychosis") is especially effective for these symptoms, whereas the older medications may make them worse.

Body Image Problems

You can't go out looking like this. You've scrubbed your face three times and reapplied lotion, but you still look blotchy and pocked. You look up and down at yourself in the mirror. The bathroom light hitting your nose looks like the sun rising over an Arizona rock formation. How can you talk to anyone when you look like this? You promised your best friend that you would go out with him, but you can see now that you'll end up hiding somewhere while he parties.

You pick at your cheeks. You grab the can of hair gel and try to finger your hair a little more. Maybe that'll soften your look so no one will notice your face.

Your friend shouts for you to hurry up. He tells you that you look fine. He says he likes your new shirt. Obviously he won't mention what a mess your face is. You slam the door and shout out to him that you're sorry, but you just can't go.

Beauty exists in the mind, as many have said, and so do the defects and ugliness that we often see in ourselves. Most of us are dissatisfied with at least some aspect of our appearance, whether it be our weight, our hair, our facial features, or skin tone. For example, studies have found that nearly half of college students are preoccupied with an aspect of their appearance. These concerns often seem exaggerated to others, and they often pass with time. Perhaps you remember being distraught as a teenager over a pimple or two, while your parents tried to reassure you that you were still cute. But for some, a minor blemish or personal feature becomes an all-encompassing disaster, a flaw that you cannot bear.

About one in a hundred individuals is severely distressed over an imagined or exaggerated defect in appearance. Psychiatrists refer to this condition as body dysmorphic disorder, which usually has its onset in adolescence. If you suffer from body dysmorphic disorder, you believe that there is something horribly wrong with your appearance. In most cases, your concern has some basis in reality, but it is exaggerated. Psychiatrists refer to this as an overvalued idea, not a *delusion*. For example, you may in fact have wrinkles around your eyes, but they are typical for your age, and most people would find them unremarkable. You might have a small birthmark on your neck, but you are the only one who finds it unattractive. You may have a larger-than-usual nose, but of the sort that most people would consider distinguished rather than hideous. In fact, you may have been oblivious to the defect yourself until something happened that drew it to your attention. Maybe your barber or beautician made a silly comment that you took to heart. Maybe your boyfriend or girlfriend left you, leading you to wonder about the possible reasons why. Maybe you developed a scar or blemish that did not fade fast enough for you to ignore.

Concerns in body dysmorphic disorder most often involve the skin, nose, and hair. You may be concerned about thin hair, balding, body hair, or facial hair (too much or too little of it). You may think that your nose is too large or disfigured. You may dislike the color, coarseness, or patchiness of your skin. You may have pockmarks, scars, moles, or birthmarks that seem to spoil your image. You may think that no one can look at you without noticing how wrinkled you have become. Other common areas of concern are the lips, chin, teeth, and shapeliness or fitness of the body. Women are often concerned about the size and appearance of their breasts, waist, and hips. Recently, men have become more concerned about having muscular chests, buttocks, and shins.

You may be concerned over more than one area of your body. Or your concern may shift from one body part to another over time. You probably have no awareness of how minor your problem seems to others. If your loved ones do not comment, you assume that they are trying not to upset you. You think you can tell, from their glances and indirect comments, that they are aware of your flaw. You think that colleagues and strangers notice your defect as you walk by. You spend hours each day trying to arrange yourself in such a way that the flaw is less noticeable. You apply makeup, comb your hair in a certain way, or wear special clothing (perhaps a hat, a turtleneck, or gloves) in order to conceal the problem. Many of the rituals and preoccupations seen in body dysmorphic disorder are remarkably similar to those seen in *obsessive*-compulsive disorder, or OCD. As in OCD, you may be unable to proceed until you feel just right. You try to satisfy yourself that people will be distracted from your flaw and not stare at you in horror. Otherwise you will stay at home, unable to socialize or work. This social *avoidance* leads to increasing *anxiety, depression,* and even *suicidal thoughts.*

Body Image Preoccupations Are a Feature of Several Other Illnesses

If you have anorexia nervosa (see "Appetite Disturbances"), you are likely to view yourself as overweight when in fact you are dangerously thin. Anorexia is very similar to body dysmorphic disorder, except that the imagined defect involves the entire body. In spite of all evidence you genuinely believe that you must lose weight. You believe that other people look at you and see a fat or misshapen person. It is not uncommon to suffer from both anorexia and body dysmorphic disorder. I once treated an underweight man who thought that he was fat and that there was something wrong with his nose. He used to pick at the skin of his nose continuously, until his preoccupations lessened with medication. His restricted eating was more difficult to treat.

In hypochondriasis and somatization (see "Physical Complaints and Pain") you may be obsessed with the belief that you have an undiagnosed medical illness. You think that something is wrong with your body, but your concern is not esthetic, as in body dysmorphic disorder. Rather, you have a large number of vague aches and discomforts that lead you to seek help from general medical doctors, hoping to find relief.

If you suffer from *depression,* you may ruminate or dwell upon certain perceived flaws. These concerns can be similar to those seen in body dysmorphic disorder, except that they arise out of the depression and resolve when the depression is treated. If you suffer from schizophrenia (see "Psychosis") you may also have imagined physical defects, but they tend to be more bizarre and in keeping with the other *delusional* beliefs that occur with the illness. For example, I treated a young man who believed he saw his nose contort itself in the mirror. He thought that demons were making it move. Psychiatrists refer to this as a somatic delusion.

Of course, dissatisfaction with your appearance or body is not always a sign of mental illness. Beauty is not entirely relative, and defects are not always imagined. There are some esthetic principles that most of us seem to agree upon. Symmetrical features, proportional body parts, and physical fitness are usually considered more attractive. Some exaggeration in the size of the lips, Adam's apple, breasts, and penis may be considered sexier. Feminine features (long eyelashes, pouting lips, smooth skin) are seen as more beautiful in both men and women. Other physical characteristics seem to go in and out of fashion or vary in attractiveness from one culture to another.

These are just general rules, and they do not predictably determine what makes one individual attractive to others. In fact, personality traits and personal style can more than compensate for the physical features that we grow up with. For example, if you ask teenagers what they consider most attractive in a partner, they will say a sense of humor. Nevertheless, you may feel that your life would be much better, one way or another, if you could only change your appearance. This aspect of *self-esteem* can be addressed in psychotherapy, with the goal of helping you to improve what you can change, and to come to terms with what you cannot.

How to Cope with Imagined Body Defects

If you suffer from body dysmorphic disorder, you eventually may try to get the problem medically corrected. In fact, most people with body dysmorphic disorder seek help from dermatologists and cosmetic surgeons, rather than from psychiatrists. Unfortunately, cosmetic surgery and dermatological interventions are almost never satisfactory in addressing this illness. Your new nose, supplemented breast or shins, suctioned waist, or planed skin are different, but rarely better, in your mind, even if the surgery proceeds exactly as planned. It was not the flaw in your appearance that needed correcting, but your irrational focus and distress. (In contrast, if you seek surgery for an objectively apparent deformity, or out of acknowledged vanity, you are likely to be happy with the result.)

The treatment of choice for body dysmorphic disorder is one of the SSRI antidepressants (see "Depression"). Approximately one-half of those treated become significantly less preoccupied with and distressed about their supposed flaw. In fact, you may no longer consider yourself to have a physical defect. It is no surprise that this type of medication is effective, since SSRI antidepressants are also used successfully to treat related conditions like obsessive-compulsive disorder (OCD), anxiety, and depression. However, body dysmorphic disorder requires treatment at a higher dose and for a longer period of time than is usually required for these other illnesses. You probably will not start to feel better until after two to three months of treatment at the highest dose.

Psychotherapy can also be helpful, especially in combination with medication. Therapy for body dysmorphic disorder uses cognitive-behavioral approaches. You may practice maintaining your composure while exposing yourself and others to your flaw, for example, by looking at yourself in a mirror or by taking a walk in public. As the anxiety builds, you utilize relaxation techniques (see "Anxiety") that you have learned in therapy, and you stop yourself from fussing with your clothes and makeup as you would normally do. Over time you learn to tolerate the anxiety and the exposure without withdrawing or wasting hours on grooming. You also explore the maladaptive thoughts that lead you to exaggerate your flaw. Another exercise could be role reversal, where you try to convince yourself that the flaw is not as bad as you think, or that it is not a flaw at all. In this way, you learn to think more positively about aspects of your appearance that distress you.

If you care about someone who has an irrational preoccupation with his appearance, you want to be candidly supportive. If you think his concern is exaggerated, you should say so. You do not need to argue with him about his bodily concern, since argument will probably not change his mind, but you can tell him that you see things differently. You can encourage him to see a psychiatrist before he wastes time and money on surgery or dermatological treatments that will ultimately disappoint him. Although he may think that a psychiatrist will tell him he is vain, foolish, or delusional, you can remind him that there are psychiatric treatments that will make him feel better. Even if his concern about his appearance is entirely justified, a psychiatrist might be able to help him feel less anxious and depressed about it.

Compulsions

As you leave for work you turn the key to the porch door all the way to the right, firmly enough to be sure that you have success-fully locked it. You want to turn it further, but if it breaks off in the lock again you'll be in trouble. You turn it back to the left, then to the right, and back and forth again four more times. Now it is safe to head to the car and strap your daughter into her car seat. To be sure that the car door won't pop open and the car seat fly out as you round a corner, you use the electric lock on the key ring to lock and unlock the back door three times. You also check the lock manually before getting into the driver's seat. You count to ten before starting the car, then off you go. That went pretty smoothly. You might make it to work on time today.

But wait! What if you left the porch door unlocked? Did you check it, or did you forget? You think you checked. You always do. You'll just have to start over to be sure. You turn the car around and head back into the driveway. You remove the keys from the ignition, unstrap and remove your daughter, and walk back to check the house. Of course, the door was locked.

You call the daycare center to let them know you'll be late again. You don't want them to worry.

A compulsion is an act that you engage in against your wishes. The act itself is not pleasurable or rewarding. It may be irrational, inconvenient, or even harmful. A compulsion is often confused with an *impulse,* which is an act that you want to engage in, even though there are negative consequences. For example, you may have a compulsion to bite your nails down to the skin of your fingertips, whereas you have an impulsive desire to eat a hot fudge sundae despite being on a diet.

Why would anyone engage in an unpleasant act? After all, we are able to exert control over most of our behaviors. Generally we give in to compulsions because they bring us some sort of relief from other unpleasant feelings. This is most evident in obsessive-compulsive disorder (OCD), an illness that affects about one in forty individuals. Obsessions are recurrent and unwanted thoughts that cause a tremendous amount of anxiety. To deal with those anxious feelings you develop ritual behaviors that are time consuming and admittedly absurd.

The most common obsessions in OCD are fears of contamination. You worry about contacting and spreading germs and dirt. To cope with those fears, you may wash your hands over and over again throughout the day. I have treated many OCD patients who came in with terribly chapped hands. Like surgeons preparing for an operation, they would scrub their hands and forearms, sometimes for minutes at a time. They would wash after touching almost anything, but especially after touching doorknobs, handrails, money, telephones, and other objects that are handled by many people. They might wear gloves when leaving home, but the gloves themselves could become contaminated either by a particularly strong contact or if the people forgot to wash before putting them on. Once contaminated, the gloves would have to be thrown away. These ritual behaviors make sense in an operating room, where sterile conditions are required, but not elsewhere.

If you have OCD, you probably also engage in checking rituals. You may be pretty sure that you locked the door or turned off the stove, but if you do not double-check you become increasingly anxious, so eventually you feel like you must give in to your anxiety. The checking is completely irrational. The uncertainty may return after checking once, and you feel compelled to check again. Eventually you develop routines that somehow seem to satisfy your obsessive doubts. For example, you may turn the light switch on and off a total of ten times, having learned that this does the trick, that a sense of certainty temporarily replaces your doubts. You may feel that no matter how many times you turn a switch, close a door, or turn a lock, you are still left with doubts. You may have to break the switch or key to achieve a sense of certainty, but then you have another problem to deal with.

Many people with OCD have a need to seek reassurance. My patients with OCD may reconfirm their appointments several times. Family members may notice that a relative with OCD asks them the same question over and over again. Though this can be exasperating at times, family members may find it easier to just answer the question again rather than argue about it. If your obsessions include violent or sexual thoughts, you may compulsively ask your therapist, your priest, or your family members to reassure you that you are not a bad person, that you have not harmed anyone, that you are not disgusting. You do this even though you know that your troubling thoughts are alien to you, that you do not ask for them or enjoy dwelling on them.

Many people with OCD are obsessed with symmetry. Things around you must be organized precisely, or you feel unbalanced. To deal with these uncomfortable feelings, you may move things around, straightening books and piles of newspapers, lining up toothbrushes and pens, hanging and putting on clothing in a precise order, and eating your food one item at a time. You may feel compelled to touch things that grab your attention, and if you touch an object with your left hand, you may feel the need to touch another with your right. Some of my patients with OCD find hand-shaking to be a nerve-wracking experience. They feel compelled to touch the person again with their left hand, which can come across as odd or impolite, unless they find a way to do so smoothly, without attracting attention. Or you may get about by keeping your arms stiffly at your side, fearful of bumping or touching an object as you walk precisely and symmetrically through doorways, down the middle of hallways, and up stairs, always one stair at a time.

Hoarding is another common compulsive behavior. In some of the more severe cases I have treated, patients were unable to throw anything away, including trash and waste (see "Sloppiness"). Their houses filled up with newspapers and bags of garbage. They saved clippings from their hair. Piles of used laundry would accumulate in the homes of people who did not own a washing machine, because they were fearful of putting their clothes in a public washer. In one case a patient had been saving his urine in glass jars around his apartment before his family brought him in for treatment. The obsessive thoughts that these severe compulsions are responding to are not always clear. They seem to involve obsessions about completeness and control. You feel that you must collect everything and not lose anything that is yours.

In the early stages of coping with obsessive thoughts, compulsions have some logic to them. They are understandable strategies for coping with irrational thoughts. But compulsive rituals tend to become ineffective over time. You may find that checking the stove ten times before you leave the house no longer relieves your doubts. You may have to check twenty times. Or you may have to check ten times while your husband watches, so that you can ask him later to confirm that you checked. Eventually you may come up with less logical rituals. For example, you might find that if you walk back and forth through the kitchen doorway ten times before checking the stove, then you have to check the stove only twice, not twenty times. In this way your compulsive patterns may change over time. Eventually you have rituals that you feel you must complete even though you do not remember how they evolved. They take on a life of their own, but you feel anxious and uncomfortable if you ignore them.

Some compulsions are carried out in your thoughts, rather than in your behaviors. You may count to yourself. You may repeat a phrase over and over again in your mind. You may recite a prayer. Even though you don't realize it, these mental compulsions can be apparent to others because you appear distracted or are noticeably moving your lips or tapping, or counting on, your fingers.

Compulsions May Occur in Illnesses Other Than OCD

Compulsive behavior can be seen in other conditions. Trichotillomania is an illness in which you compulsively pull out, play with, or chew your hair. It can lead to patchy baldness. Nail biting and nose picking are other common compulsive behaviors. You know that the end results of these behaviors are painful fingertips, disfigured nails, and nosebleeds, but you find it difficult to refrain. If you resist the urge, you become increasingly anxious. You chew, pick, and pull until you achieve a sense of completion. All three of these behaviors, which psychiatrists refer to as disorders of grooming, may be related to OCD. They also may be related to grooming instincts observed in animals. Rodents, for example, will stop fleeing and start to groom their fur when they find themselves cornered by a predator. This instinct may have survived in those of us who play with our nails and hair when anxious.

Tourette's disorder is a type of tic disorder, a neurological illness that frequently overlaps with OCD. If you have Tourette's disorder, you make involuntary *movements* and sounds, or both. Examples of motor tics include eye blinking, shoulder shrugging, and hand jerking. Phonic tics include throat clearing, sniffing, and shouting out words. Some tics are so complex that it may be hard to think of them as involuntary. For example, you may shout out obscenities, repeat what someone has just said, or make various gestures with your hands.

Unlike compulsions, tics occur without prior thought. However, many people with Tourette's disorder report that they sometimes experience an urge to indulge the tic before it occurs, and that they can sometimes delay the tic. If they do so, then their anxiety builds and the tic explodes, often in a stronger form than if it had not been delayed. This is similar to the experience of delaying acting on compulsions in OCD. Interestingly, about half of those diagnosed with Tourette's disorder experience the classic symptoms of OCD, in addition to their tics.

We often refer to certain types of sexual behaviors, drug and alcohol use, shopping, and gambling as compulsive behaviors. But these behaviors are better understood as *impulsive* responses to *cravings* rather than as compulsions. Each of these behaviors brings some immediate pleasure in its own right. We engage in them because we believe they make us feel good, even if we have mixed feelings about the long-term consequences.

If you have an eating disorder like anorexia or bulimia (see "Appetite Disturbances"), you are preoccupied with your body, your weight, and your caloric intake. Restricting what you eat, vomiting, abusing laxatives, and overexercising could all be viewed as compulsive behaviors, in that they are persistent and maladaptive. However, if you engage in these behaviors, you probably view them as essential mechanisms for controlling your weight. You may not view these behaviors, or your desire to be thin, as problematic. Bingeing on food may be a more compulsive behavior. When you binge, you realize that you are overeating and that you will regret it shortly. You do not enjoy the food itself so much as the temporary relief you experience at abandoning your self-imposed restraint. The *self-mutilation* that occurs in some psychiatric conditions can also be viewed as falling somewhere between *impulsive* and compulsive behavior.

Repetitive behaviors can also occur in autism, mental retardation (see "Learning Difficulties"), and dementia (see "Memory Loss"). For example, it is not unusual in these illnesses to rock back and forth, to call out repeatedly, or to masturbate frequently. In each of these cases, the repetitive behavior reflects the person's attempt to soothe herself or to communicate when language and social skills are poor. Psychiatrists refer to these as perseverative, rather than compulsive, behaviors. There is no internal struggle to resist acting.

How to Cope with Compulsive Behaviors

OCD can be treated with medication, cognitive-behavioral psychotherapy, or both (see "Obsessions" for a full discussion). Compulsions are unwanted and habitual behaviors, but they are not completely out of your control. With enough determination you can resist your urges and refuse to engage in compulsive behaviors. The challenge you face is that you may become increasingly anxious so long as you have the obsessive thoughts that drive your rituals. You may be able to suppress one compulsive behavior only to find yourself creating a new ritual to deal with your *anxiety*.

Throughout your treatment you should keep in mind that your rituals are arbitrary and illogical, no matter how compelling. When you have lived with a particular ritual for some time, you begin to think of it as essential. You lose perspective. Therapy and medication can help you to regain the perspective you need to enable you to see your behaviors as unnecessary and, ultimately, to conquer them.

If you experience tics as well as obsessions and compulsions, then you may have Tourette's disorder. Tourette's disorder is much rarer than OCD, but the two often occur together. If you have Tourette's disorder, you should see a neurologist as well as a psychiatrist. If you have been diagnosed with both, then your obsessions and compulsions may respond best to a combination of antipsychotic medication (see "Psychosis") and an SSRI antidepressant (see "Depression").

If someone you care about suffers from OCD, you may become involved in her rituals, for example, by repeatedly answering questions, providing reassurance, rearranging furniture, or preparing food according to certain specifications. Even if you are not asked to assist in rituals, you may find yourself changing your own habits in order to make life easier for your loved one. For example, you might be pained to see her washing her hands to the point where her skin becomes red and cracked. You may begin to open doors for her, to take off your shoes before entering the house, to discourage visitors, and to clean household objects more than you would otherwise. These are understandable acts of love, but they also send a message that the obsessive fears and compulsive behaviors are appropriate. They also reward the compulsive behaviors by enlisting your attention and support. You end up reinforcing the behaviors that you would both rather extinguish.

At the other extreme, you may become exasperated by your loved one's compulsions. You may refuse to answer her repeated questions. You may refuse to drive back home to let her check that the iron is unplugged. You may grab her hands to stop her from counting. You may shout at her and tell her that she is being ridiculous.

Generally it is best to avoid showing anger and frustration. Your loved one already knows that obsessions and compulsions are illogical. She would rather live without them. You should talk to her frankly about the steps she is taking in her treatment in order to reduce her compulsive behavior. Treatment takes place over time, step by step. Many compulsions become so habitual that they take place quickly and without much thought. Other compulsions may be wrapped up in complex fears and extreme anxiety. They may be hard to abandon, and you should be patient and tolerant as your loved one works on reducing them. However, you should never feel compelled to be an accomplice in her rituals. If you find yourself being asked to repeat yourself or to engage in other unnecessary behaviors, you should calmly point out that you are not going to participate in them. This may make her anxious for the moment, but it will help her in the long run.

Confusion

How did you end up here? A sweet nurse just came in with your breakfast and told you that you were in the hospital. You remember that you had a procedure planned—something to do with your heart—but you don't remember checking in. She said it is Wednesday, so you must have been here several days. Apparently you've been quite a handful, ripping out your needles, wetting the bed, wandering into other patients' rooms, and screaming in the middle of the night. That's not like you, but you're too disoriented to really care.

The nurse gave you some medicine before she left, and you suddenly feel like drifting back to sleep. You'll sort it out when your family arrives.

Confusion of one sort or another is a feature of many mental illnesses. Misperceptions, false beliefs, and befuddlement are common in *psychosis* and *mania*, syndromes in which one loses touch with reality. When psychotic or manic, you may behave in a hyperactive and disorganized fashion, seemingly without purpose. Your speech may be incoherent or *nonsensical*. But in these conditions, you remain alert to your surroundings in spite of being out of touch with reality. The more concerning condition, and one to which we are all vulnerable, is a state of medical delirium characterized by confusion and a diminished ability to pay attention to our environment.

Delirium is one of those words that has a different meaning in common speech, referring to a state of madness or uncontrolled excitement. For physicians, delirium refers to a temporary condition, unrelated to other mental illnesses, resulting from medical illness or *intoxication*. For example, up to one in three people hospitalized for a medical condition or surgery will experience an episode of severe confusion. The confusion develops rapidly over a few hours and resolves in a matter of days as the underlying cause is treated. The underlying cause is often located outside of the brain, for example in an infection of the bladder or an imbalance of salts in the bloodstream. It is important to recognize delirium when it occurs because it may be a sign of serious medical problems.

Delirium is primarily a problem with concentration and alertness. You are unable to sustain attention to things happening around you. Your doctor may introduce herself to you, but the name does not even register in your memory. Someone tells you where you are, but you continue to look around in a befuddled haze. You are disoriented regarding the place, the date, and even the time of day. Loved ones reassure you that you are being taken care of in a hospital, but you do not understand them and scream in panic. Your confusion may be mistaken for dementia, but you do not have *memory loss* so much as an inability to pay attention to anything long enough to memorize it. When you recover from delirium, your memory will most likely return to normal.

Doctors may perform simple bedside tests of attention span to determine whether you are delirious. They may ask you to spell a word forward and backwards, perform simple math calculations, or simply to repeat several words—which in itself may be too difficult if you are severely confused. You also may have trouble speaking clearly. Your voice may be slurred or hushed, and you may invent words. You may have false recollections of things that have not happened. For example, you may think that you have already eaten breakfast, when in fact you have not.

Delirium is usually a fluctuating condition. You may be alert and seemingly lucid one moment, but confused and drowsy the next. You wake up multiple times during the night and drift off during the day. You become agitated, fearful, and *hyperactive* at times. But you may also appear lethargic and depressed and have nothing to say. You may experience *hallucinations,* seeing things that are not present. For example, you may be observed talking to yourself even though you believe that you are holding a conversation with someone else in the room. In your confusion, you may misinterpret what others are doing around you. When someone tries to feed you or change your clothing, you may think that they are trying to poison you or tie you up.

Delirium is a very serious condition. The brain does not become so confused unless something is wrong. Delirium commonly occurs in a person's final hours before death. But it may also be a sign of a reversible medical condition that could be dangerous if it is not discovered and treated. The elderly are most vulnerable to developing delirium, especially if they already suffer from some degree of dementia. Delirium is also more common among cancer and AIDS sufferers and in patients who are in intensive care units after undergoing complicated surgery.

There Are Many Treatable Causes of Delirium

Delirium is not really a psychiatric condition. It rarely occurs in the course of psychiatric treatment. It is much more commonly encountered in hospital settings and in nursing homes, so general doctors and surgeons must be able to recognize and treat it. Unfortunately, some doctors fail to recognize confusion in their patients, fail to recognize that it is a serious development when it does occur, or mistake confusion for some other psychiatric condition like *depression, mania,* or *psychosis.* As a general rule, the onset of confusion, hallucinations, or agitation in an elderly person is most likely due to delirium and not to illnesses such as schizophrenia, which strike much earlier in life.

Fortunately, the potential medical causes of delirium are well known. Once delirium is recognized, doctors will order a series of medical tests to find out the specific cause. They will probably order blood chemistries, a blood cell count, urine cultures, an electrocardiogram (EKG), and a chest X-ray. They may also perform brain imaging, drug testing, and lumbar puncture (commonly known as a spinal tap, for evidence of brain inflammation or infection) and obtain an electroencephalogram (EEG) and testing for syphilis and HIV. They will also review your medication regimen to determine whether any of your medications could be contributing to confusion.

Medications are among the most common and easily reversible causes of confusion. Pain killers, muscle relaxants, psychiatric medications, anticonvulsants, steroids, and many other medications can cause confusion. Your doctor will simplify your regimen and try to eliminate any medication that could be having such an adverse effect. *Intoxication* with drugs or alcohol also can cause confusion, as well as sudden withdrawal from alcohol. The confusion, shakes, seizures, and fluctuations in pulse and blood pressure that occur in alcohol withdrawal are known as delirium tremens (or DTs), which can result in death if untreated.

Other common medical causes of delirium include infections, vitamin deficiencies, blood chemical (especially sodium) imbalances, thyroid problems, diabetes (due to either high or low sugar levels), and cardiac problems. Seizures, brain tumors, and strokes may cause confusion as a direct result of the disturbance or injury in the brain. The rapid onset of confusion, especially when accompanied by trouble moving or talking, may be evidence of a new brain injury. When I worked in a general medical hospital before becoming a psychiatrist, the most common cause of confusion was urinary tract infection in elderly patients. The patients would be extremely disoriented when they arrived in the hospital, but after a day or two of antibiotic treatment they would be back to normal.

The treatment of delirium depends almost entirely on the underlying cause. For example, infections are treated with antibiotics, and diabetes by normalizing blood sugar levels. Alcohol withdrawal is treated by replacing alcohol with high doses of a sedative medication like diazepam (Valium), then tapering off the drug in a controlled fashion. Regardless of the underlying cause of the delirium, a low dose of antipsychotic medication (see "Psychosis") may help reduce confusion, agitation, and hallucinations. Most physicians use the medication haloperidol (Haldol) because it does not cause confusion itself, and because it can be administered by injection. But it would be a mistake to treat the behavioral manifestations of delirium without also determining and correcting the underlying cause.

If a loved one is confused, especially in a hospital or nursing home, there are some steps you can take to help orient and calm her until she recovers. Since your loved one is likely to be distracted and fearful, your presence may be reassuring. She may not recall exactly who you are from moment to moment, but she will recognize that you are someone she can count on to watch out for her. You can calm her if she becomes frightened by the nurses and physicians who hover around her. When you have to leave for a time, you should assign a sitter to stay with her until you return. In an intensive care unit, where natural light is absent and no one ever seems to sleep, you can remind her when it is day or night. Place a calendar or clock by her bedside to help orient her. Leave family photos or familiar objects, like a comforter or stuffed animal. You may want to turn on a television or radio to help focus her attention. Return eyeglasses and hearing aids if they have been misplaced. Magazines and newspapers require too much attention. I recall examining one delirious patient who was sitting up in bed and apparently reading a newspaper, except that he was holding it upside down.

Cravings

You are proud of yourself. It has been more than a week since your last drink. You knew you had to stop when you found yourself keeping a bottle of vodka in the bedroom. Sure, you think about having a drink nearly every minute of the day. At lunchtime you find yourself walking out the door for a burger and a drink. Luckily, your secretary catches you and reminds you to call home. You get a muffin at the canteen instead, then head back to your office.

On the way home, you no longer stop at the old bar—at least you haven't been there for several days. But it's Thursday, and you know your friends will be there tonight. If you get out early, maybe you could stop by. Just to say hello. You don't have to drink anything. At least no more than a beer.

A craving is more than a desire. To crave is to desire something that you know is bad for you. You will go to great lengths to continue to get it. Soon nothing in life seems as important as satisfying your craving. You plan your day around it. You lie at work, you lie at home, and you lie to yourself. You tell yourself that you are in control, that you do not have a problem. You convince yourself that there is no real harm in it. Your craving brings you pleasure, sometimes intense pleasure. And what is wrong with enjoying life a little bit? In clear moments, though, you can see that you are not the person you used to be. The craving has become a strange parasite that has taken over your body.

At what point does alcohol and drug use, sex, gambling, or any other *impulsive* behavior become a problem? According to some religions, any use of drugs or alcohol is sinful. Most governments regulate alcohol, drugs, gambling, and extramarital sex. Psychiatrists do not describe any of these urges or activities as inherently abnormal. In fact, it is normal to find most of these activities pleasurable, which is why they are so tempting. Instead, psychiatrists focus on whether the activity is out of control, and whether it has a negative impact on your life.

All drugs are physically dangerous when used regularly. Tobacco and marijuana can cause emphysema and cancer. Alcohol can cause hepatitis and cirrhosis, among other problems. Cocaine causes high blood pressure, strokes, and heart attacks. Intravenous drug use can lead to deadly infections with HIV and viral hepatitis. And it is easy to overdose and die. Every time you shoot up with heroin, you are playing Russian roulette. If you have difficulty controlling your sexual cravings, you or your partner may become unintentionally pregnant or infected with sexually transmitted diseases like syphilis and AIDS.

Drug and alcohol use can also have a direct impact on psychiatric health. When you use alcohol and illicit drugs, you bathe your brain in toxic substances. The brain can take only so much abuse before it breaks down. Almost all drugs and alcohol can cause *depression* and *anxiety* when used regularly. If you are vulnerable to other psychiatric illnesses, like schizophrenia or bipolar disorder, then substance use may precipitate an episode of *psychosis* or *mania*. Even if you do not experience these psychiatric problems as a direct result of your drug use, you may become increasingly frustrated at your inability to exert control over your life. This can lead to a decrease in *self-esteem* and, in a vicious cycle, to further drug use to escape bad feelings.

All addictions can lead to problems at home and at work. It takes a lot of time to obtain and use drugs, to arrange sexual encounters, and to engage in serious gaming. Once you start bingeing in any of these areas, it becomes very hard to stop. You might leave home with the intention of making a quick score, then find yourself staying out all night using up all your money. When so much of your time is spent planning or engaging in these activities, you have little time left for family, friends, and work. You fail to complete assignments on time. You show up late for work. You cancel dates. You stop doing things that you used to enjoy doing. You do not live up to your potential. You may lose the trust and affection of your loved ones and colleagues.

You may engage in increasingly reckless behavior, either while intoxicated or in an attempt to satisfy your cravings. For example, you might risk your life to obtain drugs in the middle of the night in a crime-ridden neighborhood. You might have anonymous sex without a condom. You might drive home while drunk. You might withdraw your savings in the hope of winning big at the casino. You risk arrest for possessing illegal drugs or soliciting sex. You may be scared the first time that you take any of these risks, or embarrassed when you look back at them, but after a while you get used to taking chances. You may forget the danger to yourself and others.

These are all fairly direct consequences of engaging in addictive behaviors. But at a certain point cravings seem to take on a life of their own. You try to cut back, but you find that you are using more and more, and for longer periods of time, than you had planned. In fact, you have to use more of the same substance in order to get high. Your brain has grown used to the drug, a phenomenon which psychiatrists refer to as tolerance. If you stop using the drug, or cut back on your use, you begin to have withdrawal symptoms (see "Intoxication"). During withdrawal, your cravings for the drug become acute. Psychiatrists use the term dependence to refer to this pattern of increasing drug use with tolerance and withdrawal. Though sex and gambling do not have the direct chemical effect on the brain that drugs and alcohol have, people who are addicted to these behaviors describe a similar escalating craving and miserable feeling when they stop.

A common feature of all addictions is *denial*. You may tell yourself that other people have trouble holding their alcohol but not you; that marijuana is not really a drug; that snorting a few bags of cocaine a week is not so bad; that oral sex with a prostitute is not really cheating. You may tell yourself that you are in control, even though you are spending more and more money, staying away from home, and coming in late to work. You tell yourself that it will be easy to stop. If you check in for rehabilitation, you may convince yourself after a few days that you are no longer addicted, that you have changed for good. When you use again, you tell yourself and your loved ones that it was just a little slip, even as you start thinking quietly to yourself about how to get more. The first step in fighting cravings is to genuinely and consistently acknowledge the extent of your addiction.

Where Do Substance Cravings Come from?

Natural curiosity leads most people to try addicting substances at some point, usually in their youth. More than a third of us have tried an illegal drug. Approximately half of all Americans over the age of twelve drink alcohol regularly. More than one in twenty regularly smokes marijuana. Nearly thirty percent smoke or chew tobacco. Nearly one in a hundred uses cocaine. But not all users are addicted. Approximately one in ten Americans over the age of twelve is addicted to illegal drugs, alcohol, or both.

To be addictive, a substance must make you feel good (see "Intoxication"), so that you want to try it again and again. Behavioral psychologists refer to this as a reinforcing effect. Opiate drugs, like morphine and heroin, directly stimulate chemical receptors in the brain that dissolve pain and that cause you to feel relaxed and blissful. Stimulant drugs, like cocaine, amphetamine, ephedrine, nicotine, and caffeine, bind to other chemical receptors in the brain that cause a sense of mental alertness, confidence, and well-being. Sedative drugs, such as the benzodiazepines and barbiturates—sometimes called downers—work on yet another chemical receptor, replacing anxiety with tranquility. Scientists do not yet know precisely which effects of alcohol on the brain cause people to feel relaxed and giddy. All other drugs, including the hallucinogens, marijuana, and volatile substances, cause you to feel high in some manner. Most if not all drugs also stimulate the release of the chemical dopamine in parts of the brain that reinforce habitual behavior. When this brain system has been mobilized, it becomes very hard to stop using. (In laboratory experiments, mice will stop eating and drinking in order to continue pushing a lever that electronically stimulates that portion of the brain.)

Most drugs are also reinforcing because you must continue to take them in order to avoid going into withdrawal. If you have a habit and stop using cocaine, for example, you immediately become severely depressed. You feel like you are dying, and you may want to die. You will do anything to get another hit of cocaine, even if you cannot get enough to feel high. You just want to avoid feeling miserable.

Not surprisingly, we all respond to different drugs in different ways, which is why we are likely to become addicted to one drug over another, or to avoid becoming addicted at all. Alcohol abuse, for example, tends to run in families. If you have a first-degree relative who is alcoholic, then you are approximately four times more likely to become addicted to alcohol yourself, usually at an early age. You may be less susceptible to the side effects of alcohol and tolerate larger amounts. For some people marijuana causes a sense of pleasant relaxation. For others who may be less likely to use it more than once it causes *paranoia*. Some drug users prefer stimulants, while others prefer downers. Some people like the expanded sense of consciousness that hallucinogens can induce. Others find *hallucinations* frightening.

Some drugs appear to be intrinsically more addictive than others. Judging from its widespread use, nicotine may be the most addictive drug of all. A high percentage of people who try tobacco go on to use it regularly. You smoke more and more and have great difficulty stopping. Of course, nicotine is a legal drug, and it would probably be used less if it were illegal. Cocaine, in the natural form of leaves from the coca plant, which are chewed slowly, is not very addictive. However, when it is transformed into crack cocaine, it becomes highly addictive. Crack cocaine is either smoked or dissolved and injected directly into the bloodstream. In both cases, the drug reaches your brain much more rapidly, causing an intense but short-lived *euphoria*. When something makes you feel so good, it is hardly surprising that you want more. But crack users will also tell you that they never recapture the intense feeling of their first use.

There is no such thing as an alcoholic or drug-abusing personality. Everyone is vulnerable to cravings and addiction. This is most evident with nicotine. Since tobacco is not an illegal drug, and since addiction to cigarettes is still socially acceptable, we can see that a wide range of people can become addicted. Since some other drugs can be obtained only through illegal means, you are more likely to get involved with these drugs if you have *impulsive*, reckless, and *antisocial* personality traits. You may also be less concerned about the consequences of your behaviors on yourself and on others and therefore less motivated to stop. Nevertheless, many people who become addicted to drugs do not have a particular personality problem; rather, they experiment, use too much, and then have trouble stopping.

Some people are more vulnerable to drug or alcohol use because of their environments. Heavy alcohol use is encouraged in many college fraternities, for example. Marijuana use is considered acceptable by many parents, who view it as a harmless drug. Some high school students view cigarette smoking as a cool way to act like an adult. And drugs like cocaine are more readily available in some urban settings. Many military personnel who served in Vietnam became addicted to heroin, but the vast majority were able to stop using, unassisted, when they returned to America. If you are surrounded by friends who drink or use drugs as much as you do, then you may not realize that you are developing a problem.

Rates of drug and alcohol addiction are three to four times higher among the seriously mentally ill. Psychiatrists refer to co-occurring mental illness and substance abuse as a dual diagnosis. Many people with *anxiety* disorders use alcohol to feel relaxed, especially in public. If you suffer from *depression,* you may use alcohol or stimulants in an attempt to improve your mood. When experiencing *mania,* many will drink or use drugs to enhance euphoria. Since most drugs of abuse and alcohol can cause depression and anxiety, it can be difficult to sort out whether you have an underlying psychiatric illness or are experiencing the direct or indirect effects of the drugs. People with schizophrenia also are more prone to abusing alcohol and drugs. You may find that alcohol, marijuana, and sedatives provide some temporary relief from the anxiety caused by your *psychotic* symptoms. You may also be pressured by neighborhood drug dealers to purchase their drugs. You probably also consume a tremendous number of cigarettes, especially if you find that nicotine improves your ability to pay attention and think more clearly.

What Do We Crave, Besides Drugs and Alcohol?

It has become popular to refer loosely to all sorts of behaviors as addictions. To speak of a "chocolate addiction," for example, trivializes the serious cravings that are experienced in drug or alcohol abuse. At the same time, it is clear that many behaviors are powerfully reinforcing and difficult to stop, even though they do not involve drug use. Some gambling, sexual behaviors, shopping binges, and eating behaviors may be better understood if we think about them as stemming from powerful cravings. They may even share an underlying mechanism in the brain. It is no surprise that we derive pleasure from sex, food, money, and shopping, but some people lose control over these *impulsive* behaviors while knowing that they cause them harm.

Sexual cravings are very similar to drug cravings. Drug users will often compare getting high on drugs to having sex. Some of the chemicals released in the brain during drug use likely are similar to those released during fantasy and orgasm. Sexual behaviors are extremely reinforcing. They make you feel good, and you want to have more. Most people fantasize, at least some of the time, about risky or unusual sexual acts that they would never carry out in real life. But if these fantasies are more exciting and fulfilling than your regular sexual behavior, you might be tempted to try them. Some of these behaviors may be illegal, or they may pose a challenge to your long-term relationship, but if they are pleasurable, you will be tempted to repeat them (see "Sexual Preoccupations"). At some point you may lose control of your cravings and become dependent on the services of prostitutes, ever-expanding sources of pornography, sex with strangers, or the use of fetishes during sex. You may have difficulty stopping, in spite of the financial, social, medical, and legal costs.

Psychiatrists estimate that about two percent of Americans have a similar problem with gambling. The intense thrill of winning is so reinforcing that you are willing to lose over and over again in the hope that you will eventually hit the jackpot. Some people experience a similar thrill from shopping or shoplifting (see "Impulsiveness"). Food is also very rewarding, and you might binge on great quantities of food, or at great expense (see "Appetite Disturbances"). Other repetitive behaviors, like those seen in obsessive-compulsive disorder and bulimia, may be better understood as *compulsions* rather than as cravings. Compulsive behaviors are not pleasurable in themselves; they are performed reluctantly in an attempt to relieve intense anxiety.

How to Cope with Cravings

Of course, a craving is not a parasite, as described at the beginning of this topic. It is a product of your own brain. Every action that you take to satisfy a craving is an action that you choose to initiate or that you succumb to. If you genuinely decide that your addiction is a problem, rather than a source of pleasure, you can stop it. The craving comes from within you, and you can beat it, but you may need help to do so.

The first essential step is to recognize that you have a problem. At first, your cravings are easily satisfied and bring you pleasure. When you are feeling tired, anxious, lonely, bored, or angry, you have a drink or a pill, and you feel better. It may be some time before problems begin to pop up. Your family, or others around you, may recognize that you have a problem before you do. Your boss, your spouse, your therapist, or your parents may tell you that you ought to cut back. They may suggest that you see someone about your problem. You may find this advice, and the implication that you are addicted, insulting, ludicrous, or annoying. Psychiatrists refer to this as a stage of *denial*.

If you enjoy what you are doing, and you are not concerned about the impact your use has on your life, then you will not be motivated to change. Even if you are arrested and ordered into treatment of some sort, you will devote your energies to beating the system rather than to getting better. But at some point it dawns on you that you might lose your job, your marriage, or your friendships. You may have begun to worry about the amount of time and money you spend satisfying your cravings. Perhaps you have begun to notice that you do not enjoy the drug or activity as much as you used to, even though you are using more often. This is a stage of ambivalence. You do not want to give up your addiction altogether, but you think that perhaps you would be better off if you did, or if you curtailed it. You may be concerned that you find it hard to cut back. At this point you may try to stop on your own. Or you may continue to use while considering your options.

At some point you may have a sudden and dramatic realization. You realize that you must stop using, even though using brings you pleasure. You acknowledge that you are out of control, and that your cravings may never go away entirely. You recognize that you will have to take serious steps to avoid indulging them. To stop using you may have to change your lifestyle, enlist the help of your loved ones, and attend self-help groups or therapy. Sometimes a firm recommendation from your doctor or therapist, or an intervention by family members, may be sufficient to help you realize the state you are in.

If you are addicted and want to stop using, you should set short-term goals for remaining abstinent day by day. You may need to check into a detoxification and rehabilitation program in order to get through withdrawal safely (see "Intoxication"). You will engage in relapse-prevention therapy, the mainstay of treatment for addictive behaviors. You will identify your triggers for drug use and develop strategies for coping with them. For example, if you have friends who provide you with drugs, or who continue to use, then you must avoid them, unless they have joined in your decision to stop using. You also must avoid situations and places associated with your addiction. Do not drive through the neighborhood where you used to buy your cocaine; do not stop at the bar where you used to drink. You will come up with excuses to swing by these places, but you must not indulge them; it is hard enough to remain abstinent without tempting yourself.

You will learn in therapy about the nature of cravings and factors that lead to relapse. You will discuss your underlying ambivalence and ongoing fantasies. You will discuss the emotions (such as loneliness, anger, and nervousness) that have led you to use in the past. You will examine how a series of small decisions can culminate in using drugs. For example, you may identify that you feel that you deserve a reward when you stay late at work, leading you to seek drugs on the way home. You will then examine the series of decisions that lead you to stay late, to see if they can be changed in the future.

You will find yourself missing the euphoria that drugs brought you in the past. You will fantasize about using them again. For months after stopping you may have sudden and intense cravings in which the desire to get high overwhelms the risks that you had carefully considered during more sober moments. You will be tempted to use. Refuse to indulge yourself in these thoughts and impulses. Immediately remind yourself of the troubles that drugs have brought you, and distract yourself with some other activity.

The best method to avoid fantasizing and planning to satisfy your cravings is to keep yourself busy with something else. Many people who are fighting addiction take on new projects that fill up their time and keep them satisfied. Your projects must have nothing to do with your cravings, and they should keep you away from your triggers. For example, if you tend to drink when you are alone, then staying at home to write poetry would be a poor choice; the temptation to drink would be too great. Instead, during your free time you might want to volunteer at a hospital or library, where you will be surrounded by others. Consistently spending time with your family in planned activities is a good way to keep your mind from wandering while at the same time surrounding yourself with the people who support you most.

If you relapse into addictive behaviors, do not give up. Even though abstinence is the goal, nearly every user experiences relapses along the way. For example, only one-fourth of alcoholics remain abstinent in their first six months after stopping. The important thing is to resume abstinence as quickly as you can. A relapse is a serious matter, but it is also an opportunity to learn from your mistakes and to modify your treatment strategy. Even if you have avoided a relapse for many months, you should keep in mind that you are still vulnerable. The greatest risk of relapse occurs in the first year. Many self-help groups stress that you must take "one day at a time" and never believe that you are cured of your addiction. Remain vigilant, especially during times of *stress*.

Alcoholics Anonymous, commonly known as AA, was founded in the 1930s and has inspired many other self-help groups. A self-help group consists entirely of other users, though some groups are "open" and allow others to attend and offer support. Most of these groups follow a 12-step approach, which involves a gradual recognition that you have a problem and that you require the assistance of others, including God (or a "higher power"), to avoid relapse. Some other self-help groups follow a Rational Recovery model, which involves the use of cognitive-behavioral strategies adopted from psychotherapy. These groups try to help their members identify the emotional triggers that lead to relapse. Self-help groups can be very effective, in part because the group members know what you are going through, and they can tell when you are in *denial* or in need of support. They will encourage you and share painful but inspirational experiences. You will choose a sponsor, whom you can contact for support when you have a craving. These groups also encourage socialization; you can fill up your time with group-related activities, leaving you little time to think about using.

Most people find it difficult to stop using without the support of family members and friends. It may be even harder to tell your loved ones that you are an addict than it is to acknowledge this to yourself. But if you continue to fool them, it will be much easier to lie to yourself. If you involve your family, they can help monitor you and provide you the support that you need when you are experiencing cravings. You will be tempted to give in to your cravings from time to time, but if you tell your family first, and they support you in your determination to abstain, then you have a much better chance of success.

Most of these relapse-prevention strategies for coping with drug and alcohol cravings also apply to sexual and gambling urges. You must identify the triggers and fantasies that set you on the way to seeking sex, playing cards, or placing bets. Avoid these triggers, and enlist the support of friends and family. Addictive behaviors, especially sexual ones, may be embarrassing to discuss with your loved ones. But the consequences of failing to control your behaviors will be even more embarrassing. You may also find it helpful to keep a diary of your urges and behaviors, to help you monitor the extent of your problem and your success in overcoming it.

Medications Are Sometimes Helpful in Reducing Cravings

There are a few medications that can be effective in reducing drug use or cravings. Disulfiram (Antabuse) is a chemical used in the treatment of alcohol abuse. It interferes with the metabolism of alcohol so that you become sick if you consume even a small amount of it. Some people have died as a result of drinking alcohol while under treatment with disulfiram, and the treatment is safe only if you are not impulsive and are genuinely committed to remaining abstinent. The goal of treatment is to bolster your resolve to avoid drinking, not to punish you if you slip. It does not directly reduce cravings. Acamprosate (Campral), which has been used in Europe for years and which was recently approved for use in the United States, may reduce alcohol cravings once you have become abstinent and increase your chances of remaining sober. There are currently no medications proven to suppress cocaine cravings.

Methadone and LAMM (levo-alpha-acetylmethadol) are long-acting medications that can be useful in the treatment of opiate addiction. They are addictive as well, but they can be dispensed in a controlled fashion by a regulated clinic to prevent escalating use. They are also much safer than heroin, since they are taken orally rather than by needle. Even though these medications substitute one addiction for another, users are often able to remain healthy and return to the workforce. A new combination drug, buprenorphine-naloxone (Suboxone), suppresses opiate cravings and blocks opiate receptors in the brain so that heroin does not produce a high if it is used.

If you want to stop smoking tobacco, there are two medications that may be helpful. The nicotine patch, gum, inhaler, or lozenge works for tobacco addiction in the way that methadone works for heroin addiction: you replace your cigarettes with a healthier form of the drug. The patch delivers a controlled amount of nicotine into your bloodstream through the skin. The nicotine replacement helps reduce your craving for tobacco. You slowly reduce the dose of your replacement therapy over several weeks, easing the effects of nicotine withdrawal. Alternatively, you can start treatment with the antidepressant medication bupropion (Zyban). Bupropion reduces cravings for nicotine and makes it easier to quit, perhaps in part by preventing feelings of depression that typically occur during nicotine withdrawal. You have a one in three chance of successfully stopping smoking if you receive therapy and medication. Only one in ten succeed when simply advised by their doctor to stop. Tobacco suppresses appetite, so if you stop smoking, you should start exercising in order not to gain weight.

A few medications, such as the SSRI antidepressants and hormonal agents, suppress *sexual preoccupations,* but none has been sufficiently studied to prove effectiveness in a large number of people.

If you suffer from cravings, you may also benefit from medication for any underlying psychiatric illnesses, such as *depression* or *anxiety.* However, psychotherapy and medication for these co-occurring conditions are unlikely to be helpful if you continue to indulge in drug or alcohol use. The direct toxic effects of the drugs will overcome any positive effects of medication and therapy. Urine testing for drugs may be required during your psychiatric treatment to ensure that you are abstinent.

How to Cope When a Loved One Is Addicted

If someone you care about has a drug or alcohol problem, you can play a very important role in every step of recovery. You may be the first person to realize that your loved one has an addiction. It may be difficult to tell your loved one that you are concerned. Initially he will likely *deny* that he has a problem, and he may take steps to conceal his addiction from you. He may become *angry* or imply that you are part of the problem. You may fear that if you add to his stress, he will use more. The best approach is for you to be matter-of-fact about your concern and to avoid expressing anger or making threats. However, you may be able to calmly lay down conditions. For example, you might tell him that if he does not seek help, you will have to consider separating. You can offer to accompany him to meetings with a doctor, therapist, or self-help group. In those settings you may be able to provide valuable information about the extent of the problem and its impact on you and your loved one.

You should be realistic about the challenges of recovering from addictive behaviors. Cravings are very difficult to overcome, and a serious lifestyle change may be required. You can be helpful in monitoring your loved one, providing him with emotional support, and making sure that he stays busy. You may need to decide to what extent you are willing to change your life. For example, it might be necessary to move away from a particular neighborhood, or for your loved one to change careers.

Ultimately you will have to decide how much, if any, *deception* you can tolerate in your relationship. If your loved one has cravings, he is going to lie to himself and others. Even if you recognize that this is a part of the illness, you may not find it acceptable. By being matter-of-fact and practical, rather than angry and judgmental, you may be able to lay groundwork by which your loved one agrees to be as honest with you as he is with himself. If he has a craving, he agrees to tell you rather than keep it to himself. If he uses, he confesses to you and not just to his self-help group or therapist.

You have to recognize that nearly everyone who is addicted has at least one relapse following a period of sobriety. If you are willing to stick with the relationship you should be willing to help your loved one through a relapse. You can be clear about your expectations and what you expect from him if he should have a lapse. You should keep in mind that he will likely continue to use less and less so long as he is genuinely committed to stopping.

Deceitfulness

What a coincidence, you tell the man sitting next to you at the bar, you were the president of your high school class as well. You would have been the valedictorian, too, if you hadn't been so busy cheerleading. After all, that was the year that you led the squad to victory in the national competition.

He says he's surprised that you were a cheerleader. Well, you respond, of course you're not in the same shape that you were in twenty years ago, but you look pretty good for your age, don't you?

No, he says, he's surprised because his wife hadn't mentioned you. She was a cheerleader at Monroe High in the '80s. Really, you say, what was her name? He asks you to wait just a minute while he goes off to look for her. You'd love to see her, you say, before you gulp down your drink and hurry away from the bar.

Lying is not usually a sign of mental illness. After all, most of us lie every day. We would appear odd if we answered every social question as truthfully as possible. We tell white lies in order to protect our privacy, to avoid complicated explanations, and to spare people's feelings. Even if we agree that lying is ethically wrong in principle, there are many situations when telling a lie might be justified (for example, if you were to give the wrong directions to an assassin, leading him away from his intended victim). Even though deception can be commonplace, it is also a significant feature in several mental illnesses.

Pathological Lying Is Usually a Sign of Personality Disorder

When people refer to someone as a "pathological liar," they probably mean someone who has a personality disorder and finds it as easy to lie as to tell the truth. Psychiatrists do not recognize a mental illness characterized solely by compulsive lying, as if lying were a tic that could not be suppressed. When you lie, it is because it serves some useful purpose.

If you have an *antisocial* personality disorder, you lie in order to con and manipulate others and to avoid facing the consequences of your actions. You are facile with words and skillful at feigning emotions. You can trick a gullible stranger into giving you money or convince a girlfriend not to leave you after she has caught you cheating. If you are a store clerk and the manager discovers that money is missing from your cash register, you weave an elaborate story implying that another clerk took it, and that you are embarrassed to have to say so. You use deception so frequently, and with such skill, that you lie almost automatically. You are surprised when someone catches the discrepancies in your stories, but you quickly invent a new explanation. If that does not work, you pretend that you are shocked—outraged!—to be accused of telling a lie. If you protest loudly enough, most people will believe you or be too scared to say otherwise.

Lying or exaggeration is commonly seen in several other personality disorders. If you have a narcissistic personality disorder (see "Grandiosity") you may exaggerate or invent skills and accomplishments while denying your personal problems and failures. Beneath your superior veneer you feel worthless and vulnerable. You hope to convince others that you are someone important. If you have a *histrionic* personality disorder, you exaggerate almost everything. You feel that "life is a cabaret," or it should be, and you see nothing wrong with adding a little color to make your stories and your life more glamorous, more dramatic. In your stories, and to some extent in your mind, you are close friends with all of the important and interesting people, and you may hint that you have slept with most of them as well. As in narcissistic personality disorder, your *self-esteem* is actually very fragile, and you need to feel that other people are impressed by your importance and therefore want to be around you.

Sometimes People Lie About Their Symptoms

Doctors occasionally find themselves treating patients who have invented or intentionally produced their medical symptoms. For example, I once evaluated a woman who used a hypodermic needle to inject watered-down feces into her blood. The injection caused a fever, and when she presented herself to a hospital she was admitted for treatment of a bacterial infection. She did not improve, though she should have, and eventually she was caught injecting herself with a dirty needle while in her hospital bed.

Psychiatrists assume that such patients have a psychological need to be taken care of and force themselves to become ill. Perhaps they enjoy being surrounded by doctors and nurses and being treated as a puzzling medical case. Unfortunately, the condition and motivations are poorly understood, since most patients deny the deception when it is discovered and quickly flee the scene. Psychiatrists refer to the illness as a factitious disorder. Most reported cases involve women, often nurses who have medical knowledge and access to pills and equipment. In some dramatic cases, patients have undergone multiple unnecessary abdominal surgeries by going to one hospital after another and claiming to have illnesses and symptoms that were never in fact diagnosed or treated. In the past this was called Munchausen's syndrome, after a historical figure known for his tall tales. In a related condition, some parents have been caught inducing false medical symptoms in their children, presumably with the goal of receiving attention for themselves as tragic, care-giving parents.

Sometimes people pretend to have medical or mental illnesses for reasons other than to be treated as patients. In fact, they may not want to receive actual treatment at all. You may exaggerate back and neck pain after a car accident in order to make more money in a lawsuit. You may pretend to be hearing voices to avoid responsibility for a crime. You may exaggerate symptoms of stress in order to avoid returning to military duty. You may claim to be suicidal on a cold night in order to enter a hospital and receive a comfortable bed and meals. Or, if you are addicted to narcotics, you may go to one doctor after another claiming to have severe pain that does not respond to over-the-counter medications. Psychiatrists refer to this type of intentional deception as malingering. It is a rational strategy for getting needs met and is not, in itself, a mental illness.

At the other extreme psychiatrists use the term minimization when referring to a patient who knows that she is mentally ill but pretends otherwise. For example, if you tell your therapist that you are no longer suicidal, while in fact you are planning to harm yourself, then you are minimizing your depression. Minimization is common. Unfortunately, the assessment and proper treatment of mental illness depends largely on your ability and willingness to accurately describe your internal thoughts and feelings. You may be more likely to be honest if you believe that your loved ones, doctor, and therapist want to help you and will not punish you for reporting symptoms (for example, by committing you to a hospital). *Denial* is also common in mental illness but, in contrast to minimization, is not a form of deception. If you are in denial, you genuinely do not appreciate that you are mentally ill.

Lying is a common feature of drug and alcohol use, gambling, and sexual *preoccupations*. In each of these conditions you conceal your *craving* from others because you are embarrassed by your behavior, the behavior is illegal (at least in some cases), and you do not want to be asked or forced to stop. Even though you tell yourself that you want to stop using, you are afraid of losing your options if other people get involved. If your loved ones ask, you deny that you have a problem, or you tell them to mind their own business. When you arrive home late because you stopped to buy drugs, you claim that you were finishing a project or driving a colleague home. If you agree to see a therapist, you may not reveal the real source of your problems. You say only that you are depressed or anxious.

Finally, in some conditions a patient may appear to be lying when in fact she is confused. In dementia (see "Memory Loss") you are unable to remember recent events, and you may unconsciously invent stories to fill in the gaps. This is known as confabulation and is completely unintentional. In schizophrenia and other *psychotic* illnesses, you may have *delusions* or *hallucinations*. When you describe your unusual beliefs and experiences, people may mistakenly assume that you are making things up or telling tales. Even though what you describe may be false, you believe it to be true.

How to Cope with Deception

If you have a tendency to lie, then you probably are not interested in a cure. You can fool most people most of the time, and you find that lying is a useful strategy. You will be motivated to be more consistently truthful only if you think it will serve your interests. You may have such a realization if lying has begun to get you in trouble, rather than helping you to avoid trouble. You may find that your spouse, your family, your colleagues, your therapist, or the police no longer trust you. You realize that you have a credibility problem.

Since lying is an entirely volitional behavior, not a *compulsion,* no specific treatment is indicated aside from motivation. If you exaggerate your accomplishments or invent medical symptoms, then therapy may be helpful in building your *self-esteem* and assisting you to develop more effective strategies for relating to others. If you tend to minimize your symptoms of mental illness, then you should work with your care-givers to develop better trust and communication.

If someone you care about is disingenuous, you should consider whether her intention is to deceive you for some ulterior purpose, or whether she is just protecting her privacy or covering up feelings of inadequacy about her actual accomplishments and skills. If the latter, you can communicate to her that you care about her for who she really is and that you are not impressed by superficialities.

Sometimes loved ones tell minor lies to preserve a certain amount of privacy without intending to harm anyone. As a parent you may be particularly concerned when your adolescent children start to conceal things from you or lie to you for the first time. You want to communicate clearly that you do not accept this from loved ones, that it is impossible to have a relationship without trust. At the same time, try to recognize if you are being too intrusive or demanding.

If someone you know regularly tries to deceive you for gain, then you should probably avoid any significant relationship with that person. Lying is likely to be just one of a number of *antisocial* behaviors you can expect. There may be no benefit to confronting your acquaintance with her lies, unless you need to confirm your suspicions. Confrontation may lead only to denial, argument, and threats. You may be better off not letting her know you are on to her game. However, you may want to tell other friends, colleagues, or family members about your concern, since they may have been deceived as well.

Delusions

At last the time has come: the world will end on New Year's Day.

All of the signs have come together. There was the hurricane in Florida and the earthquake in Mexico. Fires are raging in California. Last night you saw seven stars form a circle around the moon.

You can tell that people are worried this year. They watch you reverently as you pass down the street. They whisper to each other and burst into tears. They know that you are a prophet and that their souls are at stake. You predicted this long ago, and it is there in your diary for everyone to read. All of the signs have been detailed, year after year. No one believed you last year, but this year they'll see. The world really will end.

Delusions are unchanging beliefs that are held on inadequate grounds. They often defy logic and persist in spite of contrary evidence. Along with *hallucinations* they are symptoms of *psychosis* and involve a break in reality. They are most commonly associated with schizophrenia but can also occur in other psychotic illnesses and in severe *depression* or *mania*.

Some delusions are bizarre and obviously false to most people. For example, you might believe that you have come from another planet. Other delusions concern matters that could happen in the real world. For example, you might develop a false belief that your spouse is having an affair or poisoning your food. Sometimes the delusions seem to have some personal meaning, while other times they seem completely out of character and unrelated to any previous experience. Delusions are often long-standing and unchanging, but some delusional beliefs come and go and change as the underlying illness waxes and wanes. The most significant feature of a delusion is that no amount of arguing will change it, since logical thinking is disturbed during psychosis.

There Are Several Common Types of Delusions

The most common form of delusion is a persecutory delusion, the belief that others are trying to harm you. You may focus on a family member, someone at work, a famous politician, the police, the FBI, or people of a particular race. You may believe that demons are pursuing you, or that people are harming you through the practice of witchcraft, voodoo, or spells. You may think that high-tech devices are being used to monitor you or control your thoughts. You may believe that people are harassing you for a specific purpose: to force you to have sex, to enlist you in a secret mission, to break down your willpower, or to drive you crazy. The unrealistic fear of being persecuted is also referred to as *paranoia*.

Grandiose delusional beliefs are the most common after persecutory delusions. *Grandiosity* is the belief that you are someone very important. For example, you might believe that you are a politician, a religious prophet, an entertainment celebrity, or an award-winning scientist. Grandiose delusions are common in both schizophrenia and in *mania*. Grandiose and persecutory delusions often occur together. After all, you must be important if so many people are out to get you. If people do not recognize and celebrate you as the important person that you are, then someone must be conspiring to keep you from becoming famous.

An erotomanic delusion is the false belief that someone, often a celebrity, loves you and intends to marry you. Many stalkers suffer from erotomanic delusions. You may continue to believe that you are in a relationship even when your victim has repeatedly taken you to court and testified against you. You may believe that you are both persecuted and desired by the object of your delusions. One of my patients believed that the president had sent the FBI to spy on him because he was having an affair with the president's daughter. Delusional *jealousy* is the false belief that your partner is having a romance with someone else.

Delusions about the *identity* of others are also common in schizophrenia. You may believe that people close to you have been kidnapped and replaced with imposters. The imposters may be robots, witches, or spies who look exactly like your loved ones. You are convinced that they are not the same people that you knew, though you may be unable to explain how you know this. You may treat your loved ones differently or even attack them. You might lock your wife out of the house or call the police to arrest your mother.

A somatic delusion is the false belief that something is *physically* wrong with a part of your body. For example, you might believe that you are riddled with cancer, even though medical tests all show normal results. You might believe that your body is the host to worms that you can feel moving about in your stomach or bloodstream. You might believe that you are pregnant even though you have not had intercourse. A nihilistic delusion is a belief that the world is about to come to an end. You may believe that the impending destruction of the world is your fault. Somatic and nihilistic delusions are more common in severe *depression* than in schizophrenia.

Some Unusual Beliefs Are Not Delusions

Even psychiatrists can be challenged to sort out delusional beliefs from normal but unusual beliefs. After all, we do not live in a perfectly rational world, and people believe many things that they might have trouble explaining. Though we might be reluctant to admit it, irrational thinking is common for each of us at times. We are most irrational when thinking about topics that are very emotional: our weaknesses, our hopes and desires, the people we love or admire. Sometimes these beliefs are referred to as fantasies. When you discuss fantasies with a family member, friend, or therapist, you can usually accept their realistic feedback. You are able to apply logic to determine whether your fantasy is realistic or just wishful thinking. This is the difference between fantasy and delusion. A delusion persists in spite of all feedback. The process of testing a person's belief to see if it responds to evidence and rational feedback is called reality-testing.

There are other beliefs that may be false but that are passed on within a culture and often go unquestioned. Prejudices, rumors, and historical myths may be believed by many people who do not have enough information, or desire, to logically challenge what they have assumed to be true. We all have prejudices, and we all form inaccurate opinions on matters about which we are relatively uninformed. These are not delusions and are not signs of mental illness.

However, a person who becomes psychotic may retain these beliefs or prejudices, and they may become exaggerated to the point of becoming a delusion. For example, if you hold racist beliefs before becoming ill you may become convinced at the onset of a psychotic episode that members of another race are conspiring against you. But delusions are particularly illogical, even when they originate in commonly held prejudices. For example, I have worked with several black patients who believed that they were members of the Ku Klux Klan.

Religious beliefs can also be confused with delusions. Religious beliefs are a matter of individual faith. They cannot be proven true or false. They are usually shared by other members of a religious community. For example, many people who are not psychotic believe that spirits of the dead, angels, and demons can influence everyday life. The leader of a religious community can assist in distinguishing between orthodox beliefs and idiosyncratic beliefs that may be due to mental illness.

Delusions Can Occur in Several Illnesses

Delusions are most commonly observed in schizophrenia (see "Psychosis"). However, some people experience long-standing delusional beliefs without hallucinations or disorganized thinking. The delusions do not change much over time, and they are not bizarre (that is, they involve beliefs that could be true but are not). Psychiatrists label this pattern of illness a delusional disorder. For example, I treated a man who believed that he was an undercover police officer and that he must protect his neighborhood. Before being hospitalized, he patrolled the area all day, asking strangers for identification. He carried an "identification card," which had obviously been printed by hand and laminated. He never heard voices, and he always spoke coherently. Delusional disorder typically develops in the fourth or fifth decade, later in life than schizophrenia, and it appears not to respond as well to medication. It tends to be accompanied by alcoholism. It is rare and poorly studied.

Severe *depression* and *mania* can cause a break in reality. Your mood may determine the content of the delusions you experience in these illnesses. Mania usually causes grandiose delusions, while depression causes morbid, guilty, or nihilistic beliefs. Delusions in mania may change from day to day.

Delusions that appear late in life may be caused by dementia, in which paranoia is a common response to *memory loss*. Drug abuse and medical illnesses (such as head injury or stroke) can also cause delusions.

How to Cope with Delusional Beliefs

Since a person with delusions does not recognize that he is delusional, he often does not go to a psychiatrist for treatment, except perhaps to request treatment for the anxiety that he experiences because of his fears. As far as he is concerned, his beliefs are real. But if he is brought to treatment by others, or if he seeks help himself, antipsychotic medication (see "Psychosis") will bring at least some relief. The delusions that occur during an episode of schizophrenia usually begin to respond to medication in a matter of weeks. The severe distress and fear that accompanies delusions may begin to subside within days of starting treatment.

Long-standing delusional beliefs are more difficult to treat. Even if the underlying belief does not go away, medication may be effective in reducing the strength of the conviction. For example, I once treated a man who believed that he was being persecuted by the Mafia. Every time a car drove down his street he would run and hide behind furniture. He installed extra locks on his doors and slept on the floor in his closet. He carried a gun in his car in case he were ever attacked. He accepted medication, not because he realized he was delusional, but because he was too anxious to fall asleep. With treatment, he continued to believe that the Mafia was following him, but he found it amusing rather than threatening. He stopped worrying that his life was in danger, and, most importantly, he stopped carrying the gun.

Psychotherapy by itself is not an effective treatment for delusions. Delusions do not respond to logical thought or discussion. In the midst of a psychotic episode you cannot think or talk yourself back to reality. However, once your thinking has begun to clear with antipsychotic medication, psychotherapy may be very beneficial in helping you to readjust to the real world, to develop strategies for distinguishing between delusions and reality in the future, and to cope with the reality that you have an illness.

If you experience delusions, you may continue to have occasional thoughts that others would find unusual or illogical, even though you are taking medication. You will learn which thoughts to share with friends or strangers and which thoughts to keep to yourself. When you think, for example, that someone might be following you, you should remind yourself that you have had similar beliefs in the past, but that nothing bad happened. There is no need to panic. You should not confront the person you suspect may be following you. Instead, you should contact your psychiatrist once you get home. You should share all of your worries in therapy.

Delusional beliefs can be a particular challenge for family and friends. We are not used to talking with people who seem to be living in a different world with different rules. For many of us, talking to a person with delusions may remind us of talking to a child who has fantastic beliefs. But if you speak to an adult with schizophrenia as if he were a child, he will probably find you condescending. He may think that you consider him a fool, and, consequently, he may become more suspicious of your intentions.

It is better to calmly discuss delusional beliefs in a respectful yet direct manner. Express interest in his views and listen to his beliefs, but acknowledge that you do not share those beliefs. You will be trusted more if you acknowledge the difference in how you see things than if you try to pretend that you share his delusional belief system. It is generally unwise to enter a delusional system to convince a loved one to do something. For example, I knew a nurse who would routinely convince a patient with grandiose beliefs of being an army officer to take his medication by pretending to telephone the president of the United States for an order. This may work in the short term, but it reinforces the delusional belief and plants the seeds of distrust in a patient who is already paranoid.

There is no point in arguing with a delusional patient. No matter how logical your argument may be, it will not prevail. In fact, you may make matters worse by showing your anger and frustration. A delusional loved one may become increasingly convinced that you are arguing from emotions rather than reason and that you do not have his best interests at heart. If he is already suspicious and fearful, such an argument may make him feel increasingly isolated, frightened, and angry.

In treating a delusional patient I often convey that I have worked with many people who have similar beliefs, and that I have found that they feel better once they have someone to talk to about their predicament. I tell them that medication will help them to feel calmer and think more clearly. I acknowledge that it takes a leap of faith for them to trust me and to give treatment a try. You may find a similar strategy to be helpful. You can acknowledge that the delusional person must be in distress because of what he believes is happening to him. You may be able to tell him that you and he have been through this before, that you think he will feel better again once he gets help from a professional. If he is not acutely ill but has persistent delusional beliefs, you can reach a truce of sorts in which you have your beliefs and he has his. You can help remind him which beliefs to act on and which to keep to himself.

Denial

You don't know why you keep these appointments. The doctor doesn't do anything except tell you to keep taking the pills. The pills don't do anything but give you a headache and make you sleepy. And sometimes they make you hear voices.

The voices were getting louder last week, so you stopped taking your nighttime dose. You're feeling better already. The voices are still there, but now they give you ideas for poems. You've been able to stay up later and later and write more. Won't your doctor be surprised when your book is published! He's probably getting jealous already. You can see it in his eyes; he's getting worried that you're coming back to life. He asks, "Have you been taking your medication? Have you been having trouble falling asleep? Are you feeling more energetic? Have your thoughts been racing?"

No, you tell him, this is the best you've felt in months.

Psychiatrists use the term *denial* to refer to a patient's lack of insight into having an illness or psychological difficulty. Denial does not arise from a lack of psychological or medical knowledge, but from a failure to recognize, appreciate, or accept in oneself what is evident to others. If you have schizophrenia, there is a one in three chance that you do not believe that you have a mental illness at all. If you have been diagnosed with bipolar disorder, depression, or general anxiety, there is a one in four chance that you do not appreciate the nature of your illness. Among those who suffer disabling symptoms of mental illness but who have not yet been diagnosed, more than ninety percent do not think of themselves as ill. This last figure probably reflects a widespread lack of understanding of mental illness in general, combined with personal denial.

The most dramatic examples of denial are seen in neurology rather than psychiatry. If you experience a stroke on the left side of your brain, you may be unable to move your right arm or leg, and you may become depressed and frustrated over your loss of function. If you suffer a stroke on the right side of the brain, however, you may also develop a complete lack of insight into the fact that your left side is paralyzed. I examined one patient who moved his right hand when I asked him to move his left. When I held up his left arm, he informed me that he was moving it, even though it was completely still. Another patient told me that the arm I was holding was not his. He suggested that it belonged to the man in the adjacent bed. If you have had a right-sided stroke, you may be surprisingly unconcerned about being in the hospital and the subject of so much attention. Neurologists refer to this variety of denial as anosognosia, which is caused by direct damage to specific areas of the brain.

In dementia it is common to be unaware of the extent of *memory loss*. Initially you may minimize your difficulties, laughing them off as signs of senility. Or you may unconsciously fill in the gaps in your memory with false recollections. For example, you might tell someone in your family that the doctor called to cancel your appointment, when in actuality you forgot to attend. In dementia, such excuses or inventions are usually not intended to be deceptive. You believe that what you say happened actually did happen. Psychiatrists refer to this as confabulation, and it seems to be the brain's attempt to create coherence as the world around you is increasingly erased from memory. As dementia becomes more severe, you may lose whatever insight you had as you progressively forget everything, including the fact that you have trouble remembering. In a sense, this denial is protective; you are less likely to become *depressed* if you do not recognize that you have a serious problem. On the other hand, you may take on unrealistic and even dangerous tasks, such as trying to drive to the mall even though you have forgotten how to get there.

Denial Is a Prominent Feature of Psychosis and Mania

If you have schizophrenia you are unlikely to recognize that you are becoming ill as you develop your first *psychotic* episode. You feel increasingly *paranoid,* but you believe it is because people are trying to harm you, not because you are misinterpreting things around you. If you *hallucinate* voices, you attribute them to ventriloquism, demons, or wireless broadcasts by secret service agents. As you become increasingly confused and distracted you assume that someone is poisoning your food or jamming your brain. The idea of seeking medical help is the last thing to occur to you. In fact, you may think that anyone who suggests this is conspiring to have you locked up.

Delusional thinking is at the root of denial during an acute psychotic episode. Your paranoid or grandiose beliefs seem to offer a better explanation for your distress than any explanation pertaining to mental illness. After all, we are all more inclined to trust our own eyes and ears and logic rather than others who have not shared our experiences. "I'm not making it up," you want to say when your parents tell you that the Mafia is not following you. "If they're not following me, then why do I hear voices whispering in Italian about me? I hear them as clearly as I hear you now." In fact, lack of insight is the most common symptom in acute psychosis, more common even than paranoia or hearing voices.

Many people with schizophrenia continue to lack insight even when their symptoms improve and they are no longer delusional. Some studies have found that as many as three out of four individuals with schizophrenia deny that they have a serious, chronic mental illness, in spite of symptoms and disability that would seem obvious. Those who lack insight are most likely to refuse to take medication or seek help when their illness worsens.

If you are no longer delusional, why would you continue to lack insight into your illness? One likely reason is that schizophrenia affects the frontal lobes of the brain, which are areas that are involved in self-awareness and rational thought. Like the neurological patient who has had a stroke, you may be unable to appreciate the nature of your illness, regardless of your intelligence, prior educational level, and explanations from your doctor and others. Interestingly, many patients can accurately point out in other patients the same signs of mental illness that they fail to recognize in themselves. As one patient told me, "Doctor, I don't need that medication, but could you prescribe something for that guy talking to himself in the corner; he's paranoid as Hell!"

Loss of insight may be the first sign that a person with bipolar disorder is on the verge of becoming *manic*. Between episodes of mania and depression you may have excellent insight into the severity of your illness and the need for medication. You may know all of the symptoms that you need to watch out for, and you may be prepared to see your doctor at the first sign of an episode. Unfortunately, once mania starts to take hold again and you begin to feel slightly optimistic, energetic, and euphoric, your outlook and your plans change. You begin to get annoyed by your doctor's insistence that you take mood-stabilizing medication. You begin to think that there is nothing wrong with feeling good. Within a matter of days you may have lost insight completely, denying that you are, or have ever been, manic. You are sure that you are just being misunderstood, that your loved ones are jealous of your potential, and that your doctor delights in controlling you.

Most People Do Not Like to Think of Themselves as Ill

Such dramatic denial is less common in other mental illnesses. However, most of us minimize our experiences with illness to some extent. Many people prefer to think of themselves as having a problem with "sugar" rather than as suffering from a serious and chronic illness like diabetes. If you suffer from depression you may prefer to think of yourself as stressed-out, discouraged, or fatigued. If you have obsessive-compulsive disorder, you may try to conceal and explain away your compulsive rituals. If you are addicted to cigarettes, you may say that you can stop any time, even though you failed to do so in several previous attempts.

You may minimize your illness for many reasons. Even if an illness affects many areas of your life, you still prefer not to be defined by the illness. You like to think of yourself as the same person you were before becoming ill. You may resent changes in your life, such as taking medication, seeing a doctor, and being monitored constantly by your loved ones for signs of relapse. To avoid further intrusions on your privacy and autonomy, you may conceal milder symptoms or come up with benign explanations for them. You do not want anyone to overreact. This is often a matter of wishful thinking rather than intentional *deception*. You may also think of mental illness as an embarrassing affliction, or you may be afraid of the stigma of being perceived as mentally ill by others. Sometimes doctors collude with a patient's desire to minimize his illness, telling him, for example, that medication is being prescribed to help him sleep or feel calm, when in fact it is for depression or schizophrenia. It is very difficult to develop insight if you know little about mental illness to begin with and your doctor does not fill you in honestly.

Some patients suffer from an exaggerated awareness of symptoms that, on the surface, would seem to be the opposite of denial. For example, if you have hypochondriasis or somatization (see "Physical Complaints and Pain") you may experience pains and discomforts that arise from vigilant attention to your body. Some doctors have characterized *depression* as an illness of excessive insight, of thinking too much about the pervasive challenges and existential dilemmas of life. Even though awareness of symptoms is heightened in these particular disorders, an accurate awareness of illness is lacking. You may not realize that your tendency to see the glass half empty is due to depressive hopelessness rather than realistic pessimism.

Psychoanalysts developed the idea that denial is not just a sign of mental illness, but also a defense mechanism. Defense mechanisms are unconscious processes that keep us from being overwhelmed by unacceptable desires or frightening realities. For example, if your mother died of cancer, you may be unable to cope with the fact that a suspicious spot has appeared on your annual X-ray. You may cancel your follow-up appointments, even though the most rational approach would be to receive a thorough workup and, if necessary, treatment. This use of the term *denial* has become popular, as when we say that someone is "in denial" about being in a destructive relationship or about the slim chances of receiving a job promotion. The use of denial as a defense mechanism can often be addressed in psychotherapy, whereas the more profound denial observed in many mental illnesses may persist in spite of the most helpful feedback and education.

How to Cope with Denial

If you have a tendency to lose insight when you are sick, then you should try to develop strategies during periods of improvement to maintain your awareness and adherence to treatment. The denial that occurs during psychosis and mania is so profound that you should prepare for your loved ones to take over when you become ill. You can develop advance directives that spell out how you would like to be treated, including your preferred medications and care settings. You will likely lose insight into the rationale for all of these plans when you are acutely ill, but after your episode resolves, you will be thankful that you planned ahead. Even if you recognize that you have a mental illness, you may have difficulty accepting the fact that you need medication. You should recognize that medication does not change your thoughts or your personality. It is not a shackle imposed on you by your physician or family. Medication, when appropriately prescribed, helps you to be in control of your thoughts and your moods. You can take medication as part of an overall plan to help you achieve stability and meet your life goals.

Unfortunately, it is extremely common for people to stop taking their medications or to skip doses. Studies have found that most people (including doctors) usually do not complete a full course of their prescribed antibiotics when they are sick. Most people with diabetes, high cholesterol, and hypertension cheat on their diets, skip doses, and sometimes stop their medication without telling their doctors.

Not surprisingly, rates of noncompliance with prescribed medications are even higher in psychiatric illness, since many people fail to appreciate that they have a chronic or relapsing illness requiring ongoing treatment. Unfortunately, half of all patients with schizophrenia stop taking their medication in the first year of treatment, and almost all who stop antipsychotic medication relapse within two years. If you have been diagnosed with bipolar disorder and stop taking your mood-stabilizing medication, there is a fifty percent chance within a year that you will become manic, and a twenty-five percent chance that you will become depressed. In most cases, you will relapse within a few months. One-third of individuals with depression relapse in the first year after stopping antidepressant medication. Even skipping an occasional pill may lead to lower levels of medication in your body and a greater chance of becoming ill again.

If someone you care about has a mental illness, you may find that he sometimes loses insight into the fact that he is ill. He may want to stop medication or stop seeing his doctor. He may resent you for reminding him that he is sick and needs to stick with his treatment plan. It may be difficult for you to strike a balance between letting your loved one make his own decisions and take responsibility for his life, and doing your best to ensure that he does not relapse. You do not want to be perceived as threatening or paternalistic. You want to try to communicate that you are a partner in managing his illness; that you can assist him because your insight into his condition does not fluctuate the way his does. You can remind him where his illness has led him in the past, and how adherence to treatment has helped him to improve. Even if he continues to lack insight into the specific nature of his mental illness, he may be able to learn from his experiences and adhere to treatment because it works. You can always tell your loved one that you understand the leap of faith and courage that is required on his part to accept that he has an illness when he does not feel ill and to follow a treatment plan even when he is uncertain of its purpose.

Specific strategies may be helpful in making sure that your loved one adheres to his prescribed medication. Some antipsychotic medications (see "Psychosis") are available in long-acting injectable forms. The injection is administered every two to four weeks, usually at a psychiatric clinic, and the medication stays in his system at least until the next appointment. The level of most other medications can be checked periodically by blood draw to ensure that your loved one is receiving an adequate dose and is taking what is prescribed. Of course, if you find pills stashed under his pillow, tossed in the toilet, or unused in his pillbox, then you must assume that he has been missing at least some, if not all, of his doses.

Depression

You thought you had defeated this beast. Life was looking pretty good. Both your daughters left for college, where they've been doing very well. Your wife seemed happy. And you hadn't missed a day at work for two years. So why are you now dreading waking up each morning, each day being more painful than the last, with no end in sight? It seems now that you were never really happy, you were just fooling yourself.

Last night you couldn't sleep at all. You lay awake in bed worrying about everything. When the sun came up, you pulled the curtains shut and got back into bed. You spent the whole day in your pajamas. The apartment is a mess, the dishes overflowing in the sink. When your wife got home, she just sighed and loaded the dishwasher. You're too lazy to help her, even though she's worked hard all day and should rest. You don't know why she puts up with you. If she left you, that would be the end.

Over dinner she tries to cheer you up. She tells you stories about her friends at work. She suggests that you both go out to a movie, but you just stare at your plate, and she knows that you don't have the energy. You hardly touch your dinner, even though you have barely eaten all day. The food seems to have no taste. You think that maybe you have cancer, but there's no point in checking. If you do have cancer, you'll die soon anyway.

For a while you tried to keep working. Your family needs the money, and at least your job got you out of the house. But your mind kept wandering off. Sometimes you had to close the door so no one would see you sitting, your face in your hands, crying for no reason. Your supervisor finally told you to go home instead of wasting everyone's time. You cried all the way home and didn't tell your wife for days.

Is life really supposed to be so miserable? Doesn't everyone realize how pointless life is? Maybe it's just you; maybe you think about things too much. But how can you ignore the fact that you've accomplished so little, that life holds nothing for you?

Everyone has experienced the blues at some time or other. When we are under stress, or when something bad happens in our life, we get upset. We wish things could have turned out differently. We worry about the future. We may even cry or curse. Friends have trouble cheering us up. These are normal reactions, and we generally recover from them soon enough, but they give us some insight into the more profound and extended feeling experienced by someone who has depression.

The word *depression* can mean many things. It can be used as a synonym for sadness, in which case it is simply a symptom. Psychiatrists use it in a broader sense to identify a syndrome of sadness, hopelessness, and sluggishness accompanied by disturbances in sleep, appetite, and sexual interest. Doctors now usually refer to this syndrome as a depressive episode, major depression, or clinical depression, to distinguish it from the healthy sadness that everyone experiences at times. Unlike the blues, major depression lasts for weeks, months, or years and causes you to resist the natural tendency to get on with life. If the blues are bumps in the road of life, depression is a rut.

Depression is one of the most common syndromes of mental illness, and it has been recognized and accurately described by physicians and sufferers for well over two thousand years. As many as one in four women suffer from major depression at some point during their lives, and approximately one in eight men. In the United States more than one in twenty people are depressed in any given year. Depression currently causes more disability in developed countries than any other medical illness.

Sadness Colors Everything

The main feature of depression is an overwhelming and pervasive change in mood to a feeling of sadness that is so heavy and oppressive that it is hard to describe. I have heard many people with depression describe this sadness as worse than any pain they have ever experienced. The pain is visible; your facial muscles sag, your eyes are downcast, and your shoulders slump. You break into tears unexpectedly. The sadness is almost contagious. When I talk with someone who is depressed I find myself becoming sad and nearly tearful.

Some people experience and express depression in other ways. Some may appear joyless and irritable. This is particularly common among adolescents and the elderly. Some people seem more anxious than sad. Others conceal their emotions and even brighten up a bit in company. You may be surprised to learn that a friend who did not appear sad when you got together actually has been depressed.

People who do not feel comfortable expressing sadness, especially men, may channel their feelings of despair into *anger* and self-destructive behavior. Someone who used to be easygoing and friendly may become sullen and curse, cancel plans, or bicker over minor matters. For others, sadness is experienced as vague *physical complaints*—such as headaches, stomach pains, faintness, or *fatigue*—that seem to have no medical cause. Depression may cause you to feel emotionally and physically empty inside, empty in a way that is not relieved by eating.

When you are depressed nothing cheers you up. You are unable to enjoy the people and activities that used to give you pleasure. I have worked with several older depressed men and women who would not smile even when visited by their grandchildren. Psychiatrists call the inability to enjoy anything anhedonia. A person with severe depression may become unable to express any emotions at all. His face glazes over, and he cannot even cry. It is as if the source of his tears has dried up.

When you are depressed, sadness also colors all of your thoughts. You feel like the world has defeated you. You feel that you can do nothing right. You feel that nothing can be solved. You feel like your life is a waste. If you are a religious person, you may feel that you have let God down, or that God has forsaken you. You feel that you are to blame for everything, even your depression. You feel that if you were a better person you would be able to overcome your lethargy and sadness. After all, other people have hard lives but do not give up. You wonder why you are so weak. Also, because depression is not widely understood, others may wonder why you do not just pull yourself up by your bootstraps and cheer up.

People with depression often feel that they are a burden to family and friends. I have treated many people with depression who wanted to kill themselves in order to spare their spouse or children the trouble of taking care of them. A depressed person may be unable to see that his death would hurt loved ones much more than any temporary inconvenience caused by his illness. Depression causes you to lose perspective and to become oblivious to the needs and concerns of others around you.

When you suffer from depression, you ruminate constantly. You carry the weight of the world on your shoulders. You worry disproportionately about your job, love life, family, relationship to God, and health. You become preoccupied with memories of bad times. You have trouble distracting yourself. You are unable to let go of trivial matters. You find yourself crying over old conversations. You are constantly apologizing. You may worry that you have lost a friend forever because you had to miss her party. You worry that you will not be able to provide for your children. You worry that your spouse will leave you.

Sometimes these worries become so extreme that they break with reality. For example, I treated a woman who worried that she had contracted a venereal disease from someone she had dated long ago, before her marriage. She was certain that she had infected her husband and child, even though there was no evidence of infection. Her belief reflected the guilt and loss of perspective that she was experiencing during her depression. When thinking breaks with reality it is called a *delusion*. Many people with depression develop a false belief that they are on the verge of bankruptcy and abandonment.

Depression causes people to lose perspective about the future. The loss of hope is profound and difficult to understand if you have not experienced depression yourself. You probably can remember a time when you suffered from a stomach virus and could not stop vomiting. At that moment you probably felt that the nausea and pain was the worst feeling in the world, and it seemed like it would never go away. Intellectually you understood that you would feel better in a day or two, but the sick feeling kept dragging you back into the present. Depression causes a similar feeling of misery, but it goes on for day after day and week after week. You think that you will never get better, or that life can only get worse. You forget what it feels like to be happy, even if you had a joyful life only a month or two earlier. You begin to doubt that anyone can help you, including your doctor and family. As you begin to lose all hope, you may begin to wonder whether life is worth living. You may wonder whether the world would be better off without you.

Depression Affects Sleep, Appetite, and Sex

Major depression affects more than your mood. It also causes a disturbance in your body's natural rhythms. Psychiatrists refer to these changes in sleeping, eating, energy level, and sexual habits as the neuro-vegetative symptoms of depression.

In most cases *sleep problems* occur alongside depression. Food loses its flavor, and eating is no longer pleasurable (see "Appetite Disturbances"). Some people with depression come close to starving themselves to death. The combination of decreased sleep, decreased appetite, and profound and visible sadness is typical of melancholic depression, a subtype that has been recognized for centuries. The name derives from the ancient Greek word for "black bile," which was thought to be the cause of depression.

Some people with another form of depression sometimes referred to as atypical depression experience the opposite change in their sleeping and eating patterns. You may have trouble falling asleep but then sleep late into the morning. When you finally get up in the morning you feel better than you do late at night, when the depression starts to return. You find yourself craving food. Since you are eating more while being less active, you may gain weight. If you have atypical depression, you may brighten when you are in the company of others.

In both men and women depression may lead to a loss of interest in sex. *Sexual performance problems* can lead to conflicts in your relationship, and your doctor may mistakenly think that you need couple therapy rather than treatment for depression. Unfortunately, many of the medications used to treat depression can cause sexual disturbances as well, prolonging the problem even after the depression has begun to recede. Women may also stop having menstrual periods during depression.

Life Slows Down During Depression

Most people who experience depression also slow down notice-ably in their thinking and *movements*. Psychiatrists refer to this as psy-chomotor retardation. Every movement seems to take so much energy. You walk slowly. You eat slowly. You speak slowly. You take long pauses and sigh between sentences. You make few spontaneous movements or gestures. I have known many patients who essentially stopped moving altogether, sitting still the entire day. You are easily *fatigued* and leave many tasks unfinished. You become *sloppy* and stop taking care of your appearance, even to the point of not washing or changing your clothes.

Speech and thinking are also slowed in depression. You speak softly and slowly and with less rhythm and tone. You may eventually be reduced to speaking one syllable at a time. People find themselves leaning forward, straining to hear you, and they may become bored or weary trying to listen to you. Your thinking is sluggish, and you are unable to follow the more rapid speech of people around you. You find it difficult to concentrate, remember, or solve problems. In the elderly slowed thinking may be confused with senility (see "Memory Loss").

On the other hand, you may feel on edge, with continuous *anxiety* and restlessness. You worry about everything, and your worries are expressed in constant movement. You pace and move objects from one spot to another. You wring your hands or slap your forehead. While frenetically occupied with these minor movements that accomplish nothing, you may be slowed in your purposeful movements. This anxious and *hyperactive* pattern of depression is more common in the elderly.

What Is the Course of Major Depression?

Depression can occur at any age. For some people depression follows a seasonal pattern. In such cases, you become depressed in the fall and winter and begin to recover in the early spring. These seasonal *mood swings* can seem natural when they are mild, but if you become sad and unproductive every winter you may, in fact, be depressed.

The first episode of depression most often occurs when a person is in his twenties. Though depression can seem to come out of the blue, it usually occurs after a stressful event, such as losing a job, experiencing a death in the family, or separating from a loved one. You may have left home or started at a new school or job. Even happy occasions can be stressful, such as the birth of a child, a marriage, or a graduation. Over several weeks or months you become increasingly nervous and unproductive. You begin to think that you are a failure. You become increasingly sad and tearful. You lose your patience easily. You cannot see a solution to your problems. As depression begins to settle in, your sleep pattern and appetite change, at which point you should seek treatment if you have not done so already.

Most people who experience depression do not seek psychiatric treatment. This is unfortunate. Without treatment, an episode of major depression usually lasts for at least six months. In some cases it becomes deeper over time until you no longer venture out of your home and you stop eating and begin to have *suicidal thoughts.* In some cases you may begin to hear voices and lose touch with reality (see "Psychosis"). With treatment, however, depression begins to lift within several weeks. Mild depression responds well to psychotherapy. More severe depression generally does not respond to talk therapy or go away spontaneously, but it can resolve with medication.

Most people have more than one episode of depression. Your chances of having a second episode increase if you are young when you experience your first episode, if you have been mildly depressed for years, if you lose touch with reality, or if someone else in your family has also experienced depression. Generally, antidepressant treatment should not be stopped if you have experienced more than one episode of depression, because of the extremely high likelihood that you will become depressed again. If you have experienced three episodes of depression, you are almost certain to have another unless you remain in treatment.

Depressed Mood Can Occur in Several Other Illnesses

Psychiatrists contrast major depression to the milder, but longer lasting, form of depression known as dysthymia. If you suffer from dysthymia, you feel unhappy and discouraged most of the time. You may feel that you have been unhappy all of your life, but you do not have trouble with your sleep, appetite, or sexual functioning, and you handle your job responsibilities adequately. Dysthymia affects approximately two percent of the population each year and does not go away spontaneously. Unless you receive treatment you are likely to remain mildly depressed for years. You and those who know you may think that depression is simply a part of your personality.

Many therapists believe that another ten to twenty percent experience milder and less pervasive patterns of depression that are nevertheless troubling. In these comparatively minor depressions you are likely to experience a variety of *physical complaints,* vague dissatisfactions, *anxiety, sleep problems,* and *fatigue,* none of which is persistent or disabling on its own. These symptoms may lead you to seek therapy, but it is unclear whether they respond as well to medication. Some people may also experience brief episodes every few weeks of recurrent depression, in which symptoms are more severe but last only a few days.

Bipolar disorder is an illness characterized by episodes of depression alternating with episodes of *mania*. As many as one out of four people who experience an episode of depression will eventually be diagnosed with bipolar disorder after also experiencing an episode of mania. Until this happens, it is difficult to distinguish major depression from bipolar depression; depressive episodes look exactly the same in both illnesses. If a member of your family has been diagnosed with bipolar disorder, or if your mood becomes elevated (see "Euphoria") when you emerge from depression, then you may be more likely to have an underlying bipolar disorder. If so, antidepressant medication may not be the treatment of choice in the long term.

After the death of a loved one many people naturally develop symptoms of depression (see "Grief"). Depressed mood can also occur for a short period of time following any major *stress* or setback. Psychiatrists refer to this as an adjustment disorder, which is a temporary inability to carry on normally.

Depression commonly occurs in women immediately after giving birth, especially after their first baby, but it is usually mild and lasts only a week or two. Mothers tend to feel irritable, fatigued, and helpless and have tearful episodes alternating with moments of joy. For about one in ten women, however, postpartum depression is more severe and prolonged. You experience most of the typical symptoms of major depression, and treatment may be needed. If you become depressed after giving birth the first time, then you are at greater risk of developing postpartum depression again after future pregnancies.

If you have schizophrenia (see "Psychosis"), you are also at risk for developing depression. Paradoxically, many patients become more depressed as their psychotic symptoms improve, when they realize that they are suffering from a serious and chronic illness.

Several medical illnesses and medications can cause depression. For example, depression commonly occurs as a direct result of stroke or thyroid abnormalities. Beta-blocker medications (such as propranolol or Inderal) that are commonly used in the treatment of high blood pressure and coronary artery disease can sometimes cause depression. Depression is also extremely common in dementia (see "Memory Loss"). Half of people diagnosed with Parkinson's disease become depressed, and one in four of those with multiple sclerosis. The psychological impact of having a serious or painful illness, like cancer, may also cause depression indirectly.

Many people who develop depression also use alcohol or illegal drugs (see "Intoxication"). Since these substances can cause or exacerbate depression, it is crucial that you stop drinking and refrain from drug use if you are going to engage in treatment for depression. Sometimes depression emerges briefly when you stop drug use, for example, during the first few days of abstinence from cocaine. The terrible feeling of depression that occurs during withdrawal is one of the reasons why it can be so difficult to stop using.

What Causes Depression?

Depression does not have a single cause. In the past, psychiatrists distinguished between endogenous and reactive depressions: the former was thought to be a biological illness that occurred spontaneously, like a heart attack or a bout of pneumonia; the latter was thought to be a psychological response to some loss or stress. We now believe that the development of depression is more complicated. An episode of depression is usually brought on by a variety of stresses in people who have a biological predisposition to the illness. You may be particularly predisposed to depression under *stress* if you have no one to talk to, if you are stuck at home, and if you are responsible for the care of others.

Most studies have shown that your chance of developing depression is two to three times higher if you have a first-degree relative who has been diagnosed with major depression. Women also seem to be predisposed to depression, with rates that are approximately twice as high as men. It remains unclear whether this gender difference is due to biological differences in women (for example, different levels and fluctuations of hormones) or to the different lives that women live, compared to men (for example, higher rates of childhood abuse, less economic power).

Experiences during childhood, such as the loss of a parent, parental conflict, or an unpredictable and abusive home life, may have left you particularly vulnerable to loss and depression in the future. Rates of depression in adulthood are much higher in these cases. On the other hand, the strengths that you have developed in overcoming early adversity may protect you from future stress.

Your underlying temperament may predispose you to becoming depressed. Are you the sort of person who blames yourself when things go wrong? Do you lack positive feelings about yourself? Are you anxious? Are you overwhelmed by setbacks? Do you tend to view failures and losses as insurmountable? Do you feel trapped by your circumstances? If so, these ways of thinking can make disappointments and frustrations more depressing. Even if your personality style has played a role in your depression, this does not mean that depression is your fault in any way. Unfortunately, depression is not a state of mind that can be overcome simply by trying harder. But by altering your ways of thinking in a more positive direction, you may be less susceptible to depression in the future.

As with several other psychiatric illnesses, psychiatrists believe that depression is ultimately the expression of a chemical imbalance. Abnormal levels of neurotransmitters, the chemical signals released by nerve cells in the brain, have been detected in depression, and antidepressant medications appear to exert their effect by blocking or augmenting the effects of these chemicals. The neurotransmitters most likely to play a role in depression are serotonin, epinephrine, and norepinephrine. Many hormones, which are chemical signals that travel through the bloodstream, also play a role in depression. For example, low levels of thyroid hormone can cause depression. Research has shown that psychological stress induces changes in hormone and neurotransmitter levels.

How to Cope with Depression

The good news is that depression is treatable. Antidepressant medication is highly effective, and psychotherapy can help you through a depressive episode, whether or not you choose to use medication. In either case you should be evaluated by a physician to receive a thorough medical workup and a proper diagnosis. Even if your symptoms are relatively mild, they may have a cumulative effect if they persist for months or years. You may become increasingly hopeless and desperate without treatment. Depression can usually be treated at home, though hospitalization is safer if you are having *suicidal thoughts*.

Psychotherapy is less likely to be effective as a sole treatment for moderate to severe depression, especially for the melancholic type of depression. In fact, it may be counterproductive to spend time talking about yourself during a severe depression, when you are likely to be morbidly self-critical and pessimistic. Antidepressant medications are more effective and work faster. But even with medication you have to be patient, since you are not likely to feel better for at least a couple of weeks. Most doctors who prescribe antidepressants are general doctors, not psychiatrists, and unfortunately they often prescribe doses that are too low, or they abandon treatment too early. If you are not feeling any better after three to four weeks, your medication dose should usually be increased.

If you have responded well to medication, then you will want to discuss with your doctor the advantages of continuing to take medication. If this was your first episode of depression, and if the symptoms were relatively mild, then you may want to stop medication after about six months and hope for a sustained remission. However, depression is a chronic and re-current illness for many people. More than three out of four will have another episode of depression within three years after antidepressant med-ication is stopped. Fewer than one in four relapse when medication is continued. If your symptoms were severe, if you became suicidal, or if you have a strong family history of depression, then it may be safer to stay on medication even after a single episode.

Psychotherapy is an effective treatment for mild to moderate depression about half the time. In therapy you will be educated about depression and encouraged in your efforts to get better. You will be reassured that you are not losing your mind and that you will get better. Depending on the type of psychotherapy, there may be more focus on monitoring and changing depressive thoughts or resolving current difficulties, especially in your relationships with other people. These are referred to as cognitive-behavioral and interpersonal techniques. Some people feel much less de-pressed after a single therapy session simply from learning about depres-sion. You may not need further treatment.

When you are depressed, try not to be too hard on yourself. Depression is not your fault. Many people before you have suffered from depression, including many famous and accomplished individuals. It will pass. Do not worry too much about others when you are depressed. Your friends and family only want you to get better, and they will understand that you are not your usual self. Concentrate on yourself until you are feeling better. You should stay as active as you can. Keep going to work if you feel better when you are busy and around other people. But keep in mind that work may be too stressful, and no one benefits if you go to work and do nothing.

You should not make major changes while you are depressed. Your depression may cloud your judgment so that minor problems appear irresolvable. When you are feeling better, your job, your marriage, and the stresses of being a parent may all seem less of a problem than they seemed when you were depressed. However, depression sometimes can serve as a stimulus to reevaluate the life you have been living. After you have recovered from depression, you should take steps to improve and to reduce stress in your life. If you are miserable in your job, you should explore other options. If you are in a relationship with someone who makes you feel worthless, you should reconsider whether the relationship is worthwhile. You can explore these options in psychotherapy if you wish. Therapy can also help you to learn how to change your life in much smaller ways that will reduce your chance of becoming depressed again in the future.

Do not be surprised if you experience feelings of depression in the future. Do not panic. Like everyone else, you will continue to feel the blues from time to time even if you are on an antidepressant medication. If sad feelings, doubts, and weariness persist or become more severe, consult with your psychiatrist. A simple increase in the dose of your medication, or restarting your medication, may prevent a full-blown episode of depression.

If you care for someone who suffers from depression, you can best help your loved one and yourself by recognizing it as an illness and learning about it. Avoid blaming the person with depression, since the depression is largely out of his control. It is not caused by a defect in willpower, motivation, or morality. No one chooses to be depressed any more than one chooses to have a heart attack or breast cancer. Fortunately, treatments exist, and you can help make sure that your loved one gets the treatment that he needs.

Even though depression is not caused by a personality defect, it does temporarily affect the personality style of the depressed person. Do not mistake temporary moodiness and loss of interest for trouble in your relationship. The person who is depressed is likely to lose interest in activities that you used to enjoy together, including sexual activities. These are symptoms of the illness, and your relationship will likely return to normal once the depression is treated. Even if your loved one says that the relationship is sour, keep in mind that depression is affecting his view of life in general. So long as he is depressed, he will see everything in the bleakest terms possible, which may arouse your resentment. You will not necessarily be able to convince him otherwise, or cheer him up, but you can remind him to be patient, since he is likely to feel differently once the depression has lifted. You need to keep your own perspective while remaining sensitive.

Of course, one of your most important roles is to support your loved one when he is feeling so depressed that he develops *suicidal thoughts*. Though suicide is the gravest risk posed by major depression, there are many other serious complications to the illness. Depression can be more disabling than many physical diseases. A parent has trouble taking care of his children, a spouse has trouble going to work, and a young adult has trouble keeping up with schoolwork. Everyone in the family is affected when someone is depressed. Your support can be invaluable in providing the practical and emotional support to other family members. You may also be able to help in other little ways, such as reminding your loved one about doctor's appointments and encouraging him to take his medication each day.

Antidepressant Medications

Antidepressant medications are highly effective in the treatment of major depression and dysthymia. According to multiple studies, major depression resolves in a matter of weeks in about two-thirds of cases treated with an antidepressant. For those who do not improve after taking adequate doses of one medication, the antidepressant can be switched or augmented. Nearly half of patients improve with the second medication that is tried. It should be noted that about one-third of depressed patients improve with placebo treatment, suggesting that some effects of medication are nonspecific. Your expectation for improvement may be therapeutic.

More than a dozen antidepressant medications have been developed since the discovery of imipramine in the late 1950s. Currently antidepressant medications are grouped into several different classes: tricyclic antidepressants, monoamine oxidase inhibitors (MAOIs), serotonin-specific reuptake inhibitors (SSRIs), and a variety of newer medications that do not fit into any of these groups. All antidepressant medications appear to be equally effective, with the possible exception of trazodone (Desyrel), which may not be as effective in severe depression.

Tricyclic antidepressants were the first to be developed and include imipramine (Tofranil), desipramine (Norpramin), and nortriptyline (Pamelor), among others. Once the treatment of choice, they are now prescribed less often because of their side effects. They tend to cause dry mouth, blurry vision, constipation, sedation, lightheadedness, and sexual dysfunction. They can also slow the rhythm of the heart, posing a danger to elderly patients and patients with certain medical conditions. This effect on the heart also makes the tricyclic antidepressants particularly dangerous in a suicide attempt by overdose.

MAOIs, including phenelzine (Nardil) and tranylcypromine (Parnate), are the least commonly prescribed antidepressants because of the potential interactions between the antidepressant medication and many common foods and medications. When taking an MAOI, you must avoid aged, ripened, or fermented food products as well as a variety of medications. Otherwise, the interaction causes a hypertensive crisis, a potentially deadly increase in blood pressure that is accompanied by a severe headache. MAOIs may be effective when other antidepressants have failed. When switching to, or from, an MAOI, it is necessary to wait several weeks with no medications prescribed (a washout period) so that they do not interact with each other.

Newer Antidepressant Medications Have Fewer Side Effects

The most commonly prescribed antidepressant medications are the SSRIs, which include fluoxetine (Prozac), sertraline (Zoloft), fluvoxamine (Luvox), paroxetine (Paxil), citalopram (Celexa), and escitalopram (Lexapro). These medications do not affect the heart and are much less dangerous in an overdose attempt. They tend to have fewer side effects, and the side effects that do occur are better tolerated. They can cause nausea, headache, anxiety, restlessness, or trouble sleeping, especially early in treatment. They also commonly interfere with sexual desire and *sexual performance*. However, sexual side effects can usually be treated with sildenafil (or Viagra). Though viewed as harmless by most doctors, these medications can interfere with the metabolism of some other medications. To prevent adverse effects, the prescribing doctor must carefully consider these potential medication interactions.

Several other antidepressant medications do not fit into the other categories. Bupropion (Welbutrin) usually does not cause the sexual side effects seen with other antidepressant medications. However, it can cause nausea and trouble sleeping in some patients. Seizures can occur at doses higher than prescribed. Venlafaxine (Effexor), mirtazapine (Remeron), and most recently duloxetine (Cymbalta) were each released in the past decade and have various side effects similar to those of the SSRIs. Another relatively new medication, nefazadone (Serzone), is rarely prescribed because of potential liver side effects.

Doctors usually prescribe a low dose of antidepressant medication initially. You may require an increase in dose every few weeks until you begin to feel better. If higher doses are still not effective, a different antidepressant medication should be tried. Psychiatrists may also recommend other strategies, such as adding lithium (see "Mania") or combining antidepressant medications, when a single antidepressant medication alone is not having the desired effect. In any case, patience is required; the positive effects of treatment with antidepressant medication are not evident for four to six weeks. Once you have found a medication that works for you, you can relax knowing that antidepressant medication is highly effective in preventing a recurrence of depression within a year.

Other Medical Treatments for Depression

For patients who suffer from seasonal depression, phototherapy (or light therapy) may be effective. Phototherapy involves the use of a special bright light, which imitates sunlight, for approximately thirty minutes once or twice a day. Phototherapy is used throughout the fall and winter months. It may be used alone or in combination with psychotherapy and medication. Half of patients with seasonal depression improve with phototherapy, usually within a week of starting treatment.

Electroconvulsive therapy (ECT), more commonly known as shock therapy, is the most effective treatment for depression. It does not have any of the side effects caused by medications, and it works much faster, often within a week or two. ECT is the treatment of choice when the symptoms of depression are so severe that the rapid relief of suffering is critical. ECT may be the treatment of choice when depression is accompanied by *psychotic* symptoms, *suicidal thoughts,* slowed movement, significant medical illness, pregnancy, or malnutrition. Three-fourths of patients improve with ECT, even in these most difficult to treat groups.

ECT involves a procedure during which an electrical current is passed through the brain to induce a seizure. This is performed under anesthesia to prevent muscular convulsions that would otherwise take place. We do not know why ECT treats depression, but depressed patients often feel better after two to three sessions. ECT is usually administered two to three times a week for a few weeks before it is reduced to a weekly maintenance treatment. Typically a course of ECT is administered over a couple of months. In the meantime, antidepressant medication may be started as a long-term maintenance treatment.

The only side effects of ECT are a brief period of confusion following the procedure and temporary loss of memory for events around the day of the procedure. Some people experience more severe *memory loss*. The anesthesia and induced seizure have potential risks, but those risks are generally small compared to the risks of using antidepressant medications, or of leaving depression untreated. Unfortunately, this highly effective treatment has a bad reputation, largely because it used to be administered without sufficient anesthesia, leading to muscular convulsions that were disturbing to watch and which could result in broken teeth and bones. Nowadays, the procedure is considerably safer, and patients who have undergone ECT for the treatment of depression overwhelmingly recommend the treatment.

There is one over-the-counter treatment for depression. The plant St. John's wort contains the chemical hypericum, which has antidepressant properties. Several research studies done in Europe suggest that hypericum is an effective treatment for mild depression, though its effectiveness for more severe depression is in doubt. Unfortunately, botanical products like St. John's wort are not regulated, have not been thoroughly tested for safety, and can have unexpected side effects and interactions. For example, St. John's wort increases the metabolism of birth control pills and several other medications, sometimes making them ineffective. The amount and preparation of hypericum in any particular brand of St. John's wort extract may vary. Because of the unpredictability of the product and its effects, many doctors are reluctant to recommend the use of this or other botanical products. Even if you do choose to treat your depression with this over-the-counter botanical product, you should still see a psychiatrist for a medical workup, assistance in monitoring your depression, and consideration whether to undergo psychotherapy.

Dissociation

You thought you had forgotten all about the mugging. But when you were walking home from work your heart started pounding and your mouth dried up. You felt like you couldn't get home soon enough. You practically ran the last block and quickly locked the door behind you.

You called your sister, and she reminded you that it has been exactly a year since you were attacked. Funny, you couldn't recollect the date of the mugging, but your body remembered. You might be feeling better if the mugger had been caught, but you weren't able to tell the cops anything about him. All you remember is the point of a knife against your back and the pain of your face being pushed against a brick wall.

Dissociation is an altered state of consciousness in which parts of mental functioning split apart and awareness is restricted. We generally experience our body and mind as a seamless, unified consciousness that retains its identity over time. In dissociation, however, you may feel like you are a stranger in your own body, or that your memories belong to someone else. You may be unable to remember aspects of frightening or fearful experiences. You may feel uncertain who you are and whether you are in control of your feelings and actions. Dissociation is usually brought on by the shock of a *traumatic* experience.

Most people experience milder forms of dissociation at some point during their lives. When you are under stress, exhausted, deprived of sleep, or famished, you may begin to feel strange about yourself. Psychiatrists refer to this as depersonalization, the sensation that you do not feel right in your body or that you are somehow disconnected from your thoughts and actions. The sensation is difficult to capture in words; you feel like you are experiencing yourself from an alien perspective. You may feel like a robot going through the motions. In more extreme cases you may feel like you have come out of your body or that you are watching yourself as if you were an actor in a play.

Derealization is a similarly strange feeling in which the world around you feels suddenly different. You feel as if you are operating at a different speed from the rest of the world. The world may seem two-dimensional, and you may feel like you are watching a movie. The air through which you walk may seem thick. Sounds are louder or softer, and colors are more vivid or faded. Objects seem highly focused or far away. One person described to me how posters in his room seemed to develop three dimensions and stand out from the wall.

Déjà vu is another common dissociative experience, in which your sense of time and memory is briefly disturbed. You feel that you are reliving a moment in your life exactly as you experienced it before. You try to play the moment back in your mind, but it is hard to capture it clearly. Another common dissociative experience is to lose track of the passage of time while performing a monotonous task. For example, you may find that you have almost completed a journey down a familiar highway, yet you have no recollection of passing the usual landmarks along the way.

In most cases these strange disturbances in your sense of *identity* and reality are temporary. In fact, you may find yourself struggling to hold on to the strange sensation, wondering if it offers you some new clue to the nature of reality. Throughout the experience you realize that nothing has really changed. You realize that you and the world around you are physically the same as they were before. (If you think that the world has really changed—for example, thinking that the world around you is just a computer simulacrum, or that an imposter has hijacked your body—then you probably have a *delusion*.) Chronic and continuous feelings of depersonalization and derealization are rare unless you have a schizoid personality disorder (see "Oddness").

Hypnosis works by inducing a dissociative state. The hypnotist focuses your attention to such an extent that you block out everything from your conscious awareness except her instructions. During hypnosis you may be able to access feelings and memories that you were not consciously aware of when you were awake. The memories that you form when you are in this impressionable state are difficult to recall when you awaken, as if they were laid down in a secret chamber of your mind. When you come out of a hypnotic state you may be surprised to learn how much time has passed. Something similar occurs during meditation. When you focus your attention on a simple prayer, symbol, sound, or your own breathing, you essentially induce a hypnotic state. Once you are in that altered state, you may have a sensation of coming out of your body, of experiencing the world from a high vantage point, of understanding deeper truths, or of being at one with the universe.

Dissociation also occurs in religious trance and possession. Many religions use rhythmic music, chanting, incense, and fasting to induce a dissociative state similar to a hypnotic or meditative state. In these trances you may come to feel possessed by a god and speak and behave in a manner characteristic of the god but uncharacteristic for you. You may speak in tongues, make pronouncements, and thrash or dance about. You may pass out, and you may not recall anything when you come out of the trance. While in a trance or possession you may be able to walk on nails or hot rocks or pierce your skin without being aware of any pain.

Dissociation Is a Common Response to Trauma

Most of us dissociate when facing a life-threatening situation. Our bodies release a variety of chemicals when we are in danger, and these chemicals help us to focus our attention narrowly on the threat. We are able to shut out distracting information, often including pain. We may concentrate on feelings and sensations that are difficult to put into words afterwards. For example, you may remember the sensation of your heart pounding, or the smell of an attacker, but you may be unable to recall what he said or describe his face. You may be puzzled afterward by these memory gaps. During a traumatic event you may also become numb or confused. You may feel like events are proceeding slowly, as if in a dream. You may feel like you are floating above your body, watching it from a distance. You may also feel numb following a shocking loss, such as the death of a loved one or news of a terminal illness (see "Grief").

Approximately one-third of those individuals who have a *traumatic* experience continue to feel as if they are in an altered state in the days and weeks following the event. Some feel that their life has taken on new meaning. For others the world feels like it has become darker and more dangerous. For many of us who were in New York City on September 11, the streets of Manhattan in the weeks that followed seemed more vivid and magical, yet also frightening. Any unexpected noise could make you panic, but every moment alive seemed richer and more valuable.

After a trauma, you may feel numb and disconnected, as though your body is just going through the motions. You may find yourself blanking out. On the other hand, memories of the trauma may erupt suddenly into consciousness, in the form of nightmares and *flashbacks*.

The more threatening and prolonged the trauma, the more likely you will have dissociative symptoms after the event, and the more likely you are to develop symptoms of post-*traumatic* stress disorder (PTSD). Many scientists suspect that dissociation is a sign that the mind is unable to deal directly with trauma and must keep it separate from conscious awareness.

Several other dissociative syndromes can occur following a psychological shock. In conversion disorder, you develop neurological impairments without any physical injury. For example, when faced with a job or relationship crisis, you suddenly become blind, mute, or paralyzed (see "Physical Complaints and Pain"). In dissociative amnesia you suddenly lose *memory* for a period of time. For example, you may forget everything about an extramarital affair you had one afternoon at a motel. If you escape from a fire that kills your family, you may behave as if you never had a family. In dissociative fugue you appear in a new town or city, having forgotten your *identity* altogether. You may assume a new identity and be untroubled by your inability to recall your previous life.

All of these syndromes appear to emerge in the face of conflicts that you are unable to resolve directly. Your loss of memory or neurological impairment serves to keep the conflict at a distance, out of conscious awareness. It is as if your mind—like a computer operating system—has crashed and is operating in "safe mode," in which very little can be accessed until the problem is fixed. Fortunately, the dissociation is usually temporary and is fairly easily treated. The use of hypnosis or anxiolytic medications (see "Anxiety") may help the therapist to uncover the psychological conflict or trauma that caused the symptoms. Once the conflict is made explicit, the symptoms promptly resolve.

Dissociative symptoms can also occur in other psychiatric conditions. For example, panic attacks may cause feelings of numbness, floating, or confusion. In *psychosis* you can experience all sorts of bizarre disturbances in bodily perceptions and identity. Many drugs can cause dissociation (see

"Intoxication"). Hallucinogens distort the experience of time and space. Ecstasy can cause physical boundaries to feel less distinct so that, for example, you may feel emotionally connected to another person when you touch his skin. Ketamine and some volatile substances can induce a sensation of floating above or outside of your body.

Dissociative feelings can occur in a number of different medical conditions, so a medical evaluation is always important. For example, seizures are often preceded by strange sensations similar to depersonalization or derealization.

Childhood Trauma Can Cause Chronic Dissociation

Prolonged abuse or neglect during childhood can lead to a number of psychiatric problems, the most serious of which is dissociative identity disorder, more commonly known as multiple personality disorder. If you are sexually abused repeatedly early in your childhood, you may have difficulty developing an integrated personality. You dissociate, or phase out, when you are abused, and your memories of the abuse may remain out of reach at other times. Your personality evolves in a compartmentalized fashion, with different experiences, memories, and temperaments evolving in response to your unpredictable environment. You may feel like one person when you are abused, and another person when you are safe. With time, you may develop seemingly distinct personalities that are capable of dealing with different situations as they arise. The splitting of *identity* is a desperate survival strategy for a child who has few other resources for coping with profound and prolonged abuse by caregivers.

As you grow older and escape from the abusive home, the splitting of identity may no longer serve a purpose, but your personality has been established and is hard to change. You probably do not realize that your identity is fractured. You may not even have a core personality that feels most like "you," with other personalities intruding from time to time. You may notice that you have blackouts. After spending time with a friend you may have no recollection of what you discussed. You may encounter items in your possession that you do not remember acquiring. Strangers may greet you by another name. Friends tell you that they have seen you doing things that you do not recall, or that seem odd to you, such as speaking with another voice.

In other cases you may have a sense of the split in your identity. You may feel that there are different aspects to your personality, and that one or another is dominant from time to time. Sometimes your thoughts seem like a conversation, with the different aspects of your personality speaking to each other. The voices may comment on you, or urge you to behave in a certain way. You recognize that the voices are a part of you and not coming from some outside source, in contrast to the way that *hallucinations* are usually experienced in illnesses like schizophrenia. People who know you may be surprised by how differently you behave in different situations. The tone of your voice, your expression of emotions, and your physical mannerisms may change depending on the personality being expressed.

Some scientists are skeptical of the existence of multiple personalities. They suspect that overzealous therapists and suggestible patients unwittingly collude in creating a syndrome that receives a lot of media attention. Patients who begin their treatment by confidently stating that they have a multiple personality disorder most likely do not. They may have an unstable sense of their own *identity* for other reasons, and they may like the idea of having an exotic diagnosis that excuses much of their behavior. The patients I have worked with who seemed to have genuine personality dissociation came into treatment reluctantly, either at the urging of their partners or with vague concerns about memory lapses. In any case, dissociative identity disorder appears to occur very rarely.

How to Cope with Dissociative Symptoms

In most cases, dissociative symptoms are temporary and resolve spontaneously. Unless your environment remains chaotic and threatening, your mind will naturally try to reintegrate fragmented experiences. When dissociative experiences persist, it is usually in cases of severe *trauma*.

There is no simple treatment for dissociative identity disorder. The aim of psychotherapy is to integrate the different aspects of your personality as much as possible. The first step is to provide a safe place in which to explore the splits in your personality and bring them into conscious awareness. Therapists who treat multiple personality disorder believe that therapy is usually successful in helping the patient to experience less dissociation and to feel more unified. However, the condition is uncommon, and treatments have not been rigorously studied.

You should be suspicious of therapists who suggest that your problems stem from being abused as a child when you have no memory of being abused. Studies have shown that significant traumatic experiences are not forgotten for years and suddenly remembered. You may not dwell on painful memories, but you can recall them if you try. Memories that are reconstructed under hypnosis or with prompts and instructions from a therapist often turn out to be false.

Euphoria

What a great show! You whistle along with all the songs and stand up and clap after every one of them. When you applaud the actors at the end of the show you feel that they deserve a standing ovation. You don't know why so many people from your section look annoyed as they get up to leave the theater. The seats were fabulous!

You feel inspired. You could write a musical like that, or even better. As you hit the avenue, you start humming tunes. You could have your first song composed by the time you get home. You step out onto the street, and a car interrupts your reverie, screeching to a halt to avoid hitting you. So what if you're crossing in the middle of the block; pedestrians have the right of way, don't they? You wonder why the driver is so grumpy. It's a great day!

Euphoria is a good feeling, a feeling of being on top of the world. We naturally feel euphoric when we are falling in love, when we are spiritually inspired, or when something wonderful happens. In many ways, euphoria is the opposite of depression. Psychiatrists use the term to refer to someone who feels too good, because of *intoxication* or an underlying illness like bipolar disorder or schizophrenia. Euphoria is one of the characteristic features of *mania.*

Euphoria is one of the earliest signs that mania is developing. Initially you feel optimistic, confident, and cheerful. You interpret things in a positive manner. Things that would have upset you in the past now seem trivial. You feel generous and loving; everyone seems to be your friend. You are bubbling with creativity. Ideas come to you easily and quickly. You begin to make plans. You feel that you will be successful in whatever you do. You reach out to people whom you do not know, or to whom you have not spoken in years. You feel refreshed, even with very little sleep. You think you look better than ever.

Psychiatrists refer to this stage as hypomania, because it is not severe enough to be considered mania. It is a pleasant state to be in, and it is no surprise that people rarely seek help when they are feeling so good. If we could all function at that level we might be more accomplished, and life would be one long parade. When you are hypomanic, people around you notice that you are more active, friendly, and enthusiastic. You are fun to be around. Unless you have been through these stages before, you and those around you may see the change as a sign of health rather than sickness.

Many people experience *mood swings* that never progress to full mania. In a milder type of bipolar disorder that psychiatrists call type II, you experience episodes of *depression* and occasional periods of hypomania. You are likely to become a bit euphoric each time you emerge from a period of depression. Understandably you may not mind the hypomanic periods, in contrast to the profound periods of depression. Other people suffer from cyclothymic disorder, in which mood swings back and forth from mild depression to hypomania over the course of days to weeks. In both cases it is important that the pattern be recognized as a variety of bipolar illness, for which mood-stabilizing medications (see "Mania") are likely to be the most effective treatment.

If you have the classic type of bipolar disorder, hypomania is likely to be a temporary stage on the way to mania. As mania progresses you become elated. You are not bothered by anything. Everything pleases and excites you. Everything is funny. You pun and make jokes. You laugh at your own thoughts, and you do not care if anyone else notices. You try to get others around you to smile and join in the fun. Your mood is expansive. You are constantly distracted by the urge to bring others into the circle of your good feeling. You approach strangers. You share the details of your life with anyone who will listen. The passing remarks of others serve as an excuse to leap into a conversation. People around you find it hard not to smile. On the other hand, your lack of seriousness and intrusive manner may begin to irritate some, and you may not recognize the effect that you are having.

Even the most modest, shy, and secular people may become extremely *religious* and *sexually preoccupied* as part of their euphoria. Love and spiritual communion can inspire a sense of euphoria for most of us. But when you are manic you may mistakenly believe that you are sexually irresistible, that others are in love with you, and that you have a unique and special understanding of God.

As mania becomes more severe, the sense of euphoria begins to be replaced by a feeling of omnipotence and irritability. You begin to feel annoyed by others rather than excited by them. Rather than spreading good will, you demand attention and reverence. Instead of feeling close to God, you may begin to suspect that you are God. Rather than feeling buoyant and sweet, you become *angry* and frustrated. Eventually your mood may become more depressed than euphoric, or the two feelings may alternate from moment to moment. Psychiatrists refer to this stage as "mixed mania," because mood is both *depressed* and manic.

Drug *intoxication* can also cause euphoria. Alcohol, nicotine, sedative medications, and marijuana, when taken in moderation, induce a gentle euphoria, or buzz. You feel content, relaxed, and happy to be with others. Some club drugs and hallucinogens can induce a euphoric feeling of being at one with humanity or the universe. Cocaine and other stimulants cause a sense of well-being when swallowed or snorted, but they can induce a more dramatic rush, or orgasmic feeling, when smoked or injected directly into the bloodstream. Heroin and other opiates (including prescription painkillers) induce a blissful and lethargic state. Essentially all substances of abuse cause some variety of euphoria, some sort of high, that makes them desirable.

There is no specific treatment for euphoria. The significance of euphoria is that it may signal an impending episode of mania. If someone you care about becomes unusually and unreasonably euphoric, you should take her to see a physician, particularly if she has experienced episodes of mania or depression in the past. If necessary, treatment can be started before the condition worsens. You will need to recognize that the person who is experiencing euphoria will not be troubled by it and may be resistant to having it treated. After all, who would want to take a medication that is supposed to make you feel less happy? Rather than arguing that point, you should try to remind your loved one of the periods of depression and manic loss of control that occur without medication.

Fatigue

You asked for a week off from work when you first picked up the flu from your cousin. Your doctor warned you that it might put you out longer, but she had no idea that you'd still be bedridden the following summer. You can manage to get out of bed to sit at your desk, but you haven't been able to do much work because you just can't concentrate. You find yourself staring blankly at your papers and forgetting what you have been reading. Sometimes your head starts pounding, and you just turn off the lights and get back into bed.

You've been losing weight, even though you had to stop exercising. A walk around the block exhausts you. You weren't depressed at first, but now you're getting frustrated and afraid you'll never get better. You think you'd feel better if only someone could tell you what's wrong.

Fatigue is a commonly reported symptom even among people who are not ill. It is a prominent feature of many psychiatric illnesses, such as depression and anxiety, and of many medical illnesses, such as anemia, hypothyroidism, and viral infection. Nearly half of Americans have reported that they have experienced distressing levels of fatigue at some point in their lives. In surveys fatigue is the most commonly reported psychiatric complaint, affecting one-third of women and one-quarter of men at any given time. In recent decades a syndrome of chronic fatigue accompanied by multiple *physical complaints* has been identified, though its causes remain unknown. In other countries, and in America in the past, chronic fatigue has been called neurasthenia, or nervous exhaustion.

If you suffer from chronic fatigue syndrome, you feel tired all day, day after day. Daily chores are exhausting, and you have difficulty taking care of them. If you exert yourself at all you quickly feel drained. You find that you have difficulty concentrating, and you may become forgetful. You are able to sleep at night, but you do not feel refreshed when you wake up in the morning. You may have headaches, stiff and achy joints and muscles, a sore throat, and tender lymph nodes. You may find that you are particularly sensitive to the side effects of medications. As many as three out of a hundred people suffer from chronic fatigue syndrome, with these symptoms lasting for several months.

Scientists do not know what causes chronic fatigue. Some believe that there may be an underlying medical cause, such as a chronic viral infection. Others assume that it is a purely psychiatric syndrome, perhaps a variety of depression or anxiety. The reality is probably somewhere in between, with many factors contributing. For example, there is some evidence that chronic fatigue tends to run in families. If you have an identical twin with chronic fatigue syndrome, you have about a forty percent chance of becoming ill as well. Scientists have found little evidence of a disturbance in the immune system, or of a specific virus. However, many people have developed persistent fatigue following a viral infection, suggesting that infection may precipitate the syndrome. Some research has found subtle disturbances in levels of stress hormones or other chemical messengers, but it is unclear if these are a contributing cause or a result of the syndrome.

More than half of individuals diagnosed with chronic fatigue syndrome have experienced an episode of *depression* prior to the onset of fatigue. A similar number have previously experienced *anxiety* disorders. These rates are high and suggest that mood disturbances and anxiety may increase the risk of developing chronic fatigue at a later date. Chronic fatigue syndrome is distinguished from major depression by the absence of typical depressive symptoms such as sadness, tearfulness, hopelessness, worthlessness, and guilt. If these features are present then you probably feel fatigued because you are depressed. It is also important to distinguish between fatigue and sleepiness. If you have a *sleep problem,* you will feel tired and irritable and have difficulty concentrating during the day. If you treat the underlying sleep disorder, you will stop feeling so fatigued.

Chronic fatigue syndrome also appears to overlap with some other illnesses in which vague *physical complaints and pain* exist without an obvious cause. For example, if you have chronic fatigue, you most likely also experience tenderness, pain, and discomfort at various trigger points and also more diffusely throughout your body. Doctors refer to this condition as fibromyalgia, which has no known cause and cannot be confirmed by specific tests. You may also experience a variety of other persistent discomforts, such as bloating, nausea, weakness, difficulty swallowing, irritable bowel, or food allergies. In addition, males may have problems getting an erection. Psychiatrists refer to persistent clusters of these symptoms without an identifiable physical cause as "somatization." Doctors may be artificially distinguishing between fibromyalgia, fatigue, and somatization based on assumptions about whether the underlying cause is medical or psychiatric. It is probably more accurate to recognize that the brain interacts with the other organs of the body, and that pain, fatigue, and other so-called physical symptoms are always influenced by psychological factors.

How to Cope with Fatigue

If you suffer from persistent fatigue, the first step is to be medically evaluated. You may find, for example, that your blood cell count is low, that your thyroid gland is not producing enough hormone, that you have diabetes, or that you have contracted a viral infection. Several patients who have come to me for the treatment of fatigue have turned out to have hypothyroidism that was easily reversed with thyroid hormone supplementation. Your doctor will also assess you for symptoms of *depression* and *anxiety*. Some medications and drugs can cause fatigue, and, if you are abusing drugs or alcohol, you will need to stop.

If a thorough medical and psychiatric workup reveals no obvious cause of your fatigue, and if your fatigue persists for months, then you probably have chronic fatigue syndrome. There are no proven medical treatments for chronic fatigue. Antiviral medications, steroids, and immune system boosting medications have not been effective. Tricyclic antidepressants (see "Depression") are known to be effective in treating some pain syndromes, and they have been somewhat effective in relieving symptoms of chronic fatigue. However, they are not much more effective than a placebo, and they may cause side effects that exacerbate your illness. You may be tempted to take megavitamins, but there is no evidence that they are effective. Some studies have shown that magnesium may be a helpful supplement, though there is no evidence of magnesium deficiency in people who suffer from chronic fatigue.

Probably the most important approach to living with chronic fatigue is to try to modify your lifestyle. You may find it helpful to simplify your life, eliminating chores and responsibilities that stress you out and exhaust you. However, you must force yourself to continue to engage in activities that you enjoy, or you run the risk of becoming increasingly isolated and inactive. This is particularly important with exercise. One of the prominent symptoms of chronic fatigue is that you become disproportionately exhausted when you exert yourself. On the other hand, physical exercise has been proven to improve mood and energy levels, in both healthy individuals and those suffering from chronic fatigue. Studies have shown that if you cautiously maintain or reintroduce exercise into your life, you will eventually feel better, even if you feel more exhausted initially.

You do not necessarily need to see a therapist if you suffer from fatigue. However, if anxiety or depression is a significant part of your illness, then psychiatric care is important, and medication or psychotherapy may ameliorate many of your symptoms as well as your overall sense of well-being. If you suffer from chronic fatigue syndrome, you probably do not view yourself as psychiatrically impaired. But you may find it helpful to discuss psychological factors that may exacerbate or perpetuate your illness, and psychological strategies to minimize your disability.

Fears

One thing you miss about living in the country: the buildings were only one to two stories high. Since moving to the city you've had to walk up and down eight flights of stairs at work and two flights at home. Most everyone around you thinks you're an exercise freak; only a few people know that you're scared of elevators.

Not that elevators are unsafe, you keep telling yourself. But once you were in an elevator when it was stuck between floors. You were trapped with four other people, and you panicked. Now your heart starts racing just thinking about it. In fact, you start to sweat just passing the elevators in the lobby. The doors innocently "bing" as they open and beckon to you.

Fear is a normal human emotion. Fears help remind us to avoid danger. Fear mobilizes our bodies to cope with the danger at hand. Scientists refer to this as a "fight or flight" reaction, which results from the release of certain chemicals (like epinephrine) into the brain and bloodstream. Our pulse quickens, our skin tingles, and our eyes focus on the danger. Some of us are temperamentally cautious, and others are born to take risks. But fear is universal. And many of us develop fears that are far out of proportion to any actual danger.

Phobias are the most common mental health problem in the United States. A phobia is an irrational fear of a specific object or situation. Approximately one in ten Americans suffer from at least one serious and disturbing phobia. Many people fear common animals or insects, such as snakes, spiders, bees, rats, birds, cats, or dogs. Many adults fear airplanes, elevators, or automobiles. Children especially may be afraid of storms, water, or imaginary monsters in the dark. And many people are afraid of blood or bloody situations (including needle sticks or injections, bodily injury, or surgery). Many of us are familiar with the medical terms for the common fear of heights (acrophobia) and closed spaces (claustrophobia). Psychiatrists call these fears "specific" phobias.

If you have to face the object of your fear, you become extremely *anxious*. Your pulse increases, your breathing becomes rapid and shallow, your mouth dries, your palms sweat, your hair stands on end, your skin develops goose pimples, and you get butterflies in your stomach. Until the fear-inducing situation has passed, you have trouble thinking about anything else. You may become flustered. You may have a full-blown *panic* attack. If you are with others, you will probably be as embarrassed as you are frightened. You may blush and stammer an apology. I have a fear of airplane turbulence, and until recently I always broke into a sweat at the first bump. My pulse would pound, and I would put down my magazine and start to pray. I would stare with concern at the flight attendants, wondering why they had not run to their seats to buckle in. I tensed all my muscles and braced for the next jolt, while the other passengers continued to calmly chat or read their books.

If you have a fear of blood, needle injections, or bodily injury, the reaction may be different. Your blood pressure drops, you become lightheaded, and you may even pass out if you are standing. This occurs commonly when medical students observe their first surgery, and when volunteers give blood. This group of blood-related phobias appears to run in families and may have a genetic mechanism.

Fearfulness is a common feature of many other mental illnesses. You may be terribly afraid of embarrassing yourself in public, and so you make great efforts to avoid being scrutinized or judged by others. Psychiatrists refer to this as a social phobia, which is characterized by *avoidance* of many social or professional situations. In hypochondriasis, you may misinterpret or exaggerate *physical complaints and pain* and begin to fear that you have a serious and undiagnosed medical condition. You may suffer from *panic* disorder and experience attacks of extreme fear out of the blue. Panic attacks may cause you to develop a general fear of going out in public; psychiatrists call this agoraphobia.

If you are afraid of, and avoid, situations that remind you of *trauma* you have experienced (such as a car accident or rape), you may have a post-traumatic stress syndrome rather than a simple phobia. If you suffer from obsessive-compulsive disorder you may be afraid that something bad will happen to you if you do not act on your *compulsions*. If you suffer from schizophrenia, you may be *paranoid* that someone, or something, is trying to harm you. The fears in schizophrenia are different from those in phobias in that you genuinely believe that you are in danger. If you suffer from phobias you are in genuine distress but you realize that your fear is irrational.

Where do phobias come from? It is commonly believed that a person develops a fear of dogs, for example, because he was once bitten by a dog. Yet snakebites are rare, and a fear of snakes is very common. Psychiatrists believe that phobias are learned, though some of us may be genetically more vulnerable than other. We learn to be afraid of objects and situations either because we have had bad experiences with them ourselves, or because others have taught us to avoid them. For example, you might have an unexpected *panic* attack in a locker room and thereafter be scared to get undressed in front of others. Or your parents might have been scared of water and raised you to believe that swimming was dangerous. Consequently, when you venture near water you become nervous, reinforcing what you learned from your parents. We learn that we remain safe and secure when we avoid the objects of our fears, and so we continue to avoid them.

Phobias Can Be Treated with Psychotherapy

The treatment of phobias involves unlearning the fear through psychotherapy. The most successful method is called exposure therapy. If you are motivated enough, perhaps because your phobia interferes with your job or your enjoyment of life, then you will trust your therapist to gradually expose you to the thing you fear most. First you will learn ways to relax yourself. These include muscle relaxation exercises, breathing techniques, and visualization of peaceful situations (see "Anxiety"). Next you will learn to remind yourself that your fear is irrational. Most likely nothing bad will happen to you if you get on an elevator, board a plane, or pet a dog. Some therapists also use hypnosis to reinforce your confidence.

Exposure therapy begins as the therapist assists you in thinking about, or visualizing, the object or situation that scares you. Some therapists use computer programs to simulate a scary situation. Gradually you become bolder and practice looking at pictures or getting close to the object of your phobia. For example, you might look at a picture of a snake, or take a trip to an airport. Eventually you feel confident enough to confront your fear directly. Once you have used your relaxation techniques successfully in an encounter, you are likely to be even more confident the next time you confront your phobia. Eventually, your fears may go away completely. The technique is slightly different with blood phobia, since you must learn to tense, rather than relax, your muscles. Otherwise your blood pressure may drop, and you may faint.

Medications can also play a role in the treatment of phobias. Beta-blocker medications (such as propranolol, or Inderal), which are usually used for high blood pressure, can be very effective, especially for treating the fear of speaking in public, commonly known as performance anxiety. Anxiolytic medications (see "Anxiety") like alprazolam (Xanax) may also have a role in reducing fears that are encountered on an occasional basis, for example if you are afraid of flying but have to take a plane trip to attend a family wedding. These medications are potentially addicting when used routinely and can have side effects such as sedation and confusion. Newer antidepressant medications (see "Depression") are very effective for the ongoing treatment of social phobia and agoraphobia, both of which involve the fear of being embarrassed in public.

Flashbacks

You are driving through town as you would on any given day when you first become aware of the burning smell. You open the car window and, almost without thinking, pull over to the side of the road. You reach for your cell phone, but you can't remember where the numbers are stored. A child is screaming. You recognize your son's voice, only you know he's much older now. You see him running down a hallway as fire licks the walls behind him. You pick him up and run out the front door, the sound of sirens cutting through the haze of smoke. Then the smoke clears and you find yourself standing on the sidewalk, next to your car, the phone still in your hands.

The smell of smoke drifts away. No one is in danger. Your son is off at college. You were probably just smelling someone's burnt breakfast from a nearby home. You lean against your car and try to breathe slowly.

"Flashback" was originally a cinematic term, but it has been borrowed by psychiatry to describe the experience of intensely recalling past experiences. If you have lived through a *traumatic* experience, you may find not only that the memories continue to haunt you, but that they remain nearly as vivid as when the event first took place. Rather than fading like other memories, they intrude and seem more real than your everyday life. When a flashback occurs, you feel as if you are reliving the experience.

Flashbacks are often triggered by something nearby that is reminiscent of the trauma. A war veteran hears a low-flying plane and thinks he is under attack from enemy soldiers. An assault victim walking along a crowded sidewalk smells a particular aftershave and recalls being pressed against a wall by a stranger's body. A car accident victim tenses his whole body at the sound of screeching car brakes, fearing that he is being rear-ended again. An adult who, as a child, was beaten by a parent experiences the same feelings of terror and anger when his boss yells at him. Even an individual's thoughts and feelings can trigger a flashback, seemingly out of the blue.

When you experience a flashback you may behave as if the event is being replayed. You may act aggressively or defensively. A war veteran may roll on the ground, run for cover, or strike out unexpectedly when reexperiencing combat memories. Those experiencing flashbacks might scream in terror or shout in anger at imagined people. They may even threaten people around them, confusing those individuals with the figures in their mind. If you have post-traumatic stress disorder (PTSD), you may also experience vivid nightmares that are similar to the flashbacks you experience while awake. You may thrash or strike out in your sleep, disturbing or even injuring a loved one who shares your bed.

Scientists believe that flashbacks are the result of the unique way in which memories are formed and stored during life-threatening situations. When you are terrified, threatened, helpless, or harmed, you pay attention to your internal experiences and your environment in a different way. As stress chemicals are released, your mind shifts into another mode. You remember some things in great detail while neglecting or immediately forgetting others.

Many people speak of trauma being "etched" or "burned" into their memories, and it seems that stress hormones do in fact cause the memories to be more intense and permanent than usual. However, your mind stores the feelings as implicit memories that are difficult to describe in words. For example, we use our implicit memory when we ride a bike; you cannot describe what you are doing, but your body remembers. In a similar manner, you may be unable to describe what happened to you during an attack, but you can relive it during a flashback. You might be able to talk about an attack without showing any emotion, yet you suddenly feel terrified without realizing why after touching fabric that has the same texture as the corduroy pants worn by your assailant. Seemingly innocuous sensations tap into otherwise concealed but vivid memories.

About one in ten people with PTSD report experiencing flashbacks. Visual flashbacks are most commonly reported, but that may be in part because visual experiences are easier to describe than smells, sounds, and emotions. You may learn to live with the occasional flashback, and you may avoid people and places that you think are likely to trigger memories.

There are no medications that specifically and consistently treat flashbacks. However, antidepressants (see "Depression") have been used increasingly in the treatment of PTSD and sometimes reduce the frequency and intensity. You may also benefit from cognitive-behavioral therapy, which helps you to identify the sensations and experiences that trigger flashbacks. You will gain confidence and recognize that you can avoid them or control your reactions to them. Eventually you may expose yourself to triggers and practice relaxing (see "Anxiety") and not overreacting. With time the flashbacks may be less intrusive and may begin to fade into the past, like other memories.

Flashbacks may be confused with *hallucinations*, which occur in several illnesses that are unrelated to trauma. Both can be experienced vividly and can compete with reality. However, if you have flashbacks from PTSD, you realize afterward (and often during the flashback) that you are living in your memories. You realize that events did not just repeat themselves, even if they briefly felt real. You realize that trauma has caused a disturbance in your memory, that your mind is not functioning properly. A person who experiences hallucinations generally does not realize that they are a symptom of illness. If you hallucinate voices, for example, you probably think that the problem is not in your mind but with the people who seem to be talking about you.

The term "flashback" can also be used to refer to the delayed effects of a hallucinogenic drug. If you have used LSD, you may occasionally experience symptoms of *intoxication* weeks or months after your last use. Scientists are not sure why or how often this happens.

Grandiosity

You are shocked; the promotion went to that lousy sycophant, when you really deserved it. You even came in on time one day last week so that you could be on hand during the new boss's visit. You also pitched in with the others to buy her a welcome bouquet, though you figured out a way to slip in a card with just your name on it. You're sure your coworkers would have done the same, if they'd been smart enough to think of it.

Well, who wants to work for such an unappreciative queen anyway? You decide to call in sick and stay away from the office for a few days. Let her think you're going to leave. Then she'll regret passing over you.

Grandiosity is an exaggerated conviction that you are a special and important person. As a uniquely special person, you feel that you deserve special treatment. You expect to be recognized by others as important and talented, even if your accomplishments are unremarkable. You expect others to do as you say and to follow your lead. You ignore rules, which you assume were made for others. You imagine that people consider you to be funny, attractive, and someone who is worth spending time with, even though the truth is that they find you to be a bore and full of yourself. You view others as objects to be manipulated. If someone makes an effort to be friendly to you, you quickly calculate whether he is important and, if not, you ignore him. You are constantly thinking of ways to become more powerful, and you imagine that others envy your skills and accomplishments. You feel that you deserve only the best, and you are insulted when others fail to appreciate as much.

Psychiatrists refer to this collection of traits as a narcissistic personality disorder, after Narcissus, a character from Greek mythology who became entranced by his own reflection in a pool. If you have a narcissistic personality you have a grandiose sense of your own importance, and you manipulate and alienate others. All personality traits exist along a spectrum, and some of these narcissistic personality traits are fairly common in milder form. In fact, it may be healthy to have a slightly exaggerated sense of self-esteem. Psychiatrists estimate that fewer than one percent of the population suffer from the full-blown personality disorder, in which these grandiose traits are a persistent and pervasive part of the sense of self and of the interactions with others.

Psychiatrists believe that the grandiose feelings in narcissistic personality disorder actually mask profound *self-esteem problems*. If you are narcissistic you are very easily hurt. You build up an image of yourself as powerful, talented, and desirable because you genuinely fear that you are worthless. Any slight or rejection, even unintentional, unsettles your self-image, throwing you into a fit of *anger* or *depression*. Any failure or loss calls into question whether you are really so special after all. You predictably have troubles at work and in romantic relationships, because others fail to appreciate you sufficiently and because you tend to behave in an arrogant and manipulative fashion.

Grandiose traits are common in some other personality disorders as well. If you have a *histrionic* personality disorder, you like to be the center of attention, and you behave in a dramatic or seductive fashion in order to keep everyone's attention. You treat others like objects to be manipulated in your own personal drama. You speak of casual acquaintances as close friends, and of friends as if they were intimate partners. If you are rejected or slighted you may throw a temper tantrum or make threats.

If you have an *antisocial* personality disorder you simply do not care about others, except to the extent that you can exploit them for your own ends. You believe that rules are made to be broken, and you break them whenever you think you can get away with it. You believe that everyone puts themself first in this world, and anyone who pretends otherwise is a liar or a fool.

Grandiose Delusions Occur in Psychosis and Mania

The grandiosity that occurs in the personality disorders reflects a pervasive and lifelong failure to empathize with others and to cope with underlying feelings of inadequacy. Grandiosity of a different sort is seen in other major mental illnesses, like bipolar disorder and schizophrenia. In these illnesses, grandiosity emerges as you lose touch with reality, regardless of your usual level of self-esteem and empathy for others. You may not be grandiose or narcissistic in the least in between episodes of mania or psychosis.

When you become *manic,* you predictably develop grandiose beliefs. You feel like you are on top of the world, and everyone should pay attention to you. You believe that you are the most interesting, exciting, and talented person around. You feel powerful, like you can do anything. People seem to want to be near you to share in your glory. Everything that you say, write, or do is remarkable. If others do not give you your proper due, you may become irritated, or you may feel that your talents are wasted on them. You talk about celebrities whom you consider to be your colleagues or supporters. You consider yourself famous, or on the verge of fame, and assume others have heard of you. You believe that you have unusual skills, such as being fluent in multiple languages. You may insist on speaking in these languages to show off your skill.

Religion and sex are common grandiose themes in mania. You may become preoccupied with *religious* salvation. You feel as if you are in a state of glory and enlightenment. The words of religious books seem to speak clearly and directly to you. You may feel compelled to spread the message of God. You may begin to prophesy.

On the other hand, you may become *sexually preoccupied.* You feel sexually inexhaustible. You become convinced that you are unusually virile and desirable. Your speech is full of sexual references. You flirt and pursue sexual contact in an arbitrary or risky manner, for example in public places with strangers. You dress in a flashy manner or put on too much make-up. You no longer feel shame, and you make sexual comments and gestures that you would never make in public if you were not manic. Religious and sexual preoccupations often occur at the same time. I recall one patient who showered me with Biblical verse before demanding that I kiss her.

Eventually your grandiose thinking becomes more extreme and *delusional*. Instead of believing that you should be famous, you become convinced that you are famous. You might begin to believe that you are someone else: the president, a pop star, or the Messiah. You may begin to experience *hallucinations,* which you attribute to the voice of God or to your name being announced over the radio. You become *paranoid,* thinking that others are jealous and trying to steal your money and reputation. At this point you are experiencing *psychosis* as well as mania, because you have lost touch with reality.

The content of grandiose delusions is partly a reflection of the times. In the nineteenth century a person with mental illness might wear a French general's hat and stick one hand into his shirt in imitation of Napoleon. Now it is more common to believe that you are a famous rap star, that you are married to the president, or that you have developed a cure for AIDS.

Grandiose delusions are also seen in schizophrenia (see "Psychosis"), in which it is common to have both paranoid and grandiose beliefs, but without other manic symptoms like rapid speech and *euphoria.* For example, you may believe that you are a nuclear scientist and that the FBI is trying to capture you to steal your secrets.

How to Cope with Grandiosity

The personality disorders are difficult to treat. The treatment of choice appears to be psychotherapy, in which you try to come to terms with underlying feelings of vulnerability. If you have a narcissistic personality, you will find it hard to trust your therapist or tolerate any critical feedback. But if you can cope with the challenges of therapy, you will begin to develop a more realistic view of yourself that is less grandiose and less vulnerable to injury. You might benefit from antidepressant medications (see "Depression") at times when you are particularly upset by seemingly insurmountable failures or rejections.

If someone you care about has narcissistic traits, you want to avoid fulfilling his self-defeating expectations. You should neither shower him with undeserved praise nor accuse him of being a self-centered monster. Instead, try to share your more balanced views with him. For example, you might tell him that the new car he bought is very nice, but do not reinforce his desire to have the most expensive car in the neighborhood. Let him know that you appreciate him for other reasons, not just because he drives a flashy car.

Grandiose delusions that occur during *psychosis* or *mania* are generally treated with antipsychotic medications and mood-stabilizing medications, respectively, or in combination. If you care for someone who has grandiose delusions, you will play a valuable role in supporting him during his treatment. You should generally avoid trying to argue with him about his beliefs, since no amount of talking will change them. You can respectfully share your view of reality and remind him that it is the nature of his illness for him to have some unusual beliefs. It may be tempting to try to counter grandiosity by putting your loved one down, but that accomplishes nothing, except perhaps to make your loved one feel that you are frustrated and that you no longer love him. You want to communicate with your loved one in a caring way, without becoming too emotional about the odd beliefs that he expresses, which are largely out of his control.

Grief

Your children are worried about you. You've been doing nothing except pacing about the house and garden during the day, and flipping through your photo albums late into the evening. You've stopped going to church.

Your kids have finally convinced you to get out of the house and have dinner with them. But you insist on going somewhere new. How could you go to your favorite restaurant without her? As it is, you keep thinking about how much she would have enjoyed the fish, how proud she would have been that your son is graduating, and how happy she would be for your daughter and her new boyfriend. No one talks about her, but she is all you can think about.

Sometimes, in our technologically advanced society, we forget about death. Americans on average live into their seventies and move away from the communities where they grew up. It is easy to avoid the sick and dying in our day-to-day life, as many of us do not live with our parents and grandparents when they pass away. It seems to us that death should be an aberration rather than an inevitable part of life. Whether this insulation from sickness and death makes us more vulnerable to grief, when death occurs, is not clear. We all experience grief differently, in part because of the different cultures we come from, the different relationships we may have had with the deceased, and the different circumstances of the death itself.

If a loved one's death was expected, then we may have started to experience anticipatory grief beforehand. There is time to share love, to say goodbye, to bring in family and friends, and to prepare for the loss. You feel lonely and sad after the death, but it is less of a shock. If a death is unanticipated, or is particularly tragic, then you are much more likely to feel surprised, numb, and tricked by fate. You feel like you have been abandoned. You pace restlessly, half expecting to happen upon your loved one. You may wonder what you did to deserve the loss. You keep telling yourself that it could not have happened, that there must have been some mistake. You may be more *angry* than sad.

The initial period of shock may last for days or weeks, but eventually you come to terms with the fact of the death and proceed with the process of mourning. After a loved one has died, you are likely to be lonely and preoccupied with memories. You frequently dream about the departed, and you may awaken disappointed to recall that she is no longer with you. You may hear her voice in your thoughts, sense her presence, or even have fleeting visions. These are like the *hallucinations* that occur in some mental illnesses, except that you realize that your loved one is not really alive and talking to you. You may mention the departed in every conversation. I met a man once who went on a cruise after his wife's death in a car accident, and he told the story again and again to everyone he met. I imagine that his children were hoping the trip would distract him and clear his mind, but he brought his grief with him.

On the other hand, you may try to *avoid* anything that reminds you of the one you lost, and you may try to avoid the topic altogether in conversation. People around you may also be careful not to mention your loved one, for fear of upsetting you. References to the departed may trigger memories that make you feel sad. You may have trouble looking at photographs or visiting the people and places that you used to enjoy together. You may feel guilty for little things that you did, or failed to do, before your loved one passed away. You feel sad and may cry at times.

These are symptoms that are usually associated with *anxiety* or *depression,* but they are normal during bereavement. In fact, it is not unusual to be sad, lonely, and preoccupied for several months to a year after a death, and sometimes longer. You may have *sleeping problems,* feel less energetic, and be bored by food. You may lose interest in activities and plans that used to fill your time. You may lose interest in being around other people or in forming new relationships. In fact, about one in three people who are grieving experience all of the symptoms of depression during normal grief.

Even though grief is a normal experience, the death of a loved one is also a serious stress that can cause mental illness. About one out of twenty grieving people develop more severe and persistent symptoms that merit a separate diagnosis of major depression. You should consider seeking psychiatric treatment if you begin to lose all motivation and energy, or if any symptom persists and seriously interferes with your life. You certainly need to see someone if you develop strong feelings of guilt or worthlessness, or if you develop *suicidal thoughts*. Guilty feelings in depression can take on an unrealistic flavor. You may feel that you caused the death, or that you are a bad person. If your grief turns into a major *depression,* then you will probably benefit from treatment with antidepressant medication, at least for several months. If you have had an episode of depression in the past, you are more vulnerable to becoming depressed during bereavement.

Children can also experience grief, or other psychological difficulties, after losing a parent. When a preschool child loses a parent, he may experience *anxiety* even though he does not understand the concept of death. An older child may also become *depressed* and disruptive (see "Antisocial Behaviors"). Children may feel they are somehow responsible for the disappearance of the loved one.

Something Like Grief Can Be Experienced in Other Circumstances

We do not have a comparable word to grief that captures the emotional experience of the person who is dying. But the process of coming to terms with your own impending death bears some resemblance to the process of grief. Most of us do not like to think about our own death. When you learn that you are not expected to live long, likely as a result of a terminal illness, your first reaction is likely to be one of *denial*. You may argue with, or disbelieve, your doctor. You may feel shocked and numb (see "Dissociation"). You may become *angry* and turn your anger toward hospital staff or family. You may refuse to think about your situation, or you may frantically pursue alternatives, no matter how unrealistic they seem. You may try to make deals with your physician, or with God, in the hope that you might live longer in exchange for trying harder.

Many people who learn that they are going to die experience a period of *depression*. This seems like a natural reaction, under the circumstances. It is hard for a person who knows he is dying to be hopeful about the future and enjoy the present. Nevertheless, when your days are limited, it is a shame to live them under a cloud of sadness, helplessness, and lethargy. Therapy, religious counseling, and even antidepressant medication (if death is not imminent) may help you to make the most of your last days, if you are unable to see through your depression. Eventually the person who is dying may come to terms with his death, an acceptance that this is the natural culmination of everyone's life. Spiritual beliefs and the love of, and hopes for, surviving relatives and friends may make the end of life less of a trial.

Some people experience something like grief if they are separated from someone that they still love, for example in a divorce. Obviously death is a more serious issue than separation, at least for the object inspiring the grief. But for the person left behind, separation may evoke similar feelings. You may find yourself preoccupied with the one you miss. You think you see her in the faces of strangers that you pass on the street. You may seek out places that she used to frequent, or you may avoid those places altogether. You may go into a *panic* if you actually run into her. After a breakup some people also experience *jealousy*.

People can experience something similar to grief when they leave their homeland. The experience is likely to be harder if the circumstances were abrupt or traumatic, for example if you were forced to immigrate to a foreign country because of war. Many immigrants seek solace in spending time by sharing memories with others from their country. On the other hand, some find this too painful and try to get on with life and forget about the past.

Grief can also be experienced upon the death of individuals other than family. The loss of a mentor or a religious leader can be very powerful. Some people are very emotionally attached to their pets and can experience periods of grief lasting for weeks or months. Entire communities may experience grief when a national figure dies, as happened after the assassinations of Martin Luther King and John Kennedy. Communities may also go through the stages of grief following any shared catastrophe, like the abduction of a child or a terrorist attack. Most of the country experienced a grieflike reaction after the terrorist attacks on September 11. Some individuals experienced *dissociation,* depression, anxiety, and *trauma,* even if they were not present at the attacks.

How to Cope with Loss

If you have lost someone you care about, you should keep in mind that it is normal to experience grief. It is okay to feel sad, lonely, and disheartened. Eventually you will stop grieving. You will begin to spend less time thinking about your loss. You will resume the activities that you used to enjoy. You will try new things. You will start to meet new people and form new relationships. Of course, you will never replace the person that you lost, but you may feel more comfortable moving on. You will start to think of relationships as fulfilling while they last, rather than as sources of future loss. You will begin to have pleasant, rather than painful, memories of the one you lost.

Most religions have specific mourning rituals that, among other things, serve to bring a community together when a loved one is lost. Though you may feel burdened by expectations that you appear in public and greet sympathizers, these rituals help to keep you socially connected when you may be tempted to retreat. If you are completely preoccupied with your loss, then you should gradually try to distract yourself by going out with friends and doing activities that you used to enjoy. If you find it too painful to think about your loss, then you should gradually expose yourself to the photos, places, and people that you fear will make you sad. A counselor can guide you in these tasks and can also refer you to further care if you seem stuck in depression.

If you care about someone who is grieving, you should generally give him time to heal. You can be available and supportive as you follow his lead. If he wants to talk about the departed, then you should listen. If he wants to avoid discussing his loss, do not force him to do so. This can be difficult if both of you are mourning the loss, since one of you may want to talk, while the other is more comfortable avoiding the issue. In that case, continuing to show affection toward each other is the best way to signal that you are available. At some point he will open up, and you should be prepared for the emotions to pour out. You may be surprised when someone who has been so stoic suddenly starts to sob uncontrollably. In fact, you both may be surprised when this happens.

Going to counseling together may be helpful if either one of you is having a particularly hard time grieving. The loss of a child can be particularly difficult to cope with, and parents sometimes separate after losing a child. Couple therapy may help you to deal with your feelings of frustration and sadness together, rather than let the feelings push you apart. If someone you care about becomes increasingly depressed while grieving, then you should encourage him to see a psychiatrist. As mentioned above, some people become increasingly depressed and so do not emerge from their grief in the expected fashion. Antidepressant medication may be helpful.

If someone you care about is dying, your job again is to be as supportive as you can be. Some people are so afraid of losing someone that they run away from the situation. You might be tempted to throw yourself into work, distract yourself with minor arrangements, or leave the scene altogether. It is more helpful to be emotionally available, to stand by your loved one as he passes through the stages on the way to accepting his death. No one wants to die alone, and your presence will be valued. If you are unsure how you can be helpful, it is okay to ask him.

You should also take care of yourself. If you are sad, exhausted, angry, or drunk, you will have trouble supporting yourself and your loved one. It may be a challenge to remain supportive and available while you are beginning to grieve in anticipation of your loved one's death. It is important to make the most of the time you have left together, and not to treat him as if he were already dead. There will be time to mourn afterward. You will eventually come to value the memories of your last days together, as difficult as they are for both of you at the time. Many people find religious faith and counsel to be reassuring when facing death or the death of a loved one.

Hallucinations

They are trying to keep you from sleeping. You are not sure who they are, but they are probably the boys from the house next door. Every time you lie down they start talking outside your window, whispering your name. They say they'll get you as soon as you fall asleep and that you had better watch out.

But those boys are quick. When you run to the window, they're not there. Sometimes you see just a shadow over by the garage, like someone staring back at you.

A hallucination is a sensory misperception. You hallucinate when you hear, see, feel, smell, or taste something that, in fact, is not there. Psychiatrists refer to these, respectively, as auditory, visual, tactile, olfactory, or gustatory hallucinations. Hallucinations are symptoms of *psychosis* and involve a break with reality. They are most commonly associated with schizophrenia, but they can also occur in other psychotic illnesses, as well as during drug use or withdrawal.

As far as the brain is concerned, hallucinations are experienced as if they were real. Even though there are no external sensory stimuli, the parts of the brain in which vision, sound, and smell are processed are activated. The hallucination starts in the brain, not in the world outside; it is as if the brain were playing a video-tape.

It is often possible to tell when somebody else is hallucinating. A person who is experiencing auditory hallucinations will often mutter, laugh, sing along, or shout back in response to what she is hearing. She may stop talking in the middle of a conversation. She may cover her ears with her hands, with cotton balls, or with a hat. I have known several patients who wore tinfoil under their hats in an attempt to block the voices that they believed were being transmitted into their brains. If a person is experiencing visual hallucinations her eyes may dart around the room or she may reach out to touch something that is not present.

How does it feel to experience hallucinations? Imagine that you are walking down the street and you suddenly hear someone calling your name. The voice sounds like someone you know. You stop and turn around, looking among the crowd for a familiar face. If you see someone else responding to the name you may feel a bit embarrassed but also reassured, and you continue on your way. But what if no one else answers, and you hear your name called again? What if you hear someone behind you comment on the way you are dressed? What if someone keeps calling you awful terms like slut or faggot? Even if you were experiencing no other symptoms of psychosis, these voices, which seem so real, would make you feel like you were going crazy. After all, what can we trust if we cannot trust our own eyes and ears? On the other hand, if you have experienced hallucinations for a long time, you may grow accustomed to seeing or hearing them every day.

When you are psychotic, and therefore not thinking clearly, it seems obvious that the voices that you hear must be coming from the people around you. You may accuse an innocent passerby of calling you names. If no one is around, then you conclude that someone must be projecting the voices from a distance. You might reason that the voices are coming from a speaker system or from someone with telepathic powers. You might conclude that God, angels, or devils are speaking to you. If you also have visual hallucinations, you might believe that you can see and hear someone speaking to you, even if no one else can. You may suspect that others can also see what you see but will not admit it.

Hallucinations Occur in Several Different Illnesses

Most people with schizophrenia (see "Psychosis") experience auditory hallucinations, which is why people often associate the illness with "hearing voices." Voices are usually heard as if they were coming from outside of the head, as if someone were actually present with you and speaking. Sometimes the voice seems to be coming from within, like a loud and intrusive thought. Most of the time the voice is recognizable as the voice of a family member or someone you know. Sometimes it seems to be the voice of God or the devil.

The voice often comments on your every move, and it is often critical. It may call you names. It may issue commands, telling you to turn around, do the dishes, turn on the television, or close the window. Some of the commands may be more dramatic, bizarre, or even violent. For example, I once treated a very devout man who believed that he heard the voice of God instructing him to attack others. He believed that God must have a reason for giving the command, and he always complied. If he were to disobey, he believed that God would punish him. Sometimes you hear your thoughts spoken as you think them, or immediately after, like an echo.

Visual and tactile hallucinations are more common in medical or drug-related conditions. For example, during alcohol withdrawal it is common to see animals in the corner of the room or to feel insects crawling on your skin. Many illegal drugs cause a wide range of hallucinations. Psychedelic drugs like LSD, psylocybin, and mescaline are best known for this effect, which can occur during *intoxication* and later during *flashbacks*. Cocaine and phencyclidine (PCP, or angel dust) can also cause visual and auditory disturbances. Cocaine users will sometimes crawl on the floor trying to pick up nonexistent white powder, or they mistakenly hear the voices of police officers outside their window. Marijuana and some designer drugs (such as ecstasy, or MDMA) can cause heightened perceptions, rather than hallucinations. Colors seem brighter, vision more distinct, and touch more sensuous.

Before certain types of seizures it is common to smell burning rubber. In most medical and drug-induced conditions you recognize that the hallucination is abnormal. In contrast, in schizophrenia you are not thinking clearly, and you reinterpret reality to explain the voices you are hearing.

Though hallucinations are most commonly associated with schizophrenia and drug use, they can also occur in *depression* or *mania*. If you are severely depressed, the voices that you hear are likely to be disparaging and morbid. They may tell you that you are worthless and that you should die. If you are manic, the voices are more likely to sing your praises. You may think that you are God's special messenger and that He is speaking to you directly.

There are times when hallucinations can be normal and not a product of mental illness, especially when you are not concentrating on the world around you. A common experience is to hear your name called out when you are on the verge of falling asleep. You wake up only to realize that no one else is home or that everyone else is asleep. It is also common, even when you are fully awake, to hear the voice of a relative or loved one in the first weeks after they have died. In some religions, hearing the voice of God may not be unusual, especially during religious ecstasy.

How to Cope with Hallucinations

The hallucinations that occur during schizophrenia, depression, or mania can be effectively treated with antipsychotic medications (see "Psychosis"). Generally, hallucinations resolve more quickly with medication than do other psychotic symptoms, but they may not go away entirely. Many people learn to live with hallucinations and to distinguish them from the sounds of the real world. If the voices make critical comments or command you to do foolish things, you can chuckle to yourself and ignore them. Many people find it useful to carry a radio and headphones to drown out the voices. Other strategies include keeping your mind occupied by reading, playing games, watching television, or doing chores. I have seen some individuals with schizophrenia pretend to be talking on their cell phone when they are pestered by hallucinations. In that way strangers are less likely to notice that they are actually talking to themselves.

Hallucinations that occur during drug intoxication are not usually treated. It may help to have a friend stay with you to talk you through a bad trip. The distorted perceptions will disappear in time as the drug leaves your body. Hallucinations that occur during alcohol withdrawal can be benign, or they may herald more life-threatening complications, such as seizure and delirium (see "Confusion"). In any case, you should receive medical attention if your alcohol use leads you to hallucinate.

Histrionics

The world is so cruel! You have been stranded here at a cocktail party, and no one is gallant enough to offer to escort you home. Don't they understand that you've been here for hours? Your poor little dog may die if you don't get home to walk and feed him. You know he misses you so much.

A girlfriend suggests you call a taxi—as if you could be seen leaving the party alone! What is she thinking? And no, you don't want her to give you a lift; you want a man to take you home. You have the espresso machine and brandy all set up in the living room. You just need to find someone . . . yes, like him—that handsome man who just walked in, the one with the movie star looks: there's no ring on his finger or woman in sight. You break off the conversation with your girlfriend and head across the room. Maybe you could stay a little longer after all.

Life would be boring without a little drama. We all enjoy being in the company of someone who is lively, funny, energetic, and flirtatious. If you have these outgoing traits you can be quite popular and successful, and you may be particularly well suited for a career in entertainment, or perhaps politics. On the other hand, if you have these traits to an extreme degree you may have what psychiatrists call a histrionic personality disorder.

If you have a histrionic personality disorder you come across as very needy. Unless someone is fawning over you or flirting with you, you feel that you are unattractive and worthless. You have bouts of despair whenever someone threatens to break off a relationship, and if you are unable to manipulate that person into staying you immediately hook up with someone new. If you are fortunate you find someone who provides the stability that you lack and who can tolerate your tendency to be seductive with everyone around you. In the meantime you fantasize about finding a powerful, famous lover who will sweep you off your feet and send you chocolates and champagne every day.

One of the most recognizable features of a histrionic personality style is the tendency to be vague and superficial while professing to have the deepest sorts of emotions. Your friends may have no clear picture of your past. Your stories may be overly dramatic and may change from one telling to the next. You may exaggerate your previous accomplishments and characterize relationships as deeper than they are. You may describe your latest boyfriend as "the most incredible guy" and "the best lover" you could ask for. Yet from your description he comes across as a cardboard character whom you are unable to characterize in any personal detail. You may not know where he is from, what kind of work he does, or what his interests are. You may respond that none of these things really matter, so long as he loves you.

Typically you fall in love at first sight, without the usual hesitant steps and explorations. You often fall for individuals who are not willing to return the favor. You may find yourself pining for your professors, your therapist, celebrities, married men, or others who are either unavailable or unlikely to commit. Your friends notice that your relationships always follow the same pattern, with rejection and disappointment predictably following a whirlwind pursuit of perfect love. When a relationship ends, or is on the verge of ending, you are thrown into a panic. You cannot imagine what you will do if left alone. You may threaten to harm yourself (see "Self-Mutilation"), or you may make a scene. You may have trouble getting out of bed and moving on unless your friends gather around to support you.

The word "histrionic" comes from the Latin word for actor, and a histrionic personality is highly dramatic and emotional. Your life seems to be one long soap opera. You express your emotions as if you are on stage. Your every experience has to be over the top. You often seem to be performing, and you feel empty without an audience.

If you have a histrionic personality, you may experience disabling headaches, back pain, trouble breathing, palpitations, and other symptoms when you are in an emotional crisis. Your *physical complaints and pain* may spare you from having to deal directly with underlying *anxiety,* loneliness, and feelings of worthlessness. You may reassure yourself and others that you missed the dance because of the flu, not because your boyfriend cancelled. Your friends recognize that you are in emotional distress when you complain, and they provide support that addresses your emotional needs as much as your physical concerns.

Histrionic personality disorder affects approximately two out of one hundred people. In clinical practice women are diagnosed with this personality style much more frequently than men. Studies have shown that therapists are likely to misdiagnose histrionic men as having an *antisocial* personality and antisocial women as being histrionic. This most likely results from masculine and feminine stereotypes: overly dramatic men are viewed as macho, reckless, and dangerous, whereas women who break rules and get into fights are viewed as emotionally out of control. In keeping with our stereotypes, only effeminate men tend to be diagnosed as histrionic. In fact, these personality styles should be distinguished not on the basis of gender but on the genuine need for affection seen in histrionic personality, as opposed to the cold manipulation of others seen in antisocial personality.

Scientists do not know what causes histrionic personality disorder. We presume that some temperamental traits, such as openness and sociability, combine with adverse experiences of neglect, overindulgence, or abuse in childhood. The result is a child who grows up with little internal sense of emotional stability and craves the recognition and affection of others in order to bolster her *self-esteem*. There is no proven treatment for histrionic personality, but most psychiatrists would recommend psychotherapy that seeks to provide a stable setting in which you can learn to better understand your emotions and the relationship patterns that you tend to fall into.

Histrionic Traits Are Sometimes Evident in Other Mental Illnesses

If you have a borderline personality disorder (see "Self-Esteem Problems") you also tend to be very dependent on the affection of others and highly dramatic in your expression of emotions. However, the ability to form even a superficial relationship with others is usually impaired. From the beginning, relationships are fragile due to ambivalent feelings and frequently expressed *anger*. You are not content to stay in a superficial fairytale romance; you are driven to test whether it is based on a deep commitment to stick with you no matter how you behave.

In bipolar disorder, or manic-depressive illness, you experience episodes of elevated mood, which psychiatrists refer to as hypomania and *mania*. During these episodes your mood becomes increasingly *euphoric,* and you express your emotions unreservedly to anyone who will listen. Even if you are naturally timid you may find yourself flirting, cursing, and making a spectacle of yourself. You become increasingly *grandiose,* and you may become angry when others do not give you the respect and attention you believe you deserve. Though some of these features seem histrionic, they are a result of your temporarily disturbed mood and are not reflective of your underlying personality. Psychiatrists can also distinguish mania on the basis of other symptoms, such as trouble sleeping, increased energy levels, and rapid speech.

Temper tantrums in children typically involve histrionic emotional out-bursts, agitation, oppositional behavior, and minor destructiveness (see "Antisocial Behaviors"). Sometimes children engage in tantrums because they are genuinely distressed. For example, you may be frustrated by a school assignment because you are having *learning difficulties,* or you may be upset after the death of a parent (see "Grief"). Sometimes children throw tantrums because they have learned that they are effective. If your parent always gives you ice cream to quiet you, then you may have a temper tantrum several times a day. Generally, parents should calmly send children to time-out and not reward them for losing their temper. The frequency of tantrums will fade with time.

Hyperactivity

You can tell that your dad is getting frustrated. You tried to mow the lawn, but you left rows of tall grass crisscrossing the yard, and you forgot to do the other side of the driveway altogether. At one point your mom called out to you to ask what you wanted for lunch, and you went to her to respond, leaving the motor running until your brother noticed and told your dad.

Things are even worse with your homework. As you stare at your math problems, you can't concentrate long enough to reach the end of an equation. You keep jumping out of your chair to peek at basketball scores on the television. You would like to pull out a video game, but your mom said you had to wait until you finish your assignment. But you are overwhelmed with boredom. You bounce the pencil up and down on the table. You reach for the eraser and lob it across the room into the wastebasket. "Score!"

Then you pull out the video game.

Hyperactivity refers to excessive, purposeless, and rapid movement. Physical hyperactivity is often accompanied by mental distractibility. Both your mind and your muscles leap from one task to another, accomplishing little along the way. Hyperactivity is a relative term. High energy levels are expected in toddlers, and children often become loud and physically active when they are excited or under stress. In fact, half the parents in the United States describe their children as hyperactive. But in some children, hyperactivity and distractibility persist into the grade school years and interfere with school performance, behavior at home, and bonding with family and friends. Psychiatrists refer to this as attention-deficit hyperactivity disorder (ADHD). ADHD often persists into the adult years but always has its onset during childhood. Several other mental illnesses can cause hyperactivity or physical agitation in adults.

If you have ADHD, you have difficulty sitting still, staying quiet, and sticking with an activity until it is finished. You tend to squirm in church, run about in class, and interrupt games with friends. You never clean up after yourself around the house, and your room is always a mess. Your parents may complain that you never quiet down, even when told to take a break. You may be viewed as impatient and *impulsive*. It seems as if you are unable to pause and think before you act. You tend to have accidents while running about or riding your bike. When you want something, you demand it. You become frustrated easily and get into frequent arguments. Instead of waiting your turn, you jump ahead in line. If you think of an answer to a question that your teacher asks a classmate, you shout it out anyway, forgetting until afterward to raise your hand.

Inattentiveness, the other half of ADHD, refers to your inability to concentrate. At school you lose track of what is being taught. Your mind wanders all over the room, or out the window. You doodle when you should be taking notes. You have trouble concentrating on games and activities with friends. You don't notice the soccer ball flying right past you while you watch cars drive by the field. When playing board games you forget to take your turn, or you neglect the rules. Your mother asks you to pick up milk on the way home, but you stop to play with a dog on the sidewalk and forget the milk entirely. You forget to do your homework, or you start it but give up after a few minutes. Or you complete your homework but leave it at home the next day. You may be quite smart, but you find your school assignments draining, time-consuming, and boring.

When your parents try to sit you down for a talk, you fidget, listen to the television blaring in the other room, and miss half of what they say. They think you are willful, since you can sit for an hour watching MTV or playing a video game but you cannot sit quietly at the dinner table or complete a simple set of chores. At school your teacher thinks that you are misbehaving or ignoring her on purpose. Your parents and your teachers complain that they have to ask you to do things over and over again.

Approximately one in twenty children suffer from ADHD during the school years, though some scientists believe that the number is much higher, as many as one in ten. ADHD is much more common in boys, though symptoms are often overlooked in girls, who tend to be more distractible and inattentive rather than hyperactive and impulsive. Most children with ADHD have symptoms of both hyperactivity and attention problems, but one or the other may predominate. Recent studies have found that the inattentive type, without hyperactivity, is more common than previously thought, and this group is largely unrecognized and untreated.

Some scientists think that both the motor and mental aspects of the illness may be related to difficulty inhibiting impulses. When an urge to move, run about, or shout occurs, you find yourself acting on the urge before you realize it. Likewise, when a distracting thought, sight, or noise enters your mind, you abandon the old and follow the new train of thought. Many suspect that the frontal lobes of the brain, where impulses are normally inhibited, may be subtly disturbed in ADHD. The brain chemical dopamine plays a role in communication between the frontal lobes and the rest of the brain, and the stimulant medications used to treat ADHD enhance dopamine and norepinephrine function. But scientists do not yet know specifically what causes ADHD.

The disorder tends to run in families, and inheritance has been estimated to explain about half of the risk of developing ADHD. Presumably other factors, such as the home environment and exposure to infections or toxins, determine whether the genetic predisposition is expressed. There is no evidence that food additives or sugar cause ADHD, as once suspected. Sometimes children may be hyperactive and inattentive because they are having trouble seeing or hearing, so all children suspected to have ADHD should receive hearing and vision screenings, as well as psychological testing. In rare cases a child may be hyperactive purely because of the chaotic environment in which he is being raised. Once his home life stabilizes, symptoms may disappear altogether.

Learning and Conduct Problems Commonly Accompany ADHD

Not surprisingly, children with ADHD generally experience academic difficulties. If you are unable to concentrate or stay still, you will have problems learning to read, write, calculate, or cooperate with your classmates. About one-third of children with ADHD are also diagnosed with a reading disorder, and they commonly fall behind their classmates by a year or two in reading skills. *Learning difficulties* may also arise from the same subtle brain problems that cause ADHD, rather than as secondary effects of poor concentration. In those cases, special education may be necessary even if the symptoms of ADHD are successfully treated.

Though all children with ADHD have some behavioral problems, about half will be diagnosed with oppositional defiant disorder when there is a consistent pattern of opposing the wishes of others. This diagnosis is more common in boys with ADHD. If you have ADHD and oppositional defiant disorder, you will be irritable and moody at times. During preschool years you may have frequent temper tantrums. At school you may get into fights with other children. For example, you may interrupt a board game, and when your classmates tell you to go away, you may kick the board or push them. You may hit or fight with your siblings on a regular basis. If your mother asks you to take out the garbage, you may talk back to her or drop the trash on the floor. When your teacher gets frustrated at you for leaving your seat and orders you to sit down, you may respond by throwing a book or some other item across the room. Because of these intrusive, disruptive, and aggressive behaviors, you may be unpopular at school. Unfortunately, even the most well-meaning of parents and teachers may yell at you, criticize you, or order you about, and so you feel like you are the problem child and that you cannot do anything right. When confronted on your behaviors, you blame someone else.

One-third of teenagers with ADHD are also diagnosed with a conduct disorder, and about one-quarter of those with ADHD and conduct disorder will have an *antisocial* personality disorder as an adult. If your ADHD symptoms are treated early, you have a better chance of learning to get along with, and respect the rights of, others.

Many children with ADHD understandably experience *self-esteem problems*. You probably think that classmates view you as troublesome, clumsy, and perhaps stupid. No one wants to be your friend. Teachers treat you differently. You seem to be the one who brings the class down. Your report cards always describe you as talking too much, moving too much, and failing to concentrate on your work. No one ever seems to have anything good to say about you. Even your parents treat you as a challenge to their patience, requiring special rules and attention. You seem to be a burden to them. Some studies have found that adults with a childhood history of ADHD continue to have lower self-esteem, poorer jobs, fewer friends, and more *suicide* attempts as adults.

Several Different Conditions Can Cause Hyperactivity in an Adult

Until the past decade, scientists were uncertain whether ADHD persists into adulthood. But research has shown that children typically do not grow out of ADHD. About two-thirds still have significant symptoms as adults, especially trouble completing tasks at work and around the house. You may head for your desk with the intention of paying some bills but instead end up picking up toys, gathering laundry, and logging onto the Internet. By the end of the day you have skipped from one chore to another without finishing any of them. At work, piles of paper accumulate on your desk, assignments are rarely completed on deadline, and you forget to prepare for, or attend, meetings. Your boss has to remind you over and over again. You feel *anxious* and overwhelmed and have difficulty succeeding in your goals.

Though symptoms can persist into adulthood, ADHD never has its onset during the adult years. If you did not experience ADHD as a child, any hyperactivity or distractibility you experience must have another cause.

Hyperactivity is a common feature of bipolar disorder. When you swing into *mania,* your thoughts race, and you become increasingly physically active. You make a multitude of plans, but you are unable to concentrate on any one of them long enough to accomplish anything. You run from one activity to another. In milder cases, your hyperactivity and distractibility may be mistaken for a personality style. People you work with may think that you are a bit intense, that you bite off more than you can chew. Or they may notice that you alternate between periods of activity and periods of slothfulness and pessimism. In more extreme cases, your hyperactivity is unmistakably abnormal. You may forget to eat meals, you may stop sleeping altogether, and you may become dehydrated from overexertion. At this point in your illness, your speech is probably increasingly rapid and *nonsensical.*

Hyperactivity can also occur, paradoxically, in *depression.* Depression typically causes you to lose energy, speak softly, and move slowly. Many people, however, experience a more nervous form of depression, in which you constantly fret and move about. You may wring your hands and putter needlessly about the house rearranging items. You may pick up the phone, hang it up, pick it up again, and hang it up again. Similar symptoms are seen in generalized *anxiety*.

If you suffer from dementia (see "Memory Loss"), you may move aimlessly about your house or nursing home. You may feel that something is wrong, that you have forgotten something important, but you do not know how to go about solving the problem. You may feel lonely, disoriented, or afraid. Or you may find yourself reliving your past, having forgotten more recent memories. All of these thoughts and feelings may lead you to wander, ask questions, or cry out over and over again. Even if someone reassures you that everything is fine, you quickly forget and resume pacing, questioning, and calling. If you suffer from delirium, you may be even more dramatically *confused*. You may scream and fight with your loved ones and with nurses. You may tear out your intravenous line and run up and down the hospital hallways. You may also inadvertently harm yourself due to your confused and agitated behavior.

Hyperactivity can be a side effect of medication. Many of the antipsychotic medications used in the treatment of schizophrenia (see "Psychosis") can cause an internal sense of restlessness. You fidget and bounce your legs while sitting. You may be unable to remain sitting for more than a few seconds. Instead you pace about, trying to release pent-up energy. Patients often describe the feeling as "ants in my pants." Psychiatrists refer to this medication side effect as akathisia. It may be difficult to tell whether your restlessness is a side effect of the medication, or a symptom of your mental illness. If it is due to your antipsychotic medication, your doctor can treat the side effect by lowering the dose, changing the medication, or adding a beta-blocker medication, such as propranolol (Inderal), that treats akathisia.

Finally, hyperactivity can be a manifestation of drug *intoxication*. Stimulant drugs, such as amphetamines and cocaine, cause you to be jumpy and energetic. You may feel like running out and doing something—anything to keep pace with your mind, which is racing. You may feel like staying up all night, doing more and more drugs until you eventually crash. The effects of PCP (phencyclidine) can be even more dramatic. I have known patients who ran out into the streets in a manic and confused rage, stripping off their clothing, kissing strangers, and getting into fights until they were arrested or hospitalized. Even a few cups of strong coffee can cause extreme restlessness and jitters. Many people also become more active, and sometimes belligerent, when drunk on alcohol.

How to Cope with ADHD

Medication is the most effective treatment for the symptoms of ADHD. Hyperactivity, impulsiveness, and trouble concentrating resolve with medication in as many as ninety percent of cases. Even though stimulants are now widely prescribed, many children who could benefit unfortunately do not receive medication. However, medication alone does not always solve the social and academic problems that have developed during the course of the illness, and some parents would prefer that their child not take medication. Behavioral therapy techniques, which can be taught to parents and teachers, can be very helpful either as a sole treatment in mild cases, or in combination with medication. When therapy and medication are combined, lower doses of medication may be needed.

If you are the parent of a child with ADHD, you are likely to feel less stressed and more confident after learning behavioral management skills in a parenting group. You learn to think about the reasons for your child's behavior and how to respond so that appropriate behaviors are reinforced, and misbehaviors are discouraged. You learn new ways to encourage your child, rather than focusing on the negative. For example, you may develop a token system in which your child earns points for good behavior (such as completing chores or homework), and can cash in points for daily rewards (such as television watching privileges). Your child's teacher can give you a daily report card so that you are aware of your child's behavior throughout the day. You will also learn helpful techniques for working with your child, such as dividing tasks into a series of short steps with simple, serial instructions.

Individual psychotherapy is generally not effective in the treatment of symptoms of ADHD, but a child who engages in psychotherapy may benefit simply from having a positive and nurturing relationship with a counselor. On the other hand, he may feel that it is yet another thing that marks him as being different from other children. Tutoring may help a child catch up with his studies, and special education may be necessary for any specific *learning difficulties*.

If you have trouble with attention and hyperactivity, there are some strategies you can use to minimize your symptoms. You should try to make a list of things you need to do and concentrate on just one task at a time. You will find it helpful to work in a calm room where you are not distracted. If you have a big job to take care of, do one small part at a time and take a short break between each part before moving on to the next. If you are confused about what you are supposed to do, ask someone. Try to organize your possessions and keep them in the same place so that you do not lose or forget them. You may find it helpful to keep a notebook in which you can write down important information, including lists of things you need to do. Leave notes for yourself where you will see them.

If you have a child with ADHD, you may find it helpful to contact a national advocacy group, or attend a local support group. You may be relieved to find that other parents have experienced the same challenges and stresses that you feel. They may be able to share with you their experiences and strategies for dealing with the illness and its treatment, and you may then feel more confident in understanding your child's behaviors and feelings.

There are many challenges in raising a child with ADHD. You have to set limits on inappropriate behavior. A diagnosis is not an excuse for your child to be violent or mean. However, you will want to recognize that your child needs more time and encouragement to complete tasks that come easily to his siblings. You should communicate to your child that you understand how difficult it is for him to concentrate. You want to reinforce his ability to overcome these challenges, rather than emphasize the fact that he has a disability. All children face challenges, which are a part of growing up. Even though a diagnosis may provide answers, it can also reinforce his feeling that he is different from other children. He may also resent having to take medication, even if he recognizes that it helps him to do his work and get along with others. You should ask him what he thinks about the medication and reassure him that he is not crazy.

Stimulant Medications

The symptoms of ADHD can improve dramatically with stimulant treatment. When abused in large amounts, stimulants can cause hyperactivity, but they improve concentration and reduce restlessness and impulsivity in people with ADHD. They probably work by stimulating the brain chemical dopamine, which plays an important role in inhibiting impulses. They induce calmness without sedation. All of the stimulants can cause headaches or nausea at higher doses, but they are generally well tolerated. They may suppress growth in children and adolescents, so physicians sometimes prescribe a "drug holiday" during summer vacation, so that natural growth is recovered. Stimulants, just like caffeine, can interfere with sleep, so the medications are usually prescribed only in the morning and early afternoon.

Amphetamines (in the form of Benzedrine) were the first stimulants used in the treatment of children, early in the last century. Dextroamphetamine (Dexedrine) and methylphenidate (Ritalin) are currently the most commonly prescribed stimulant medications, with methylphenidate being the most thoroughly studied. A dose is taken in the morning, before going to school, and at lunchtime. Concentration begins to improve within a couple of hours of taking the dose, and the medication remains effective for several hours. An afternoon dose may be taken in order to help with the completion of homework, but then you may have some *sleeping problems*. Pemoline (Cylert) is another effective stimulant, but it is prescribed less frequently due to possible liver side effects.

The first stimulant medication tried will be effective in more than two-thirds of cases. If one medication is not effective, or causes side effects, then you should try another. People often respond differently to different medications, even from the same chemical family. Studies have shown that stimulant medication can lead to improvements in all areas. You are able to concentrate in class and on tasks at home. You stop fidgeting and running about. You become more cooperative and attentive when working with parents, teachers, and classmates. You begin to form friendships and catch up on academic performance. You may feel completely normal.

Stimulants are commonly prescribed for adults with ADHD, but they generally should not be prescribed if you have problems with drug use and addiction. Stimulants can be *intoxicating,* and you can develop *cravings* for the medications if you take them in doses higher than prescribed. However, there has been no evidence that properly prescribed stimulants for ADHD have ever caused addiction. Stimulants may not be the treatment of choice if you suffer from tics, which are involuntary *movements* that can be exacerbated by stimulants.

Atomoxetine (Strattera) is a nonstimulant medication that has recently been released for the treatment of ADHD. Atomoxetine works by boosting norepinephrine, another brain chemical thought to be involved in inhibiting impulses and organizing thought. Like the stimulant medications, atomoxetine can suppress appetite and cause headaches and nausea. It shows no sign of being addicting and has been approved for use by adults with ADHD. Studies have shown that it is effective throughout the day even if it is given in a single morning dose, so you may be able to avoid taking medication while at school. However, like many other psychiatric medications, it must be taken daily for about two weeks before it starts to work.

Some antidepressant medications (see "Depression"), including the tricyclics and buproprion (Welbutrin), appear to have some effect in improving concentration and reducing hyperactivity in ADHD. However, they are not thought to be as effective as the stimulants, and they tend to have more side effects. They are usually prescribed only if stimulants are contraindicated or ineffective.

Identity Confusion

Your girlfriends have been talking nonstop about the dance.
They've each got an eye on some guy they want to take. You play
along, but guys really aren't your thing; you're too busy with
homework and track practice. You don't tell your friends, but
you'd much rather go to a track meet than to a prom.

The last time the team went out of town, you shared a room
with the captain. You stayed up all night talking about everything.
Everything but guys. Your friends think the captain is gay, but she
looks like a movie star when she dresses up. She's not like other
girls who have a crewcut and the build of a linebacker — not that
there's anything wrong with that. It's just hard for you to under-
stand; you've always thought of yourself as a girl. You like wear-
ing dresses and getting your hair styled, but that never kept you
from outrunning the boys at recess.

It would be kind of neat if the captain were a lesbian (What
would that mean about you?). You think about her all the time.
You wonder if she's going to the prom. Maybe you could double
date? You're not that interested in any guys, but you could play
along. It might be fun. You'll try to bring it up after practice and
see what she says.

Identity refers to a sense of self that is stable over time. Typically
most of us explore and establish many aspects of our own identity
during adolescence. Sometimes what appear to be normal growing
pains in a teenager may in fact be the first signs of *depression*,
schizophrenia (see "Psychosis"), or drug and alcohol abuse or *in-*
toxication. In other mental illnesses a stable sense of self is disrupted. You may feel unanchored, seeing yourself differently de-

pending on your mood. You may be vulnerable to the overwhelming influence of another person. Your memories may be fragmented, leaving you with an incomplete sense of yourself. You may struggle against expectations that you should behave in a certain way because of your gender.

In borderline personality disorder (see "Self-Esteem Problems") you may feel that you have little control over your identity. It is as if you are stuck in the perpetual turmoil of adolescence. You feel good about yourself only when other people give you positive attention. If someone neglects or abandons you, you immediately become overwhelmed with a sense that you are worthless and unlovable. You feel like you have no core personality, and you seem to borrow your identity from others around you.

Sometimes a person becomes impressionable and susceptible to developing a mental illness through identifying with another person who dominates her life. For example, if your father develops a *paranoid* belief that the FBI is following him, and you live alone with him and depend on him, then you may develop the same delusional beliefs. Psychiatrists refer to this as folie à deux, from the French term for a shared delusion. I once evaluated a woman who convinced her adolescent children that witches were persecuting her, and her children, who were otherwise healthy, joined her in her attempts to cast protective spells.

Something similar happens in cults and prolonged kidnappings, situations where you have little contact with the outside world, and powerful figures exert control over every aspect of your life. If you have been kidnapped, you may find yourself growing sympathetic with your kidnappers, even to the point of voluntarily assisting them in their criminal activities. In a *religious* cult, you are isolated from friends and family and spend all of your time with other members of this group. The cult leader is usually very charismatic and able to influence his followers' thinking and behavior. Any attempt to assert your own identity within the cult is discouraged, while assimilation leads to a feeling of security and love. This process of indoctrination and loss of individual identity is commonly referred to as brainwashing. Something similar occurs on a much larger scale under totalitarian regimes.

If you have been severely abused during childhood, you may develop a *dissociative* identity disorder. In this rare condition, formerly known as a multiple personality disorder, your sense of identity is fractured. You may have several different aspects to your personality and switch from one to the other depending on the situation. In a *dissociative* fugue, you forget who you are and assume a new identity, often in a different town where no one would recognize you. Your prior identity and memories are not forgotten completely but are temporarily submerged and not accessible to conscious thought. Fugue is rare and easily treated once your loved ones are tracked down and you are confronted with your past.

Some people confuse schizophrenia (see "Psychosis") with a split- or multiple-personality disorder. In fact, identity is fairly stable in schizophrenia, in the sense that you usually feel like you are the same person during and between acute episodes of the illness, even though your thoughts and perceptions are disturbed. When you are psychotic you may experience *delusions* related to your identity, believing, for example, that your body or mind has been taken over by some outside force, that you are actually someone famous, or that you have changed from a man to a woman, or vice versa. You may develop delusions about the identity of others, such as believing that your wife has been replaced by an imposter.

Sexual Identity Encompasses Gender Role, Gender Identity, and Sexual Orientation

Among all of the categories by which we define our identities, gender and sexuality seem to be the most fundamental. Most cultures expect boys and men to behave somewhat differently from girls and women. These expectations are called gender roles. Of course there are some genetic, anatomic, and developmental differences between men and women, but there are more similarities than differences. Societies may try to reinforce stereotypical gender roles by claiming that differences are biologically or religiously preordained. In fact, the roles are always changing, and there will always be some men and women who challenge our expectations about how the genders should behave.

There is nothing inherently wrong with having behaviors and interests that are generally thought to be more typical of the opposite sex. If a boy is called a sissy, or a girl is criticized for being a tomboy, then the problem is not with the boy or girl but with the bullies who are acting out the prejudices they have learned from adults. Children should be encouraged to explore their own personal interests and to be tolerant of differences in others. You may understandably worry that your children will grow up to be homosexual, effeminate, or butch if you tolerate different gender roles. In fact, most children grow up to be heterosexual and to fulfill gender role expectations (such as having children) regardless of their style and interests at an earlier age. Some effeminate boys do have a greater chance of growing up homosexual, but their orientation appears to be established early, and there is likely little you can do to change it.

In rare cases boys and girls feel that fate has played a trick on them: a few boys think they should have been born in a girl's body, and a few girls think that they should have been born in a boy's body. These children not only follow gender roles of the opposite sex but also feel uncomfortable with their anatomy. As a boy you may feel that your penis is an embarrassment. You may prefer to wear girls' clothing and play with other girls. As a girl, you hate your breasts and wish that you had a penis. As you grow up you begin to think of yourself as a member of the opposite sex.

Psychiatrists refer to this rare condition as gender identity disorder. In the past it was known as transsexualism, and the term is still used commonly, especially in reference to those patients who seek to alter their anatomy. The treatment of gender identity disorder aims at helping you to feel comfortable in your preferred gender. The sense that you are not really a man or a woman, in spite of your anatomy, cannot be changed in therapy. Most transsexuals choose to adopt the dress and lifestyle of the other gender. Men dress as women, wear makeup, and seek romance with men. Women bind their breasts and dress as men. (Women wearing men's attire is much more acceptable in American society than men dressing as women; perhaps this is why women seek counseling for gender identity problems less often than men.) Cross-dressing feels natural to you. You do not cross-dress flamboyantly as an assertion of your sexuality, as some homosexuals do. Nor do you find cross-dressing sexually exciting, as occurs among heterosexuals with transvestism (see "Sexual Preoccupations"). Your goal is to fit in, but as a member of the other gender. If you fall in love or have sexual relations with a member of your own sex (as happens in most cases), you usually think of your interest as heterosexual.

If you have gender identity disorder you may feel more comfortable simply as a result of adopting the dress and lifestyle of your preferred gender. If not, you may try hormone treatment to suppress your natural features and bring out traits of the other gender. If you were born a woman, you can take testosterone to lower your voice, enlarge your clitoris, shrink your breasts, coarsen your skin, and induce facial hair growth. If you were born a man, you can take estrogens and progesterones that will shrink your testicles, stimulate breast tissue, soften your skin, and raise the pitch of your voice. About one in ten individuals with a gender identity disorder will go on to have irreversible transgender surgery. Surgeons can remove the breasts, uterus, and ovaries and create a penislike appendage in women. Men may undergo removal of the testicles and penis and creation of a vaginalike pouch. In the vast majority of cases patients are pleased with the results of surgery.

Sexual orientation is quite different from gender role and gender identity. A minority of homosexual men and women do have stereotypically feminine or masculine traits, respectively, but most definitely identify themselves with their gender at birth, and most behave in a typically masculine or feminine manner.

Sexual orientation refers to whether one is attracted more to members of the same sex or to the opposite sex, or to both. This method of categorizing sexual interest is somewhat overemphasized in our time and culture. Many societies expect people to be attracted to, and capable of receiving sexual pleasure from, either sex. Nevertheless, if you find yourself romantically or sexually interested in another person of your gender, you are likely to struggle with the question whether you may be gay, lesbian, or bisexual. Regardless of how you define yourself, you should know that sexual fantasy or arousal with a member of the same sex is natural and not a sign of mental illness (see "Sexual Preoccupations").

Impulsiveness

Your friend leans in and speaks to you almost in a whisper. She tells you that she has a special deal to offer you, that she wants you to have first shot at it. You have to put some money down now, but you're almost guaranteed to get it back tenfold. All you have to do is convince ten more people to join.

The waiter arrives with the food and warns you to be careful: the dish is very hot. You immediately reach out and touch it. "That was stupid," you joke as you jerk your hand back.

"So how much do I give now?" you ask, reaching for your checkbook.

An impulse is an urge to act. Impulsiveness is the term psychiatrists use to describe a tendency to respond quickly, without a plan, and without thinking about the consequences. You may react to something in your environment, such as a stranger who steps on your foot. Or you may respond to an internal state, such as a craving to drink alcohol. Often an external event triggers an automatic internal feeling, such as anger, desire, or desperation, that sets your impulse in action.

We feel good at first when we respond to impulses; they can bring pleasure as well as relief from unpleasant feelings. But we usually inhibit our impulses long enough to decide whether it is wise to give in to them. If they are likely to cause us trouble, or to harm others, we may suppress them. We may confine our urges to fantasy instead. For example, you may want to yell at your boss when she criticizes your work, but you bite your tongue, make the requested changes, and curse her silently in your mind. You may see someone sexy on the street, but you wait till he walks past to take another look, rather than whistling or making unwanted gestures. You may be tempted to buy a flashy designer outfit, but you think about the cost, and how little you will wear it, and you pass it by. Scientists believe that this ability to think before acting derives from the frontal lobes of the brain, the most evolved and distinctively human portion of the brain.

Some people are in the habit of indulging, rather than controlling, their impulses. In many cases, impulsiveness is a temperamental trait. You may have been easily bored and prone to seek stimulation from an early age. You may have difficulty with concentration and planning. Often impulsiveness is a temporary condition resulting from the use of drugs or alcohol, which cloud judgment. Some people become impulsive as a result of a head injury, especially to the frontal lobes of the brain. In rare cases you may have a specific impulse that is difficult to control, even though you are more moderate and reflective in other areas of your behavior.

Several Psychiatric Conditions Are Characterized by Global Impulsiveness

Impulsiveness is a common feature of childhood and adolescence. Children are quick learners, but you have to protect them from their own curiosity and urges until they learn what is dangerous and can utilize their own judgment. If a child remains unusually impulsive, both in school and at home, then you may suspect that he has a conduct disorder or attention-deficit *hyperactivity* disorder (or ADHD). Some scientists believe that ADHD is primarily a disorder of impulse control. If you have ADHD you are constantly distracted by thoughts, urges, and things that you see or hear, and you respond to them automatically, for example by suddenly jumping out of your seat at school to look out the window during the middle of class.

Adolescents may be less impulsive than infants and children, but they have more independence and can do more damage to themselves and others. Adolescents are at high risk for car accidents, gunshot injuries, venereal disease, unplanned pregnancy, unintentional overdoses on drugs and alcohol, and *suicide*. Even though impulsiveness is a normal teenage developmental feature, it may also be a sign of an emerging personality disorder.

A disregard for rules and lack of empathy for others characterizes *an-*

tisocial personality disorder. You engage in many impulsive and reckless behaviors. You drive without a license while drunk, and you insist that your friends join you for the ride. You lose your temper easily and start a fight over nothing. You are likely to abuse drugs and alcohol and to get into frequent trouble with the law. You skip school or work on a whim. Even though it is your behavior that is out of control, you are likely to deny that you have a problem and blame others (in contrast to most other illnesses in which impulsive behavior is followed by feelings of guilt and shame). In adolescence, these personality traits and behaviors are called a conduct disorder. The diagnosis of antisocial personality disorder is made if they persist into adulthood, which happens about one-third of the time.

Some people are characteristically impulsive without having the other features of an antisocial personality. For example, you may be foolish, inconsiderate, and hasty in your actions, though your intentions are good. You may just have poor judgment and difficulty learning from mistakes. Your family may be frustrated by your seeming inability to live up to your obligations, expectations, and potential.

Borderline personality is a disorder characterized by extremely poor *self-esteem* and impulsive behavior. When you feel rejected or abandoned by others, you may cut yourself (see "Self-Mutilation"), attempt *suicide,* overindulge in alcohol or drugs, or embark on a series of impersonal sexual encounters. You are prone to shouting, arguing, and bursting into tears. You make rapid and foolish decisions in response to the tumultuous swings in your emotions. You may storm off a job one moment and then ask to be reinstated the next day. You view your actions as out of your control. When you have an urge to act on your emotions, you see no alternative but to do so.

Impulsiveness is also increased in bipolar disorder. When you are *manic* you are energized, and you fail to realize how disturbed your thinking is. You may make hundreds of long-distance calls or purchase numerous unnecessary luxury goods. Impulsiveness is also increased in post-*traumatic* stress disorder (PTSD). In PTSD, you are always tense and on edge. You startle easily and overreact. You may be irritable and quick to lose your temper. You may fear your potential to strike out, leading you to *avoid* others and to conceal your emotions.

Impulsiveness is also seen in a variety of neurological conditions, ranging from head injury to dementia (see "Memory Loss") to epilepsy. You may become aggressive or sexually inappropriate. Some individuals with epilepsy typically become disinhibited for several hours after having a seizure.

Intoxication usually increases impulsiveness. Alcohol and sedative drugs (also known as tranquilizers) have a disinhibiting effect. When you are drunk or high, you tend to act without considering the consequences. You do things that will embarrass you when you are sober again. You may overestimate your abilities, for example thinking that you can safely drive home even though your reaction time, vision, and motor skills are all impaired. Judgment is similarly affected by the use of marijuana. Alcohol, cocaine, and amphetamines can make you more irritable, which increases the likelihood that you will respond in a hostile fashion to minimal provocation. Stimulants and cocaine also increase your level of arousal generally. You are more active, alert, and wired. You respond quickly to whatever catches your attention.

Scientists disagree as to whether we should recognize an intermittent explosive disorder characterized by frequent loss of temper followed by guilt and shame. In most cases, such an inability to control *anger* is better explained by a personality disorder or drug or alcohol problem.

Some Mental Illnesses Are Defined by a Difficulty in Inhibiting Specific Impulses

Kleptomania is a condition in which you are driven to steal. As a child you may steal items from your mother's purse or from school. As an adult you pocket items from stores and from your place of work. Obviously, most theft is not a result of mental illness. But in kleptomania, you tend to steal items that you do not need and that you could easily afford. You may throw the stolen items away or hoard them unused in a closet. You return to stealing again and again, even though you are sometimes caught, resulting in penalties and embarrassment. Genuine kleptomania is a rare condition, and some scientists wonder whether it exists at all. Individuals who steal in order to enrich themselves may pretend that they have no control over their impulses, in order to receive more sympathetic treatment from judges, juries, and prosecutors.

Pyromania is a rare condition characterized by urges to set fires. You love to strike matches and watch objects as the flames consume them. You are thrilled to see people rushing to put out a blaze and by the sounds and sights of fire trucks. You may enjoy fireworks and blowing things up. Of course it is an almost universal pleasure to stare into flames, but if you have pyromania, you fantasize about fire in an almost sexual fashion. You set larger and larger fires and then hang around to see how people respond. You continue to set fires even after you have been caught and punished. Most individuals who set fire do so accidentally, recklessly, or with criminal intent. Some may not experience an urge to set fires so much as an urge to cause mayhem or to be viewed as a hero after "discovering" the fire and helping to put it out. These are *antisocial* behaviors suggestive of a personality problem. But most scientists believe that there are a small number of people who genuinely suffer from pyromania.

Addicting behaviors all involve impulses, more commonly characterized as *cravings*. Once your use of drugs or alcohol becomes habitual, you must give in to your impulses, or your cravings escalate. You become preoccupied with thoughts of using and plans to obtain the drug. You eventually give in to your impulses in an attempt to recapture a pleasant high and to stave off unpleasant withdrawal symptoms. It takes a great deal of self-control, and usually the support of others, to resist these impulses for any period of time.

Sexual behavior is also impulsive by nature. Evolutionary biologists, behavioral psychologists, Freudian analysts, and religious thinkers would all agree that the sexual instinct is among the most powerful human urges (probably following sleep, thirst, and appetite). Most of us set aside our sexual urges and indulge them only in private, often in the context of an intimate relationship with another person. But it is human nature to occasionally give in to a sexual impulse, for example by having an affair. On its own, such behavior is not a sign of mental illness, even when it leads to a variety of problems. But some people are troubled by *sexual preoccupations* and persistent sexual impulses (for example, to touch others or expose themselves) that they have trouble inhibiting and which may result in arrest and harm to others.

Psychiatrists differentiate between impulses and *compulsions*. Compulsions refer to unwanted urges to engage in unpleasant behavior. Impulses, on the other hand, bring immediate relief or pleasure, even if the long-term consequences are negative. Nevertheless, compulsions and impulses share many features and overlap in practice. If you suffer from trichotillomania, for example, you experience unwanted urges to pick and chew your hair. Something similar occurs in habitual nail biting. Both of these activities have unpleasant consequences: progressive baldness, intestinal hairballs, worn-down teeth, and ugly and painful fingernails. Nevertheless, you experience a building sense of tension until you indulge these urges and a pleasant sense of relief and satisfaction once you give in. Likewise, in obsessive-*compulsive* disorder (or OCD), you may find many of your ritualistic behaviors reassuring, no matter how nonsensical they seem to others. *Self-mutilation* is often characterized as an impulsive behavior, bringing prompt relief from unpleasant moods, but it is also compulsive in the sense that you are ambivalent about hurting yourself.

How to Cope with Impulse Problems

The treatment of impulsiveness usually depends on the underlying illness. Cognitive-behavioral therapy may be helpful for most conditions in that it focuses on teaching you to tolerate frustration and utilize problem-solving skills. You may benefit from relaxation techniques (see "Anxiety") that help you to respond with calmness and equanimity in the face of *stress* and provocation.

Medication may also sometimes be helpful. Stimulant medications (see "Hyperactivity") can increase your ability to concentrate and plan, at least if you have ADHD. Mood-stabilizing medications (see "Mania") sometimes dampen impulsiveness, buying you time to think before you act. They seem to be especially helpful in cases of brain injury, along with the beta-blocker medication propranolol (Inderal). Antidepressant medications of the SSRI type (see "Depression") may help settle internal feelings of rage, sadness, and emptiness that predispose you to impulsive behaviors. Some scientists believe that impulsiveness arises from a deficit in brain serotonin levels, which the SSRI antidepressants specifically remedy. Anxiolytic medications (see "Anxiety") may also be helpful temporarily, but they are generally not prescribed to impulsive individuals because they can be addicting and disinhibiting.

Intoxication

The night has been going on forever, but it has become all a blur.
You started at the pizza parlor, where you drank pitchers of beer
with your friends. Now, somehow you've ended up at some party
dancing with someone you don't even know. Not really dancing
so much as rocking back and forth while the room shakes around
you. Every time you tip over, you just pretend it's a dance move.
Nobody else seems to notice.

Your dance partner offers you a joint, and you put it in your
mouth and inhale deeply. Somebody else is feeling your body, but
you're not sure who. Not that you care. One more hit, and you
could pass out. You wonder if you'll remember any of this in the
morning.

The word "intoxication" derives from the Latin for a state of
being poisoned. Physicians use the term to refer to a state of altered feelings and behavior that is induced by consuming a foreign
substance. All sorts of substances can cause intoxication. Some
mind-altering substances, like alcohol and nicotine, can be consumed legally, even if their use is regulated. Others are illegal, like
heroin and crack cocaine. More than one-third of adult Americans
have used an illicit drug, most often marijuana. Some can be prescribed for legitimate medical purposes but are intoxicating at
higher doses, like sedative (Valium, Librium) and narcotic (morphine) medications. Some mind-altering substances are found in
nature, like opium, ephedrine (or ma-huang), and marijuana.
Some substances, like volatile glue and gasoline, were never intended for consumption and have permanent dangerous effects.

Humans have used drugs and alcohol throughout history. In

fact, there is archeological evidence that people valued intoxicating substances even before the dawn of written history. Most intoxicants cause a pleasant sense of *euphoria,* relaxation, or a change in consciousness. Though precise mechanisms are not always known, most of these substances appear to have direct chemical effects on brain cells that are presumed to be responsible for inducing changes in mood, perception, and behavior. Because these substances make you feel good, one use is often not enough. You find yourself experiencing *cravings* for the drug. You want to use it again and again, and your brain soon grows used to the substance. If you give in to these cravings, you may find yourself increasingly dependent on the drug, until you feel like you cannot live without it. Not everyone responds the same to each of these drugs, but all of them can be addicting.

Alcohol, Opiates, and Downers Have Sedating Effects

The effects of alcohol are generally well known, since alcohol is so widely used. Approximately half of all Americans over the age of twelve regularly drink alcohol. It can be purchased in the form of beer, cider, wine, or spirits, and it also can be brewed at home. After a drink, alcohol is absorbed into the bloodstream, reaching a peak concentration in about an hour. It is absorbed more quickly on an empty stomach. The body is able to clear alcohol at a rate of about one small drink per hour. However, many people, especially of Asian or Native American ancestry, have lower levels of the enzyme that metabolizes alcohol, so that intoxication can occur after consuming even a small amount.

Alcohol causes a pleasant sense of relaxation when taken in moderation. You become less anxious, more gregarious, and perhaps a bit drowsy. After a couple of drinks, however, you may begin to lose control. You become clumsy, and your speech becomes slurred. You have trouble concentrating and remembering. You may become belligerent, tearful, or sexually loose. You say things that you would not say when sober. Your judgment becomes impaired, and you may not realize the extent to which you are intoxicated. By this point it is dangerous to drive or engage in other tasks that require judgment and dexterity.

You are much more likely to abuse or become addicted to alcohol if you have more than two drinks per day (for women) or three (for men). Nearly one in five adults has experienced problem-drinking, men more than women. You may start to drink heavily as a teenager or young adult and then begin to feel out of control by your thirties. You begin to have trouble in your relationships and at work. You are more likely to become unemployed and divorced and to attempt *suicide* or be involved in car accidents. You may experience periods of *memory loss, sexual performance problems, jealousy,* and difficulties controlling your *anger.* You may develop hepatitis, cirrhosis, stomach ulcers, and pancreatitis. You develop a typical flushed appearance with swollen nose and broken capillaries on your skin.

Many prescription medications used for the treatment of *anxiety* have effects that are similar to alcohol. These include the classes of medication that physicians refer to as benzodiazepines (such as Valium, Librium, and Xanax), barbiturates (such as Seconal, Nembutal), and the barbiturate-like Quaalude. The barbiturates are rarely used as treatments for anxiety any more, because they are more dangerous, but they are prescribed for seizure disorders and are sold illegally on the street. These medications can all cause relaxation, drowsiness, clumsiness, disinhibited behavior, and poor judgment. About one in ten adults have been prescribed sedative medications, and as many as one-third become addicted if the medications are taken for several months.

Opiates are painkillers chemically derived from, or related to, opium, a natural product of the poppy plant. Morphine was first developed from opium in the nineteenth century, followed by codeine, heroin, and synthetic drugs such as Demerol, Dilaudid, and methadone. Heroin is illegal but has been used by between one and two percent of adults at some time in their lives. Though opiates can be swallowed, snorted, or injected under the skin, they have the most powerful effects when they are injected directly into the bloodstream. In prescribed doses, they relieve pain while inducing a pleasant sense of relaxation. When abused in larger amounts, they induce a sense of warmth and *euphoria.* Your body feels heavy, and you lie still, caring about nothing, until you fall asleep.

When you use opiates for the first time, they can cause nausea and vomiting. If you overdose on opiates, you may choke on your own vomit or you may stop breathing. Opiates can also cause constipation, loss of appetite, *sexual performance problems,* and constricted pupils. If you inject, you may have multiple skin sores and needle tracks over your veins. You may develop medical complications from infection with hepatitis or HIV. You may leave your friends and family behind to hang around with other users. You may have to resort to prostitution and robbery in order to support your habit. If you are addicted to opiates, your risk of death is very high; about one in a hundred untreated addicts die each year. Fortunately, about half stop on their own, often after using for several years.

Marijuana is the most commonly used illegal drug. About half of all young adults admit to having used marijuana at least once, and one in eight adults continue to use. It is derived from the hemp, or cannabis, plant and is referred to by many names, including pot, grass, weed, and hashish. Marijuana is usually smoked, though it can also be ingested with food. The effects of smoked marijuana are evident within minutes but last several hours. When you smoke marijuana, you usually experience some *euphoria*. You feel relaxed, mellow, and content with life. Everything around you seems funny, interesting, or profound. Life seems to slow down, and you sense things around you more intensely. You see objects in greater detail, and colors more deeply. Some users, however, become *anxious* or even *paranoid* rather than relaxed. Common physical effects include reddening of the eyes, dry mouth, and food cravings. You may become clumsy and slow to react. Your clothing may carry the distinctive aroma of marijuana.

Long-term effects of marijuana use include troubles with alertness and memory and possibly a decrease in motivation. It is unclear if these are permanent effects or side effects of ongoing intoxication. The vast majority of marijuana users do not become addicted.

Some other botanical products can cause sedating and relaxing effects. Kava is a derivative of a pepper plant that has been used for its intoxicating and relaxing effects in the South Pacific. It is now sold in pill form in America as a relaxing and sedating over-the-counter pill. Like other botanicals, the quality and efficacy of these pills has not been well studied. Kava can cause skin rashes and hepatitis. Valerian is a plant product that is reputed to cause mild sleepiness.

Cocaine and Amphetamine Are Stimulants

Cocaine appears to be the most addicting of the illegal intoxicants, probably because people enjoy the unequaled high that it can produce. Cocaine is derived from the coca plant of South America, where the plant's leaves are commonly chewed for their mildly stimulating effect. Converted into cocaine powder, the drug is usually inhaled into the nose with a straw. Cocaine has its strongest effects when it is transformed into crack or freebase cocaine that can be smoked or injected directly into the bloodstream. These methods deliver potent quantities of the drug to the brain faster, leading to a more intense high, as well as to more dangerous side effects. About one in eight adults has used cocaine.

The intoxicating effects of cocaine last for no more than an hour. You feel alert, excited, powerful, and happy. Some users compare the *euphoria* to an orgasm. The enjoyable effects can quickly be overcome by less pleasant psychological effects, especially as you use more often and in higher doses. You become more suspicious. Sometimes *paranoia* is evident in excessive worries about the police, drug dealers, and other people who are around when you are using. You may become nervous, irritable, and angry. You may engage in oddly compulsive and repetitive behaviors, like searching the floor over and over again for something you think you have dropped. You may see flashes of light or experience *hallucinations*. With repeated uses you are less likely to experience the pleasant high and more likely to be anxious, paranoid, and wired. You may start to drink alcohol or consume downers in an attempt to be less anxious.

Cocaine enhances the release of chemicals in the brain that lead to higher blood pressure, faster pulse, dilation of the pupils, chills, muscular tics, and palpitations. When you consume a large amount you may experience a stroke, heart attack, or seizure. I have treated men in their early thirties who ended up in intensive care units with these devastating cardiovascular conditions that usually afflict much older men. Many had permanent brain injuries.

Amphetamines are less potent than cocaine but have similar stimulating properties. Amphetamines were synthesized in imitation of ephedrine (or ma-huang), a plant derivative that has been used as a stimulant since prehistoric times. It is still sold in over-the-counter products, especially for weight loss. Synthetic versions, including pseudoephedrine (Sudafed) and propranolamine, are used in the treatment of nasal congestion, but they can be stimulating if taken in excess. In the late nineteenth century, amphetamine was synthesized and used in the treatment of asthma. It was then used, and continues to be used, in wartime to keep soldiers awake and energetic while on long missions. Today various amphetamines (such as Dexedrine and Ritalin) are prescribed in the treatment of attention-deficit *hyperactivity* disorder. Amphetamines are synthesized and sold illegally as speed, crystal, crystal meth, and ice (which can also be inhaled through the nose, smoked, or injected).

In low doses, amphetamines increase alertness and attention while holding off sleepiness. They may lead to irritability, *hyperactivity,* and *sleeping problems.* I evaluated one man who began to get into arguments as a result of his use of weight loss pills, not knowing they contained ephedrine. Amphetamine abusers often become *angry* and get into fights. When these drugs are abused in higher doses, their psychological and physical effects are the same as those seen with cocaine.

Caffeine is a socially accepted and widely consumed intoxicant with stimulant properties. A cup of coffee leads to a feeling of contentment while increasing alertness and concentration. After several cups of coffee, however, you may experience jitteriness, restlessness, *sleep problems,* muscular tics, nausea, and diarrhea. Doses of caffeine equivalent to ten cups of coffee have been known to cause *confusion.* Caffeine and related chemicals are present not only in coffee, but also in teas, soft drinks, chocolate bars, and over-the-counter cold remedies, diet pills, and sleep suppressants.

In other parts of the world stimulants are regularly consumed in the form of guarana (Brazil), mate (Argentina), kola (Africa), khat (Yemen), and betel nut (throughout South and Southeast Asia and the Pacific).

The nicotine found in tobacco is mildly stimulating. It causes a sense of well-being while increasing alertness and concentration. It can also cause nausea, stomach cramps, dizziness, and headaches when consumed in excess. Of course, other chemicals released during the smoking or chewing of tobacco can lead to cancer and cardiovascular disease. If you use tobacco regularly, your risk of death doubles. There is a one in three chance you will die before the age of sixty-five. You can reverse some of the risk immediately when you stop using.

Hallucinogens, and Many Other Substances, Cause Perceptual Disturbances

Hallucinogens, or psychedelics, are named for their ability to induce *hallucinations* and other symptoms of *psychosis.* Though chemically different, they each cause a distortion in the perception of reality. The most commonly used hallucinogens are lysergic acid diethylamide (or LSD, a synthetic drug, also known as acid), psilocybin (found in psychedelic mushrooms) and mescaline (derived from the buttons of the peyote cactus of the American Southwest).

Within an hour of consuming a hallucinogenic drug you begin to experience colors more vividly and more intense emotional feelings. Time slows down, and space seems to bend around you. Sensations may cross over each other, so that you "hear" colors or "see" music. Visual hallucinations are common, though they are usually shapes and colors rather than the distinct people and objects experienced in schizophrenia. Tie-dye shirts were designed to capture the vivid, swirling, reduplicated geometrical perceptions experienced on acid. You may also experience a distortion in your sense of yourself and your relationship to the universe; some people experience a mystical sense of oneness with the universe, or a *religious* revelation. Others feel frightened and alone. Hallucinogens can also cause sweating, an increase in pulse, muscular shakes, dilation of the pupils, and blurry vision. The drug effects last for several hours and can recur as *flashbacks* days or months later.

Phencyclidine (or PCP, also known as angel dust) was developed originally as an anesthetic agent but has properties similar to LSD. It is obtained in the form of drops on a paper blotter, or sprinkled as a powder onto tobacco or marijuana. In mild intoxication, you may feel tipsy and tingly. But PCP often causes a more severe *psychosis* with wild swings in mood and behavior. If you are intoxicated with PCP, you may appear to be having an acute episode of schizophrenia. You may become intensely withdrawn and preoccupied with *hallucinations* and disturbed thoughts. Or you may become extremely agitated, running about screaming, crying, and *confused*. You may engage in dangerous, *impulsive,* or socially inappropriate behaviors, such as running into traffic or stripping off your clothing in public. Increases in temperature and pulse, abnormal muscle movements, and stiffness can occur even at low doses. Higher doses can lead to death from overheating, seizure, or cessation of breathing. If you are fortunate the effects of PCP intoxication resolve within a day of use, but sometime the psychosis can last for a week or more.

Ketamine, sometimes referred to as special-K, is another anesthetic agent that has become a popular drug of abuse, especially in clubs. Users experience a sense of floating outside of their body. MDMA (or methylene-dioxymethamphetamine, more commonly known as ecstasy) is chemically related to amphetamines. After taking ecstasy, you may feel like the boundaries between your body and other people and objects have become fluid. You find yourself deeply moved by tactile sensations, and you touch everything within reach. Users often report a desire to hold, curl up with, and rub against other people, though in a way that is not perceived as particularly sexual. Nitrous oxide, or laughing gas, is a dental anesthetic that also induces a sensation of floating. Amyl nitrite (commonly referred to as poppers) is another type of club drug that induces a mildly pleasant altered state, possibly increasing sexual feeling. All of these club drugs can be potentially dangerous, especially when they are combined with other drugs or alcohol, and when you become dehydrated on the dance floor.

Several common plants contain atropine, a natural poison that can induce mild perceptual disturbances in small doses. Seeds or leaves of these plants have been used over the centuries as poisons but also in spiritual rituals for their mildly hallucinogenic properties. Occasionally teenagers consume them in an attempt to get high, and this can lead to *confusion,* severe agitation, coma, and death.

Industrial solvents, glues, and fuels were not developed as drugs of abuse, but unfortunately they have the ability to make some people feel high. They are all volatile chemicals that can be inhaled, often by pouring them into a bag that is held up to your nose and mouth. They are cheap and easily obtained and are commonly abused in the poorer parts of the world. Five percent of Americans have used volatile substances, but usually only once or twice. Solvents usually cause a pleasant out-of-body sensation of floating. When larger amounts are consumed, you may experience *hallucinations.* You may become agitated or completely oblivious to things around you. You may become deeply *confused.* You may become clumsy, slurred in speech, and dizzy. You may go into a stupor and remember nothing when you wake up hours later. People around you may smell the traces of gas on your body, or recognize irritated skin around your nose and mouth. These inhaled substances are extremely poisonous and can damage the liver, kidneys, and muscle as well as brain cells. They can also cause coma or death during use.

Drug Abuse Can Be Confused with Other Mental Illnesses

Intoxication refers only to the short-term effects of a substance while it is still in the body. Intoxication usually lasts a number of hours, depending on the substance. When drugs or alcohol are abused over a longer period of time, over days to months, then there are additional effects. Drugs and alcohol have a poisoning effect on the brain, leading to a whole range of psychiatric problems that are described elsewhere in this book, such as *anxiety, depression, mania, memory loss,* and *psychosis.*

Anabolic steroids provide an interesting example of the long-term effects of drugs. Steroids are not intoxicating and do not induce a high. They are abused because they enhance muscle bulk. They also have long-term psychiatric effects. If you use steroids, you may become irritable and depressed. You may have outbursts of *anger*. You may even become manic or psychotic. Physical side effects include worsening acne, shrinking of the testicles, and development of breasts in men.

Sometimes it can be difficult to determine whether psychiatric problems have been caused by on-going drug abuse, or whether drugs have been used in a misguided attempt to treat an underlying mental illness. For example, many people who suffer from *anxiety* or *depression* will drink alcohol in an attempt to alleviate some of the pain of their illness. But ongoing alcohol abuse also causes depression and anxiety. Regardless of which comes first, a vicious cycle of increasing use and increasing depression develops.

Some people become psychotic while using drugs. When that is the case, the symptoms of *psychosis* sometimes improve quickly in the hospital simply as a result of your being off drugs. This is good news only if you take steps to prevent relapsing into drug use when you leave the hospital. If you use drugs again, you will probably become psychotic again. Some people who become psychotic during drug use do not improve quickly. Symptoms persist for several weeks in spite of treatment and recur when medication is stopped. In that case, the psychosis is probably not just from the drugs but from an underlying schizophrenia. Drug abuse may only have brought the illness to the surface.

The Symptoms of Withdrawal Are Usually the Opposite of Intoxication

One of the most serious long-term consequences of drug use is the risk of becoming dependent. When taken on a regular basis, all of the drugs discussed above can be addicting. Because they make you feel good, you experience *cravings* to use them again and again. But you also become dependent on drugs because your brain grows used to them, and it is too painful to stop. Drugs and alcohol eventually change the chemistry around and within your brain cells, and when a drug is removed your brain cells experience a shock. The psychological and physical effects are known as withdrawal.

Withdrawal from alcohol or sedative drugs can be dangerous. If you are a heavy drinker, you have a five percent chance of experiencing the seizures and profound *confusion* known as delirium tremens (or DTs), which can lead to death. Otherwise you may become irritable, *anxious,* and tremulous and have *sleeping problems* within hours of your last drink. Withdrawal from heroin and opiate painkillers is very unpleasant but not dangerous. You will experience flulike symptoms including stomach cramps, diarrhea, shakes, chills, and a runny nose. Your muscles ache, and you feel terrible all over. You will be angry and depressed. When you crash after using stimulants or cocaine you may find yourself sleeping for several days in a row. You feel depressed, and you may even have *suicidal thoughts*. Nicotine withdrawal also causes depression (and bupropion, or Zyban, one of the treatments for nicotine cravings, is actually an antidepressant medication).

The *craving* to obtain more drugs is very powerful when you are experiencing withdrawal. You know that, in the short term, only more drugs will bring you relief from the unpleasant feelings. Your urge to have a drink or use drugs immediately when you wake up in the morning is a result of early withdrawal. Even after you have survived detoxification, extreme cravings may persist or come on suddenly for months after.

How to Cope with Intoxication and Withdrawal

There is little that you can do for yourself when you are acutely intoxicated. In most cases, intoxication will erode your good sense, and you may behave in ways that you never would while sober. The best you can do is remove yourself to a safe place, away from stimulation and opportunities to cause harm. Do not drive a car or engage in any other activity that requires concentration, coordination, and fast reactions. Try to avoid making decisions that require good judgment or that have serious consequences, such as having sex or spending money. Drink lots of water and keep yourself comfortable.

Ambulances and emergency rooms use naloxone (Narcan) to immediately reverse the effects of opiates during an overdose. This reversal works only for a few hours, and it causes the instant onset of withdrawal symptoms in anyone who has been using heroin, pain-killers, or methadone on a regular basis. There are no other drugs that safely reverse the effects of drug abuse. You usually just have to wait out the effects of intoxication.

There are also few medical treatments for withdrawal. Alcohol, benzodiazepine, and barbiturate withdrawal is treated with sedative medications prescribed in sufficient doses to prevent seizure and confusion, and these are tapered off over several days. This treatment is generally accomplished in a hospital because withdrawal can be dangerous. Sometimes clonidine (Catapress) eases the symptoms of opiate withdrawal a little bit.

Once you are sober, look closely at your drug or alcohol use and try to determine whether you have lost control. It may be time to realize that you have a problem and that you need to stop. If you have trouble cutting back, if you need to use when you first wake up, or if you feel guilty about your use and become annoyed when others comment on your use, then you probably have a problem (see "Cravings"). Friends and family, or a counselor, can help you to examine the extent of your problem and get you into treatment.

If you are with someone who is intoxicated, you should help her to stay comfortable, hydrated, and secure. By no means let her drive. She may be upset with you at the time, but she will thank you when she is sober, and no one will be injured. If someone you care about becomes severely anxious, agitated, threatening, or *suicidal* after using drugs, you should bring her to a hospital for emergency care. She may need antipsychotic medication (see "Psychosis"), medical evaluation, and treatment or just supportive care in a secure environment. Hospital staff will be able to treat her more effectively and quickly if you can tell them what drug was used. A situation in which someone becomes unresponsive after using drugs may constitute a medical emergency, and treatment in a hospital may be needed to prevent coma, seizure, or cardiac or respiratory arrest. A person may become unresponsive after consuming more drugs (or a more potent variety of drug) than she is used to, or after combining drugs, often with alcohol.

Generally you should try to avoid getting into an argument with anyone who is intoxicated. Many drugs cause people to be irritable and belligerent and to act unpredictably. If you stare at, or argue with, someone who is high or drunk, you run the risk of unintentionally provoking a fight. Keep in mind that the person who is intoxicated is probably acting in a way that she would not if she were sober, and the next day she might not even remember what happened. If you ignore her she will probably forget about you and move on to behaving foolishly somewhere else.

Jealousy

The ringing of the phone wakes you up. You turn to see why your wife hasn't picked it up, and you see that her side of the bed is empty. You pick up the phone. A man asks for someone you don't know. Wrong number, you tell him, and you hang up. But his voice sounded familiar. Your wife should have been home by now. You call her unit, and they say she left a few hours ago.

Suddenly the door opens. You hear her moving around in the kitchen before she comes to the bedroom. You ask her where she's been, and she says that she was buying groceries for the week. She didn't call because she didn't want to wake you. "Well," you tell her, "you should have told your boyfriend not to call, either." She looks at you blankly. She's not going to indulge you on that subject. She undresses and heads for the shower. You pick up her uniform from the floor and sniff it for traces of aftershave.

Jealousy refers to an unreasonable fear of losing an important relationship. You may be preoccupied with suspicious thoughts about your partner and so you monitor her every move. You may be resentful of any time she spends with others. You suspect that her platonic friendships have erotic potential. You may use angry or desperate threats to intimidate or entice your loved one. You may feel betrayed without reason and strike out angrily at your partner and at the imagined intruders into your relationship. Psychiatrists refer to this as pathological jealousy, to distinguish it from the more typical, milder feelings that commonly accompany love. It is quite normal, of course, to worry about losing your partner's affection, to expect emotional fidelity, and to feel angry, hurt, or betrayed when a relationship is compromised.

Pathological jealousy is often a sign of a personality disorder. In borderline, dependent, and histrionic personality disorders, you have extremely poor *self-esteem*. Your opinion of yourself from one moment to the next depends on your ability to hold onto another person. You are in the uncomfortable position of being fully invested in the relationship yet constantly fearful of abandonment. You are sensitive to any sign of betrayal, and you overreact. You provoke and test your partner, leading to escalating arguments or violence. If you have a *paranoid* or *antisocial* personality disorder, you tend to be suspicious of others generally, and you often suspect you are being cheated. You are likely to suspect infidelity in your partners with little cause. In each of these personality disorders your difficulties are complicated by the fact that your past relationships have indeed turned out poorly and that you continue to have poor judgment in choosing romantic partners. You may have good reasons for your poor expectations.

Pathological jealousy can also be a sign of a *psychotic* illness, when the jealousy is completely out of touch with reality. The type of delusional disorder in which extreme jealousy is the essential feature is sometimes referred to as Othello syndrome, after the tragic Shakespeare character. In delusional jealousy you develop a fixed belief that your partner is cheating on you. Like all *delusions,* the belief is formed with no basis in fact and is impervious to reason. For example, I once treated an elderly man who was convinced that his wife of many years was having a sexual relationship with their grown son. If you have delusional jealousy, you may spend time searching for proof, sometimes of a bizarre nature, to confirm your suspicions. I treated one man who believed that he saw semen in his wife's panties many hours after she supposedly had a tryst. You may confront your partner repeatedly with such "proof" and accusations, but no amount of denial or explanation will change your mind.

Psychiatrists do not know what causes delusional jealousy, as distinct from other types of delusions. Presumably you have a brain disturbance that affects your ability to distinguish useful information from misleading clues. You pay heightened attention to anything out of the ordinary, yet you ignore relevant information that would disprove your suspicions. In some cases a jealous delusion may be just one feature of a broader mental illness, such as schizophrenia (see "Psychosis"). Jealous delusions also occur in dementia, which may result in part from your attempts to make sense of the gaps in your *memory*. You may think that your wife is out with a lover, when in fact she has been sitting at home all afternoon. You do not remember seeing her, and you leap to a jealous explanation.

Erotomania is another variety of *delusional* illness, in some ways the opposite of delusional jealousy. If you have an erotomanic delusion, you falsely believe that someone is in love with you. In most cases, you become focused on someone famous or powerful who is usually married or otherwise unavailable. Erotomanic delusions are different from the wishful fantasies of teenagers. Like other delusions, an erotomanic belief is firmly held without any good reason and in spite of evidence to the contrary. I have evaluated many men and women who continued to pursue their delusional love even after being arrested repeatedly for stalking, harassment, and contempt of court. Even when their victims testified against them in court they attributed this to pressure from the police or family and not to the victim's genuine wishes. If you have an erotomanic delusion, you may become quite *angry* and threatening when thwarted in your attempts to be with the one you love. In spite of your belief that she loves you, you may be jealous of your victim and attack her actual loved ones.

Jealousy from all causes has been associated with domestic violence, but especially if you have an *antisocial* personality disorder. You may be contemptuous and domineering, but you may also threaten, hit, or rape your partner to express your *anger* and to make an attempt to enforce fidelity. You may intimidate or attack those whom you believe are seeking to intrude on your relationship. After the breakup of your relationship you may stalk and harass your ex-partner. Even if you were not particularly jealous earlier in the relationship, the *stress* of the breakup may overwhelm your usual coping strategies, and you may behave in a desperate fashion. Depending on your cultural values you may be particularly ashamed to be seen as a victim of infidelity. Unfortunately, newspapers report nearly every day on distraught individuals who have killed their ex-partners, and sometimes themselves and others, out of jealousy.

Jealousy does not always refer to a romantic or sexual relationship. Children sometimes display sibling rivalry, a platonic form of jealousy, after their mother gives birth to a younger child. You may start to behave younger than your age and throw temper tantrums in an attempt to retain your parents' attention. Sibling rivalry usually fades with time.

How to Cope with Jealousy

If you suffer from jealous *delusions,* you may benefit from treatment with antipsychotic medication (see "Psychosis"), though you are unlikely to seek treatment on your own initiative. If you have personality traits that leave you vulnerable to jealous feelings and preoccupations, you may benefit from psychotherapy aimed at improving your *self-esteem* and teaching you to test the veracity of your suspicious thoughts. You may also benefit from couple therapy in which you and your partner learn to communicate in a calmer fashion about your mutual needs for affection, loyalty, and independence.

If you are involved in a relationship with someone who is unduly jealous, you should try to understand what motivates his jealousy. If he is lacking in self-esteem and fearful of being abandoned, you can make an extra effort to remind him of your love for him even when you exercise your independence, for example by spending a night out with your girlfriends. If he is *paranoid* in general or completely unreasonable in his accusations, then you may find there is little you can do except guide him to a psychiatrist. You may find it easier to get him to attend couple therapy even if you think the problem is his alone. If your partner threatens to harm you, or has abused you, then you should seek help from a domestic abuse hotline, a support group, or the police. The intimidation and violence is likely to continue, especially if your partner has an *antisocial* personality.

Learning Difficulties

Moving you to the front of the classroom hasn't helped much. You can see the figures on the blackboard just as well, but you still don't know how to read them. There are too many lines and circles, and you can't tell where one word begins and another ends. And now you can't hide. The teacher calls your name and slaps the board with her pointer. Is that where the sentence starts? You see the letter a. *And that curled letter that crosses itself must be a* p. *You make a hesitant guess: "Ap . . . apple?"*
"No. No. It's 'bat,' " she says. " 'He sees a bat'!"

Learning begins long before you step into a classroom. Babies are born with the capacity to hear sounds and make noises. They quickly discover that the sounds they make have an influence on the people around them who bring food, comfort, or attention. Within six months an infant is able to recognize his name. In his first year he is able to pay attention to music and speech, to babble, and to nod his head with meaning. He begins to develop more of an interest in the world beyond him. By his first birthday he has spoken his first word.

During his second year of life a child begins to learn the meaning of individual words and the names of common objects. He is beginning to walk and to learn to feed himself. By the age of two he is using two or three words together in simple, childlike phrases. He has learned how to express affection, sadness, anger, and anxiety and how to gauge the emotions of others. He begins to play symbolically with toys and dolls. He begins to use reason to understand the explanations provided to him by adults. By the age of three he is speaking in sentences and has a vocabulary of nearly one thousand words. By the age of five he is ready to start kindergarten. Every child develops at a slightly different pace, but these are some of the typical landmarks in a developing child.

Autism and Mental Retardation May Be Detected During the Preschool Years

During the preschool years some problems with learning may become apparent. Autism, a disorder characterized by problems with social interactions and communication, is usually diagnosed during infancy. About one in every thousand children has autism, boys much more often than girls. Rates may be five times higher if you include less severe variations of autism, including Asperger's disorder (see "Oddness").

During his first year of life a child with autism may seem unresponsive. He is difficult to soothe, and he does not mold his body to anyone who holds him. He fails to babble or make eye contact. Instead he may make odd, repetitive noises.

Autistic children seem oblivious to the presence or attention of their parents, whom they treat like strangers. Children with autism never seem to show recognizable emotions. As they begin to speak, they may use invented words or repeat what others say. They may learn to read by imitating others but without having any idea what the words mean. Instead they may prefer listening to music and humming tunes.

Children who have autism also engage in a variety of *odd* behaviors. Though disinterested in people, they develop attachments to inanimate objects around the house. Unlike other children, they do not play with toys in a symbolic manner. For example, autistic children do not pretend that their dolls are speaking to each other. Instead, they may manipulate them in a mechanical way, by lining them up or spinning them. Autistic children may entertain themselves by rocking or spinning their bodies. Or they may sit quietly doing nothing.

Most autistic children make odd physical *movements,* such as arm flapping; have unexpected behavioral outbursts, such as screaming, laughing, or crying; and engage in *self-mutilating* behaviors such as head banging and biting. Many of these behaviors seem to come out of the blue. They seem to be extremely sensitive to stimulation. They may enjoy the sensations of endlessly stroking someone's hair, rubbing fabric, or running their fingers across a window screen. On the other hand, they may suddenly cover their ears and scream in response to unexpected noises. They require consistency, and any changes in the environment or routine may trigger an outburst. They insist on doing things in the same order (for example, eating before showering and not after), and they may find it difficult to switch from one activity to another. They may become quite upset if someone has rearranged the furniture or if they have to take a ride in a different car.

Mental retardation also can be detected during the preschool years, at least in more severe cases. Mental retardation is an intellectual deficiency that can arise from a variety of causes. People with Down's syndrome, the most common genetic cause, have a characteristic flat face and epicanthal eyelid folds that may be recognized at birth. Many other syndromes of mental retardation likewise have characteristic appearances. If no such obvious physical features are present, mental retardation may become evident in the second year of life when language skills are delayed. Unlike children with autism, mentally retarded children express typical emotions and are interested in communicating with their parents and with others. However, they learn to do so more slowly than other children.

Mental retardation is defined by a low intelligence quotient (IQ) score along with poor functioning compared with other children of a similar age. An average IQ is defined as one hundred. People with low IQ scores may nevertheless be quite capable of taking care of themselves and of interacting appropriately with others. Mental retardation is diagnosed only in those who have significant practical impairments.

Approximately two out of a hundred children are mildly retarded, with IQ scores between fifty and seventy. Those with mild mental retardation may not be recognized until they are in school and have difficulty in mastering reading and other more advanced tasks. These individuals may tend to think more simplistically and have difficulty reasoning and understanding others. They may not realize when someone is being sarcastic or is exaggerating or joking. With the support of family, educators, and social workers, they should be able to achieve a grade school education and hold a job as an adult. They should be able to live at home with relatives, if not on their own. Fewer than four out of one thousand children have more severe mental retardation, with IQ scores below fifty.

Specific Learning Disorders May Become Evident in School

In processing information children can have a number of difficulties that lead them to perform worse in school than you would expect from their intelligence. You may have an average or above-average intelligence but still have difficulties with reading, writing, or mathematics. You may also have specific difficulties with fine-motor coordination or social skills. When these learning disabilities are detected early you can receive additional educational assistance in order to reach your full potential. Learning disorders are thought to affect as many as one in ten schoolchildren. They have been diagnosed much more commonly in boys than in girls, though more recent studies suggest that rates may be similar.

If you have a reading disorder, you have difficulty recognizing written letters and words, and you make multiple errors when attempting to read them. You may confuse letters that look alike, such as *b* and *d*. You have difficulty putting together groups of letters to form specific sounds (or phonemes). You may have difficulty distinguishing left from right, and you may read letters or words in the wrong order (a condition popularly known as dyslexia). You read slowly and skip words. In most cases your understanding of spoken language is good, even though it is difficult for you to read. Many of these difficulties become apparent by the first or second grade, when reading skills are first taught. If you are particularly bright you may be able to compensate so that the problem is not recognized until later.

Writing disorders are usually recognized a couple of years after reading disorders become evident. If you have a writing disorder you have difficulties with handwriting and with spelling. You fail to learn basic rules of grammar and syntax; your sentences are clumsy and confusing, and your paragraphs are poorly organized when you grow old enough to write essays.

If you have a mathematics disorder you may begin to have problems in the early grades with simple counting and arithmetic. Later you may have difficulty understanding mathematical symbols and the increasingly complex and abstract equations in which they are used. You may lose track of quantities and figures or fail to group them properly when performing calculations. You may have difficulty in thinking of symbols and shapes in space, and in manipulating them in your mind.

Some children are clumsy from an early age due to a disorder of learning coordination. During the preschool years, they may have difficulty mastering milestones such as walking, feeding, and getting dressed. Also, they tend to drop or bump into things. At school they are clumsy in sports and games and may have difficulty using pencils, crayons, and paintbrushes. Handwriting is a particular challenge, even if their language skills are otherwise fine. Other learning problems may involve memory and organization. They may lose their homework, forget assignments, or require numerous repetitions to retain a new concept.

Learning disorders often occur together with coordination problems and language disorders (see "Speech Problems"). The disabilities are not caused by intellectual deficits, hearing or visual impairments, or specific neurological illnesses. Rather, they arise from subtle deficits in perceiving and processing information. The specific disabilities are diagnosed with standardized tests for reading, writing, mathematics, and fine motor skills. Children whose performance on these tests is significantly worse than their performance on IQ tests should receive targeted remedial education. Without special training they are likely to fall further and further behind in learning compared with their classmates, and school will become increasingly frustrating. Children who are unable to perform up to their intellectual capacity tend to develop poor *self-esteem*. They may ultimately skip classes, refuse to complete homework, or even drop out of school.

What Causes Developmental and Learning Disorders?

A multitude of genetic and environmental factors influence the development of intellectual and social functioning. Intelligence, as measured by IQ tests, appears to be determined by genetics at least as much as by other factors. However, the rules of genetic mixing are such that even bright or below average parents tend to produce intellectually average children rather than increasingly bright or retarded children.

There is a wide range of causes of mental retardation. Down's syndrome is the most common genetic cause, accounting for approximately ten percent of mental retardation in America. The next most common genetic cause is fragile X syndrome, which also results in a distinctive appearance featuring an elongated head and protuberant ears. Viral infections or syphilis during pregnancy can lead to retardation in the child, as can exposure to alcohol, drugs, or some medications. If you drink heavily and regularly during pregnancy, there is approximately a one in seven chance that your child will develop fetal alcohol syndrome, resulting in mental retardation, *hyperactivity,* and a characteristic facial appearance. Complications around the time of delivery, such as a premature birth or compromised supply of oxygen, increase the chance of mental retardation in the child. Infections of the brain during childhood, such as bacterial meningitis or viral encephalitis, can cause retardation in a previously normal child. Hypothyroidism and exposure to lead are rare but important causes of mental retardation. Head injuries from falls, physical abuse, or car or bicycle accidents can also produce mental retardation.

The causes of the specific learning disorders are not known. Presumably many of the same conditions that cause mental retardation could also insult the brain in a less global fashion, affecting the development of information processing skills. Co-occurring psychiatric illness during childhood could also interfere with the normal development of learning skills. In fact, there is a great overlap between learning disorders and other childhood conditions such as attention-deficit *hyperactivity* disorder (ADHD) and Tourette's disorder (see "Compulsions"). Whether these other conditions indirectly interfere with learning, or whether the learning disorders share with them a common neurological deficit, is unclear. We also do not know why boys have a higher incidence of learning disorders, mental retardation, and autism than girls.

It is unclear to what extent a neglectful, psychologically abusive or deprived home environment can cause mental retardation or learning disorders. Some children may be slow to develop communication skills, coordination, and social skills in such settings, but as they grow up or move into other environments they predictably begin to catch up with their peers.

The precise causes of autism are unknown. The illness appears to be largely genetic; an identical twin has a one in three chance of sharing the disorder. There is evidence of structural and chemical brain abnormalities in many children with autism, and about one-quarter develop seizures during adolescence. There is no evidence that deficient parenting styles can cause autism. It was assumed in the past that most children with autism are also mentally retarded, but recent studies have shown that two-thirds are not. Though possessing normal intelligence, these children have difficulty communicating with, and appreciating the feelings of, others.

Cognitive Problems May Develop Later In Life

Cognition is a psychiatric term for thinking. Cognitive problems can include disorientation, distractibility, *memory loss,* intellectual difficulties, and problems with abstract thought and reasoning. Global impairments in thinking, like those seen in mental retardation, can also occur in adults. These syndromes, seen mostly in the elderly, are known as dementia, and the primary problem involves a progressive loss of *memory.* The most common cause of dementia is Alzheimer's disease. Unfortunately, many children with Down's syndrome also develop Alzheimer's disease during their fourth decade of life.

During a severe episode of *depression* you may also appear to have dementia. You may be unable to learn new information or solve problems. Psychiatrists refer to this as pseudo-dementia, since it resolves once the depression is treated. If you are caring for someone who is depressed, you may find that you need to speak more slowly and repeat information for it to be learned.

Physical trauma to the head can cause a variety of cognitive problems, including *memory loss,* distractibility, trouble thinking abstractly, coordination problems, and difficulty learning new information. You may become more *impulsive,* especially with injuries to the frontal lobes of the brain. In more severe cases impairments may be global and persistent, leading to a diagnosis of dementia.

Cognitive problems are also common in schizophrenia. Difficulties with abstract thinking, problem solving, insight, and attention are among the "negative" symptoms (see "Oddness") that may be apparent even when *psychotic* symptoms have been fully treated. It is these thinking problems that often make it difficult for patients with schizophrenia to achieve the same degree of independence and job satisfaction as they would have otherwise. Many patients benefit from rehabilitation therapy, which provides peer support, vocational training, coaching, and coping skills with the goal of reintegrating as much as possible back into the community.

If you suffer from the cognitive impairments of schizophrenia you may benefit from a change in medication. The new generation of antipsychotic medications (see "Psychosis") is often effective for the cognitive problems that tend to persist during treatment with the older medications. They also have fewer side effects that muddy thinking. Clozapine (Clozaril) is often the most effective medicine at restoring your ability to think clearly and abstractly as you used to before developing schizophrenia. Some patients with schizophrenia appear to think more clearly while smoking cigarettes, and scientists are trying to develop new medications that might have the same effects without the risks associated with tobacco use.

How to Cope With Learning Problems

Learning disabilities are treated with direct educational instruction. Children with a reading disorder should receive extra coaching in identifying letters, connecting them with sounds, and blending them to form words. Parents should spend more time reading with them, and they must practice on their own as well. Those with a writing disorder will probably benefit from practicing reading and spelling. They should also receive teaching that focuses on helping them to refine their writing skills, for example by putting together a written essay on a topic they have chosen. These children may find that they are a more fluent writer when they use a computer to compose sentences and paragraphs. Those with a mathematics disorder may benefit greatly from individualized instruction that focuses on problem-solving methods rather than on trying to guess the right answer. It may be easier to reach solutions with a calculator than by hand. Those with coordination problems should receive additional instruction and should practice difficult tasks.

If you are a parent of a child with a learning disorder you should realize that your child is not stupid, lazy, or willful. He will be able to perform up to his potential once he receives special educational assistance.

The goal for people with mental retardation is to learn skills that help them to communicate with others and to cope with everyday tasks. They generally receive this training in special education classes or in other programs for the mentally retarded. They will flexibly pursue some degree of independence while continuing to benefit from the support of others. Rates of other mental illnesses are much higher among the mentally retarded, with one in three developing behavioral problems, so additional therapy or medication may be indicated for those additional symptoms. Behavioral problems may also reflect poorly communicated distress, discomfort, or desires.

Children with autism benefit most from the early initiation of intensive, year-round specialized education and behavioral interventions. The goal of education is to help the child acquire some basic social skills, such as communicating with others in a nonaggressive manner. These interventions are most successful for those individuals who are not also mentally retarded. With intensive treatment, they may learn to communicate their needs both verbally and nonverbally by the time they reach school age. Behavioral training throughout childhood focuses on developing social skills. In small groups they practice conversations, role-play, and problem-solve how to handle specific social situations. Unfortunately, about two-thirds of children with autism require ongoing institutionalization as they grow up.

Some of the symptoms of autism improve with medication treatment. Autism has been associated with abnormal levels of the brain chemical serotonin, and the SSRI antidepressant medications (see "Depression") that target this chemical have been found to reduce ritualized behaviors, mannerisms, and irritability. However, some people with autism are very intolerant of the side effects, so low doses should be used. Stimulant medications, such as those used in the treatment of *hyperactivity*, are commonly prescribed to children with autism. However, there is little evidence that they are effective in reducing autistic behaviors, and they may increase irritability and tics. Antipsychotic medications (see "Psychosis") may be used to treat agitation and aggressive outbursts. Anticonvulsant medications (such as carbamazepine) are used to prevent the seizures that commonly occur in autism, but they also have mood-stabilizing properties (see "Mania") and can reduce irritability and agitation.

If you are a parent of a newborn your first instinct may be to turn away from him if he has some of the physical features suggestive of mental retardation. You may feel *grief* for the loss of the normal child you had expected. Later you may feel ashamed, angry, depressed, and guilty. However, mentally retarded children are usually very affectionate, and you will find yourself loving your child in spite of your initial disappointment and fear. In fact, you may be tempted to indulge your child more than necessary, rather than fostering his independence. You may go through similar emotional stages of rejection, anger, guilt, and *depression* upon learning that your growing child has autism or specific learning disabilities. These are normal reactions to a *stressful* situation.

If your child has mental retardation, autism, or a learning disability, you should educate yourself as much as possible about the disorder and available disability programs. You should not feel guilty about your child's condition or about your inability to help your child reach goals as fully or as quickly as you would have liked. You should realistically develop new goals, in consultation with educators, therapists, and other parents, so that you help your child to function to the best of his ability. Raising any child is a challenge, and raising children with intellectual or learning disabilities present different, but not impossible, challenges.

When you speak with your child, remember that he is more experienced than is reflected in his mental or academic age. If you treat him or speak to him like a baby when he is a child, or like a child as he grows into adulthood, he will probably feel that you are condescending. If you speak to him in a normal fashion but provide additional explanations as needed, then he feels more responsible and is stimulated to learn more. For similar reasons children should generally not be held back in school if it results in them joining classmates who are less socially mature. They should receive whatever tutoring or special education they require while attending classes with their social peers.

Most children realize when they are not able to perform as well in some area as their peers, and they may be shunned or teased by their classmates. You want to communicate frankly with your child about the specific disabilities that he has while making it clear that you do not see him as disturbed or damaged. Children with learning disorders should be told that they are just as intelligent as their classmates and that with extra time, attention, and practice, they will be able to catch up.

Mania

It has been a difficult winter, but now the sun is out and flowers are in bloom and you feel good. You put on your best outfit, buy a newspaper, and sit down to scan the job listings. You don't have a résumé with you, but you're a good talker and you look fine. When you leave the café, you leave a tip that is nearly as large as the bill.

The first office you approach turns you away because you don't have an appointment. Their loss. You leave your phone number with the secretary, but she won't give you hers, even though you ask her several times. You don't really want to work in an office anyway. Passing a computer store, you realize that you have missed your calling: you should be a writer, and if you had a computer you could complete your great novel in no time. You buy two laptops and put them on your credit card. You can pay it off after you sign your first book deal.

It is past midnight, but you're not ready to sleep. You've already written at least thirty pages of your novel. You can't sit still. It's time for a break, so you dress up and head to a disco. You have a couple of drinks, and you buy several for the friends you make at the bar. Your conversation is sparkling. The club keeps playing your favorite songs. You get up on the stage with the other dancers and start to sing along. Security asks you to leave. They say you're embarrassing yourself. But how many people in their forties can break-dance? They must be jealous.

You return home, but you're still not ready to sleep. You pull out your address book and start to call your college friends to tell them about your new book. The first two hang up after reminding you that it's the middle of the night. So you start calling friends in Europe. They should be awake by now.

Another day has passed, and you still have not slept. Who can sleep when so many great ideas are flowing? You've completed one hundred pages. It's going to be an American classic. The best publishing houses are on the other side of the country, so you order a ticket to fly out in the morning. Because you're buying your ticket on such short notice it costs a thousand dollars, but it's worth it. You'll find a hotel when you get there. You call a taxi to take you to the airport. Along the way you notice that people in the streets are waving to you and pointing at you. They can tell you're going to be big. You wave out the window and scream out to them, "I'll be back soon."

Mania is the term psychiatrists use to describe a state of elevated mood, rapid speech, grandiose thinking, and agitation that can occur in several different illnesses, but which is the hallmark of bipolar disorder, previously known as manic-depressive illness.

Psychiatrists sometimes use the dictionary definition of mania, which refers to any abnormal desire or compulsion. For example, trichotillomania is an illness characterized by the compulsion to pull out your hair, and erotomania is the persistent and false belief that someone else is in love with you. In this chapter mania is not being used in that sense. The similar sounding term "maniac" has no psychiatric meaning at all; it is used in common speech to mean someone who is driven to behave in a crazy way.

The primary symptom in mania is *euphoria,* meaning an elevation in mood. In many ways mania is the opposite of depression. You feel unusually happy, hopeful, confident, and enthusiastic rather than sad, pessimistic, worthless, and withdrawn. As mania progresses you become elated, and eventually you begin to feel like you are losing control. You may begin to have violent mood swings, laughing one moment and then threatening to harm yourself or others in the next.

Rapid speech is the most notable feature of mania. As you become manic, your thoughts begin to flow more rapidly. Eventually thoughts seem to pop into your mind faster than you can keep track of them. You are constantly distracted by exciting ideas and new observations. You find it difficult to stay focused on one subject. Others notice that your speech has become rapid and loud. They may ask you to slow down or to speak more softly. They may have to keep reminding you. People are unable to follow your conversation because you keep changing the topic, seemingly without realizing it. At a certain point it becomes almost impossible to interrupt you. Psychiatrists refer to this as pressured speech, when speech is rapid, disconnected, and difficult to interrupt. As your speech and thinking become more disorganized, doctors may be unable to distinguish whether you are suffering from mania or *psychosis,* which also produces *confusion* and *nonsensical* speech.

When you become manic you also become more physically *hyperactive.* You find it impossible to be still; you bounce your legs, shake your head, and sway to an internal beat. You may be so distractible that you leave one task unfinished while rushing to another. You become untidy in your grooming and attire. You try to pack as many activities into the day as possible but abandon plans as something new grabs your interest. You may eat more than usual, or you may be in such a rush that you neglect to eat at all. In severe cases you may become physically exhausted or dehydrated. In fact, before medication was available, one in five hospitalized with mania died, usually from exhaustion.

Sleep problems are one of the earliest signs of mania. As you become increasingly manic, you find that you do not feel sleepy. You lie in bed, but you cannot quiet the thoughts that are flowing through your mind. As mania progresses, you may stay awake for several days at a time. You feel energetic in spite of getting so little rest. It is important to recognize trouble sleeping because sleep deprivation is not only a symptom of mania but also a cause. If you have bipolar disorder and you stay up all night, you might precipitate a manic episode.

When you become manic you become *grandiose,* believing that you are a unique and great person. You often become *religiously* and *sexually preoccupied.* I have worked with several patients who were very modest before becoming ill but who, when manic, ran around the hospital trying to kiss or fondle others, or took off their clothing at every opportunity. Other patients sang the praise of God almost continuously. As mania progresses, you lose touch with reality and develop *delusions* and *hallucinations.* For example, you may believe that you are the Messiah and hear what seems to be the voice of God. The voices may tell you that you have special powers.

Poor judgment is very common at all stages of mania. You often become extravagant, *impulsive,* and impractical. You might reach your spending limit on several credit cards in a series of big purchases. I have treated patients who had bought several cars shortly before being hospitalized.

You might purchase plane tickets to fly around the world. You might spend hundreds of dollars on phone calls. You wear gaudy, mismatched clothing and bright makeup. You might drink more alcohol, or use more drugs, than you are used to, at which point it becomes difficult to tell if you are manic or experiencing the effects of *intoxication*. You might take risks you would not normally take because you are convinced of your success or because you ignore the consequences. For example, you become reckless in your driving and in other activities that require caution, such as having sex without a condom.

One of the classic features of mania is that the person who is manic has no idea that anything is wrong. Psychiatrists refer to this as a lack of insight, or *denial*. It is virtually impossible to convince a manic person that she is sick and in need of treatment. It can be equally difficult to convince her that she cannot accomplish something that she has decided to do. If you point out that she does not have the skills, she will think that you are underestimating her. If you say that she does not have enough money, she will reassure you that money does not matter, or that she will have enough by the time the bill arrives. If you argue that an activity is thoughtless, illegal, or unsafe, she will say that you are being too cautious. She may become *angry* and resentful that you are placing limits on her.

Mania Is the Hallmark of Bipolar Disorder

Until recently bipolar disorder was commonly known as manic-depressive illness, reflecting the fact that virtually all people with bipolar disorder experience episodes of *depression* as well as episodes of mania. These severe changes in mood are quite different from the normal ups and downs that we all experience from time to time as good and bad things happen in our lives.

Approximately one percent of the population develop bipolar disorder during their lifetime. The risk of developing the illness is approximately ten times higher if you have a close relative with bipolar disorder. The illness is as common among men as women, and it occurs in all cultures and ethnic groups.

Bipolar disorder does not always first manifest itself with an episode of mania. Many people with bipolar disorder experience depression long before they become manic. In fact, one out of every four people initially diagnosed with depression eventually develop a manic episode, at which point the diagnosis should be changed to bipolar disorder. Women with bipolar illness usually experience an episode of depression first, whereas men usually have a first episode of mania. Since bipolar disorder tends to run in families, you should suspect that you have bipolar disorder if you develop depression but other family members have a history of becoming manic.

You are likely to have your first episode of mania any time between your teenage years and your thirties. Some episodes may be relatively mild, without a break in reality, which psychiatrists refer to as hypomania (see "Euphoria"). If you become manic you will almost certainly need to be hospitalized to protect you from your own poor judgment and reckless behavior. If untreated, mania typically lasts for several months before mood returns to normal. In the meantime you may lose your job, your marriage, and your savings. Left untreated, manic episodes are likely to occur again and again, with greater frequency and severity. Nine out of ten have a further mood episode. Mania can unfortunately be fatal. Studies have shown that at least one out of every four people with bipolar disorder attempt *suicide*.

With medication treatment, a manic episode will begin to resolve over a couple of weeks. Though medications reduce the risk of future episodes, some recurrence is likely. People with bipolar disorder usually experience an episode of either depression or mania every two to four years. This represents, on average, four episodes in the first decade after being diagnosed.

Most of the time a person with bipolar disorder returns to normal mood between episodes of mania and depression. But sometimes mood may not return to normal at the end of a manic episode. If you were manic, you may switch to depression, which can occur over just a few days. Suddenly you feel that you are no longer at the top of the world. Instead the world seems to be on top of you. You become hopeless and despondent. Though you were unable to stay still several days earlier, now you can barely move. Some people switch back and forth between mania and depression several times in a year. Psychiatrists refer to this as rapid cycling. Approximately one out of ten individuals with bipolar disorder experience rapid cycling.

Bipolar disorder is often misdiagnosed. Bipolar depression is indistinguishable from major depression. Hypomania, a less severe alteration in mood, is often overlooked because patients do not recognize that it is an abnormal mood state and that it provides a clue to proper diagnosis and treatment. According to one study, half of the patients with bipolar disorder reported only their depressive, and not their manic, symptoms to their psychiatrists. Mania can be confused with drug or alcohol *intoxication,* especially since both often occur at the same time. The *impulsive* and destructive behaviors that a person engages in while manic may lead to a diagnosis of a personality disorder if the psychiatrist does not realize that the person's usual personality is quite different. Finally, bipolar disorder may be indistinguishable from schizophrenia when a patient appears initially for treatment in a severely *psychotic* state. In fact, episodes of mania and depression also occur in an illness related to schizophrenia, which psychiatrists refer to as schizoaffective disorder. The difference is that people with bipolar disorder do not have psychotic symptoms except when they are severely manic or depressed.

For any of these reasons, the proper diagnosis may not be reached until several years into treatment, which can delay the implementation of the most appropriate treatments. On average, individuals with bipolar disorder are seen by three to four doctors over an eight-year period before they receive an accurate diagnosis. If you suffer from fluctuations in mood, you should try to explain in detail the mood patterns that you have experienced, to help your psychiatrist make an accurate diagnosis.

What Causes Bipolar Disorder?

As with most mental illnesses, we do not know precisely what causes bipolar disorder. We do know that there is a very large genetic component to the illness, more than in most other psychiatric illnesses. Researchers have been searching for the gene, or genes, that might cause the illness, so far with limited success. You are approximately ten times more likely to develop bipolar disorder if a close family member has the diagnosis. If your identical twin has bipolar disorder, there is more than a fifty percent chance that you too will have it. Even though these rates are very high, it is clear that not everyone with a genetic predisposition develops the illness.

As with depression, bipolar disorder may be a manifestation of an imbalance in signaling between neurons, the cells in the brain. Medications used in the treatment of bipolar disorder affect nerve cells and brain chemicals in a variety of complicated ways, and it is common to refer to bipolar illness as a chemical imbalance that can be corrected with medication.

One thing we can be certain of: mania is not the result of a personality flaw. Whether you are normally shy or gregarious, energetic or quiet, law-abiding or rule-defying, you may be vulnerable to developing bipolar disorder. If you engage in behaviors when you are manic that you later find embarrassing, shameful, irresponsible, or disgusting, you should recognize that you were in an altered state. You did not behave that way because you were raised poorly or because you have a weak personality. Of course, there are some people who engage in *antisocial* or *histrionic* behaviors even when they are not manic, and their behavior may become more outrageous when they become sick.

Many people find that their mood is seasonally influenced. Depressions occur most often in the fall and winter. Mania may develop in the spring. The body is presumably reacting to the amount of daylight, which changes with the seasons. If you have noticed a seasonal pattern to your illness, it may help you to prepare for predictable alterations in your mood. For example, you may not need medication except during certain seasons, and your depression may respond best to phototherapy, or light therapy (see "Depression").

To some extent episodes of mania may be precipitated by *stress*. As with depression, serious losses often precede the onset of a new episode. In fact, you may become manic after an event that you would expect to make you depressed, such as the death of a parent. As bipolar disorder progresses, episodes seem to occur more frequently and more spontaneously, without any obvious precipitating stressors.

Some medications, such as steroids, can cause mania. Antidepressant medication (see "Depression"), not surprisingly, can precipitate mania or make mania more difficult to treat. If this happens to you, you probably have an underlying, unrecognized bipolar disorder that antidepressant medication simply uncovered.

Several medical illnesses can also cause mania. If you first become manic when you are more than fifty years old, your illness more likely has an underlying medical cause. Medical conditions that affect the brain, and that have been known to cause mania, include hyperthyroidism, lupus, stroke, multiple sclerosis, and AIDS. For this reason your psychiatrist should perform a full medical workup before starting treatment. If you develop mania during the course of one of these illnesses, you may not have an underlying bipolar disorder or need treatment with mood-

Another example of a cause for
B. P. D in someone 45yrs to older

stabilizing medications. Treatment of the underlying medical condition may be sufficient.

How to Cope with Bipolar Disorder

If you have been diagnosed with bipolar disorder, there are several ways you can keep yourself healthy. First, you must recognize that you have an illness and that you are prone to experience episodes of depression and mania again in the future. Your goal is to maintain an even keel. When you are manic you may do things that shock or embarrass you when you return to health. As mentioned earlier, you should not conclude from this that you are a bad person. If you wish to be responsible, you should take steps to receive appropriate treatment so that you do not lose control in the future. This involves taking your medication, avoiding drugs and alcohol, reducing stress in your life, and enlisting the support of others.

Most importantly, you will need to be consistent in taking your medication. You and your doctor will work together to find the best medication that treats your illness while minimizing side effects. You will be tempted to stop medication from time to time. You may miss the euphoric feeling of being manic, you may dislike the side effects, or you may feel fine and forget that medication is the key to staying that way (see "Denial"). Even if you insist on stopping your medication against your doctor's recommendations, it is essential that your doctor know, so that she can continue to monitor your illness with you, and possibly point out to you any symptoms if they recur. The greatest risk of recurrence into mania occurs in the first few weeks after abruptly stopping medication.

If you have experienced only a single episode of mania, you and your doctor could consider stopping your mood-stabilizing medication. This decision should be based on an understanding that relapses are common. If your first manic episode was particularly severe, or if you became suicidal or dangerous to others, then the risk of relapse may be too great, and you may choose to remain on medication. If you choose to stop medication you should wait until at least four months have passed, since an untreated manic episode would probably last three to four months. Your medication should then be tapered slowly over at least a month. If you begin to develop some recurrent symptoms, then the medication should be resumed.

Medication is highly effective in shortening the duration of a manic episode and in preventing future episodes. Unfortunately, about half the people with bipolar disorder will experience a recurrence in spite of taking medication as prescribed. If a recurrence is detected early, a simple adjustment in the dose of medication may bring the episode back under control.

People who live with bipolar illness have found it helpful to make changes in their life that will reduce *stress* and promote stability. You should think about whether you are in a job that allows you to relax, or whether your job places too many demands on your thoughts and time. If you have a job that requires you to work odd hours, or to stay up through the night, you run the risk of becoming manic as a result of losing sleep. If you have a high-pressure job in which there are serious consequences for each little judgment you make (for example, in surgery or stock trading), then you may be under too much pressure. When you get sick, and your judgment becomes impaired, you may make bad decisions that harm others. If you choose to remain in a job of that sort, it is important that you have people around you who can monitor your judgment and remind you if your mood is changing or your work skills are faltering.

You will want to learn your own personal warning signs indicating that you are becoming ill. Everyone experiences mania and depression somewhat differently. You may notice that you first become overly optimistic, energetic, and excited about projects. You may start to wear more makeup than usual. (I have treated several women for whom a change in the shade of lipstick was a sure sign.) You may start pondering whether life is worth living. You may notice changes in your sleep habits. You should learn to separate these early warning signs from the regular ups and downs that you will continue to experience from day to day. You may want to keep a diary of symptoms, side effects, medication doses, and stressful events. Friends and family can be particularly helpful in providing an independent assessment of whether you are becoming too excited or depressed. Listen to them.

Psychotherapy, or talk therapy, can be very effective for some other psychiatric illnesses, but it is not very helpful when you are in the midst of a manic episode. One of the hallmarks of mania is the inability to think logically and to utilize insight, both of which are very important in psychotherapy. However, psychotherapy can be very helpful during recovery from manic and depressive episodes.

If someone you care about has been diagnosed with bipolar disorder, you should take several steps to preserve the quality of life that you share. Mood swings can batter a relationship, and people with bipolar disorder run the risk of losing the relationships that are important to them. Your greatest role may be in helping your loved one to monitor symptoms and treatment. From time to time she may lose sight of the fact that she is ill (see "Denial"). In fact, this may be a warning that she is on the verge of becoming manic. At this stage a simple adjustment in medication may lessen the severity of the episode. Whenever possible you should try to attend psychiatric appointments together so that you can share your observations.

It can be a lot of fun to spend time with someone who is hypomanic. She may be engaging, funny, adventuresome, creative, and energetic. You find yourself smiling and laughing when you are in her company. But keep in mind that her jovial and expansive mood is very fragile, and the truth is that she is severely ill and in emotional and, likely, financial distress. It is only a matter of time before the bubble bursts.

If your loved one becomes manic you should try to convince her to go to either the psychiatrist or the emergency room. Avoid escalating the situation by becoming loud, demanding, or threatening. In fact, a person who is manic is most likely to become violent when someone prevents her from following her urges. When manic, a person feels all-powerful and entitled to do whatever she wishes. If you need to set limits, do so calmly and supportively. For example, you might inform her that, if she is unwilling to see the psychiatrist with you, you would like to speak to the psychiatrist yourself.

Many people with bipolar disorder will, while either manic or depressed, attempt suicide, and some are successful. You should take any signs of *suicidal thinking* very seriously.

You and your loved ones should make plans, when both of you are well, to prepare for periods of illness. The house should be free of alcohol and weapons. You should take steps to protect your finances, perhaps by limiting the number of credit cards you keep and by restricting access to cash accounts that you share. Otherwise, a manic shopping spree could lead to debt as well as embarrassment.

Mood-Stabilizing Medications

Mood-stabilizing medications are the mainstay of treatment for bipolar disorder. The mood-stabilizers include lithium and several anticonvulsant medications that were originally developed for the treatment of epilepsy. The mood-stabilizers can treat a manic episode rapidly, sometimes within just a few days of starting medication. When taken on a regular basis, they also prevent the recurrence of manic and depressive episodes.

Lithium carbonate (Eskalith) is a simple molecular salt. In fact, it was used in the past as a replacement for common table salt, until people realized that it could be dangerous when consumed in large amounts. Lithium was found to have mood-stabilizing properties in the 1950s. It has a variety of effects on cells in the brain, and no one knows for sure why it is an effective treatment for mania. One of the suspected mechanisms is that it binds to chemicals inside nerve cells that are involved in the regulation of communication between the cells. In general, this has a stabilizing effect on the cells. Studies have shown that half of manic episodes resolve with lithium treatment.

For reasons that are not yet clear, several anticonvulsant (anti-seizure) medications used in the treatment of epilepsy are also effective mood-stabilizers. They probably work by binding to receptors on the surface of nerve cells that control chemical communication between cells in the brain. The most commonly used and most studied anticonvulsant mood-stabilizer is valproic acid, also known as divalproex sodium or sodium valproate (Depakene, Depakote). Half of the time a manic episode responds to valproic acid, and perhaps faster than to lithium. Carbamazepine (Tegretol) is also an effective treatment for bipolar disorder, but it can be difficult to use, since it often interacts with the metabolism of other medications that may be prescribed for you. Psychiatrists are currently studying several other anticonvulsant medications that may have mood-stabilizing properties.

For most of the mood-stabilizers, the level of the medication in the blood is more important than the dose or number of pills taken. Levels are checked weekly when treatment is started, then less frequently once an effective and safe dose has been reached. Most of the mood-stabilizers cause similar side effects: nausea, indigestion, diarrhea, tremor, sedation, and weight gain. Everyone responds to each medication differently, and you may experience no side effects at all. For some people, even minor side effects can be disturbing, and it is important to find a medication that you are willing to take consistently every day.

Other Treatments for Mania Exist

Antipsychotic medications (see "Psychosis") have always been useful in the treatment of severe mania with hallucinations, delusions, or agitation when combined with a mood-stabilizer. Recently some of the newer antipsychotic medications have been found to possess mood-stabilizing properties even when used alone. Antidepressant medication (see "Depression") is not used alone in the treatment of bipolar disorder because of the risk of precipitating mania, but it may be added cautiously during periods of depression. Anxiolytic and sedative medications (see "Anxiety" and "Sleep Problems") also play a role in the treatment of bipolar disorder by promoting sleep, slowing racing thoughts, and reducing agitation.

Electroconvulsive therapy (ECT) is a safe, effective, and rapid treatment for mania. If manic symptoms are particularly severe, or if a person has responded well to ECT in the past, then a psychiatrist may recommend the use of ECT. Electroconvulsive therapy involves two to three sessions per week for three to six weeks. At each session a series of electric pulses are administered to the head while you are asleep under anesthesia (see "Depression" for more details). Once the manic episode has resolved, ECT can continue on a weekly basis or be replaced with a mood-stabilizing medication as maintenance treatment to prevent future manic or depressive episodes. Eighty percent of cases respond to ECT, even among those who failed to improve with medication. This is probably the highest response rate for any treatment for any mental illness.

Memory Loss

You don't know why your children are making such a fuss. You already saw your doctor last month. Why do they want you to see a specialist? You feel fine. You think your memory's pretty good for someone your age. So you keep misplacing your keys. Who doesn't? You hardly need them anymore, since you prefer to stay at home. The streets around town have gotten so confusing lately.

It's probably your son-in-law who's behind this. What's-his-name would just love to put you in a nursing home. Now, what time did they say they were coming by to pick you up? You wrote it down somewhere.

Memory loss is a common problem among the elderly, occurring in approximately one out of five people over the age of sixty-five. As memory problems become more severe they are usually accompanied by impairments in other areas of thinking and functioning. Psychiatrists refer to this chronic and progressive deterioration as dementia. In common usage to refer to someone as demented is to call her stupid or mad. But physicians use the term dementia to refer to a specific syndrome of cognitive decline, which can have a number of causes. Alzheimer's disease is the most common cause of dementia, diagnosed in approximately one in twenty adults over sixty-five and about one in five over eighty-five.

Memory loss is usually the earliest and most obvious sign of dementia. At first you begin to have difficulties with short-term memory. For example, you forget phone numbers, the names of people you have recently met, and appointments. You forget that you have left food either out of the refrigerator or cooking on the stove. You lose your keys and other items. Earlier memories of important events are more resilient. You may be able to talk at length about your service in the war and tell stories about old friends and family, but not remember what you ate for breakfast. Well-learned tasks, such as how to ride a bike or turn on a shower, are also slow to disappear. The last to go are core biographical memories, such as your name and date and place of birth.

As you develop dementia, you may be unaware of the impairments that are evident to others (see "Denial"). You may become frustrated when you cannot find the word you are looking for, when you cannot locate an object that you were holding moments earlier, or when you forget the name of the person you are talking to. But you get angry at the situation rather than recognizing that it is your abilities that have declined. You may become skillful at changing the topic of conversation or telling jokes to distract from your difficulties. You find a lighthearted way to say "never mind" whenever something escapes your memory. Those around you will notice that you confabulate. For example, you might say that you had a lovely fish dinner, when in fact you forgot to eat dinner altogether. When introduced to someone for the first time, you may say you have already met. These are unconscious strategies, of the sort that we all use to smooth over awkward social situations. If you are bright or well educated to begin with, you will find it easier to conceal your memory loss.

As dementia progresses, other cognitive skills deteriorate. You may develop troubles with language, forgetting how to read and write. You may have trouble remembering what to call different objects. Your thinking slows, and you may stop talking altogether. You develop difficulties with calculations and telling time. You may have trouble judging distances and drawing simple shapes. You have trouble solving problems in general, which may be frustrating to you. You repeat questions over and over. Eventually, you may require assistance in completing even simple tasks such as tying shoelaces and eating.

Not surprisingly, personality, mood, and behavior also change as dementia progresses. You may develop suspiciousness and irritability. You may become frankly *paranoid,* believing that your caregivers are trying to harm you. I have treated several patients who locked their family members out of the house, believing that they were imposters. You may have unexplained outbursts of *anger,* tears, or laughter. On the other hand, you may become increasingly withdrawn and apathetic. You may behave in a socially embarrassing manner. For example, you may disrobe or scream in public. You may make inappropriate sexual advances toward anyone who walks by, including your nurses and relatives.

You fail to wash yourself or clean your clothes; you are oblivious to how you appear to others. Your house or apartment may become a mess, with dishes and trash accumulating everywhere. I have treated several patients who had been discovered living among their own feces. You may display increasingly bad judgment, for example by giving away large sums of money to strangers. You may wander away from home, getting lost on foot or in a car, if you can remember how to operate one. You tend to trip and fall. In many ways your behavior becomes regressed, so that you act like a young child.

In about a quarter of cases, dementia is accompanied by *depression*. You may become sad and tearful. You may feel worthless and be worried about being a burden on your family. It can be difficult to recognize depression in someone suffering from dementia, since many of the symptoms overlap. Apathy, slowed thinking, and *sleep problems* commonly occur in dementia even when mood is otherwise unchanged. It is perhaps surprising that not everyone with dementia becomes depressed, and perhaps it is fortunate that many do not realize how much their function has declined. Visual *hallucinations* are also common in some forms of dementia.

Dementia ultimately progresses to the point where you have little meaningful interaction with the world. You may be unable to move on your own or speak. You may show no sign of being aware of what is going on around you. You require assistance in order to eat, dress, and go to the bathroom. You do not recognize your children or loved ones. In most cases, dementia is accompanied by progressive difficulties with muscular movements, so that even swallowing may become difficult. You become vulnerable to choking, pneumonia, and bedsores. A diagnosis with dementia shortens life expectancy; on average, individuals live for about ten years after being diagnosed with Alzheimer's disease.

Several Different Illnesses Can Cause Dementia

Alzheimer's disease is the cause of approximately half of all cases of dementia. The diagnosis can be confirmed after death microscopically on the basis of protein clumps and tangles that are found throughout the brain. The brain atrophies as brain cells and their interconnections die off. Alzheimer's is thought to have a genetic component and is four times more likely if you have a first-degree relative with the illness. Alzheimer's is sometimes referred to as a cortical dementia, because it primarily effects higher brain functions such as memory, language, and problem solving.

Vascular dementia is the next most common cause of dementia. Previously known as multi-infarct dementia, it is caused by small arterial blood vessel disease within the brain. Inflammation, cholesterol deposits, and blood clots, of the sort that cause angina and heart attacks, are also thought to cause vascular dementia. Brain tissue becomes starved for oxygen in affected areas and dies off. This may occur in the form of multiple strokes, with either a stepwise deterioration in functioning or gradually, as diffuse areas of the brain deteriorate. Brain imaging reveals numerous small- and medium-sized injuries throughout the brain. If you suffer from vascular dementia, you probably also suffer from high blood pressure, high cholesterol, and other cardiovascular problems.

Huntington's disease and Parkinson's disease both affect the basal ganglia, a part of the brain that controls muscular movements. For this reason, the dementia that they cause is sometimes referred to as a subcortical dementia, with slowing of thinking and *movement problems* but relatively intact language skills. Dementia is seen in only one-third of the cases of Parkinson's disease but is inevitable in Huntington's disease. In both illnesses abnormal movements are likely to become apparent before memory loss. *Depression* is also very common in both illnesses, as well as *psychosis* in Huntington's disease.

Other degenerative illnesses also cause dementia, but their clinical features are similar to Alzheimer's. Lewy body dementia, which may be the underlying illness in as many as a quarter of cases, usually causes vivid visual *hallucinations* and fluctuations in alertness. It may be difficult to distinguish this form of dementia from delirium, an acute medical condition that causes profound *confusion*. Infection with HIV or syphilis can also cause dementia, as can multiple sclerosis, heavy alcohol abuse, and head trauma.

In the vast majority of cases, dementia is a progressive and irreversible illness. There are, however, some causes of dementia that are reversible if discovered early, such as brain tumors, thyroid abnormalities, and vitamin deficiencies. These make up no more than five to ten percent of all cases of dementia. If you have been newly diagnosed with memory problems, or dementia, you should have brain imaging and blood work done to look for these treatable causes.

Dementia Is Not the Only Cause of Memory Problems

Psychiatrists distinguish between dementia and amnesia. Amnesia is a loss of memory for a discreet period, or difficulty in forming new memories, in the absence of other problems with thinking and functioning. Unlike dementia, it is often a temporary condition. An example of amnesia is the memory loss that occurs during an alcoholic blackout. If you drink too much you may wake up the next morning and have no recollection of what happened while you were drunk. You have no difficulty forming new memories, but the events of the night before are lost to you forever. Psychiatrists refer to this as retrograde amnesia, the inability to remember something from your past. Anterograde amnesia refers to the inability to learn new information. Benzodiazepine medications, used in the treatment of *anxiety* and *sleeping problems,* when taken in high doses, can cause difficulties with forming new memories. I have known people who took a benzodiazepine medication to help them sleep after a long-distance airline flight and forgot most of what happened on their first day abroad.

One of the more common causes of amnesia is an injury to the head. If you have been hit in the head, you may lose memory for a period of time leading up to the injury, and you probably do not recall receiving the injury itself. Your prognosis is good if some of your memory returns over the next few days, but complete recovery may take months.

Deficiency of the vitamin thiamine can cause amnesia, and this is commonly seen in cases of severe alcohol abuse, because you fail to eat adequately. Sufferers typically forget events a few minutes after they occur, and sometimes they forget past events. They tend to be oblivious to their memory problems. Psychiatrists refer to this illness as Korsakoff's syndrome. In more severe cases, thiamine deficiency leads to gross *confusion* and troubles with muscular coordination, known as Wernicke's encephalopathy. When detected and treated early enough with vitamin supplementation, these problems may resolve over weeks. But sometimes lost memories are never recovered. If alcohol abuse and malnutrition persist, full dementia may develop.

Vascular strokes can cause isolated problems with memory, even in the absence of full dementia. Short of a stroke, you may experience transient episodes of amnesia resulting from intermittent reductions in oxygen supply to the brain. Physicians refer to these episodes as transient ischemic attacks, and they are similar to strokes except that you recover function after a few minutes. Memory problems are among the many symptoms caused by these attacks, as well as loss of consciousness and muscle weakness. If you have a stroke or a transient attack, you should see a doctor immediately.

Psychiatrists have long believed that memory can be suppressed for psychological reasons, even in the absence of a physical injury. In fact, it is common knowledge that our brains hold many more memories than we are consciously aware of at any given moment. We are surprised by memories that occur to us after years. The memory may be triggered by an unexpected association: a stranger who reminds you of an old boyfriend, a snippet of music that reminds you of an old song, a smell that takes you back to your grade school cafeteria. In very rare cases you may temporarily lose your memories of a specific period, or of a specific event, following a shocking experience. Presumably the recollection is too upsetting for you to keep in your conscious awareness (see "Dissociation"). Some individuals have even forgotten their own identity entirely for a period of time, and psychiatrists refer to this as a fugue state.

Severe *depression* can mimic dementia as you become withdrawn, slow, and unmotivated. You perform poorly on cognitive tests, and you seem to have a decline in your ability to remember information. However, these symptoms resolve as the depression is treated. If you suffer from *psychosis* or *mania,* you may be so internally distracted (by hallucinations and racing thoughts, for example) that you have trouble paying attention to the real world around you. As a result, you may not be able to remember many things that happened to you while you were acutely ill, even once you recover. Finally, treatment with electroconvulsive therapy (ECT, see "Depression") can cause a loss of memory of events around the time of the treatment.

How to Cope with Dementia

If someone you care about has dementia, you want to provide her with the assistance she needs to function at the highest level that she can manage. This level may change from month to month as her dementia progresses. If you provide too much assistance she may fail to exercise the abilities that she still has, and she may become bored and depressed. If you provide too little, she may become increasingly frustrated by tasks that are beyond her abilities. As language skills decline, it may become more and more difficult to understand the needs of your loved one. Like a child, she may express herself through behaviors rather than words. She may shout repeatedly when she is lonely. She may strike out at you when she is frustrated or frightened. She may wander when she is bored or needs to go to the bathroom. She may accuse you of stealing something from her when she has forgotten where she left it. It can be difficult to decipher these behaviors unless you remind yourself that she is unable to remember or communicate in her usual fashion.

There are steps you can take to make the environment less confusing for a loved one with dementia. You want to create a home where safe areas are clear and negotiable. Remove distracting objects. Use colors, signs, and familiar pictures. Set up a path in the house and outside where she can wander safely without getting lost. If there are doors and cabinets that she should not access, install concealed locks. Try to eliminate distracting noises from buzzers, alarms, radios, and televisions. A television can provide interesting stimulation and distraction, so long as it is set on a mellow channel. You may want to set up a closed circuit monitor or alarm in her bedroom to let you know if she gets up in the middle of the night.

Try to find tasks that are appropriate to your loved one's current abilities. You can involve her in household activities, such as assisting in cleaning her room, and this will make her feel more useful and less isolated. Be patient and recognize that she will have difficulty with complicated tasks. Provide her with instructions one step at a time. Try to avoid quizzing her and testing her memory, which will only reinforce her fears and feelings of frustration. We explain things to children in the hope that they will learn to exercise their judgment rather than simply follow directions. But as dementia progresses, lessons are lost rather than learned. Rather than reasoning or arguing, you may want to help her make connections. For example, if she becomes suspicious of a young man in the house, remind her that he is the son of her best friend. She may not remember that he comes to the house every day to take care of her, but she may remember the name of her childhood friend, and this will be reassuring. If your loved one tends to forget who you are, do not take it personally. Get in the habit of reminding her who you are automatically.

As needs become more basic, and behavior more childlike, remember that your loved one still values human contact. You can provide affection by giving a backrub, massaging her hands, brushing her hair, or spending time talking to her in a soothing tone. Try to avoid introducing sudden changes in her care or environment. Try to avoid showing anger. Even if she acts in a disinhibited manner, or strikes out at you, recognize that she is not angry or spiteful but confused and frightened. Be aware that many people with dementia do strike out at their caregivers from time to time, and they are not always as frail as you might think. When helping her to dress or complete other tasks, you should place yourself in such a way that you cannot be kicked or punched in the face. If she becomes agitated while performing a task, try to calmly reassure her, distract her, or assist her.

Eventually your loved one may need nursing home care. Trained staff can ensure that your loved one receives adequate fluids and nutrition and exercise to prevent bedsores and muscular contractures. Since dementia is progressive, you should prepare for the death of your loved one. It may be more appropriate to ensure her comfort and general care rather than pursuing aggressive medical and surgical interventions as health problems develop. You should consider in advance whether your loved one would want to be revived after a cardiopulmonary arrest, and whether you should use antibiotic medications or place a feeding tube as her condition worsens. At a much earlier stage you should consider pursuing legal guardianship in order to deal with her financial and medical needs.

Therapy is not an effective treatment for dementia, but it can be very helpful for caregivers. You may feel helpless, guilty, or burned out in your efforts to cope with your loved one's illness and declining functioning. Studies have shown that dementia is perhaps the most *stressful* of all illnesses for caregivers. You are more vulnerable to experiencing *depression, sleep problems,* and declining health. Caregiving interferes with your work attendance, vacations, and opportunities to pursue promotion. You run the risk of arranging your entire life around your caregiving responsibilities, often at great financial cost. You may find it helpful to learn more about dementia and coping strategies from other family members in similar situations, by joining a local family support group.

Cognition Enhancing Agents

Scientists have been working hard to discover treatments for dementia. Currently there are several medications, most of them known as cholinesterase inhibitors, which can improve the course of dementia in some cases. Even though there are several different microscopic causes of dementia, most seem to involve a deficit in acetylcholine, a brain chemical that is important in nerve signal transmission. Medications that inhibit the metabolism and elimination of this chemical can improve thinking. Medication appears to slow the progress of the illness in about one-third of patients, so that functioning is no worse up to a year later. This prolongs the quality of life and delays the need for more intensive caregiving and nursing home placement.

Tacrine (Cognex) was the first of these medications to be released but is now rarely prescribed because of side effects like nausea and vomiting. Alternatives include donepezil (Aricept), rivastigmine (Exelon), and galantamine (Reminyl). These medications also seem to produce improvements in other symptoms of dementia, such as agitation, irritability, suspiciousness, wandering, hallucinations, and depression. Caregivers notice that treatment helps their loved one to remain more in touch with the world around them. Even though they were initially tested only in cases of Alzheimer's disease, these medications appear to be at least as helpful in the treatment of several different types of dementia. Unfortunately, most patients do not benefit significantly.

Memantine (Namenda), which blocks the brain chemical glutamate rather than boost acetylcholine, is similarly effective for a minority of patients with dementia. It was recently approved for use in the United States after being prescribed for more than a decade in Germany. The combination of memantine and a cholinesterase inhibitor may be doubly effective. Several other types of medications are currently undergoing clinical trials. Some people have used vitamin E or a botanical product derived from the leaves of the gingko biloba tree, but controlled studies of their effectiveness have provided mixed results.

A number of other psychiatric medications can be helpful in managing some of the behavioral and mood symptoms of dementia. Individuals with dementia are typically very sensitive to medication side effects such as *confusion,* tremors, or stiffness. The use of psychiatric medications should be reviewed regularly. Nevertheless, some can be used safely in lower doses. The newer antidepressant and antipsychotic medications can be used, respectively, for significant symptoms of *depression* and *psychosis,* the latter most commonly including *paranoia* and visual *hallucinations.* Buspirone (Buspar), a treatment for *anxiety,* can be effective in reducing nervousness, irritability, pacing, and wandering. Trazadone (Desyrel) or zolpidem (Ambien) can be helpful for *sleeping problems.* Benzodiazepines (see "Anxiety") are rarely used because of the increased risk of *confusion* and falls.

Mood Swings

The past few days have been the best of your life. Several of your friends came over for your birthday, and you insisted on going out to party on the town. Maybe you had a little too much to drink, but everyone had fun, and you didn't get into any fights. While you were out you ran into an old girlfriend, and you made plans to go hiking over the weekend. At work the next day you completed a project ahead of schedule and left early. Things were looking up.

But now, a day later, you are exhausted because you couldn't sleep the night before, and your head is pounding. Just as you finally doze off your date calls and you curse at her for waking you up. So much for your weekend plans. You slam the phone down and sleep through the afternoon.

To some degree mood swings are a part of life. It is normal to become sad in response to everyday *stress* and happy in response to achievements. Some people are more inclined to become frustrated and resentful and to see the glass half-empty. Others see setbacks as opportunities for personal growth. Yet another group of people are extremely temperamental, swinging back and forth between these two ways of viewing the world. Like a boat without a rudder, they are tossed about by their emotions. This sort of moodiness can occur in several different psychiatric conditions.

The most dramatic extremes of mood occur in bipolar disorder. You may spend months in a profound *depression*, alternating with months of *mania*. At the extreme you may have *suicidal thoughts* or lose touch with reality. These are mood swings on the grand scale, swinging from one episode to another over the course of months to years. Within an episode, however, your mood is fairly consistent. You do not swing from one extreme to another over the course of a day.

Psychiatrists have recognized that people who are extremely temperamental from day to day may suffer from a variation of bipolar disorder that is called cyclothymic disorder. If you have cyclothymia, you and those around you have probably recognized that you are a moody person. You have probably been moody since you were a teenager. You experience periods of *euphoria,* in which you are excited, uninhibited, fun-loving, thrill-seeking, restless, and self-confident. These periods may last weeks or days. Then you wake up to discover that you are exhausted, irritable, tearful, and pessimistic. Though you do not become fully manic or fully depressed, these alternations in mood wreak havoc in your life. You make and break relationships. You start and abandon jobs. You move from one town to another. You drink and use drugs to try to control your mood.

Some psychiatrists recognize a variant of cyclothymia in which mood is almost always elevated. You impulsively and energetically pursue relationships and projects without ever seeming to crash. Therapists refer to this as a hyperthymic style. You may be irritated when your plans fail to materialize, and your friends and colleagues may find you uncritical and unreliable, but you are unlikely to seek therapy since you are rarely in distress.

Even though these types of moodiness could easily be confused with a personality style, it is important to recognize them as mood disorders because they may improve when treated with mood-stabilizing medication (see "Mania"). Medication may bring stability to a previously chaotic and tumultuous life. One-third of those diagnosed with cyclothymic disorder eventually receive a diagnosis of bipolar disorder, after they have experienced a full-blown manic episode. Manic episodes have serious consequences, including hospitalization, job loss, and suicide. Prevention of possible manic episodes is another good reason to consider a trial of mood-stabilizing medication.

Some women experience mood swings that predictably coincide with their menstrual cycle. For approximately a week before the start of menstruation you may experience headaches and breast tenderness, feel bloated, and become easily fatigued. Your mood is irritable, anxious, or depressed. You lose your temper and cry easily. You may want to stay home and avoid activities that you otherwise enjoy. You may have trouble *sleeping,* or you may sleep too much. You may also binge on food. Most of these symptoms are seen in *depression,* but in premenstrual dysphoria they occur only for a week or so, and only prior to menstruation. The symptoms predictably fade by the time bleeding has stopped.

Doctors are not certain what causes premenstrual dysphoria, commonly known as premenstrual syndrome, or PMS. Presumably the fluctuations in several hormones at the time of ovulation, preceding menstruation, cause the psychological and physical symptoms. Almost all women have experienced premenstrual symptoms at some point. Nearly half experience some symptoms on a monthly basis. Doctors estimate that about one in ten women experience symptoms that are severe and predictable enough to merit treatment with medication. Some of the SSRI antidepressant medications (see "Depression") have proven to be effective in reducing premenstrual complaints. You may need to take the antidepressant medication only during the premenstrual period rather than every day of the month.

Moodiness Is Commonly a Reflection of Personality

The world would be a boring place if we all had the same personality traits. Fortunately, some of us are shy, while others are outgoing. Some of us are energetic and dramatic, while others are calm and work behind the scenes. Some of us feel things passionately and act on impulse, while others are steadfast and wise. None of these personality styles is inherently better than another. But psychiatrists recognize that some people have lifelong personality traits that are extreme and maladaptive. Many personality disorders are characterized in part by moodiness. Mood may change from day to day, or from hour to hour, and usually in response to interactions with others.

If you have a borderline personality disorder you probably have poor *self-esteem* and stormy relationships with others. You may consider someone your best friend one moment and hate her the next after some minor slight that you view as a catastrophe. You may yell at your friend, throw things, or take out your anger on yourself (see "Self-Mutilation"). You probably feel like you have no control over your mood at all, that you can only react. You see yourself as a victim, and you are *angry* and hopeless about it.

If you have a *histrionic* personality disorder, you like to be the center of attention. You express extreme emotions, but you display them like an actor on stage. One moment you are shouting and swearing in anger, and the next you are hugging, kissing, and professing your enduring love. People who know you well learn not to overreact to your mood swings, since you get over them quickly.

Moodiness can also be seen in post-*traumatic* stress disorder (PTSD). PTSD is not a personality disorder, but serious trauma can alter how you relate to the world. If you suffer from PTSD, you may spend much of your time frightened and tense. Relatively minor stress can set you off, and you may explode in *anger*. Afterward you may feel helpless and sad. You feel like your nerves are wound too tight, and you have trouble controlling your emotions.

Moodiness of the sort seen in personality disorders can also occur in reaction to virtually any illness. When we get sick we become more self-centered, irritable, and needy. Sometimes we want to be taken care of, and sometimes we want to be left alone. Pain and discomfort interfere with our sleep and concentration and keep our nerves raw. We may be angry one moment, depressed the next, and grateful at yet another.

Mood Swings Can Occur During Drug and Alcohol Abuse

Drugs and alcohol can change your mood faster than just about anything. A little bit of alcohol or marijuana will make most of us feel relaxed, content, and friendly. Drink or smoke a bit more, or use cocaine, and you can become *euphoric*. These are among the reasons why some people enjoy drugs and alcohol. But the effects of *intoxication* on your mood are not always predictable. In many cases, you will progress from feeling happy to becoming irritable, suspicious, and quick to fight. Or you may become hopeless and tearful. Psychiatrists refer to this as mood lability, a state in which moods change quickly from moment to moment.

Your moods will swing again when you are withdrawing from drug or alcohol use. You are likely to become increasingly short-tempered, especially if you are unsuccessful in getting high again. You may become profoundly depressed, and even have *suicidal thoughts*. Friends and family may be shocked to see you crying, shouting, and making demands. In fact, your mood swings may provide the first clue to others that you are having a drug or alcohol problem.

How to Cope with Mood Swings

If you suffer from mood swings or persistent moodiness, you should consult a mental health professional. You might benefit from different types of treatment, depending on whether you have a mood disorder, a personality disorder, or a drug or alcohol problem. Mood-stabilizing medications (see "Mania") may be the treatment of choice in most cases, along with psychotherapy. Therapy will help you to understand what triggers the changes in your mood, and how you can learn to control your reactions, rather than feeling out of control. You may especially benefit from *anger* management therapy.

If you are experiencing mood swings during the course of drug or alcohol use, you will first have to stop using these substances. No matter what medications you take, or how much therapy you engage in, your mood will not stabilize if you continue to use. It may be that you have an underlying mood disorder that would benefit from medication treatment, but this is difficult to determine, and even more difficult to treat, during active use of drugs or alcohol.

If someone you care about experiences mood swings, try to help him to get treatment. In many of the conditions discussed above, the person may not realize that he has a problem. It may seem to him that things are happening to him that are out of his control. He may not realize that he could regain control by taking medication, engaging in therapy, or stopping drug and alcohol use.

It can be draining to live with someone who experiences mood swings. You find yourself riding the emotional roller coaster with him. You try to remember the good times when he is irritable, frustrated, and hopeless. You hope that the bad times will pass quickly. You will need to learn to set limits so that both you and your loved one know how much you are willing or able to provide when he is irritable. You should ensure that you have time to yourself, for work and fun, so that you do not get sick and exhausted yourself. You may find it helpful to join a support group in which you will learn that you are not alone, that others have had similar experiences. You may learn from others who have had to cope with problems like yours.

Movement Problems

This medication is going to kill me, you think. You begged the doctor to increase the dose because the voices have really been bothering you, but after taking the new dose you can hardly move.

Your father helps you into the car and drives you to the clinic. On the way there you have trouble looking out the window because the back of your neck is tight, pulling your head back, and your eyes feel like they're glued to the ceiling. Your father helps you get out of the car, and then you shuffle slowly to the clinic door. The nurse looks at you with concern, but you can't form any clear words. You just stare straight ahead while pointing at your tongue with your shaking finger.

The nurse nods and helps you to an examination room. She tells you not to worry. In a minute she returns with a needle, and soon you're feeling better.

Movement problems commonly seen in psychiatry range from muscle stiffness to tremors and tics, and from the general slowing to the acceleration of movement. In many cases the problem is caused by psychiatric medications, and these side effects are easily recognized and generally treatable. Some movement disturbances are symptomatic of an underlying psychiatric illness and are likely to improve with treatment of that disorder.

Depression frequently causes a general retardation in movement. If you are depressed you lack energy and motivation. Your posture is slumped, your voice is soft, and you move slowly, if at all. In severe cases you may lie in bed or sit in a chair and not move for hours at a time. On the other hand, if you have *mania*, which is at the opposite emotional extreme, you are constantly in motion. You find it difficult to stay still, as new ideas are constantly occurring to you, and you often act on them with little thought. Psychiatrists refer to the slowing of movement in depression and the acceleration of movement in mania, respectively, as psychomotor retardation and agitation. Confusingly, some depressed patients actually become hyperactive, puttering about aimlessly and nervously but constantly in motion. *Hyperactivity* is also seen in attention deficit-hyperactivity disorder (ADHD), which has its onset in childhood.

If you have obsessive-*compulsive* disorder (OCD) you may engage in ritual movements. For example, you may have to stop and count to ten before you pass through a doorway, or you may have to pass back and forth through the doorway several times. You may feel compelled to land on every step of a staircase, or every floor tile as you cross a room. I have treated many patients who are afraid to step on cracks in the pavement and so they adopt an awkward gait on the sidewalk. You may have to arrange your body in a certain manner when you sit down, and you may have to get dressed in a specified order, performing odd rituals along the way.

Some people with OCD are also diagnosed with Tourette's disorder, a neurological condition characterized by tics, which affects nearly one in one thousand people. A tic is an involuntary movement, and tics can range from shoulder shrugging and nose scratching to throat clearing and cursing. Most tic disorders consist of a single tic that goes away within a year or two. If you have Tourette's disorder you have multiple tics, and the movements and vocalizations can be quite embarrassing, at least when they occur in public or in front of strangers who are not aware of your condition. You may develop the habit of trying to suppress your tics, in which case they usually come forth eventually, usually in a more dramatic fashion, perhaps with a series of jerks or expletives. Or you may try to cover them up by pretending that the tics were intentional. For example, if your shoulder jerks, you may reach up and scratch it. Or if you keep clearing your throat, you might explain that you have a cold. Tics worsen when you are nervous.

Many of the movement disturbances seen in schizophrenia (see "Psychosis") are related to medications. However, even before antipsychotic medications were developed, people with schizophrenia had been observed to have a number of odd movements presumably caused by the underlying brain illness. Schizophrenia can cause you to stand in an un-usual position, for example with one arm raised over your shoulder or with your head always turned to one side. Psychiatrists refer to this as posturing. You may also have a habit of repeating certain movements predictably. For example, you may clap your fingers together as you walk, or you may grimace before starting each sentence. Psychiatrists refer to these movements as stereotypies. You may also start movements, like reaching out to shake a hand, only to stop and reverse. This may happen several times in a row. These unusual movements were seen more fre-quently in the past, before treatments for schizophrenia had evolved.

Catatonia is another psychiatric condition that affects movement. Cat-atonia is a state of minimal movement and responsiveness. When cata-tonic, you lie still completely, never blinking, talking, or moving your muscles. If someone moves your limbs, they stay in place where they are left, even hanging in the air, as if you were a wax figurine. If you speak at all it is only to mimic what is said to you, which psychiatrists call echolalia. If you move at all, it may be to reflect movements made around you. For example, when I reach out to shake the hand of a patient who is catatonic, he may extend his left hand to me, fingertip to fingertip. Psychiatrists do not know what is going on in the mind of someone who has catatonia, though we suspect that it is a frightening state of mental paralysis. Cata-tonia can occur in schizophrenia, *mania,* or *depression,* and it can some-times be caused by another underlying medical condition. It is most rap-idly treated with a course of electroconvulsive therapy (ECT, see "Depression"), but it also often responds to medications used in the treat-ment of the underlying psychiatric condition.

Outside of psychiatry, movement disorders are commonly caused by strokes, seizures, or degenerative brain conditions such as multiple scle-rosis. Parkinson's disease and Huntington's disease cause abnormal move-ments and are often treated by psychiatrists because of associated demen-tia (see "Memory Loss"), depression, and psychosis. Some muscular conditions, like restless leg syndrome and nocturnal myoclonus, are less evident during the day but can cause *sleep problems.* If your abnormal movements are different from those typically seen in psychiatric illness, or if they persist in spite of psychiatric treatment, then you should probably be evaluated by a neurologist to make sure that you do not have a separate condition that might benefit from neurological interventions.

Many Movement Disorders Are Caused by Drugs or Medications

The first generation of antipsychotic medications (see "Psychosis") commonly cause a number of muscular side effects. Your muscles may become stiff so that you have difficulty moving. Your legs shuffle, and your arms hang straight down as you walk. Your posture is slumped. You move slowly. The muscles of your mouth and throat can also stiffen so that you have difficulty speaking clearly or swallowing. Your facial muscles become rigid, giving you a masklike, emotionless appearance. You develop a tremor of your hands and arms, which rock at a frequency of three cycles per second. Because of the manner in which the hand and fingers move, the shaking is referred to as a "pill-rolling" tremor. All of these symptoms are also seen in the neurological illness known as Parkinson's disease. Both Parkinson's disease and antipsychotic medication cause a reduction in transmission of the chemical signal dopamine in the extrapyramidal tracts of the brain. For this reason the side effects are sometimes referred to as extrapyramidal symptoms, or EPS.

Sometimes, especially when you first start taking medication, the muscular stiffness can be particularly acute. Your eyes may roll up in their sockets. Your neck may twist backward painfully. Doctors refer to these reactions as an oculogyric crisis and torticollis, respectively. Needless to say, these side effects are very frightening, and they usually happen shortly after you take your first doses of antipsychotic medication. The good news is that they are easily treated with medications such as benztropine (Cogentin) and trihexyphenidyl (Artane). These medications are sometimes prescribed in advance, to make sure that you do not have a bad experience when you first start your antipsychotic medication. In an emergency they can be given by injection. These medications have few side effects themselves, but they can cause drowsiness, blurred vision, and constipation.

The newer antipsychotic medications, commonly referred to as atypical antipsychotics, are distinguished in part by how rarely they cause these muscular side effects. Risperidone (Risperdal) is the only newer medication likely to cause stiffness and tremor, though generally only at higher doses. In the past, patients taking antipsychotic medications were frequently described as zombies, in large part because of the odd appearance of walking stiffly and having no facial expression. With the newer medications this effect is much rarer. You no longer look like you are overmedicated. People may be able to tell you are on medication by how well you are doing, rather than by observing the obvious unpleasant side effects.

A related medication side effect is the internal sense of restlessness, known as akathisia, that some antipsychotic medications cause. You may have difficulty remaining seated for very long, you may bounce your legs or drum your fingers, and you may pace back and forth. You feel like you have ants in your pants, or like your skin is crawling. Since *hyperactivity* is a common symptom of mental illnesses, doctors often fail to recognize when it is a side effect of medication. Fortunately the side effect will go away if your dose is decreased, or if you are switched to another antipsychotic medication. Alternatively, you may feel better with the addition of a beta-blocker medication, such as propranolol (Inderal), which treats akathisia.

There is one antipsychotic medication side effect that occurs late in treatment and that is not always reversible. Tardive dyskinesia (TD) is a movement disorder caused especially by the older antipsychotic medications. TD is quite different from the tremors and stiffness described above. What emerges are puckering and grimacing movements of the mouth and face, and undulating snakelike movements of the fingers and limbs. Generally the movements are first seen in the tongue and muscles around the mouth, but in more severe cases even the trunk of the body twists and rocks. Fortunately, if you have TD you may not be particularly troubled by it. In fact, you may be unaware of the movements, and when they are pointed out you come up with explanations that minimize the problem (see "Denial").

In the past tardive dyskinesia affected about one-third of patients treated with antipsychotic medications. The disorder is much rarer now that the newer medications are in widespread use. Unlike other side effects, TD rarely occurs early in treatment ("tardive" means late). Rather, it emerges years into treatment, especially when high doses of medication have been used. Elderly patients appear to be more vulnerable and develop TD after taking medications for a shorter period of time and at lower doses. There is only one proven treatment for TD: a switch to the unique antipsychotic medication clozapine (Clozaril). Otherwise your physician will try to treat you with the lowest dose of medication possible and perhaps prescribe some vitamins, which may be helpful. Generally it is better to avoid TD in the first place by taking the newer medications, rather than to count on treating TD once it develops. It often does not resolve completely when medication is stopped; in fact, it may worsen temporarily, since antipsychotic medication can mask some of the movements.

While antipsychotic medications may cause a pill-rolling tremor, several of the mood-stabilizing medications (see "Mania") cause a more rapid tremor. The tremor caused by lithium, valproic acid (Depakote), and carbamazepine (Tegretol) is much finer, similar to the shaking that you might experience when extremely cold or frightened. It may not be evident when you are resting, but if you reach for an object, like a coffee cup or lipstick, the shaking becomes more obvious. A mild tremor commonly occurs even in the normal dose range of these medications. If the tremor becomes more severe, such that your arms, legs, and shoulders are shaking, then it may be a sign that your medication levels are too high. Fortunately the tremor is usually easily treated with propranolol, the same medication used to treat akathisia.

Illegal drugs can also cause movement problems through their effects on the nervous system. Alcohol *intoxication* famously causes impairments in coordination, leading to difficulty walking, driving, and using machinery. Alcohol, marijuana, and opiate drugs can slow your reaction time, leading to similar problems. Stimulants, including cocaine, can make you jittery. You move around a lot, and quickly. Your muscles may shake or jerk, reflecting nervous system irritability. You may have difficulty slowing down, relaxing, or *sleeping*. Withdrawal from alcohol can also cause jerks and shakes. In more severe cases, alcohol withdrawal and cocaine intoxication can cause seizures, in which case you may lose consciousness while your entire body convulses. If you are a heavy alcohol user and become deficient in the vitamin thiamine, you can develop Wernicke-Korsakoff syndrome, with *confusion, memory loss,* clumsy gait, and incoordination.

Nonsense

What is wrong with this doctor? You wonder how many times you will have to repeat yourself before he understands you. Doesn't he speak English? Or French? Or Dijon?

You hope they serve French fries with lunch. You're starving. And star-crossed. Fate is responsible for you being here today. It was a "fate accompli." If only you weren't so accomplished, they wouldn't have taken you to the hospital in the first place. Second place. Third.

Psychiatrists pay particularly close attention to speech. It is through speech that we understand what is on a person's mind. You tell a story about your concerns and how they developed, and psychiatrists extract from this a pattern of illness. How you speak is often as revealing as what you say. Your mood may be evident in the volume and speed with which you talk. Your accent and word choice may provide clues to your cultural and educational background. Fears and shame may be implied by what you avoid discussing. But in each of these cases speech still makes sense.

In several major mental illnesses, on the other hand, speech begins to fall apart. Words and sentences become increasingly disorganized and disconnected in meaning, with the result that others may think you are speaking complete nonsense. Disorganized thinking, along with *delusions* and *hallucinations,* is a common feature of *psychosis.*

If you have disorganized thinking you probably do not realize it. You may continue to speak fluently but without making much sense. People who speak with you will notice immediately that you are unable to stay on topic or put coherent thoughts together.

When mildly disorganized you tend to veer off the subject. You shift from one topic to another without seeming to notice, a pattern that psychiatrists refer to as tangential thinking. It is as if everything you say reminds you of something else, and you find the intruding thought too interesting to ignore. Psychiatrists describe psychotic speech as being characterized by loose associations—in other words, the absence of logical connections between words and phrases. In its most severe form, known as word salad, there are no coherent sentences at all; every word is unrelated to the one that follows.

Sometimes psychotic speech can be like a Lewis Carroll poem, a Dr. Seuss story, or certain rap lyrics. If you listen to a person who is severely psychotic, you may notice clang associations, in which one word triggers a similar sounding word. For example, a patient once told me that he was "a man with a plan to jam with the band." Though this sounds like it could be a song lyric, it emerged in the middle of a completely unrelated discussion about medication. The rhyme, rather than the meaning, dictated the direction of his speech, and he was unable to return to the original topic. In fact, he became louder and increasingly nonsensical. Sometimes a person will invent (or combine) words, or he may use real words in unusual ways. He may even be genuinely surprised if you do not understand his neologisms. For example, one patient said she could not understand me because I was speaking "jewberish." (She may have assumed I was Jewish, or thought of psychiatry as a Jewish profession.) Echolalia is another form of speech and refers to a tendency for psychotic patients to simply repeat back what is said to them. Nonsensical speech and odd behaviors are most commonly seen in the disorganized subtype of schizophrenia, which used to be called hebephrenia.

Loose associations are also commonly observed in *mania*. As you become manic, your thoughts begin to flow more rapidly. You speak loudly and are difficult to interrupt. You become oblivious to social cues, including the give and take of conversation. Psychiatrists refer to this as pressured speech. Sometimes a manic patient will babble incoherently while believing that he is speaking a foreign language or speaking in tongues. I once treated a woman who spoke to me in what she insisted was Hebrew, and which she was sure I could understand. I later observed her speaking what she called "African" to another doctor. Rapid and loose speech may also occur during *intoxication* with stimulant drugs, such as cocaine, caffeine, and amphetamines.

Thought blocking is another form of disordered thinking that is common in psychosis. If you are suffering from thought blocking you stop abruptly in the middle of a sentence, forgetting the subject of discussion. You may have been distracted by a *hallucination,* or by an intrusive thought such as, "The doctor is about to cast a spell on me." Or you may have simply lost your train of thought before you could express it. You may be unable to explain what was on your mind when you stopped speaking. You may have a *delusional* belief that someone sucked the thought out of your brain. Some patients also experience poverty of thought, a condition in which you have little on your mind and little to say. You may give only yes or no answers to questions, or you may not answer at all. Poverty of thought also occurs in severe cases of *depression.* In the extreme you may become completely mute and catatonic (see "Movement Problems"), even though you are physically capable of speaking.

Psychosis and Mania Are Not the Only Causes of Nonsensical Speech

When a person's speech is disorganized, you might think this reflects an internal state of confusion. However, psychotic patients will often say that they are not confused, just frustrated by the inability of others to understand them. They are often attentive to their environment and aware of what is going on around them. They may be able to tell you what day it is, even though they cannot put together a coherent sentence. This is in contrast to the state of *confusion* that doctors refer to as delirium. When delirious you become disoriented and unable to pay attention to your environment. You lose track of time, and you may forget where you are. Delirium is an acute state of confusion that often has an underlying medical cause that requires emergency evaluation and treatment.

Stroke is an example of a medical illness that can directly impair speech. If you have a vascular event in the left side of your brain, for example, your ability to read, speak, and comprehend the speech of others may be affected. You may suddenly be unable to speak, or your speech may be slurred or incomprehensible. You may use words incorrectly. Neurologists call this aphasia. It is distinguished from psychiatric conditions in part by its rapid onset.

Dementia may also be a cause of nonsensical speech. Dementia is an illness in which you progressively lose your *memory*. You may start to make up words, or use words incorrectly, as you begin to forget what things are called. For example, you might wear a "time" on your wrist or write with a "pointy thing." Your loved ones notice that your speech is increasingly filled with gaps and inaccuracies.

In more severe dementia you may talk constantly without saying much. You may repeat yourself over and over, which is called perseveration. You may ask a question, receive an answer, and promptly forget it. Your loved ones may become irritated as you ask the same question again and again. You may repeat what someone else has said to you, or perhaps something you hear on the radio or television. Eventually you may babble continuously or stop talking altogether.

Incoherent speech and meaningless vocalizations can also occur in autism and severe mental retardation, two disabling conditions that are first diagnosed in childhood (see "Learning Difficulties").

Tourette's disorder is an illness commonly treated by neurologists, though many of its symptoms are psychiatric in nature. If you have Tourette's disorder you may experience *compulsions* to shout out or repeat words and phrases. These are called vocal tics. You are perfectly capable of speaking in a normal, fluent, and coherent fashion most of the time, but your speech may be peppered with these verbal outbursts. You may shout out curse words. You may repeat something that you have just said or heard. You may grunt, snort, or clear your throat. Sometimes you utter complete but irrelevant phrases, such as an advertising jingle. In contrast to other illnesses, in Tourette's disorder you are fully aware of your nonsensical speech and so are probably thoroughly embarrassed.

How to Cope with Nonsensical Speech

There is no specific treatment for disorganized thinking. The organization and flow of thought usually improves as the underlying condition is treated, usually with antipsychotic medication (see "Psychosis"). Fortunately, disorganized thinking usually improves more rapidly than other psychotic symptoms such as hallucinations and delusions. However, in some cases, especially if you have the disorganized subtype of schizophrenia, nonsensical speech and disorganized behaviors may be your most prominent symptoms, and they may persist to some degree in spite of treatment.

If someone you care about speaks in an incoherent fashion, you should try to be supportive and clear in your communication with him. You can tell him that you are having trouble understanding him. You can encourage him to slow down and to speak just one sentence at a time. If you need to speak to him about something, and he goes off on a tangent, you can gently redirect him by saying, "I see; but let me ask you again about this." It is okay to point out that he is straying from the subject, but try not to give the impression that you are being critical. The direction of his thoughts and the quality of his speech are largely out of his control. He is not trying to annoy you.

You should be alert to the possibility that your loved one is becoming frustrated with your inability to understand him or with what he may perceive as your attempts to control his speech. If he becomes louder, more insistent, or angry, you should ask for a break rather than continuing to struggle to understand him. You can apologize for being unable to understand him, and you can acknowledge that this must distress him.

If you have been through this before, you may be able to guess what your loved one is trying to communicate, even if you do not know exactly what he is saying. You may find it helpful to tell him what you think he is saying, so that he can tell you if you have understood him more or less. He may be able to say yes or no even if he has difficulty putting together more complicated answers. I find that a psychotic patient is often greatly relieved to realize that someone has understood him, since the world has otherwise become such a lonely, frightening, and confusing place.

Obsessions

You ask yourself if you dressed appropriately. Everyone else is wearing a conservative suit or dress. You knew you shouldn't wear blue. Is blue conservative? From your seat next to the podium, you look around the auditorium, counting the number of people wearing blue. It's a memorial service, not a funeral, but you feel ashamed. You might as well have come in your underwear.

Suddenly you close your eyes, blood rushing to your cheeks. Can they see your underwear? You pull your legs closer together, imagining yourself on stage without pants. What a sick thought!

In a minute you have to stand up and give a short speech, and you can't remember your first line. You'll reach for the microphone and say something ridiculous. What if you tell the audience to check out your underwear? You can't seem to think of anything else. You start to count backwards from ten. By the time you reach zero, you think, you'll be able to picture yourself with your pants back on, and you'll remember what to say.

Ten, nine, eight . . .

Obsessions are unwanted thoughts that you cannot get out of your mind. All of us have unwanted thoughts at times, but they are usually fleeting. Perhaps we imagine hurting someone we love or fondling someone we should not. We worry that we might pass gas in an elevator. We wonder what would happen if we raise our hand at an auction when we do not intend to place a bid. We worry whether we have remembered to lock the door or turn off the iron, or whether we have come too close to someone with a bad cold. We wonder if it's a good idea to fly on Friday the thirteenth. But we weigh these thoughts quickly and dispense with them. If you suffer from obsessive-compulsive disorder, however, the thoughts will not go away. Even if you realize that the thought is ridiculous, that your worry is unfounded, you are unable to stop thinking it.

Obsessive-compulsive disorder (commonly referred to as OCD) is an illness that combines obsessions and *compulsions*. The compulsions are time-consuming, seemingly superstitious rituals that you use to manage your obsessive thoughts. If you carry out the ritual, you hope that the obsession will fade. OCD was once thought to be a rare condition. We now know that approximately one in forty people suffer from disabling obsessions and compulsions. That makes OCD one of the most common psychiatric illnesses, following depression. Effective treatments now exist, but more than half of people with OCD do not seek treatment.

Obsessions in OCD Are Most Commonly About Illness, Doubts, and Symmetry

The thoughts that occur in OCD seem bizarre. In fact, many people who suffer from OCD never tell anyone because their intrusive thoughts are just too silly or embarrassing to discuss. Even though they seem bizarre and idiosyncratic, they are not. Obsessions fall into several very well recognized patterns. If you tell a psychiatrist your specific thoughts, she will probably tell you that you are not unique, that she has treated several other people with the same obsessions. You may suffer from only one type of obsession, but most people with OCD experience several different types, sometimes at different points in the course of their illness.

Probably the most common obsession is an irrational *fear* of germs. You worry constantly about where objects have been and who has touched them. You try to avoid touching handrails, money, and mail, since you can picture them being held by endless numbers of strangers. You feel uncomfortable in a doctor's office, and you certainly do not pick up any of the magazines in the waiting room. Who knows what you could catch? You keep cleansers in every room and carry antibiotic hand lotion with you at all times. You hate it when you have to shake hands, and you try not to touch anything else until you can wash. And public bathrooms are a real trial. You develop elaborate rituals for flushing, washing your hands, and getting out of the bathroom without directly touching anything that might be contaminated.

Germs are microscopic organisms that no one can see, but to you they are almost palpable. You are constantly mindful of what objects might be contaminated or dirty. But your concerns about germs are not rational. The contamination you fear is transmitted almost magically. For example, you might fear getting sick simply from reading a book about germs, even if the book itself is sterile. You may feel like you have been contaminated after speaking on the phone with someone who is sick. You might recognize that a certain illness, like AIDS, cannot be transmitted by touch, but you obsess over whether you were exposed to it by riding the subway. Even though the likelihood of transmitting germs is low, you may fear that you have passed on an illness from a stranger to your child, even after washing your hands many times.

A related obsession is the thought that you actually have contracted an illness, or that something is physically wrong with you. For example, you may be unable to get the idea out of your mind that you have cancer. If you think about it logically you realize that you have no reason to suspect you are ill. Although you may feel fine, you nevertheless cannot get rid of the thought. Obsessions of this sort are also seen in hypochondriasis (see "Physical Complaints and Pain"), but if you have OCD you experience numerous other obsessions, not just about being ill.

Obsessive doubts are also extremely common in OCD. Did you lock the door? Did you turn off the lights? Did you give someone the correct phone number? Did you get the time right? We all have these doubts from time to time, but we generally settle the matter quickly by double-checking. Sometimes we recognize that our doubts are based on such a slim chance of error that we can ignore them. But these doubts are unbearable in OCD and are not easily resolved by double-checking. If you have OCD you have to check the locks over and over again. You telephone again and again to make sure that you have received and given the correct information. You realize that you probably did everything right the first time, but that nagging doubt persists and grows stronger and stronger. You may spend much of the day arguing with yourself over the pros and cons of every possible action.

Obsessive doubts are usually accompanied by a catastrophic fear that something terrible will happen as a result of your neglect. The house will burn down, a burglar will break in, your pet will starve, you will miss your plane, or the babysitter will be late. If you fail to phone your wife every hour, maybe she will have a car accident or be kidnapped. I have treated a few patients who would drive around the block every time they hit a bump, just to double-check the area to make sure that they had not run over someone. Even though they could tell from looking at the rear-view mirror that no one was lying in the street, they would not be reassured until they had driven around again to confirm.

Many people with OCD have obsessive feelings about symmetry. The world around you must be ordered and even, or you begin to feel uncomfortable. For example, I have worked with patients who find it almost intolerable to sit near a pile of papers or magazines without straightening the piles and setting them at precise distances from the sides of the table. Pencils and pens must be laid exactly parallel to each other. You might worry that your car will be scratched if you do not park it in the exact middle of the parking space. A friend of mine would not let you touch him on one side of his body unless you were willing to do the same to the other side; a friendly tap on the back would send him into a nervous frenzy to find someone who knew enough to tap him a second time. The obsession in this case is more a sensation than a thought. You feel restless, unsettled, and awkward until symmetry is restored, at which point you achieve a feeling of satisfaction.

Some of the most fascinating obsessions in OCD are recurrent thoughts and images of a violent, sexual, or sacrilegious nature. All of us have irreverent or nasty thoughts from time to time. We may imagine or picture situations in our mind that we would find very troubling if they were to happen in real life. Either we quickly suppress these thoughts and images, telling ourselves that they are unwanted, or we simply forget about them. In OCD, however, these images and thoughts keep intruding. And even if they occur rarely, you obsess about what they mean to you. You feel guilty and ashamed. You worry that you are disturbed or disgusting for having such thoughts. OCD plays a dirty trick: it brings to mind the images and thoughts that you specifically find most upsetting. If you are a modest person, then you imagine people naked. If you are peaceful, you picture people beaten and bruised. If you are a *religious* person, you keep thinking about curse words, especially when you are in church. You may go to confession over and over again for seemingly trivial concerns. If you are *sexually* conservative, then you may imagine situations that you consider taboo. I have treated mothers who kept picturing their children in sexual poses. They had no related sexual urges and derived no satisfaction from these thoughts; on the contrary, they felt sick, guilty, and ashamed.

Repetitive Thoughts Can Occur in Several Other Illnesses

Obsessions that occur in OCD are different from healthy preoccupations and from the ruminations that occur in other mental illnesses and during times of stress. The word "obsession" derives from the Latin "to sit upon," or "to besiege." Obsessions are like invading thoughts that come from somewhere else. They make no sense. You wish they would go away. This is quite different from how the word obsession is sometimes used in common speech. We sometimes speak of being obsessed with someone or something that we desire. In this sense, we may be obsessed with *Star Trek*, with Ming Dynasty pottery, with the latest supermodel, or with the captain of the school football team. These obsessions may cause heartache if they are unfulfilled, but we enjoy them in a bittersweet way.

Sometimes obsessive interests may be an early sign of a developing mental illness, especially if they displace other hobbies and activities. Prior to developing schizophrenia (see "Psychosis") you may develop odd interests in conspiracy theories, paranormal phenomena, or unusual religions. This may just be a sign of *identity confusion* of the sort that many of us experience transiently during adolescence, when we are trying to define ourselves as different from our parents. But it may also be a sign of confused thinking and difficulty in forming relationships that precedes more serious illness.

Obsessive interests are also common in Asperger's disorder (see "Oddness"), which is often thought of as a variant of autism. If you have Asperger's disorder you probably have an idiosyncratic interest in some body of knowledge. For example, you may be obsessed with dinosaurs, calendar dates, sports scores, or movies. You may be so obsessed that you think and talk only about your area of interest, to the exclusion of other social activities. These interests are different from OCD obsessions because they are not unwanted or intrusive to the person who experiences them.

If you have an erotomanic *delusion,* you develop an unrealistic obsession with another person, believing that, in spite of all evidence, she is in love with you (see "Jealousy"). You may resort to stalking and harassing the object of your obsession. When she rebuffs your interest, you may get angry.

During times of *stress* we become preoccupied with worries. Will I get the job? Did I say the right thing? Is my future son-in-law good enough for my daughter? These thoughts can be distracting and may cause you to lose sleep. These preoccupations are a reflection of your *anxiety,* but they are not obsessions. They have a logical connection to your current circumstances. Once your problem is resolved, the worries go away.

Rumination is another word psychiatrists use to refer to recurrent thoughts. Ruminations lie somewhere between anxious preoccupations and obsessions. They take up a lot of your mental time, to the exclusion of other thoughts. But unlike obsessions they do not come out of the blue, and they are not necessarily unwanted. For example, you may have pessimistic thoughts if you suffer from *depression.* During all your waking hours you reflect upon how worthless and hopeless you feel. You may dwell endlessly on past events that make you feel guilty or ashamed. If you are *paranoid,* then you are preoccupied with fears of being harmed by others. These ruminations are different from obsessions in that they make some sense in the context of the underlying disturbance in mood and thinking. To the person who is depressed or paranoid, the thoughts seem completely reasonable.

You may have recurrent, troubling thoughts if you have experienced a *traumatic* event such as combat or rape. You may dream about the event or experience *flashbacks* when you are awake. But you may also think about the event over and over, trying to figure out if you did something wrong. Thinking about the event may make you angry, sad, or anxious. You do not like these feelings, but the thoughts and memories keep recurring. In some ways these flashbacks and thoughts are similar to the obsessions experienced in OCD, except that they make more sense in light of the trauma you have experienced.

Sexual urges and drug *cravings* are also recurrent, and in some ways unwanted, like obsessions. If you smoke, drink, or use drugs the cravings may come to you again and again, even after you have decided that you must stop using. *Sexual preoccupations* are also very difficult to suppress. But in contrast to obsessions, cravings focus on something enjoyable. Even if you know that drug use, sex, or gambling is bad for you, you still get a thrill of anticipation when you think about them. The obsessions of OCD, on the other hand, are in no way satisfying.

There are several psychiatric conditions characterized by obsessions about the body. In both anorexia and bulimia (see "Appetite Disturbances") you are preoccupied with your body weight and shape. In body dysmorphic disorder you obsess about other aspects of your *body image,* ranging from the shape of your nose to the size of your muscles.

Finally, obsessive thinking is a feature of what psychiatrists refer to as an obsessive-compulsive personality, which is different from OCD, though the names are confusingly similar. In some other countries, the term "anankastic personality" is preferred. If you have an obsessive-compulsive personality disorder, which affects about two of one hundred people, you are overly perfectionistic and controlling. Everything in your life has to be organized and regimented. You obsess about following rules and routines. When presented with opportunities for spontaneous fun you become anxious and irritable. This does not endear you to others, and you may have trouble making and keeping friends. Even at work your perfectionism is not valued. You may obsess about details to such an extent that you can never finish a project. You may have difficulty seeing outside of the box. You insist mindlessly on following a process rather than on achieving the desired outcome. You may be intolerant of the work styles of others and insist on doing things your own way. OCD and obsessive-compulsive personality disorders can occur together, but they are usually separate. In fact, many people who suffer from OCD are *sloppy* and disorganized, since their rituals and thoughts distract and overwhelm them.

What Causes OCD?

Obsessive-compulsive disorder is a fascinating illness, in part, because the symptoms seem so Freudian, even though the underlying causes are neurological. You obsess about dirt, sex, and violence. You imagine scenarios that represent your worst fears and strongest taboos. Somehow the brain finds the subjects that you least want to dwell upon and then makes you consider them over and over again. One might think that such symptoms have their origin in childhood, when we learn to suppress our primitive urges. But there is no evidence that childhood development is disturbed in those who go on to suffer from OCD later in life.

There appears to be a genetic component to OCD. Your risk of developing OCD is four times higher if you have a first-degree relative diagnosed with the illness. OCD also tends to occur more commonly in certain neurological conditions. For example, about half of those diagnosed with Tourette's disorder (see "Compulsions") will also develop OCD. Some children develop OCD after a strep throat infection, and their symptoms sometimes resolve with antibiotic treatment. The basal ganglia, a part of the brain that manages communication between the cerebral cortex and the more primitive parts of the nervous system, may be the site of OCD symptoms. Scientists believe that a deficit in the chemical brain signal serotonin, and possibly dopamine, plays a role. The most effective medications for OCD are those that boost serotonin.

OCD usually has its onset during the teenage or early adult years. Often the symptoms appear quickly and unexpectedly. The symptoms may wax and wane over time, even without treatment. The types of symptoms may also change. For example, you may have concerns about contamination for many years, but then become more obsessed with doubts. Your ritual compulsions also evolve over time, as you try to develop new strategies for coping with your anxious and obsessive thoughts. Most doctors assume that symptoms become more pronounced during times of stress, but sometimes they seem to come and go without any rhyme or reason.

Psychotherapy and Medication Can Be Effective for OCD

Psychiatrists once thought that OCD was an untreatable illness. Fortunately, as we have since learned that OCD is a relatively common illness, we have also discovered that certain medications and cognitive-behavioral therapy can be effective treatments.

The SSRI antidepressants (see "Depression") are the medical treatment of choice for OCD. The tricyclic antidepressant clomipramine (Anafranil), which also has a strong effect on serotonin levels in the brain, is just as effective as the SSRI antidepressants but tends to have more side effects. As with depression, improvement in the symptoms of OCD is seen after four to eight weeks of treatment. Approximately half of those treated with medication experience significant improvement, though symptoms often do not disappear entirely. If medication is not effective initially, you may require a higher dose or a trial of a different medication. Medication does not cure OCD. Even if symptoms disappear entirely with medication, they may recur when medication is stopped.

Even though medications can be very effective, many who suffer from OCD prefer to undergo psychotherapy, either alone or in combination with medication. Cognitive-behavioral therapy is the only psychotherapy that has been demonstrated to be effective, and it is just as effective as medication and may provide a longer-term cure. You will need to complete homework exercises in between sessions as part of your therapy. It is not clear whether the combination of medication and therapy is better than either treatment alone, but most doctors believe that a combination of the two therapies may bring faster and more sustained symptom remission.

If you decide to engage in therapy, you and your therapist will make a detailed list of all of the obsessive thoughts that you experience, as well as all of the compulsive behaviors that you practice. You will trace back your behaviors to the specific obsessions that drive them. Rather than struggling to suppress your thoughts, you will strive to detail and monitor them. You will practice exposure and response prevention. For example, you might be asked to touch an object that you consider dirty and then not allow yourself to wash your hands. You might be asked to refrain from adjusting your chair or the objects around you, even though they have been purposefully left in asymmetric positions. The techniques are targeted to your specific obsessions and rituals.

These techniques may cause anxiety initially, even though you will eventually find the obsessions to be less intense and easier to ignore. To better manage the initial *anxiety* you may learn to use relaxation techniques. You will also use cognitive techniques in which you review your specific anxieties and fears with your therapist, revealing the illogical and magical thinking behind them. It is much easier to resist an urge when you have acknowledged to yourself the extreme improbability that something catastrophic will happen as a result. You must remind yourself, for example, that if you fail to double-check the door you are unlikely to be robbed. You will prove to yourself that thinking bad things does not bring them to life.

Neurosurgery has been tried rarely in extremely severe cases in which obsessions and compulsions do not respond to other treatments. However, outcomes have been poor, with persistent symptoms, repeated surgeries, and, in some cases, *suicide*. Surgery should not be considered except in the most desperate cases.

If someone you care about has OCD, you should be mindful of his attempts to involve you in his *compulsive* rituals. For example, if he asks you the same question repeatedly, you should tell him calmly that he knows the answer and that it is not helpful for you to reassure him needlessly. He may feel more anxious initially, but ultimately he is likely to obsess less as a result of not being indulged.

Oddness

From your station in an aisle of your uncle's grocery store you watch him take care of the customers. He can ring up prices and give directions all at the same time; you can barely keep track of the items to which you've already attached price labels. Your mind tends to drift off, and you find yourself standing in the middle of the floor with your price gun pointing aimlessly at rows of cans. Mothers pull their curious children around you, shushing them.

Every so often a customer asks you a question, and you try not to bungle it. Lately a lot of kids have been asking you whether the hamburger is kept with the hams or with the burgers. You tell them that they are with frozen foods and that you don't think they have ham in them. The kids laugh, so maybe that's the wrong answer?

Oddness can be a very nonspecific sign of mental illness. People will find it odd if you mumble to yourself while hearing voices, if you start to panic in the middle of a crowd, or if you start sobbing out of the blue, unless they know you and realize that you are suffering from, respectively, hallucinations, panic attacks, or depression. This chapter refers to an aspect of oddness that is more difficult to explain or understand: many people with chronic mental illnesses such as autism and schizophrenia have a profound difficulty in engaging with others in a normal fashion. They have difficulty negotiating eye contact, personal space, and conversation.

Schizophrenia is defined primarily by symptoms of *psychosis,* especially hallucinations and delusions. People with schizophrenia often also experience what psychiatrists call negative, or deficit, symptoms. Negative symptoms are defined as the absence of certain traits that are typically present and include *avoidance* of social interactions, apathy, poor hygiene, diminished emotional responses, and subtle impairments in thinking. The impairments in thinking, or cognitive impairments, include troubles with abstract thinking, problem solving, and maintaining concentration (see "Learning Problems").

If you have negative symptoms of schizophrenia, which affect about one-third of those diagnosed, you spend much of the day sitting by yourself, excited by little around you. Some might think you are *depressed,* but you do not feel sad so much as disinterested. You may have trouble understanding other people. You may pay less attention to your grooming and dress than you used to. Your hair may be bizarrely combed or simply neglected, and your clothes may be mismatched. It is these subtler symptoms, rather than the more obvious hallucinations and delusions, that sometimes make it difficult for a person with schizophrenia to obtain and keep a job, to make friends, or to date.

In the past, psychiatric hospitals were filled with patients suffering from negative symptoms of schizophrenia. People who visited the hospital for the first time would understandably wonder why everyone looked like a zombie. The new generation of antipsychotic medications (see "Psychosis") and rehabilitation programs have improved the treatment of negative symptoms and have made it possible for many patients to get out of the hospitals and become active again in their lives.

About one-fourth of people with schizophrenia develop characteristic poses and movements that doctors refer to as posturing or stereotypical movements. For example, an individual might walk around with one arm raised behind his head, or he might repeatedly tap his arm while talking. A patient who engages in these unusual *movements* is often unaware of them, but they are fairly obvious to others and contribute to an impression of oddness.

Psychiatrists have recognized a couple of personality disorders that are characterized by odd ways of viewing the world and interacting with others. Personality disorders are defined as lifelong and maladaptive styles that are not caused by another major mental illness. People with schizotypal and schizoid personality disorders do not suffer from *hallucinations* and *delusions* but have traits similar to those seen in schizophrenia.

If you have a schizotypal personality disorder, you tend to have odd beliefs and interests, unusual perceptual experiences, unusual emotional reactions, general suspiciousness, and difficulty developing friendships. You tend to be a loner, perhaps because others view you as strange. The woman down the street who wears the same rumpled dress every day and who makes no decision without consulting her Ouija board probably has a schizotypal personality disorder. About one in a hundred people have this personality type, and some eventually develop schizophrenia, which is probably genetically related. Antipsychotic medications, which are the treatment of choice for *psychosis,* may also help diminish unusual pre-occupations and perceptual experiences in this personality disorder, if they are considered troublesome.

If you have a schizoid personality disorder, on the other hand, your *avoidance* of others comes from your lack of interest in relationships. You pursue your own interests in isolation and care little for the opinions of others. Someone with schizoid personality disorder is likely to live with his parents as an adult and to work in a storage room or back office where he does not have to interact with customers or co-workers. Schizoid personality also occurs in about one percent of the population. There is no known treatment for this personality style, nor do most individuals with this disorder desire treatment. If you have it, you are happy to be left alone.

Autism is a developmental disorder characterized by difficulties from infancy in interpersonal communication and relationships. As many as one in one thousand children suffer from autism, or perhaps five times that number if less severe disorders of interpersonal development (such as Asperger's disorder) are included. From an early age you find it difficult or impossible to communicate verbally or with gestures, to demonstrate expected emotions, or to engage in playful activities. You become fixated on certain objects and interests and display unusual and rigid habits and movements. You have profound *learning problems.* In most cases you are viewed as seriously disabled, rather than odd.

Asperger's disorder is a higher functioning variety of autism and is named after the physician who first described the illness. If you have Asperger's disorder, you do not have difficulties with language or learning, but you have difficulties relating to others in social interactions. You do not pick up on social cues or appreciate the intentions, discomforts, and needs of others. For example, you may not realize that the person you have engaged in a monologue is trying to politely end the conversation. You tend to be verbose, speak loudly and with little inflection, and go off on tangents. You may make poor eye contact, hold peculiar postures, and have an odd gait. You may dress oddly and have unusual habits. You may show no interest in, or awareness of, the emotional feelings of others. You may learn to say "thank you" and "excuse me," but you use the terms automatically, without appreciating why you should be grateful or sorry in a particular situation.

As in autism, you are likely to have certain fixed preoccupations, interests, and habits. For example, you might be obsessed with dinosaurs, including the exact number of bones that have been identified for each species. I worked with one patient who was obsessed with writing a detailed history of his life, including every mundane detail of every day. He wrote pages each day, but it seemed unlikely that he would ever catch up with the present. Some individuals with Asperger's disorder have remarkable talents for exact drawings, instant calculations, or photographic memories. You may also be rigid in your habits, and you may be prone to losing your temper when your routine is disturbed, or when you misunderstand a social situation. You may not recognize how your behavior has disturbed others.

The prevalence of Asperger's disorder is not well known, since individuals are often viewed as just odd, but not mentally ill, and do not come to the attention of professionals. When seen by a mental health worker, they have often been misdiagnosed as having a schizoid personality disorder. If you have Asperger's disorder you might benefit from treatment with SSRI antidepressant medications (see "Depression") or antipsychotic medications (see "Psychosis"), which can reduce your tendency to become rigidly preoccupied and eliminate some unusual habitual movements and gestures. The ability to recognize and empathize with the emotional responses of others is more difficult to treat, though intensive social skills training starting in childhood may help.

If someone you care about has negative symptoms of schizophrenia, schizotypal personality traits, or autism, you probably do not think of him as odd. You think of him as having his own distinctive ways of thinking and behaving, and they may make sense to you even if they seem odd to others. If you find yourself embarrassed by your loved one's behavior, especially in public, it may be because you feel it reflects on you. Many people may not understand the disability from which the unusual behaviors arise. Generally it is best to encourage your loved one to conform to those social expectations which are reasonable for him, such as putting on clean clothing before going out, while being understanding and matter-of-fact about other behaviors that may be out of his control, such as frequent tics. Strangers will take their lead from you and are less likely to gawk or become worried if you give the impression that nothing is out of the ordinary. Remember that most people know little about mental illness.

Panic

This wasn't the first time, you tell the emergency room doctor.
The first attack came on when you were shopping at the mall.
Suddenly you started to sweat, and your pulse was racing. You
were on the verge of passing out, but somehow you got outside
and felt better in the cold open air. You thought it was over.

Tonight you were celebrating after the football game. You were
smoking with some friends when, suddenly, your chest started to
hurt. Your heartbeat was pounding. You're twenty-five and in
good shape, but isn't that what a heart attack is like? Your head
was throbbing and you slipped to the floor. Your friends got you
into the car, but you don't remember much else.

You're starting to feel a little better now, but you are scared.
Are you going to die, you wonder? Or are you going crazy?

Panic is an attack of intense anxiety, accompanied by physical
symptoms, which can last for up to an hour. Psychiatrists estimate
that as many as one in ten people experience a panic attack each
year. Typically an attack builds up over a minute or two, starting
with a vague sense of anxiety or fear. You begin to sweat, tremble,
and feel numb or tingly. You might experience chills or be flushed
with heat. Your heart feels like it is racing, pounding, or beating
erratically. You feel your pulse throbbing in your head. Your chest
hurts, and you feel like you are having trouble breathing or swallowing. You experience belly cramps or butterflies in your stomach, and you think you might throw up. You may feel unsteady
or even faint. You are confused and have trouble engaging in a
conversation with others. Most disturbing is the absolute terror
and dread that accompanies the attack. You probably think that

you are about to die, or that you are having a heart attack or stroke. It may seem to you that you are losing your mind.

In most cases panic attacks seem to come out of the blue. As far as you know, you were not anxious or scared about anything in particular just before the attack came on. Some researchers have noted that, in fact, panic attacks are more likely to occur during times of *stress,* especially following a divorce or separation from a loved one. Some psychiatrists believe that a precipitant to the attack can usually be uncovered in psychotherapy. For example, you might be nervous about an upcoming meeting with your boss and so you panic when you see someone dressed like your boss on the street. You may not be consciously aware that you were nervous in the first place, or that the stranger reminded you of your boss. But suddenly you are in the midst of an attack.

It probably would be easier to cope with panic attacks if they occurred only under certain conditions. Then you could prepare for them or avoid those situations. In fact, most people who suffer from frequent panic attacks end up avoiding crowded or confined places far from home. Having a panic attack in a public place can be embarrassing. You feel like you are losing control in front of everybody. You feel trapped by the closed spaces and bodies around you. You may feel like you cannot escape or get help. Many people respond by *avoiding* congested streets, malls, subways, buses, tunnels, bridges, and public events. You may increasingly stay at home or go out only with a friend or partner. Psychiatrists refer to this as agoraphobia, or a *fear* of public places.

Of course, if you have panic attacks often, or if they are severe, you may get into the habit of feeling anxious between attacks as you constantly await the next one to occur. This sort of anticipatory *anxiety* may make you more vulnerable to another attack, and you may be caught in a cycle of fear. Between attacks you may worry that you are going crazy or losing control of your life. You may cut back on your usual activities. You may develop symptoms of *depression* or have *suicidal thoughts.* You may start to drink or abuse drugs in order to dampen the constant anxiety.

Panic Can Occur in Several Different Illnesses

If your panic attacks occur as frequently as once a week, or if the fear of having a panic attack interferes with your lifestyle, then you probably have panic disorder. Two to three percent of Americans suffer from panic disorder during their lifetime. Half who have panic disorder also develop agoraphobia.

Panic disorder is the primary psychiatric illness in which panic attacks occur. The illness usually develops during young adulthood and affects women twice as often as men. About half the people with panic disorder have another family member who also suffers from the disorder, suggesting a strong genetic component. Panic attacks can be produced in vulnerable individuals by exposing them to chemicals like lactate or carbon dioxide, which are naturally produced in the body during physical exertion and hyperventilation. Hyperventilation is a symptom of panic, but it can also bring on an attack. This suggests that your body is primed to experience panic symptoms under stressful or frightening circumstances.

Panic attacks are unanticipated, at least initially, and seem to come out of the blue. As you have more and more attacks, you may begin to recognize some of the situations in which they are more likely to occur. Nevertheless, they are not predictable responses to specific *fears*. If you are scared of dogs and have panic symptoms only when you are around a dog, then you have a phobia and not a panic disorder.

The panic that occurs in some other illnesses may be very similar to the symptoms seen in panic disorder. If you have post-traumatic stress disorder (PTSD), you may panic when you are reminded of your *traumatic* experience. For example, a combat veteran might be overwhelmed with anxiety when he mistakes the noise from a car backfiring for a gunshot (see "Flashbacks"). If you have a borderline personality style, you have poor *self-esteem* and may panic when rejected by a loved one. If you suffer from obsessive-compulsive disorder, you may panic when you try to resist the urge to act on your *compulsions*. Generally, the panic attacks that occur in these other illnesses are different in that the cause of the panic is obvious. You are less likely to feel like you are dying, losing control, or going crazy. The physical sensations may be less pronounced than the anxiety.

Several drugs can cause panic attacks. Stimulants like caffeine, nicotine, amphetamine, cocaine, ephedrine, and theophylline (a treatment for asthma) can predispose you to suffering a panic attack, presumably because they stimulate the release of the same chemicals that are involved in panic. Psychiatrists refer to these chemicals, which are found both in the brain and the bloodstream, as adrenergic chemicals, including epinephrine or adrenaline. They are released in fear-inducing situations. Paniclike symptoms can also be seen during withdrawal from alcohol, sedatives, or opiates and during *intoxication* with hallucinogens or psychedelic drugs.

How to Cope with Panic Attacks

It is crucial that you receive a complete medical workup when you first experience a panic attack. Those who suffer panic attacks feel like they are dying, because many of the physical sensations of a panic attack can also occur during a heart attack, seizure, asthmatic attack, or pulmonary embolus (blood clot in the lung). Your symptoms could also be caused by a number of other less obvious medical problems, such as an endocrine disorder or vitamin deficiency. The onset of panic symptoms later in life should raise the suspicion of an underlying medical condition rather than a primary psychiatric problem.

There are three approaches to treating panic attacks, and they can be used separately or together. Psychotherapy can be effective in many cases. A counselor can help you to control the catastrophic thinking you have during a panic attack. You learn to remind yourself during an attack that you will not, in fact, die or lose control. You will practice relaxation techniques (see "Anxiety"), including training yourself to breathe slowly and evenly using the diaphragm throughout an episode of panic. You keep a diary of attacks, the situations that precipitated them, and your reactions. You practice breathing through a straw to induce panic symptoms so that you learn that you can handle them and even suppress them at will. You slowly begin to expose yourself on a daily basis to the situations that worry you. The panic attacks become less frightening and easier to manage. Eventually they decrease in frequency or stop altogether. Psychotherapy may also be helpful in exploring any stresses or internal conflicts that may have made you vulnerable to the attacks in the first place.

Antidepressant medication (see "Depression"), when taken on a daily basis, is also highly effective in preventing panic attacks. Most psychiatrists now use the SSRI antidepressants, because they have fewer side effects, and the tricyclic antidepressants are probably less effective. Both types of medication can cause an increase in anxiety when they are first prescribed, for which reason the starting dose is usually very low. Antidepressant medications also have the advantage of treating the symptoms of depression which commonly accompany panic disorder. Usually an antidepressant medication is prescribed for about a year, at which point it may be possible to stop the medication. However, panic disorder appears to be a chronic illness, and panic attacks recur in most who stop medication. The combination of antidepressant medication and psychotherapy is the most effective treatment for panic attacks.

The third approach to treating panic attacks is to use an anxiolytic medication (see "Anxiety") for the prompt relief of a panic attack at the first sign of an episode. The benzodiazepines that work most rapidly (for example, alprazolam or Xanax) can be very effective in the short term. Unfortunately, the panic attack may be well under way, or over, before the medication kicks in. Sometimes anxiolytic medications are used on a daily basis to suppress panic attacks before they occur, especially if they are frequent. This method of treatment is not recommended, since the medications are potentially addicting, and panic attacks will re-emerge when the medication is eventually stopped.

Paranoia

You knew it was a mistake to let her talk you into going to this restaurant. The waiters were looking at you funny as you walked to the table. What's the big deal? So you can't afford the fanciest shoes. You make enough money to eat their food.

Your girlfriend orders the daily special without asking for the price. Doesn't she know by now how these places work? The specials are designed to rip you off. You ask the price, and the waiter glares at you. Now he'll probably go back and piss in your soup. You know you should just get up and leave, but part of you wants to stay so you can yell at him when he comes back.

Paranoia is an unwarranted feeling that others are trying to harm you. The word comes from the ancient Greek for "out of your mind," and it originally had a broader meaning. If you are paranoid you may believe that someone, or some group of people, is deceiving you, manipulating you, talking about you behind your back, or insulting you. In more extreme forms you may believe that your life is in danger.

Some degree of suspiciousness is healthy. Although the world is full of good people who like to help others, there are also con artists, criminals, predators, and opportunists. Some people are nice among friends but mean to strangers. Politicians, businessmen, and others in positions of authority sometimes betray our trust. And sometimes those closest to us hurt us, intentionally or not. To be of psychiatric concern, paranoia must be persistent and out of proportion to the evidence. Paranoia can be seen in a wide range of psychiatric conditions. For some people suspiciousness of the intentions of others is a pervasive part of their personality style. If you have a paranoid temperament you probably have had lifelong difficulties in getting along with others. Rather than recognizing your own faults and limits, you blame others when things go wrong. If you fail to get a promotion at work it is because the boss is out to get you. If a date goes poorly it is because you were set up with a jerk. If the cops arrest you for speeding, it is because they are prejudiced. It seems like everyone in the world wants to screw you. With such an attitude it is difficult to make friends and form close relationships with others. You may keep to yourself, or you may hang out only with others who share your view of a hostile, dog-eat-dog world.

If you believe that everyone is willing to stab you in the back in order to get ahead, then you are likely to want to defend yourself. You may treat others as objects to be manipulated. You may deride others behind their backs, on the assumption that they do the same to you. You may misinterpret the benign comments of others as being malicious or sarcastic. For example, if a colleague compliments you on a project, you may suspect that he is buttering you up while preparing to steal your idea. I worked with one patient who could not tolerate any disagreement. If I ever expressed a difference of opinion with him, I was not just wrong, I was lying. To him, the world was full of liars and only very few people, like himself, who were always truthful.

You may lose your temper easily. You may hold grudges for months or years. You are *jealous* and possessive of loved ones, fearing that they will betray you or move on to something better at the first chance. You may spend an inordinate amount of your resources making complaints and filing lawsuits.

Psychiatrists refer to this disturbance in temperament as a paranoid personality disorder. It appears to be a lifelong style that occurs in approximately one percent of the population. It is poorly studied, in part because individuals who are so paranoid are unlikely to seek treatment or participate in research studies. You do not recognize that you have a problem, aside from the way you believe others treat you.

There appears to be a genetic component to paranoia, with paranoid delusions and personality styles tending to cluster in families. Paranoid personality is also more common among men than women. Therapists think that paranoia arises from an exaggerated sense of self-consciousness. You are sensitive to the views of others and think that others are paying as much judgmental attention to you as you do to them. While constantly monitoring others you misinterpret or exaggerate the significance of minor comments, gestures, and coincidences. Being regarded by others makes you feel ashamed or embarrassed, and you respond with *anger*.

Drug and alcohol use can also cause paranoia in some people who are otherwise not particularly suspicious. For example, after smoking crack cocaine you may begin to suspect that your dealer is cheating you or that the police are outside your door. These are certainly not bizarre beliefs, under the circumstances, but they develop as a side effect of the drug. Once the drug has cleared out of your system you realize that your fear was exaggerated. Paranoia can also occur during *intoxication* with marijuana, hallucinogens, or PCP (phencyclidine). The chronic use of alcohol and stimulant drugs (for example, amphetamine) can also cause paranoia.

Persecutory Delusions Are Common in Psychotic Illnesses

In psychotic illnesses paranoia breaks with reality to such an extent that it is considered a *delusion*. Persecutory delusions are the fixed and false belief that others are trying to harm you. Persecutory delusions are usually accompanied by other signs of paranoia, such as *anxiety*, vigilance, edginess, and a reluctance to disclose too much. These paranoid features are most commonly seen in schizophrenia (see "Psychosis"), but also in *mania* and delusional disorders.

Why are persecutory delusions so common in schizophrenia? All of us are on guard at times, and, in the real world, it is easy to make a mistake or to be taken advantage of if you are not paying attention. In schizophrenia, this instinct for self-preservation becomes exaggerated. When you become paranoid you begin to notice little details and subtle signs of the intentions of others. Things that you might ignore when you are feeling well take on huge significance. If someone coughs or scratches her nose, you think she is sending a signal, perhaps a warning. If a phone company makes repairs in your neighborhood, you think that they are installing surveillance bugs. If a doctor prescribes medication, you suspect that it is a tranquilizer to render you helpless. Once you start noticing and misinterpreting little details, they begin to reinforce each other. All of the pieces of the puzzle seem to come together, leading to the inevitable conclusion that everyone is out to get you. Once you feel this way it is very hard to trust that anyone actually wants to help you, including your family, friends, and doctors.

As you become paranoid, it is common to believe that random or unrelated events are directed at you in particular. Psychiatrists label these beliefs "ideas of reference." For example, you might believe that a television commercial advertising mouthwash was played in order to inform you that your breath stinks. Pop stars seem to be singing and rapping about you on the radio. When you see people talking on the street you think they are talking about you. It is even easier to develop this sort of delusion when you are *hallucinating*, hearing your name called everywhere you go.

Other common paranoid beliefs are related to the feeling that your mind is vulnerable to the actions of others. Most of us feel like our thoughts are private and safely concealed inside our skull. But when you are psychotic that barrier seems to dissolve. You believe that people can hear what you are thinking. You believe that others are able to place thoughts into your mind. You believe that someone is able to force you to act in certain ways beyond your control. Psychiatrists refer to these beliefs, respectively, as thought broadcasting, thought insertion, and thought control. For a person experiencing these sorts of delusions, a simple walk down the street can be terrifying. You feel that you have lost all privacy and all control. You lose the feeling of boundary between yourself and other people.

One of the most common paranoid beliefs is the fear that you are being raped or prostituted. In the initial stages you may simply believe that others want to have sex with you. This is not a pleasant feeling; rather, you feel like you are under attack. Regardless of your usual sexual preferences you may feel that you are being "turned into" a homosexual. You may believe that your family members are trying to have sex with you as well. As you become more psychotic you become convinced that you actually are being raped, perhaps while you are asleep. I know one person who was convinced that he could feel himself being raped from behind as he sat in a chair with no one around.

Paradoxically, as you become paranoid, you are likely to become most suspicious of those who are most intimate to you. We all have strong emotions regarding our parents, lovers, and children, and they know our secrets and weaknesses. When you begin to suspect someone close to you, all of the old fights and disappointments come back to life in your mind.

You experience a painful sense of betrayal. Your paranoia regarding the rest of the world is reinforced when you realize that even your family is against you. You may feel safer in the company of strangers. If you become sufficiently frightened you might even attack the people that you love most.

At some point nearly every patient with persecutory delusions comes to believe that there is a conspiracy against him. The nature of the conspiracy depends on the culture in which you live. In the past, in countries that were predominantly Protestant, it was common for paranoid patients to fear the forces of the pope. Since the Cold War ended, patients seem to be less concerned that they may be the target of the KGB, though this was a common delusion when I was in training. The CIA and FBI continue to be popular in the persecutory beliefs of patients. Probably the most common belief is of being harassed by the Mafia. I have heard this fear expressed by patients from around the country, from other countries, in all age groups, and from a variety of ethnic groups. This is probably a reflection of the popularity of Mafia stories on television and in films.

How to Cope with Paranoia

If you suffer from feelings of paranoia, you are unlikely to seek psychiatric help. You are more likely to blame others and avoid self-reflection. However, if you seek treatment for anxiety, or if you are brought into treatment by colleagues or family, then you may be able to find some relief. Psychotherapy can be helpful if you have a maladaptive tendency to view the world suspiciously, so long as you are willing to try to change. A therapist can help you to try to gain a different perspective on your interactions with others. You may learn to be more objective and self-reflective, rather than leap to a paranoid interpretation every time you are disappointed. This sort of therapy is not easy. You are probably very sensitive to criticism, and the therapist will have to maintain your trust while at the same time challenging your long-established way of thinking.

If you suffer from episodes of paranoia as part of an underlying illness like schizophrenia, then the treatment of choice is antipsychotic medication (see "Psychosis"). Antipsychotic medications will almost immediately bring some relief from the anxiety and fearfulness that you experience because of your paranoia. However, several weeks of treatment are usually required before the underlying belief (for example, of being chased by the

Mafia) begins to soften and disappear. Sometimes persecutory delusions persist in spite of medication, but they become less pervasive and intense, and you are able to shrug them off most of the time.

If someone you care about suffers from paranoia, you should try to help him get treatment. This may be difficult, since he is already suspicious of strangers and authority figures and quick to perceive criticism. You want to help him, but he may sense an attempt to control him, and this may make him angry or frightened. Whenever you are dealing with someone who is paranoid, you should be as honest as you can be. Your loved one will be on alert for any sign of deception or manipulation. It is better to calmly state how you perceive things, and to acknowledge that you do not think your loved one is being persecuted. You should communicate that you realize he feels persecuted, but that you see it somewhat differently. You should point out that you can tell he is in distress and that you would like to try to help him in some way. Even if he does not believe he has a mental problem he may be willing to see a psychiatrist to help him deal with *anxiety* and *sleeping problems*. In your interactions with someone who is paranoid, you want to avoid showing too much emotion. If you argue angrily, then you may appear desperate. This may reinforce his belief that you are trying to control him, not help him.

Physical Complaints and Pain

You are fed up with doctors. You've seen seven in the last month, and not one of them has been helpful. Each had some different test to run on you, and all the tests have come back normal. Or so they say. You know that you are in so much pain that there must be something causing it. First it was your back, but now your knees and neck are hurting as well. One doctor put his stethoscope to your chest, and you screamed in pain. He asked whether it was a sharp pain or whether you felt burning or pressure. What kind of question is that? It was all of the above!

Now your colon problem has been coming back. You feel gassy all day. Your food doesn't seem like it's digesting properly. Maybe you have an ulcer? And with all these problems, you really don't feel up to having sex any more. It's just too uncomfortable.

You explained all this to the last doctor, but he said he wasn't going to do another exam. He said he'd like you to see a colleague of his, a psychiatrist. He said that the problems were all in your mind. As if you could imagine such pain!

There has always been a temptation to distinguish between illnesses of the mind and illnesses of the body. If a physician is unable to find a specific medical abnormality he may conclude that a patient's complaint is not real. The patient is either faking or mentally disturbed. But physicians are increasingly aware that the distinction between physical and psychiatric illness is artificial. When we feel pain, discomfort, and other changes in sensation, we experience them in our brain. The brain can amplify or dampen these sensations. Depending on our prior experiences and cultural background we may interpret discomfort differently. Sadness may be perceived as a queasy sensation in the stomach. A tremor of muscles may be experienced as nervousness. The brain can also influence the other organs of the body through nerve cell transmission or the release of hormones into the bloodstream. For example, psychological *stress* can precipitate a heart attack or depress the immune system. Though there are practical reasons for separating psychiatric and other medical illnesses, we must recognize that our mental state greatly influences how we develop, perceive, and communicate physical complaints.

Pain Is a Complex Physical and Mental Experience

Pain is probably the most common medical complaint. Acute pain serves a useful purpose, calling our attention to injury or disease. But many people suffer from continuous or intermittent pain that can last for months. Such pain no longer serves a useful purpose and may be disabling and costly. Affecting more than ten percent of Americans each year, pain syndromes such as back pain, headaches, and pain stemming from cancer or surgery bring millions of patients to their doctor. If pain persists, either with or in spite of treatment, then you may also develop *depression, anxiety,* and *sleep problems.* You may have difficulties in your relationships with others, becoming more helpless, hopeless, dependent, manipulative, irritable, or withdrawn.

Several different types of pain have been recognized. The most easily understood is somatic pain arising from injury or inflammation to nerve cells in the skin, muscles, and bones. This is the pain we feel when we slam a door on a finger or when we spill lemon juice on a cut. Our nerve cells send a transmission to our spinal cord, and the spinal cord immediately sends a signal to our muscles to withdraw from the source of pain. This reflex takes place even as the signal continues to our brain, where we identify the feeling as painful. Somatic pain may also arise from less obvious muscular tension or inflammation. There may be tender trigger points that you can touch, even when there is no visible injury.

Visceral pain arises from inflammation, tension, or damage to nerve cells in the deeper organs of the body. You probably cannot pinpoint the part of your body from which this pain arises, though you may experience a dull, pressing pain in a diffuse area far from the injury. For example, you may feel shoulder, arm, or jaw pain during a heart attack. When experiencing visceral pain you may feel clammy and nauseated. Similar diffuse discomforts are frequently experienced during psychiatric illness. *Depression, panic attacks,* and general *anxiety* are often accompanied by headache, vague abdominal pain, and queasiness. It is probably impossible to determine whether your mood is stressing your other organs, or whether you are interpreting uncomfortable emotional feelings in the more familiar physical terms of pain and nausea. In either case you genuinely feel discomfort.

Neuropathic pain arises from damage to the nervous system, rather than to the organs and tissues that the nerve cells monitor. You usually experience neuropathic pain as a grinding pressure, dull ache, stabbing pain, electrical shock, burning sensation, or combination of these feelings. When a nerve cell has been severed, for example during an amputation, you may experience neuropathic pain as well as a strange sensation that the severed limb or appendage is still present.

Many of the chronic pain syndromes that plague patients and frustrate doctors do not fit easily into these categories. You may have trouble describing your pain, or you may experience a variety of discomforts, ranging from pinpoint tenderness to diffuse aches, to sudden stabbing sensations. Your doctor may be unable to find any other abnormality on physical exam or in laboratory and radiological studies. In fact, if he does find an abnormality it may be unrelated to your pain. Scientists have found, for example, that spinal disc abnormalities detected on scans are usually unrelated to whether or not you experience back pain. Fibromyalgia is a common pain syndrome characterized by painful trigger points and diffuse body aches. It has no identified cause and frequently overlaps with chronic *fatigue* syndrome.

Premenstrual syndrome (also known as PMS, premenstrual dysphoric disorder, or late luteal phase dysphoric disorder) is another syndrome with both psychiatric and physical symptoms. Those who suffer from PMS can experience irritability, exhaustion, sadness, tearfulness, headaches, cramps, unusual hungers, sleeping difficulties, and bloating during each menstrual cycle (see "Mood Swings"). The symptoms usually peak in the week prior to menstruation, then disappear altogether for at least a week afterward.

Somatoform Disorders Are Characterized by Exaggerated Physical Concerns

Somatization disorder is a chronic illness characterized by multiple physical complaints that appear to have no medical basis. The disorder used to be called hysteria under the mistaken belief that it was caused by the uterus and affected women only. It is still diagnosed much more frequently in women, with approximately one out of a hundred suffering from the illness. Somatization disorder is difficult to cure. Most patients continue to seek medical attention.

If you suffer from somatization you have probably been sick most of your life, complaining of multiple symptoms since at least your teenage years. You may have seen more than one doctor in the hope of addressing refractory or recurrent problems with all parts of your body. You may have undergone extensive medical workups and treatments, and you may have been referred to a psychiatrist when your physician decided that your complaints were in your mind. Your symptoms are manifold and change from time to time. You have pain, *sexual performance problems,* gastro-intestinal disturbances, and neurological complaints such as weakness and blurry vision. You may have difficulty describing your experiences in a consistent or logical fashion, giving others the impression that your complaints, though intense, are vague, shifting, and overlapping. You may impress others as being *histrionic* and hungry for attention and validation.

Hypochondriasis is similar to somatization disorder but is found equally among men and women. If you suffer from hypochondriasis you are convinced that you have an undiagnosed medical illness. For example, you may be certain that you have cancer, AIDS, or another systemic infection, even though your medical workup is clean and you remain healthy. You may have a number of unexplained physical complaints but typically not as many as you would have in somatization. Rather than complaining about everything, you have a particular set of complaints and a specific illness that you suspect you have contracted. Someone close to you may have recently died or been diagnosed with a serious illness, or you may have just recovered from an illness yourself, so you feel that you know what you are talking about. You suspect that your doctor must not be looking hard enough. In time you may abandon one concern only to develop another. As many as one in twenty may have hypochondriacal fears.

Psychiatrists are not certain what causes somatoform disorders such as somatization, hypochondriasis, chronic pain, and, perhaps, chronic *fatigue*. Bouts of these illnesses often come on or are exacerbated during times of *stress*. There is some evidence that individuals with these illnesses are more sensitive to physical sensations. Most of us ignore the minor aches or cramps that we experience every day. If we feel a bit fatigued we work through it. If our heads starts to throb we try to distract ourselves with another activity. If we have a cough, diarrhea, or nausea, we wait a couple of days to see if the symptoms resolve on their own, rather than rush to the doctor's office. If you have a somatoform disorder, though, these common sensations and symptoms may trigger worries and be interpreted as harbingers of serious illness. You may have learned that, when you complain about these symptoms, your loved ones and your doctors support you and try to reassure you. You may not be accustomed to getting attention any other way. You may also benefit from having a reason to take off some time from work or to avoid chores, though you certainly would not say that you are enjoying yourself as a result.

Body dysmorphic disorder is a condition in which you are convinced that aspects of your *body image* are obviously disfigured. You do not believe that you have an illness, as you would in hypochondriasis, but you are intensely bothered by your looks. You may seek surgery to correct your supposed defects, but you will almost certainly be dissatisfied with the results.

Both hypochondriasis and body dysmorphic disorder arise from false beliefs, but they are generally not thought of as delusions. You are able to discuss your belief that you are ill or disfigured in a manner that does not completely break from reality. On the other hand, somatic *delusions,* which generally involve more bizarre beliefs, can occur in schizophrenia and severe *depression*. For example, while *psychotic* you may believe that your body is infested with parasites or that your organs are rotting. The physical complaints of psychotic patients should not be ignored, especially since individuals with severe mental illness are often more vulnerable to serious medical illnesses. I once treated a patient with schizophrenia who complained of a pain in his throat, which he attributed to being forced to swallow glass. His belief about swallowing glass was delusional, but his pain and trouble swallowing were real, and we found an esophageal tumor during a medical workup.

Conversion disorder is a rare condition in which a person responds to a psychological stress by suddenly developing a neurological problem. For example, you may suddenly experience paralysis of your legs after surviving a rape. Or you may become blind after witnessing a murder. The symptoms come on abruptly and appear to result from the *dissociation* of, or inability to confront consciously, a terrifying memory or conflict. Your symptoms may resolve abruptly once the underlying psychological conflict is explored in therapy or elicited during hypnosis.

How to Cope with Pain and Physical Concerns

If you suffer from persistent pain or multiple physical complaints, a medical evaluation is necessary. The goal of a medical workup is not to determine whether your complaints are real. The goal is to find out whether there may be specific underlying conditions that can be treated, hopefully leading to some relief from your symptoms. A medical workup should include screening for psychiatric illnesses, like *depression* and *anxiety,* which might underlie or exacerbate your condition.

If you have a tendency to feel that you are recurrently ill, in the absence of any probable medical cause you may be diagnosed with a somatoform disorder such as hypochondriasis or somatization. You may be referred to a psychiatrist or therapist to help you understand how you express or satisfy your emotional needs in the form of physical complaints and contact with caregivers. A therapist will avoid trying to reassure you, which is unlikely to be effective, but will help you to see the overall pattern of your illness. You will come to recognize that there is no need for you to fear the worst when you experience vague discomforts. You may learn to monitor your body somewhat less vigilantly and to forgive the occasional gassy cramp, headache, or back spasm. Relaxation therapy (see "Anxiety") may help you to better manage these physical sensations and accompanying fears. These and other cognitive-behavioral interventions can be effective about half the time in reducing symptoms, worries, and visits to the doctor.

If you have a somatoform disorder you may be inclined to go to many different physicians. You may feel that specialists should address your many different complaints. You may find that one doctor is more sympathetic when another does not take you seriously enough. The result is that no doctor has a complete picture of your illness, and your care becomes fragmented. One of the first steps in your treatment is for you to select a single physician to address your concerns. You may need short, regular visits as often as once a month so that you feel your health is being adequately monitored. Your doctor will get to know you well and will help guide you through the waxing and waning of your condition. He will recognize that you can get sick just like anyone else, so an occasional test or consultation may be necessary. However, you and your doctor should try to avoid repeated and invasive workups that are unlikely to uncover anything new or provide you with much reassurance.

If you care for someone who tends to be somatic, you should recognize that her discomfort and distress is real, even if it does not arise from a treatable medical condition. You should be supportive of her emotional needs without getting carried away in her quests to obtain medical relief. For example, you can discuss with her how she feels about missing an engagement because of painful cramps, but you should not rush her to the hospital. You should encourage her to help herself rather than rely on others when she feels disabled. Sometimes the medical problem becomes a distraction for both the patient and her loved ones from their own emotional conflicts. You should try to steer your loved one into therapy, where these issues can be addressed, and encourage her to stick with one medical doctor. You may be able to provide useful information to any doctors and therapist about the pattern of illness and associated psychological stresses or emotional problems.

Pain and physical discomfort can be psychologically stressful, whether they stem from identifiable medical problems or not. You may find that your loved one's personality traits are put to the test during the course of a serious or chronic illness. Most people become more dependent on others during an illness, even if they were previously very independent. Many also become irritable and frustrated, if not depressed. You may feel that you are giving more while being appreciated less. You should recognize that this is a temporary situation resulting from illness, and not a permanent change in your loved one's personality. Do not take it personally. You should not get angry or avoid your loved one. Instead, remind her that you need to take care of other business from time to time but that you will be available when she needs you. You should make time for yourself to relax or to do things that you enjoy.

Analgesic Medications

There are a variety of medical treatments for pain. The physician who manages the cause of your pain usually prescribes the treatment. For example, you are more likely to receive your pain treatment from a family doctor, internist, or surgeon than from a psychiatrist. However, your psychiatrist may be involved if your symptoms arise from, or are complicated by, *anxiety,* trouble *sleeping,* or *depression.* In more complicated cases of chronic pain a multidisciplinary team, sometimes including anesthesiologists and psychologists, may work together to find treatments that bring you some relief. It is most important that, if you have more than one physician assisting you with pain relief, they coordinate the care that they provide. Otherwise no single physician understands the full picture of your illness, and the treatment prescribed may be incomplete or inappropriate. You may also risk legal problems, as some pain medications are potentially addicting and tightly regulated.

The most commonly used pain relievers are over-the-counter products. Acetylsalicylic acid, commonly known as aspirin, has multiple uses. It relieves pain by inhibiting chemicals that are released when tissues are injured or inflamed. It also reduces fever and blood clotting. Nonsteroidal anti-inflammatory drugs, such as ibuprofen (Motrin), have similar properties. Both types of anti-inflammatory medications can cause gastric irritation and bleeding, though the risk may be lower with some of the newer medications (such as celecoxib, or Celebrex), which are available only by prescription. Acetaminophen (in Tylenol and many cold preparations) also relieves pain, probably through direct action on chemicals in the brain; it does not reduce inflammation. Even though many of these medications are sold over-the-counter, they are not harmless, particularly if they are taken with other medications. For example, the nonsteroidal anti-inflammatory drugs can dramatically increase lithium levels. Acetaminophen can be toxic to the liver. Each of these medications may be more dangerous if you drink a lot of alcohol.

Opium, derived from a type of poppy plant, has provided pain relief for thousands of years. Morphine was extracted from opium in the nineteenth century, and many other opiate medications have been extracted or synthesized since (including codeine, hydrocodone, hydromorphone, and methadone). Opiates work by attaching to chemical receptors in the brain and on nerve cells throughout the body, leading to a suppression of pain sensation. Unfortunately, opiate medications are potentially addicting, and even if you do not experience addiction you may develop tolerance and require increasingly higher doses to achieve the same degree of pain relief. Opiates are available only by prescription and are closely regulated as narcotics. In spite of the potential for abuse, opiate medications are tremendously effective and can be used safely in most cases. Neither physicians nor patients should be afraid of using opiates for the short-term relief of acute pain. They have also been used successfully in the treatment of chronic pain from cancer and arthritis when other treatments fail. Side effects include sleepiness, sadness, nausea, itchiness, constipation, and, at very high doses, trouble breathing.

Tramadol (Ultram) is a synthetic medication that has effects and side effects similar to the opiate medications, even though it is chemically different. It can induce seizures and should be used cautiously with certain other medications, such as antidepressants.

Narcotics Are Not the Only Treatments for Pain

A variety of psychiatric and neurological medications are sometimes used in the treatment of pain, even though they are not primarily analgesic medications. The tricyclic antidepressants (see "Depression") are useful in relatively low doses for the treatment of chronic pain. The SSRI antidepressants do not seem to have the same analgesic effects, though they are effective in the treatment of premenstrual syndrome (PMS). Anticonvulsant medications, such as gabapentin (Neurontin) and carbamazepine (Tegretol), are particularly effective for chronic neuropathic pain. Cyclobenzaprine (Flexeril) and baclofen (Lioresal) are muscle relaxants that can be useful in the treatment of back pain arising from muscle spasm. However, they are potentially addicting and should not be used for chronic pain.

There are two topical treatments for pain. Lidocaine patches can be applied directly to areas of the skin afflicted by pain. They have proven to be especially useful in the treatment of sharp, burning pain associated with herpes outbreaks. They are worn for twelve hours at a time and then removed for twelve hours. They may not become fully effective until they have been worn for a week or two. Capsaicin is a derivative of the hot pepper plant. The FDA has not rigorously tested this natural product, and its efficacy is uncertain. When first applied, it causes an intense burning pain. If you have ever rubbed your eyes while cooking with fresh hot chili peppers, you know the sensation. With prolonged use, however, capsaicin is thought to exhaust the release of natural chemicals that create the sensation of pain. Capsaicin cream can be rubbed into painful areas afflicted by arthritis or other chronic sources of pain.

Several nonpharmacological approaches to pain relief can also be tried. Your body releases natural pain-relieving chemicals when you exercise. If you can engage in exercise without worsening an injury, you may find it ameliorates pain, elevates your spirits, and gives you a sense of being able to overcome adversity. Yoga and massage may help stretch muscles and joints and bring relief to points of tenderness or tension. Some people experience relief from acupuncture or chiropractic adjustment of the spine, though physicians often do not recommend these unproven treatments. Finally, the application of cold packs or heating pads may bring some soothing relief or distraction from muscular and skeletal pain.

Psychosis

You have noticed that something odd is happening. When you walk down the street people whisper to each other. Store clerks stare at you when you pass their windows. Women smoking in the doorways of buildings look at you and then look at each other and laugh. What are they looking at? You showered and put on clean clothes. Your hair is combed. Then you notice that some people pucker their lips together or wink at you when you cross the street or enter a coffee shop. That never happened before. Are your organs getting bigger or putting out some smell? Maybe your roommate has secretly added something to your laundry detergent.

Several weeks go by, and you are having trouble sleeping. You hear music from somewhere nearby, and it is getting louder; the walls pulse in time to the music. In the darkness of your room you see a pulsing light. Some ritual is taking place in another room, and something frightening could burst through into your room at any minute. You close your eyes, but you can still see the light. You start to pray silently, but your voice comes back at you from the wall. You think, "My God," and the word "God" echoes across the room. In horror you hear a voice asking whether God exists. What if they can hear you in the other room? What if God can hear you?

You grab a jacket and run out of the apartment. On the street you see shadows flying back and forth between the buildings. You run to a police car at the corner. The police officer rolls down his window, and you explain to him that something evil is happening in your apartment. He says that he cannot understand what you are saying. He asks if you need help. You start to repeat your story.

Then you hear a voice from the back seat of the police car. You lean closer to see who is speaking. Someone in the shadows mutters, "You can get her now, or you can get her later." You turn and run, dropping your jacket. You don't dare look back.

Psychosis is an old but commonly misunderstood psychiatric term that has a very simple meaning. To be psychotic is to be out of touch with reality. We have all awoke from a dream where the impossible is happening, but it seems real. For example, most of us have had dreams where we are able to fly, become other people, speak fluently in another language, or have a relationship with someone famous. We have also had dreams where we are being chased, perhaps by someone whose identity changes several times. Maybe those closest to us are trying to hurt us. Those dreams seem so real that, even after awakening, we wonder if they could hold some truth.

Psychosis is experienced like a dream. Rules of logic bend or evaporate. Random occurrences become significant. The impossible seems plausible: spells, poison, telepathy, mind control, and superhuman ability. When you experience psychosis you feel trapped in a nightmare. When you recover you may be unable to remember what happened when you were psychotic. On the other hand, you may be able to look back on what you experienced with complete clarity, amazed that the impossible could have seemed so real.

When we dream, we usually do not realize that we are dreaming. Unfortunately, the same is true of psychosis. When you are psychotic everything seems real. You are convinced that you are doing the best you can to make sense of the confusion around you. If someone tells you that you are being unrealistic, or that you are acting crazy, you think that they do not realize what is really going on. You may begin to suspect that they are trying to hide something from you, that they are in on the plot.

In common speech the word "psychotic" is used inaccurately to refer to someone who is evil or unpredictable, such as a "psychotic killer." This is not at all what psychiatrists mean when they use the term. To a doctor psychotic is simply the word used to describe someone who is experiencing psychosis. It does not imply that the person is evil or beyond help. On the contrary, there are treatments that are very effective for psychosis.

Psychosis is a syndrome, a cluster of symptoms that affects thinking and perception in several different ways. These include hallucinations, delusions, and disorganized thinking. *Hallucinations* are false perceptions, such as hearing voices or seeing things that are not, in fact, present. *Delusions* are false beliefs that are maintained with no evidence, or in spite of evidence to the contrary. Disorganized thinking is usually evident by *nonsensical* speech, or by what psychiatrists refer to as loose associations. If you are suffering from disorganized thinking you may be strangely unaware of how bizarre you sound, or you may experience a profound *confusion*.

Psychosis Is Most Commonly Seen in Schizophrenia

Psychosis is classically associated with schizophrenia, though it can be seen in several other illnesses as well. Schizophrenia is not, as commonly believed, a split personality, though that is close to the literal meaning of the word. People with schizophrenia do not switch back and forth between two or more distinct personalities (something like that happens in multiple personality disorder; see "Dissociation"). Rather, schizophrenia is a chronic medical illness of the brain characterized by psychotic episodes. Schizophrenia occurs in approximately one to two percent of Americans, but it causes ten percent of permanent disability in the United States.

Anyone can develop schizophrenia. It does not matter if you are intelligent, well educated, wealthy, raised by loving parents, or otherwise healthy. When I was in college a bright student in my dormitory became ill with schizophrenia. A Nobel laureate in economics suffered from schizophrenia. Your chances increase tenfold if a close family member has schizophrenia. Schizophrenia is somewhat more common in cities, perhaps because rural communities provide more support and less stressful lifestyles to those who show early signs of the illness. Or people who develop schizophrenia may move from the countryside to the cities, increasing the urban rates. Research has shown that schizophrenia is a universal illness that presents itself in a similar fashion and at similar rates in every country and among every ethnic group.

Schizophrenia typically begins during the teenage or early adult years. On average, men develop the illness about ten years earlier than women. Before becoming psychotic, a person with schizophrenia may experience what psychiatrists call prodromal symptoms, or early signs of the illness. School grades deteriorate. You have trouble completing assignments. You have trouble getting to work on time. You stop dating. You lose touch with friends. You start to develop interests in odd subjects like extrasensory perception, mystical cults, conspiracy theories, or aliens. You begin to drink or use drugs. You lose your temper and get into fights. You may become *religiously preoccupied*. Your sleep, hygiene, and eating habits change. You appear perplexed, distracted, and downbeat. Your speech becomes vague, and you have difficulty making plans. There may be other explanations for these behaviors, such as *depression* or an evolving drug problem (see "Intoxication"), but in some cases these are early signs of schizophrenia.

The first episode of psychosis may develop over several weeks or months, often following a stressful event such as the death of a close friend or relative, the birth of a child, an arrest, leaving home for college, studying for final exams, or running out of money. You may realize that something is wrong, though you may believe the problem lies outside of yourself, in how others treat you. You are unlikely to realize that you are sick and in need of treatment (see "Denial"). You may think that everyone goes through similar growing pains. You probably have no knowledge of mental illness, and your thinking is confused. However, if you have watched a family member struggle with mental illness you may realize that you need help. On the other hand, you may be frightened and hide from the truth.

If you live or work with a person who is becoming psychotic, you may realize that something is wrong. You may think she is just going through a phase, coping with *stress*, or having a spiritual crisis. You may think that she is behaving differently on purpose, and that you have no right to interfere. If you do try to intervene she may tell you it is none of your business. If she is *paranoid* she may be secretive, distrustful, and disinclined to let you and others know what she is experiencing. For all these reasons it may be possible for her to conceal the illness from herself and others until it becomes severe. In that case no one realizes how sick she has become until she is no longer able to hide the fact that she is hearing voices and is frightened and confused.

What happens during a first episode of schizophrenia? At some point it is likely that you will be brought to medical attention, perhaps by family, friends, colleagues, teachers, or even the police. Depending on the severity of symptoms and your ability to participate in treatment, you may be referred to outpatient treatment, or you may be admitted to the hospital.

Medication is essential to the treatment of schizophrenia. You will be treated with medications that make you less anxious almost immediately. Over a few days you begin to make more sense when you speak. You become less confused. Your sleep, hygiene, and appetite improve. Over a couple of weeks the hallucinations become faint and less frequent. Over a month or two the delusions fade. You realize that no one is trying to harm you. It may take more time and education before you truly understand that so much that seemed real was caused by mental illness. Sometimes these changes take place very quickly; you may be back in touch with reality in just a few days or a couple of weeks.

Generally, psychotic symptoms that come on rapidly are likely to respond quickly to treatment. If the illness comes on slowly over many months, then it may take longer to respond to medication. The longer that a person is psychotic during any episode, the more difficult it becomes to treat, and each new episode of psychosis may be more difficult to treat as well. For these reasons it is very important, if you have responded well to treatment, for you to take preventive measures to avoid becoming psychotic again. In most cases the way to avoid becoming psychotic in the future is to stay on medication.

Even before medications were available for the treatment of schizophrenia, some psychiatrists observed that the prognosis after a first episode of psychosis varied. Approximately one-third of the patients never experienced a second episode. Another third of the patients had a relapsing course with several future episodes. Between each episode these patients did fairly well. Finally, about one-third of the patients continued to experience psychotic symptoms that worsened over time. This observation probably does not apply today for two reasons. First, it is likely that many of those patients would not be diagnosed with schizophrenia today. Those who recovered completely in a short period of time might be diagnosed with *mania* or with a brief psychotic disorder. Second, we now prescribe medications that significantly improve the course of illness for virtually all people with schizophrenia. More recent studies have found that only about one in ten recover completely from schizophrenia, but also only one in ten fail to improve at all with medication.

For most patients schizophrenia is a chronic illness with a relapsing course. With medications and therapy it is possible for some people with schizophrenia to function largely free of symptoms. It is possible to hold a job, marry, and have children. For many, some residual symptoms persist, even with medication. People with schizophrenia often experience what psychiatrists call negative or deficit symptoms of schizophrenia, and these are particularly evident between acute psychotic episodes. Negative symptoms include social withdrawal, apathy, poor hygiene, diminished emotional responses, and subtle impairments in thinking (especially abstract thinking, problem solving, and maintaining concentration). These symptoms contribute to an appearance of *oddness,* even for those patients who are otherwise symptom free.

Finally, in spite of medications, about one in twenty patients experience ongoing severe symptoms, which may get worse with time. This outcome has become rarer as new medications have been developed.

Psychosis Can Occur in Several Other Illnesses

Some people become psychotic for a short period of time in response to severe *stress.* This is an example of what many people would refer to as a nervous breakdown. You may get better after the stress has passed, even without medication. You do not experience a subsequent psychotic episode. Psychiatrists refer to this as a brief psychotic disorder if it lasts less than a month. Some people become psychotic during drug use (which may be a normal effect of the drug), but the psychotic episode persists for several days after the drug is consumed. In both cases, a diagnosis of schizophrenia is not made unless the psychotic episodes occur again.

Schizophreniform disorder is a diagnosis that is made when you have the signs and symptoms of schizophrenia, but the psychotic episode lasts for less than six months. This is a provisional diagnosis. In most cases psychotic symptoms persist or recur, eventually leading to a diagnosis of schizophrenia. Even if symptoms do not last long enough to merit a diagnosis of schizophrenia, you should take steps to reduce the risk of becoming psychotic in the future: reducing the stress in your life, eliminating drug and alcohol use, and getting adequate rest.

Both *depression* and *mania* can become so severe that you eventually lose touch with reality. When this occurs, it does not mean that you have schizophrenia. However, you may need to be treated with antipsychotic medications temporarily, in addition to antidepressant and mood-stabilizing medications. Schizoaffective disorder is an illness like schizophrenia in which episodes of depression or mania also occur while the patient is psychotic. Schizoaffective illness is nearly as common as schizophrenia. It is important to differentiate between schizophrenia and schizoaffective disorder because the mood swings may be best treated with antidepressant or mood-stabilizing medications, in addition to antipsychotic medications. If you have schizoaffective disorder your first-degree relatives are at higher risk of developing schizophrenia, but half are also likely to have depression or bipolar disorder (see "Mania").

Some people experience long-standing delusional beliefs but are never troubled by hallucinations or disorganized thinking. The *delusions* do not change much over time, and they are not bizarre. Psychiatrists refer to this less common pattern of illness as a delusional disorder. It typically develops later in life than schizophrenia. If you develop new psychotic symptoms abruptly late in life, you are much more likely to be suffering from delirium (see "Confusion") due to an underlying medical illness. Delirium is a medical emergency that requires a complete physical workup. Often the underlying cause can be treated.

What Causes Psychosis?

We do not know what causes schizophrenia or other psychotic illnesses. Clearly there is a genetic predisposition, since the risk of schizophrenia increases dramatically within families and among identical twins, even if they have grown up with different families. Some schizophrenic traits are commonly found in family members, and some may have *paranoid* or schizotypal (see "Oddness") personalities. But scientists have not discovered the genes that cause the illness. And genes could not tell the entire story, since schizophrenia does not always develop in those who have a genetic predisposition. If one identical twin has schizophrenia, the other will develop schizophrenia only half of the time.

The prevailing theory has focused on the chemical signal, dopamine. Medications that treat schizophrenia are known to block the effects of dopamine in the brain. Some drugs that cause delusions and hallucination (such as cocaine and psychedelic drugs) boost the effect of dopamine. This theory is one reason why doctors and patients tend to speak of a chemical imbalance in the brain. Glutamate and serotonin are two other brain chemicals that may play a role.

Other theories focus on brain anatomy and development. There are several neurological indications that people with schizophrenia have diminished functioning in the frontal lobe of the brain (the section directly behind the forehead). This may be because some brain cells that are stimulated by dopamine reach into the frontal lobe. It may be because brain cells develop differently in at least some people with schizophrenia. Since most people with schizophrenia are treated with medication, often for years, it is difficult to distinguish between the effects of the medication and the effects of the underlying disease when studying their brains.

There are some indications that schizophrenia could be caused by a viral infection or exposure to chemicals or malnourishment in the womb. Later in life a head injury or drug use might precipitate schizophrenia in someone who has a genetic predisposition. Fluctuations in the mother's hormone levels in childbirth may also rarely precipitate a psychotic illness known as postpartum psychosis.

There has been some research into the social stresses that may exacerbate schizophrenia. The theory that blamed emotionally distant mothers for the schizophrenia of their children has long been discredited. Subsequent research has shown that episodes of illness are often preceded by a major stressful event such as the death of a family member. However, individuals with schizophrenia have not had a greater number of stressors in their life than others who do not develop schizophrenia. A family environment in which anger and other emotions are expressed openly and frequently may contribute to psychotic relapses but does not cause the illness.

How to Cope with Psychosis

Contrary to general opinion schizophrenia is a treatable illness. Medication is essential, and symptoms are generally reduced or eliminated with medication. Approximately seventy percent of patients suffering from schizophrenia improve with the first medication prescribed for their illness. The sooner treatment is started, the better the long-term outcome. Unfortunately, most people with psychotic illness do not take their medication consistently, and many experience a recurrence. If you have schizophrenia and stop your medication, you will most likely have a recurrence within a year, and almost certainly within two years.

There are several reasons why you may stop medication. No one likes to take medication, whether they have a mental illness or not. All medications can have unpleasant side effects, even if they are mild, and doctors sometimes do not pay enough attention to side effects. Side effects are usually most severe in the first week or two of treatment, whereas the benefits of medication are often not evident for several weeks. Some paranoid patients believe that the medication is intended to harm them. Finally, nearly every person with schizophrenia has doubts about her diagnosis at one time or another and stops her medication because she believes that she no longer needs it (see "Denial"). For many, lack of insight into the nature of their illness and the need for medication is a persistent or recurrent problem. Education and family support are important in maintaining medication compliance.

Typically, when a psychotic episode recurs you experience the same symptoms that you experienced in previous episodes. Learn which symptoms appear first: for example, trouble sleeping, vague worries, suspiciousness, headaches, or difficulty concentrating. Your warning signs will be unique for you, and your family, friends, and doctor will help you to identify them. If those close to you notice changes before you do, pay attention to them. They may notice when you are becoming more isolated or irritable. It can be annoying when other people tell you that you are getting sick, but you need that outside perspective when you are not thinking clearly.

If you have chronic or "negative" symptoms (see "Oddness") between psychotic episodes, then you may need some assistance in daily living. You may live in a sheltered residence and work under supervision. You may engage in rehabilitation therapy to learn to communicate with others, reduce your symptoms, avoid stress, and manage your medications.

Most individuals with schizophrenia also have difficulties with the abuse of alcohol or drugs. Psychiatrists refer to this as a dual diagnosis. You may benefit from specific treatment of your *cravings*, especially since drugs and alcohol tend to exacerbate psychotic symptoms.

There is also a high rate of *suicidal thinking* among people with schizophrenia, and suicide does not always occur during a psychotic episode. Sometimes it is the reality of living with a serious illness that leads to hopelessness and despair. With proper support and treatment you can live a good life with schizophrenia. But if you become hopeless and sad or begin to feel that life is not worth living, it is crucial that you tell someone immediately. Go to an emergency room if no one else is available to help you. Antidepressant medications (see "Depression") may help relieve feelings of sadness and hopelessness before you become desperate and suicidal.

If someone you care about has been diagnosed with schizophrenia, you should learn as much about the illness as you can. Schizophrenia is a chronic and often severely disabling illness, and you should be realistic in your expectations about your loved one's potential to function at the same level as before she became ill. You should be optimistic about treatment and rehabilitation, but accept that there is no cure. You may experience *grief* over the loss of potential. You may grieve for the loss of the relationship that you used to have, if your loved one has changed in her personality style and ability to communicate and enjoy things that you used to enjoy together. You may also feel guilty, even though the illness is no one's fault. Because many people do not understand schizophrenia, you may feel embarrassed or ashamed when your loved one behaves peculiarly in public.

You should try to maintain an attitude of equanimity and acceptance when coping with your loved one and the unusual behaviors that are common in schizophrenia. If she withdraws to her room, has difficulties with chores, dresses strangely or starts to shout, do not panic and do not get angry. If she has *delusions,* respond honestly but do not try to argue with her. If you understand her symptoms, then her behaviors do not seem so odd. You will learn to be flexible while at the same time encouraging your loved one to be reasonably socially appropriate. You want to treat her naturally, not as if she were a child or someone stupid.

One of your most important roles is to help monitor for fluctuations in her symptoms. She is likely to lose insight into the nature of her illness as she becomes more psychotic, so you may be in the best position to recognize that she needs to see a doctor. You should be alert for warning signs, which may be similar from one episode to the next. Nervousness, irritability, moodiness, trouble sleeping, social withdrawal, and a perplexed appearance are typical warning signs in general.

You may find it helpful to join a self-help group or advocacy organization to meet other families who cope with schizophrenia. You may find the experiences and tips of other families useful in coping with your loved one's illness. You may find other families supportive during times of crisis.

Most of us are frightened by the possibility of psychosis in ourselves or in others. To some extent being around someone who has schizophrenia reminds us of the disturbing fact that we are vulnerable to losing our mind. We also feel uncomfortable in the presence of someone whose behavior and interpersonal skills are odd. But more frightening is the fact that we have all heard on the news about people with mental illness who have committed bizarre and violent crimes. In fact, the vast majority of people with schizophrenia do not harm others, especially if they are taking their medication. People with severe and persistent illnesses like schizophrenia are much more likely to be the victims of violence. Most people with schizophrenia live in poor neighborhoods with high crime rates. They are often perceived as easy targets. People with schizophrenia are more likely to be sexually assaulted and to exchange sex for money, food, or drugs. They are also more likely to be the victims of discrimination in housing, employment, and medical care.

Antipsychotic Medication

The mainstay of treatment for schizophrenia and other psychotic illnesses is antipsychotic medication. The first antipsychotic medication was discovered around 1950 and revolutionized the treatment of mental illness. For the first time it was possible to treat schizophrenia, and thousands of people benefited. State hospitals were able to discharge patients who had been in a psychotic state for decades. Before medications were invented schizophrenia was "treated" through dubious methods such as wrapping patients in cold, wet blankets or injecting insulin to induce temporary comas. Psychiatry has come a long way since then. In the last fifty years, many antipsychotic medications have been developed. These have been referred to in the past as neuroleptic medications or tranquilizers (terms that are somewhat frightening and misleading because they refer to the side effects, rather than the beneficial effects, of the medications). In the past decade several new antipsychotic medications with unique properties have come on the market, and these have further improved the quality of life for people with schizophrenia. Antipsychotic medications are among the safest medications in use today. The side effects are typically mild and reversible (they go away when the medication is stopped or switched). Without medication, psychosis usually gets worse.

The first generation of antipsychotic medications includes, for example, the commonly prescribed haloperidol (Haldol), fluphenazine (Prolixin), and chlorpromazine (Thorazine). Since these medications are all equally effective at treating psychosis they are usually distinguished only by their most common side effects. Medications like haloperidol and fluphenazine may cause stiffness, tremors, and an internal sense of restlessness (known as akathisia). Medications like chlorpromazine may cause dry mouth, blurry vision, constipation, and sedation. These side effects are easily treated, in most cases, by reducing the dose or by adding another medication to treat the side effects. Each of these first-generation medications is effective at treating hallucinations, delusions, and disorganized thinking. Long-acting injectible forms of haloperidol and fluphenazine (known as depot or decanoate preparations) are available for those patients who have difficulty taking pills on a daily basis.

Another side effect, known as tardive dyskinesia (commonly referred to as TD), usually takes years to develop and appears only in a minority of patients. Patients can develop sinuous, rolling *movements* of various body parts. TD usually starts in the tongue, face, and fingers but can extend to the arms, legs, and trunk. All antipsychotic medications, with the exception of clozapine, can cause TD, but it occurs most commonly with the first generation of antipsychotic medications. All antipsychotic medications can also cause problems with *sexual performance*.

Newer Antipsychotic Medications Have Fewer Side Effects

The second generation of antipsychotic medications is commonly referred to as the atypical antipsychotics, because they have different effects on the brain. These atypical medications, which include risperidone (Risperdal), olanzapine (Zyprexa), quetiapine (Seroquel), ziprasidone (Geodon), and aripiprazole (Abilify) have become the first-line treatment of schizophrenia. They generally have fewer side effects than the first-generation medications. Also, unlike the older medications they treat the negative symptoms of schizophrenia. Individuals who have been withdrawn, apathetic, and sloppy seem to come back to life. Many of these newer medications can cause weight gain and sedation. Some can also sometimes precipitate diabetes, though sugar levels usually improve if the medication is stopped. Risperidone is now available in a long-acting injectible form.

Clozapine (Clozaril) is a unique antipsychotic medication. About half the individuals who have not improved when treated with other antipsychotic medications respond well to clozapine. It treats the negative symptoms of schizophrenia and reduces the risk of *suicide* and violence. Like the other second-generation medications, clozapine does not cause stiffness or tremors. And clozapine appears to be the only antipsychotic medication that does not cause tardive dyskinesia; in fact, it treats TD. The improvement that some patients experience on clozapine is almost magical. Many patients consider it a miracle drug because it helps them to feel like they did before they developed schizophrenia.

Why isn't everyone treated with clozapine? Clozapine is not the initial treatment for schizophrenia because it has some serious side effects. For many years, clozapine was not approved for release in the United States because several patients treated with it in other countries had died unexpectedly. It turned out that clozapine can rarely (in one out of one hundred cases) cause a dangerous drop in the level of infection-fighting white blood cells. Doctors refer to this as agranulocytosis or leukopenia. The drop is reversible if it is detected early. Because of this risk clozapine was approved for use in the United States only under the condition that every patient treated with clozapine have blood drawn on a weekly basis to check the level of white blood cells. Of course, this can be expensive and inconvenient. The risk of agranulocytosis is greatest during the first six months of treatment. After that, blood draws are reduced in frequency to every two weeks.

Other side effects of clozapine include sedation, weight gain, drooling, and, at high doses, possible seizures. In spite of these side effects and the inconvenience of blood draws clozapine is clearly the most effective antipsychotic medication available, and it has transformed the quality of life for many people with schizophrenia.

The second generation of antipsychotic medications is more expensive than the first generation, because these medications have not been around long enough to be available in generic preparations. However, studies have repeatedly demonstrated that these newer medications, including clozapine, are more cost-effective than the older medications, because they reduce hospitalization time, suicide rates, and overall disability. They also improve quality of life in a way that is difficult to price.

Religious Preoccupations

"O come, let us sing to the Lord!"

You stand in the middle of the street with the Bible held over your head. Why isn't everyone singing? Commuters honk and drive around you. Children on their way to school scurry by you nervously. Don't they realize that God could come today?

The voice came to you in the middle of the night: "Send out thy light and thy truth." You stayed up all night. You turned on all the lights in the house and the garage. You carried candles out to the street and lit them. You stuffed newspaper into a garbage can and were about to light it when the sun started to rise. You took that as a sign that God was pleased, and you took to the streets to announce his arrival.

Religious beliefs play a healthy, perhaps essential, role in most people's lives. Religion in its broadest meaning is a sense of awe and usually involves faith, worship, and a shared system of belief about the universe. Religious feeling is a highly individual trait that often combines traditional inherited beliefs, personal transcendent experiences, and a willingness to believe that which you cannot prove to others. Scientists of the mind have sometimes tried to explain away faith as a product of emotional need and delusional thinking, but that ignores the reality that, for many people, religious faith makes life worth living.

Perhaps because religion is so powerful in people's lives psychiatric symptoms often have a religious flavor. Especially during a *manic* episode, which can occur in bipolar disorder or manic-depression, you feel as if you have come close to God. Early during the onset of mania you may become more fervent in your religious feelings. You may carry the Bible or Koran everywhere you go and quote from it to strangers. You may stay up late reading chapters and hymns. You may go to your synagogue or church every day, or kneel to pray every few minutes. Your religious practices and convictions may depart dramatically from your usual. For example, I have treated several Christians who became convinced that they were Jewish and adopted Orthodox hairstyles and outfits throughout their hospitalization. You may become preoccupied with the religious beliefs, identity, or salvation of others. I treated one woman who repeatedly voiced her intention to save my soul.

During a manic episode you may feel as if you are on the verge of receiving a personal revelation yourself. The ancient statements of saints, mystics, and prophets suddenly seem to have been written about you and current events. You feel that you have been chosen as the vessel of revelation to others. You may come to believe that you can see through the differences between religions, that you will bring all people together in one universal belief. You may stand on the street shouting out wisdom, sharing your experience with others. This feeling of transcendence, revelation, and oneness with others is an aspect of the *euphoric* mood that is characteristic of mania. The belief that you are a Messiah or God is an example of a *grandiose* delusion.

It is also common to experience *hallucinations*, or false perceptions, of a religious nature. Perhaps it is only natural to assume that a seemingly disembodied voice comes from God. Sometimes voices tell you that you are the Messiah. The voices may tell you that you have special powers, that you have been resurrected, and that you cannot die. You may experience visual hallucinations that appear to be of a personal savior or a radiant angel. If you suffer from schizophrenia (see "Psychosis") you may also experience more frightening hallucinations that seem to come from the devil or demons. I have worked with many patients who feel cursed and tormented because of the frightening and hateful voices that they hear.

Distressing religious feelings also can occur in major *depression*. As your mood becomes more profoundly depressed you feel increasingly hopeless, worthless, and guilty. You may feel abandoned by God or that you are the world's greatest sinner. You may feel that all of the problems of the world are your fault. You may feel that the world is coming to an end. These *delusions* of guilt and nihilism are characteristic of severe, psychotic depression. Depression alters the way that you think, making you pessimistic and sometimes bleakly rational. You may have a crisis of faith, concluding that God does not exist and that life has no meaning. If you are considering *suicide,* then the loss of a relationship with God, or with your religious community, increases the risk that you may attempt to kill yourself. On the other hand, preexisting religious faith may sustain you or restrict you from considering suicide as an option.

Some individuals with obsessive-compulsive disorder (OCD) have religious symptoms. You may *obsess* about being a sinner. You may experience intrusive thoughts and images of a disturbing and sacrilegious nature. You may have *compulsions* to confess your sins, or nonsinful trivialities, repeatedly to your priest.

Drug *intoxication* can sometimes induce religious experiences. The hallucinogens, like LSD, can cause hallucinations and perceptual distortions that may seem to have spiritual significance. Both the hallucinogens and ecstasy can cause a feeling of being at one with other people or with the world around you. You may experience this as positive and mind-expanding or as frightening and chaotic. Many societies around the world have used naturally occurring mind-altering substances in their religious rituals, to put the practitioner directly in touch with the sacred world.

Religion may also play an important role in your life if you are trying to stop using drugs or alcohol (see "Cravings"). Most of the self-help groups for achieving and maintaining sobriety are built upon spiritual faith. As a first step in fighting addiction you are expected to acknowledge that your behavior is out of control and to submit to God or other "higher power." For most groups this acknowledgment of faith does not have to be within a particular denomination, or even explicitly religious. It is the attitude of humility and surrender that is important.

Psychiatrists use the term hyperreligious to characterize the religious preoccupations, expressions, and beliefs of a manic or psychotic patient that are clearly different from the person's usual pattern of beliefs and experiences. However, we must be careful not to misunderstand and incorrectly label a person's religious strategies for coping with illness. Most people seek solace in prayer during episodes of mental illness, just as they do when coping with a medical crisis. This is a normal, healthy response and not a sign of the underlying illness. A rabbi, imam, minister, or other leader from the patient's religious community can help a psychiatrist differentiate normal religious practices and beliefs from those stemming from mental illness.

Of course, if idiosyncratic beliefs were always attributed to mental illness, most religions would be deprived of their prophets. Hearing the voice of God or experiencing angelic visitations, demonic torments, personal revelation, and an expansive concern for the spiritual needs of others are features in the lives of almost all historically important religious figures. Psychiatrists and religious leaders must be cautious of concluding that a religious experience stems from mental illness in the absence of other harmful or disabling symptoms.

Ultimately, religious faith is not affected by medication. If you have experienced religious delusions or hallucinations during the course of your illness, you will recognize the oddness of your beliefs once you have recovered. You may be embarrassed by what, in retrospect, were sacrilegious beliefs or behaviors.

Sometimes a change in religious practices is a sign of other psychological adjustments or difficulties. You may be at a stage in your life where religion no longer seems to be relevant. You may find that you no longer have faith, or that the nature of your faith has changed. You may leave the church that you grew up with, or you may find another religious community that seems more relevant to your evolving beliefs. On the other hand, you may have begun to feel that your life is without meaning, and religion, which you have previously neglected, seems to provide some answers. You may explore one religion after another. These changes in religious practice and belief are often initiated during times of personal crisis or *stress*. Divorce, childbirth, separation from loved ones, or financial setback, for example, may precipitate a reexamination of your relationship to God and your ties to a religious community.

Teenagers and young adults may be particularly open to explore new spiritual ideas because they are at a stage in life when their sense of self is still wide open. People with mental illness may also be drawn to alternative spiritual organizations where they feel less stigmatized, or where their own unusual experiences may be validated. Unfortunately some coercive cults target the vulnerable and exploit their fragile sense of *identity* and poor *self-esteem*. Cults isolate members from family and community and strictly enforce a group identity and common action. Cult leaders use religious faith and charisma as a cover for manipulating and exploiting the financial and personal resources of cult members. Some cult leaders have led their followers in mass *suicide* or homicide. If you suspect that someone you care about is becoming involved in a cult, rather than in a genuine religious community, you should stay as involved as you can in that person's life, providing them an alternative viewpoint and lifestyle that contrasts with the enforced routines of the cult.

Self-Esteem Problems

What an angel! She is your very best friend ever. You met your new boss just yesterday, but you can tell she is the greatest! It's your second day at a new job, and she brought you coffee and muffins. She's so thoughtful and sensitive! You can tell that she's the sort of person who would never hurt you.

Not like that ass you worked for at your last job. You stayed at work for long hours working on that report, and he never even noticed. He asked you to change one of the charts; he said it was inaccurate. Well, it wasn't your fault! He gave you the data. If he wanted you to double-check his sources, he should have said so. And you told him as much.

You told him that if he had the least bit of decency, he would have stayed up late with you to help you finish. Why did he have to race home? As if his wife couldn't spare him for one evening. He must think that you don't have a life, that you have nothing better to do than work late. Well, you've had plenty of boyfriends. You could have a different one every night if you wanted.

You should have said that. Maybe you'll call him up tonight and give him an earful. But for now, you'll just have one of those muffins.

Self-esteem is one aspect of personal identity. It reflects the extent to which you feel good about yourself. Healthy self-esteem strikes a balance. You must be able to realistically acknowledge personal weaknesses and accept mistakes you have made in the past. At the same time you need to feel that you are basically a good person and that your life is worthwhile. Most of us grow up with a feeling that we are valuable, perhaps even special. Presumably we first learn to feel that way from our parents, who seemed to love us unconditionally, even when they scolded or criticized us.

Several mental illnesses are characterized, in part, by a disturbance in normal self-esteem. *Depression* causes you to see everything in a more negative light. You may feel that you are a worthless failure. You may dwell on past mistakes. For example, you might feel guilty for making a sarcastic comment to a friend years earlier, even though she has forgotten about the incident altogether. Poor self-esteem can become so exaggerated that you come to feel that you are responsible for many of the problems in the world. You feel that you have ruined your own life and the lives of those you love. You may begin to feel that you would be better off dead and contemplate *suicide*. If you have an *avoidant* personality disorder you are shy and afraid that others think poorly of you.

At the other extreme, *mania* can inflate self-esteem. You may feel that you are the greatest person in the world. You surprise yourself with your brilliance, sense of humor, and accomplishments. You feel that you can do anything. As mania progresses you may develop *grandiose* delusions of being famous. You may even come to think of yourself as an omnipotent God in human form. This exaggerated self-esteem disappears quickly once mania is treated, or when your mood swings back into depression.

Self-esteem is also artificially elevated in narcissistic personality disorder (see "Grandiosity"). If you have narcissistic traits you may portray yourself as a uniquely competent and accomplished individual with impeccable tastes and remarkable interests. You condescend to most people while seeking out the company of the glamorous and powerful. This veneer of self-importance conceals the underlying feeling that you are unimportant and vulnerable. You fear that even the most pedestrian people are happier and better adjusted than you. You worry that no one will like you unless you make yourself out to be something better. Expressed self-esteem is similarly inflated in *histrionic* personality disorder, again to cover up underlying feelings of inadequacy.

Some people have an overdeveloped conscience and set unrealistically high standards for their own behavior. They criticize themselves when they fail to be as perfect as they think they should be. Therapists have traditionally referred to this as a neurotic character style. (The term "neurotic" has been used more broadly to refer to a wide range of psychiatric difficulties, usually in contrast to "psychotic" conditions. Psychiatrists rarely use the term now because it is so imprecise.) If you have a neurotic style you are probably articulate, competent, reliable, persistent, precise, accomplished, and moral. You may be somewhat controlling and emotionally inhibited, but you view these as positive traits, seeing yourself as someone who follows the rules and always behaves rationally rather than impulsively. Psychiatrists do not label neurotic style as a mental illness, since it is neither disabling nor particularly distressing. However, if you have neurotic traits, you may seek therapy in your quest to more fully understand yourself and your perceived inadequacies or to cope with mild feelings of anxiety or failure. In therapy you explore the roots of your high expectations, and you receive reassurance for being only human.

In some cases mental illness leads to poor self-esteem indirectly, as a result of shame and stigma. For example, if you suffer from *learning difficulties* as a child, you may feel incompetent and stupid compared to your classmates. If you have *panic* attacks in public, you may feel ashamed. If you are addicted to drugs, alcohol, or sex, you may be embarrassed by your inability to control your *cravings*. In anorexia, bulimia, and other disorders of *body image,* you are certain that everyone is appalled by your appearance. Even though mental illness is better understood today than ever before, many people still view the mentally ill as odd, deficient, or dangerous. You may share some of those prejudices yourself and fear that your symptoms are a sign of some weakness in your character. As with other disabilities you need to understand your illness, approach it realistically, and not let it define your life. Educate yourself, your family, and your friends about the illness, and attend self-help groups to meet others who have learned to cope with illness.

Self-Esteem Is Exceedingly Fragile in Borderline Personality Disorder

In the middle of the past century early psychoanalysts began to describe a personality type that they found particularly challenging to treat. These patients initially appeared to be neurotic, functioning well in society but having difficulties with self-esteem. However, in therapy they demonstrated intense rage and desperation and often abandoned treatment. Psychiatrists observed that these patients sometimes seemed to lose touch with reality when overwhelmed by their emotions. Their condition, though poorly understood, was labeled as being on the borderline between neurosis and *psychosis*. The name has been retained, even though many psychiatrists no longer think of borderline personality disorder as an in-between condition.

Borderline personality disorder refers to a constellation of traits that tend to be enduring over time and that deeply disturb your ability to form relationships with others. At the core of the problem is a disturbance in self-esteem. If you have a borderline personality, you feel deeply inadequate. You feel as if you were born into a world with personal deficiencies that keep you from being able to relate to others on an equal footing. You constantly compare yourself with everyone else, and you always find yourself lacking. You feel that you are a reject and a loner, and that you are deeply unlikable. You feel different. You may feel ugly, not just in appearance but at the core. At times you may tell yourself that you are just a piece of shit. The feeling is visceral and painful. You would like to be admired, loved, and accomplished, but you feel that you can never meet anyone's standards.

Family, colleagues, and therapists may be surprised at the depth of your sense of inadequacy. By many measures you may appear to be successful. You may be talented and accomplished at work. You may excel in self-employment or in job situations where you are able to direct others. You may be financially secure. You may seek out volunteer work, where you feel that you are selfless and immune to criticism. You may be physically attractive by most objective measures, and you may go to great lengths to keep up your appearance. You seem to have many acquaintances, and you spend time socializing, at least in groups in which you are not expected to be the center of attention.

Emotions and Behavior Are Poorly Regulated in Borderline Personality

If you have a borderline personality disorder you not only feel different and inadequate, but also emotionally desperate. Every day you feel unhappy and miserable. This chronic feeling is different from the heavy, drowning sadness experienced in clinical *depression*, though you are prone to developing depression as well. The miserable feeling experienced in borderline personality disorder is often described as a chronic feeling of emptiness. You feel that your life is without meaning. You feel that something is missing. You feel constantly anxious, irritable, bored, and listless. You can enjoy activities when you are caught up in them, but the pleasure does not last. Whenever you start to feel good you immediately start to worry that something will go wrong.

In addition to these constant anxious and empty feelings, you are prone to sudden *mood swings*. A profound feeling of worthlessness can sweep over you in a moment, reducing you to tears. Then the phone rings and you become *euphoric* that a friend has called just to say hello. Then you fly into an *angry* rage when the call is interrupted by the delivery of the pizza you had ordered earlier. Within minutes of these mood swings you may recover and dismiss your outburst as if nothing had happened. You wonder why anyone would care that you lost your temper, since you feel fine now. You do not view yourself as a moody person. Rather, you feel that you are doing the best you can to respond to circumstances that are completely out of your control.

Your behavior is also *impulsive*. You act without thinking, responding quickly and in an exaggerated fashion to the tidal changes in your emotions. If your boyfriend breaks up with you, you may pick up your chair and throw it at him. If you score poorly on an exam you may go home and scratch yourself with a razor (see "Self-Mutilation"). If your therapist takes a vacation you may go out in anger, get drunk, and drive into a fire hydrant. You have difficulty thinking of less dramatic ways to soothe yourself when you are feeling bad; you tend to use drugs, drink alcohol, or sleep around. These things make you feel better, but only for a little while. You fail to think about the consequences of your actions. When the situation seems unbearable, you feel you have no choice but to act. Sometimes you genuinely want to die, and you may attempt *suicide*.

Borderline Personalities Desperately Distrust and Depend on Others

Desperation characterizes your interactions with others. If someone expresses any interest in you, you get swept away with unrealistic expectations that he will be the one to rescue you from your life of misery. You ignore early warning signs and skip over the tedious initial steps in negotiating a new relationship. Your new interest will either commit himself to you entirely, or he is a rotten, inadequate, withholding and betraying jerk, just like others you have dated and worked with. If you begin to detect hesitancy on his part, you panic and take desperate and manipulative actions to keep him interested and involved. I have worked with several young women who lied to their boyfriends about being pregnant to continue the relationship. You may threaten to harm yourself if he leaves. Both men and women may stalk their partners after a breakup, harassing them at home or over the phone. If your attempts at reunion fail, you may be embarrassed by the extent to which you feel you have demeaned yourself. You feel that you opened yourself up only to have your inadequacy and undesirability thrown back in your face.

Some individuals with a borderline personality style become terribly dependent on significant others. Fearing rejection or abandonment, they may go to great lengths to please their partners. You may tolerate verbal and physical abuse. You may feel that you deserve as much, and that submitting to abuse is the only way that you can keep a relationship going. I once treated a man who let his partner bring home other boyfriends for sex. He felt lucky on those occasions when his partner would include him. You may feel that you have little personality of your own, and you judge yourself and your interests through your partner's eyes. Your sense of *identity* changes, as you follow the suggestions and guidance of the person whose attention you are afraid to lose. You feel that your opinion and accomplishments are not worth much anyway. You think that if he takes the trouble to mold you, he must care for you. Sometimes psychiatrists refer to this vulnerable style as a dependent, rather than borderline, personality disorder.

At the other extreme, most individuals with borderline personality become suspicious when relating to others. You have come to realize that loved ones always fail to live up to your expectations. Relationships always end with hostility. You learn again and again that you are a bad person incapable of being loved. You remind yourself that relationships are dangerous that way. The closer people get, the more damage they can do. Yet you are terrified of being alone. So when someone reaches out to you, you are torn between clinging to him and pushing him away. You test him over and over again, challenging him to betray you. You act *angry,* entitled, *jealous,* and resentful. Sometimes you find it easier to keep your relationships shallow. You have a series of one-night stands that make you feel, briefly, more attractive and less lonely. Sometimes you just head to the shopping center so that you can be around people without relating to them.

Why Do Borderline Personality Traits Develop?

Most therapists believe that an ambivalent sense of self and others is central to borderline personality disorder. Deep down you lack a stable and integrated view of yourself as someone with both strengths and weaknesses. You live on a daily basis with a sense of your own badness. But this feeling is intolerable. In a process that therapists refer to as projective identification, you cast these bad feelings onto others. You blame your partners, friends, and bosses for making you feel bad, for failing you, for persecuting you. You feel that you are in a constant power struggle, and that you are always the victim. Everyone around you becomes trapped by your tendency to view things in black and white. Your view of yourself and others shifts constantly from one extreme to another. You are rarely able to describe yourself, or anyone you know, in balanced detail. Everyone is either "the greatest" or "just a jerk."

Scientists do not know exactly how or why these attitudes develop. Most patients in treatment for borderline personality disorder report having an abusive childhood. Research has shown that childhood abuse and neglect greatly increase the risk of personality disorders in adults, especially borderline personality disorder. However, a history of abuse or neglect is not always present. Most therapists presume that borderline personality disorder is caused by a developmental failure in early childhood. You may be born with temperamental traits, such as *impulsiveness* and moodiness, that make it more difficult for parents to relate to you. Or your parents may be cruel or distant. Not surprisingly, sexual abuse by family members, combined with parental cruelty, seems to produce the greatest disturbance in personality when the child grows up. The child is unable to distinguish between love and abuse, since she experienced them together. She learns to view people as threatening and unpredictable at the same time that she relies on them for affection.

Approximately two percent of Americans have a borderline personality, and another one percent would be diagnosed with a dependent personality disorder. Both are diagnosed more frequently in women than in men. Women may be more at risk because society encourages women to be more dependent and emotionally vulnerable. On the other hand, it is possible that clinicians fail to detect borderline personality traits in some men because of stereotypes about men being less emotional.

How to Cope with Borderline Personality Traits

Traditionally, therapists have been pessimistic about the prognosis for borderline personality disorder, but research has shown that treatment is helpful. If you have borderline personality traits you may be viewed as a therapeutic challenge because of the intensity of your expressed emotions, your unpredictability, and your constant need for validation. The therapist tries to provide, in therapy, a safe space where you can vent your emotions without being exploited or criticized. However, you will probably be distrustful, angry, and *paranoid* at times and provoke your therapist to betray you in the manner in which you feel you have been betrayed by others.

Every therapist will be frustrated at times by these challenges, but the skillful therapist will kindly direct your attention to the *anger* you are expressing and the effect that it has on others. When she tolerates your hostility and explores its origin, you begin to learn that rejection is not the only way people can respond to you. You slowly develop greater trust, and you realize that if you can trust your therapist there must be other people in the world you can trust as well.

Your therapist will establish some rules early in treatment, not to annoy you but as a part of your treatment. You will be expected to keep your appointments and to limit contacts between sessions. You will negotiate what sorts of contact are permissible, and how to get help in an emergency. You may feel that you need your therapist to be available for you at all times, but you will learn that when you leave a session you are not being abandoned or rejected. When you become overwhelmed with emotions you will be tempted to harm yourself (see "Self-Mutilation"). Part of your treatment will involve learning to talk about your feelings rather than acting on them. Your therapist will discuss with you ahead of time how she will respond to keep you safe if you try to harm yourself. Sometimes it may be necessary to enter a hospital for a few days if you are losing control and posing a danger to yourself.

There are several different styles of therapy that appear to be useful in the treatment of borderline personality traits. Some deal with your everyday problems and focus on providing safety and nonjudgmental support. You will learn how to avoid situations that disturb you, and you will explore healthier ways to cope with distressing feelings. Other therapies are more analytic, with the therapist frequently interpreting how your behavior in the therapy session reflects your experience with others in the outside world. One particular type of cognitive-behavioral therapy, known as dialectical behavior therapy (DBT), was inspired by principles of Zen meditation and has been proven to reduce self-destructive behavior. DBT teaches you to be more mindful of your emotional triggers so that you can think before, or instead of, acting on your impulses. In all forms of therapy for borderline personality disorder setbacks are common along the way.

Some medications also appear to be helpful in the treatment of borderline personality disorder. Antidepressant medications, especially the SSRIs (see "Depression"), appear to reduce impulsivity, irritability, and feelings of emptiness. You may find that you feel less desperate and needy, that you are able to tolerate being alone. Sometimes a low dose of antipsychotic medication (see "Psychosis") may be helpful if you are prone to lose perspective and become *paranoid* and enraged over trivialities. Mood-stabilizing medications (see "Mania") are also helpful in reducing impulsivity, mood swings, and self-destructive behaviors. None of these medications cure the underlying personality disorder, but they make the symptoms more tolerable.

Studies have consistently found that most patients who are willing to stay in therapy for an extended time will improve. Improvement occurs slowly, as one might expect when the goal is to change lifelong attitudes and patterns of thinking and relating to others. Approximately half of all patients experience a remission after two years, and another quarter experience it after six years. Even in remission you will continue to experience feelings of sadness, emptiness, and worthlessness, but these emotions are less oppressive, and you learn to live with them. You may still feel angry and suspicious from time to time, but you learn not to overreact. You develop a better sense of control over impulsive behaviors such as having one-night stands or using drugs and alcohol. You stop threatening to kill yourself and engaging in self-destructive acts. You begin to feel that you are in control of your life and not at the mercy of your emotions and outside forces. You may begin to reestablish some personal relationships, or you may simply feel more comfortable when alone with yourself.

If someone you care about has a borderline personality disorder, you will find yourself challenged and provoked. Your loved one will often be uncertain whether to idealize you or devalue you. One moment you are her favorite relative or best friend, the next moment you are being accused of being unreliable and hateful. You will be exasperated by these swings in her view of you. It is best to be honest about your feelings but also to try to be calm in your response so that the accusations do not escalate. If you respond to her hostility by becoming sarcastic or critical, then you will have played the role she laid out for you. You may find it helpful to be a little unpredictable yourself. If she expects you to get angry, be thoughtful. If she expects you to be saintly, admit that you are upset. If you find yourself becoming enraged, then take a break to calm down. Above all, try to maintain your equanimity.

You may also feel that your loved one manipulates you by making demands and threats. She may demand that you stop everything to spend time with her. She may demand that you spend less time with others. She may threaten to stop being your friend, or to harm herself. You should decide what sort of behaviors you are willing to tolerate and be clear about what you are not willing to do. If you are calm, consistent, and supportive when setting limits, and if you set them ahead of time, your loved one may feel less rejected. You should not panic when she expresses from time to time a desire to harm herself (see "Self-Mutilation"). You may want to let her know that you are willing to listen to her when she feels like hurting herself, but, if talking will not help, you are prepared to call an ambulance or to take her to the hospital yourself. When dealing with any impulsive behaviors you want to encourage her to take responsibility for the choices she makes, rather than taking on the role of monitoring and rescuing her.

Self-Mutilation

She said she'd come over right after work, but she still isn't here. You call her office and then her home, but no one answers. You're convinced she went out with her old boyfriend.

You light another cigarette. It was stupid of you to get involved with her. You knew this sort of thing would happen. Your head is pounding with anger, and you feel like it will lift right off your body. You lay your arm out on the table in front of you. Your other hand turns the lit cigarette around and brings it down at the end of a row of puckered little scars.

The searing from the cigarette nails you in place. Your eyes focus, and your head stops pounding. A wave of warmth courses up your arm and down to your legs. You breathe deeply and toss the cigarette out the window.

You walk over to the front door and double-lock it. When she shows up, let her knock until her hands are raw.

Self-mutilation is the deliberate infliction of injury to the body without the intention of dying. The injury may be temporary, for example when hairs are pulled out of the scalp, or permanent, as a result of scarring. Self-mutilation is different from other acts of deliberate self-harm and *suicide*. Though it can sometimes be difficult to distinguish a genuine suicide attempt from a "cry for help" or from an act of self-mutilation, those who engage in self-mutilation are usually not trying to kill themselves, and their behavior is unlikely to result directly in serious physical injury.

Some types of self-mutilation are culturally accepted and are not a sign of mental illness. Tattoos and piercings have become common for both men and women. Along with tanning, athletic body sculpting, hair dyeing, and depilation, ankle tattoos and navel rings say more about changing fashions and cultural affiliations than they do about mental health. Male circumcision is another example of a form of mutilation that is accepted either for its supposed hygienic benefit or as a sign of religious contract. Scarification—the laceration or puncturing of the skin to produce decorative scars—is rare in America but common in parts of Africa.

The most common type of self-mutilation seen in psychiatric illness is superficial laceration. You may use a razor or piece of broken glass to make small cuts in your skin. This is most often done to the back of the forearm, but you may also cut your thighs or other areas that you can conceal more easily. The cuts are usually just a couple of inches long and barely break the surface. They may bleed slightly, but the cuts are made far from the arteries that one would cut in a suicide attempt.

You may prefer to inflict small burns, for example with the lit end of a cigarette. This can also leave a number of small, clustered scars. Other types of self-harm include sticking the skin with needles, pinching or bruising the skin, creating a friction burn with a rope, and repeatedly picking at an old sore so that it cannot heal. A more extreme form of self-mutilation involves swallowing objects or inserting objects into other body orifices. I have treated patients who swallowed batteries or stuck ballpoint pens up their rectums. Hospitalized patients sometimes scratch their skin with staples or paperclips, but in more serious cases they may slide the object under the skin as well. These behaviors can be much more dangerous if they end up puncturing the gastrointestinal tract or causing infections, even though that is usually not the intention. Sometimes surgery is required.

Little is known about the prevalence of self-mutilation. Failed suicide attempts are a common reason for patients to be seen in the emergency room, but most people who engage in self-mutilation do not require medical care and may not come to clinical attention. Some studies have found that about one in twenty-five young adults have deliberately harmed themselves at some point. Rates are thought to decline later in adulthood as life becomes less tumultuous and better coping strategies are learned. Men appear to be as likely to engage in self-mutilation as women.

Self-Mutilation Is Often a Sign of a Personality Disorder

Self-mutilation seems to serve several purposes. Some people report that it makes them feel better. You may feel anxious until you cut yourself, at which point the nervousness and restlessness melt away. You may feel a building sense of tension until you decide to give in. You may feel numb and disconnected, and the burn to your skin wakes you up. You may feel ashamed, guilty, or angry at yourself and deserving of punishment. You may be *angry* at others but take out your rage on yourself instead. Cutting yourself may communicate, passive-aggressively, the sentiment, "See what you made me do!" You may be afraid of being alone and cut yourself in order to compel others to care for you. You may be uncertain precisely why you harmed yourself, and you may be vague and contradictory when explaining yourself to a doctor or your loved ones.

These motivations and emotional states are characteristic of borderline personality disorder, an enduring personality style characterized by extreme *self-esteem problems, impulsiveness,* and chronic feelings of rage, emptiness, and loneliness. Self-mutilation is essentially a maladaptive coping mechanism. It is an unhealthy, but sometimes effective, method of dealing with intolerable emotions and tumultuous relationships. Though self-mutilation is similar in some ways to suicidal behavior, it seems to be associated more with feelings of *anxiety* than of depression. It may also be a response to *dissociative* symptoms, such as feeling out of touch with your body and the world around you. Psychiatrists have observed that people who were sexually abused as children are more vulnerable to dissociation, borderline personality disorder, and self-mutilation than those who did not experience this form of abuse.

Self-mutilation is also more commonly seen among individuals who have an *antisocial* personality disorder. Impulsivity and rage are characteristic features of antisocial personality, but self-esteem is not a problem. In fact, if you have an antisocial personality you care about others only to the extent that you can use them. If you harm yourself, it is usually with the goal of *deceiving* and manipulating others. For example, you may cut yourself with a razor in jail in order to force correctional staff to send you to the hospital. I have worked with several prisoners who swallowed razors or burnt their forearms in attempts to prove that they were mentally ill (when, in fact, they were not) or to protest jail conditions.

Self-Mutilation Can Occur in Several Other Psychiatric Conditions

In personality disorders self-mutilation is a habit. But some individuals engage in self-harm only once or twice, in response to a particular crisis. You are most likely to harm yourself, for example, if a romantic relationship has just ended. In these cases the self-destructive act is an impulsive reaction to feelings of anger and loss. You may be uncertain whether you really want to harm yourself, whether you are trying to attract attention and help, or whether you are trying to prove that you cannot live without your partner. The self-destructive behavior is evidence of your inability to find better ways of coping with the situation, which may or may not reflect an underlying personality problem. Psychiatrists see this as evidence of a *stress,* or adjustment, disorder for which brief, problem-solving counseling may be helpful.

Some individuals with autism or mental retardation (see "Learning Problems") demonstrate self-destructive behaviors, which they may find soothing. For example, an autistic child may bang his head repeatedly, and a retarded adult may masturbate to the point of soreness. If you suffer from trichotillomania, you have a *compulsion* to bite or pull out your hair, sometimes resulting in progressive baldness. Nail biting habits are similar. If you have a *body image problem,* you may pick at your skin or engage in other self-destructive behaviors such as fasting and abusing purgatives.

More bizarre self-mutilation is sometimes seen in schizophrenia (see "Psychosis"). For example, I evaluated one patient who cut off his genitals under the *delusional* belief that he was a woman, and another who did the same in response to a *hallucination* that he believed was a command from God.

Many *impulsive* behaviors, ranging from sexual promiscuity to drug abuse, can be viewed as inherently self-destructive. Most of the time you pursue these activities because they are pleasurable, and you focus on the immediate relief from *cravings* rather than on the long-term consequences. But occasionally you may engage in these activities with the clear intention of harming yourself. Drug and alcohol *intoxication* also decreases judgment and increases impulsivity, so that you are more likely to engage in other potentially harmful activities. Most *suicide* attempts and acts of deliberate self-harm occur when an individual is intoxicated.

How to Cope with Self-Destructive Behaviors

If you resort to self-mutilating behaviors, the goal of therapy is to help you develop more effective strategies for avoiding and coping with interpersonal stress, loneliness, and anxiety. With your therapist you try to identify the situations and emotional states that you experience leading up to an act of self-mutilation. You discuss alternative reactions that are less likely to be harmful, such as phoning your therapist, seeking support from family and friends, or utilizing relaxation techniques (see "Anxiety"). One particular form of therapy, known as dialectical-behavioral therapy (DBT), has been proven to reduce acts of self-harm among individuals with borderline personality disorder. DBT teaches you to be mindful of your emotions and to exert control over your responses, inhibiting what might feel good at the moment.

There are no proven medication treatments for self-mutilation. Most psychiatrists would consider using an SSRI antidepressant (see "Depression") or mood-stabilizer (see "Mania") because of the tendency for these medications to reduce impulsivity and moodiness.

If someone you care about is in the habit of harming himself, you may be exasperated by what appears to be a repeated and puzzling behavior. You probably find it viscerally disturbing to think of your loved one cutting and burning himself. The behavior may be transparently manipulative, and you resent being held hostage to threats. You may be tempted to just ignore the behavior when it persists, and that may stimulate your loved one to engage in even more dramatic acts to catch your attention. The best approach is to be matter-of-fact with your loved one when confronting him on his behavior. You want to avoid being perceived as shocked and desperate for a solution. This may be the reaction that your loved one finds reassuring. Rather, you should clearly set limits on what you will tolerate, and, as much as possible, leave it up to your loved one to take responsibility for his behavior within those parameters. He will not die from a cigarette burn. A relapse into such behavior may be cause for inquiring about his progress in therapy rather than insisting on a trip to the emergency room. Get into the habit of talking to your loved one during more stable moments about his strengths and interests, rather than responding only in a time of crisis.

Sexual Performance Problems

Your husband has been working longer and longer hours. When he gets home he says he just wants to eat and fall asleep. At first you didn't notice. You were too busy worrying about the baby to even think about sex. But the baby sleeps through the night now, and you wish you could spend more time together.

You try to get yourself ready for him, showering after work and putting on your make-up, but he doesn't seem to notice. When you cuddle up to him in bed, he rolls away. Sometimes you notice that he gets an erection in the middle of the night, but when you tried to have sex last week, he couldn't keep it up. He said that he was too upset about work to concentrate.

You know he works hard; he always has. But is something else going on? Does he no longer find you attractive? You're just fitting back into the clothes you used to wear before you got pregnant. Does he think you're fat? Or is he seeing someone else? Your girlfriends always said that you should keep an eye on him.

Sexual feelings and practices are an important part of daily life for most people, at least from the early teenage years until late in life. In its broadest sense the word "sexual" refers to much more than intercourse. Sexuality encompasses desires, fantasies, urges, experiences, and a wide range of sexual behaviors that we engage in alone or with others. Sexuality also sometimes refers to our sense of ourselves as, for example, masculine or feminine, gay or straight, curious, abstinent, adventurous, faithful, or sexy.

Even though sex is universal we are reluctant to talk about it in a serious fashion. Sex is a private matter for most of us. We feel comfortable discussing pregnancy and constipation, but not vaginal and anal intercourse. Virtually everyone engages in the pleasant and harmless act of masturbation, but teachers and public health officials have lost their jobs for even mentioning the word. Doctors are not immune to the taboos that keep us from talking about sex. Even though sexual behaviors are important in health and illness, physicians often neglect to ask their patients about sexuality or limit the discussion to a few simple questions. Not surprisingly, patients are often shy about bringing up their sexual concerns, even to a doctor.

In surveys about four out of ten woman and three out of ten men report being dissatisfied with sex. That means that sexual problems are among the most common psychiatric concerns. Sexual intercourse seems like a very simple, almost reflexive, behavior. Every day people figure out how to have sex without instructions. The seeming inevitability and ease of the sexual act hides the fact that it requires several physiological and psychological systems to act together. A problem in any part of the process can lead to a failure in sexual desire, arousal, or orgasm.

Diminished Sexual Desire Is a Common Problem

The normal sexual response starts with sexual desire. Clinicians have estimated that approximately one in eight adult men, and as many as one in four adult women, report that they are not interested in sex. If you have hypoactive, or diminished, sexual desire, you may have few, if any, sexual fantasies and make no efforts to engage in sex. In the vast majority of cases this is a change; you have had sexual desires and have enjoyed sexual behavior in the past. It may be that your lack of interest is a temporary problem. Perhaps you are preoccupied with other matters and happy to do without sex for a while. But in many cases something has happened that has led you to think of sex as unexciting, if not unpleasant. You may have stopped thinking of yourself as someone who can be sexy.

Marital discord is a common cause of diminished sexual interest. If you and your partner are upset at each other, or not communicating well, then you may find it hard to enjoy the intimacy of sex together. After a while the failure to have sex, or to talk about your sexual dissatisfaction, becomes another sore point in your relationship. You may be caught in a cycle of increasing alienation and blame, in which the thought or mention of sex leads to anxiety rather than excitement. On the other hand, many couples continue to have a good relationship in spite of having little sex for other mutually agreed upon reasons.

You can lose interest in sex when you are under serious *stress*. If you have been hospitalized for a medical illness, if you were fired or demoted, if you are going through a divorce, or if you are struggling to raise children on your own, then you may be too anxious and busy to give much thought to sex. If you suffer from *depression* you may lose interest in sex altogether during your illness, even if you had a strong sexual desire before becoming sick. Doctors suspect that many people who report decreased sexual interest may have undiagnosed depression. Since women suffer from depression more than men, this may also explain, in part, the higher rate of impaired sexual desire in women.

Problems with *self-esteem* and *body image* can also inhibit sexual desire. Men often worry that their penis is too small and that their partner will be disappointed. Women worry that they are not voluptuous enough, or not thin enough. After a major change in your life, for example a divorce or being fired from a job, you may feel unattractive or powerless. You may think you are no longer sexy as you grow older. After undergoing surgery you may have scars and disabilities. I have treated men who lost interest in sex after undergoing a colostomy, with placement of a fecal waste bag on their belly. (But to emphasize that sexiness is in the eye of the beholder, surgeons tell me that some patients enjoy using the colostomy hole for intercourse.)

In more extreme cases you may hate or fear sex. The thought of having sex is distasteful, disgusting, or upsetting, and you strive to avoid having sex altogether. Psychiatrists refer to this as sexual aversion. It may result from a very bad sexual or violent experience such as rape. Some women feel like they never want to have sex with a man again. Painful conditions such as surgery or radiation therapy in the genital area may also lead to a strong distaste for sex, and the fear of pain may persist even after the physical condition has improved.

In a few cases abnormal hormone levels may be the cause of diminished sexual desire. Both men and women require a minimum amount of testosterone, commonly thought of as a male hormone, in order to experience sexual interest. Testosterone levels may be low enough to inhibit sexual desire even in the absence of outward signs of hormone deficiency. Birth control pills may reduce testosterone levels and therefore inhibit sexual desire in some women. Elevated levels of prolactin, a hormone produced by the brain, may lead to diminished sexual desire in both men and women. Women experience an increase in prolactin following childbirth and during breastfeeding, and this may, in part, be responsible for decreased sexual interest during this time.

In some cases partners have different degrees of sexual desire. You may both enjoy sex, but one of you would prefer to have sex every night while the other prefers it on a monthly basis. Some studies have shown that most couples have sex on the average of once or twice per week. However, there is a wide variation of sexual frequency, and there is no such thing as normal. What is right for you depends on the expectations you both have. You may also disagree about what is sexually exciting, or what sorts of sexual acts you are willing to practice. In these cases sexual desire is impaired only in a relative sense. One partner may be accused of lacking sexual interest, while the other may be perceived as too demanding.

Both Men and Women Experience Problems with Sexual Arousal

Even if you have strong sexual desires, you may have trouble achieving sexual excitement, or arousal.

During normal sexual arousal, both men and women experience increased blood flow to the genital region and breasts. Nipples usually become erect. In women the clitoris becomes thicker, the vagina lengthens, and the labia swell and redden. Men develop an erection of the penis, and the testicles become larger and tense. Both men and women produce lubricating fluids that make intercourse more comfortable. Disruptions in these physiological processes can make intercourse difficult.

Women produce lower levels of estrogen, a sex hormone, during menopause or after surgical removal of the ovaries. Estrogen is responsible for maintaining the elasticity of skin and the release of natural moisturizers and lubricants during sexual arousal. Menopausal women may develop dry and atrophied skin in the genital region and may stop producing lubricants during sex. As a result, the genital region may become itchy, irritated, or painful during intercourse.

For men, intercourse is a matter of hydraulics. During arousal blood flow into the penis increases, while outward blood flow is reduced. The penis becomes tense enough to maintain its erect shape even as it pushes through the tight muscles of the outer third of the vagina (or through the two anal sphincters during anal intercourse). You can have an orgasm and ejaculate without an erection, but it may be impossible to have intercourse.

As men get older they have more difficulty obtaining and maintaining an erection. The muscles and fibrous structures of the penis are less elastic. Blood vessels may become constricted, especially if you are a smoker or suffer from diabetes, high blood pressure, or high cholesterol. In fact, by the age of fifty half the male population experience erectile dysfunction.

Medication side effects are another cause of impotence in men and of decreased arousal in women. Medications used in the treatment of hypertension or *depression* are most commonly responsible. Alcohol *intoxication* and abuse of almost any illegal drug can also lead to impotence. Since there are many other potential medical causes of sexual dysfunction in men and women, a thorough medical evaluation is important. In men there is a simple way to determine whether you are physically capable of having an erection. Normally men have erections during REM sleep (see "Sleep Problems") regardless of whether they are having an erotic dream. If, during the night, you wake up and notice an erection, then you do not have a physical problem.

Psychological factors play an important role in arousal, as they do in sexual desire. You may feel guilty about having sex. You may feel that it is sinful. You may be nervous about performing well. You may have had previous embarrassing sexual experiences. These expectations can be self-fulfilling. If you are preoccupied with fears of impotence, then you may have trouble getting an erection. If you think you will not enjoy sex, you will be tense and distracted and remain unaroused.

You may have experienced pain and discomfort during sex in the past. Women who are afraid that sex will hurt may unconsciously tighten the muscles of their vagina (which doctors refer to as vaginismus). Both men and women may tighten the anus in fearful anticipation of anal sex. If these muscles tighten, sex may in fact become more painful, and those expectations are reinforced. Relaxation is also necessary when taking the entire penis into the mouth during oral sex, or a gag reflex may result if the penis touches the back of the oral cavity. This may take some practice.

Dyspareunia is the medical term for pain experienced during sex, a condition that affects one in every five to ten women. Pain in women can be caused by a medical condition, including urinary tract infections, endometriosis, or genital skin conditions. Hemorrhoids or sores can cause pain during anal intercourse. In parts of the world where the labia or clitoris are circumcised or sewn together, sex can become very painful for the women affected. If you have been sexually abused as a child, or raped, you may re-experience this pain during sex, even if there is no ongoing physical damage. Since you associate sex with pain, you may avoid having intercourse altogether.

Orgasm is the Climax of Sexual Response

Orgasm refers to the intense physical and psychological experience at the peak of sexual excitement. In both men and women tension mounts as you breath faster, and your pulse and blood pressure rise. Men realize a few seconds before orgasm that they are about to ejaculate, at which point orgasm becomes inevitable. You feel *euphoric*, and a wave of warmth and tingling sweeps over you, followed by a feeling of peacefulness and relaxation. During female orgasm the vaginal muscles tighten rhythmically for several seconds (along with the anal sphincters in both sexes). Other body muscles may tighten or shake. Your skin flushes, and you may break out in sweat. During mutual sexual activities, simultaneously bringing rapture to your partner adds to the excitement of orgasm.

Most men and women experience their first orgasms during their teenage years. Women in studies decades ago often reported that they did not experience orgasms until they were married, but almost all had experienced orgasm by mid-life. While failure to have ever experienced orgasm is very rare, both men and women may have difficulty achieving orgasm at times. The rates are higher among women, with as many as one in four reporting trouble reaching orgasm. In most cases inhibited orgasm is a problem during intercourse but not during masturbation. Sexual desire and stimulation with a partner may be good enough for you to achieve arousal, but not exciting or prolonged enough to lead you to orgasm. You may have learned to have orgasms only under certain conditions, and you may need to be in control of the pace and stimulation. Or you may have ambivalent feelings about sex, body fluids, pregnancy, or the person with whom you are having sex. These feelings may inhibit orgasm.

Medications are a common cause of failure to ejaculate or reach orgasm. Psychiatric medications are most often at fault; both antidepressant (see "Depression") and antipsychotic (see "Psychosis") medications commonly impair ejaculation or orgasm.

A more common sexual problem, especially among younger men, is premature ejaculation, which affects as many as one in three. Premature ejaculation is the inability to sustain arousal and delay orgasm long enough for you and your partner to be satisfied. In most cases you find yourself at the point of inevitable orgasm shortly after making physical contact with your partner. You may ejaculate in your pants during foreplay or immediately after inserting your penis into the vagina, anus, or mouth. Because it is difficult to sustain an erection and continue having intercourse following orgasm, you worry about failing to please your partner. Most mental health workers assume that premature ejaculation is a learned behavior, perhaps from early experiences of having to rush during sex. It also seems to involve a failure to control the pace of arousal during an intense sexual experience.

There is a stage following orgasm that physicians refer to as resolution. Normally after orgasm, genitals and breasts return to their usual size over a number of minutes. Skin flushing disappears, and pulse, blood pressure, and breathing return to normal. Men experience a refractory period for several hours in which it is difficult to have another erection and orgasm. Women, on the other hand, are able to have more than one orgasm in a row.

If orgasm does not occur after a prolonged period of arousal, then the resolution phase can be disrupted. Swelling and congestion of the testicles may persist for hours, and some men experience a crampy discomfort commonly referred to as "blue balls." This phenomenon is not well studied, and it is not clear whether anything comparable occurs in women. In addition, both men and women can experience headaches after sex, which may relate to the changes in pulse, blood pressure, and hormone levels.

Treatments Exist for Many Sexual Difficulties

Both psychotherapy and medications can be helpful in the treatment of sexual performance problems. Individual therapy may help you to feel more confident about your sexual interests, attractiveness, and abilities. In couple therapy, a therapist helps you and your partner to explore any expectations, conflicts, and misconceptions that interfere with your sexual relationship. In sex therapy, which is a type of couple therapy, you may be given homework assignments intended to reduce performance fears and increase communication skills. For example, you may be asked to engage in extensive erotic touching without having intercourse. You are instructed to pay attention only to your partner and not monitor your own arousal. Eventually you develop confidence in foreplay and in a variety of sexual positions, and you learn to communicate with your partner in a way that builds trust rather than frustration.

Some special behavioral techniques may be useful in specific conditions. If you suffer from premature ejaculation, you and your partner train to prolong the stage of arousal. If you find yourself on the verge of orgasm, you or your partner can squeeze the head of the penis to prevent ejaculation. Alternatively, you can withdraw from physical contact as orgasm approaches. Or you can enter the vagina or anus and then avoid thrusting, to grow used to the sensation. With practice, you learn to control and delay orgasm until you and your partner are ready.

On the other hand, if you or your partner have difficulty reaching orgasm during intercourse, you can practice masturbating together to the point of orgasm, or you can combine masturbation and intercourse. Women who have difficulty reaching orgasm may benefit from greater stimulation of the clitoris with a finger, tongue, or dildo. If you experience spasm of the vaginal or anal muscles during penetration you will be instructed in relaxation techniques, and you or your partner will be encouraged to lubricate and gently massage and dilate the area on successive occasions before trying full penetration.

A small number of men and women who lack sexual desire may benefit from hormone supplementation with testosterone, but only if testosterone levels are measured and found to be low. Excess testosterone does not improve performance. Women who are deficient in estrogen (for example, during menopause) may find sex more comfortable if they take estrogen supplements, after discussing the risks, such as a higher rate of certain cancers, with their physician. Estrogen creams may also be effective when spread on the vagina and labia.

Men who are unable to achieve an erection should have a thorough medical examination. If you can get an erection when masturbating, or with another partner, or if you wake up with an erection at night, then erectile dysfunction is more likely due to psychological factors. Sildenafil (Viagra), vardenafil (Levitra), and tadalafil (Cialis) are remarkably effective treatments for erectile dysfunction, regardless of the medical or psychological cause. They work by stimulating the expansion of blood vessels in the penis, leading to tumescence, and they are taken on an as-needed basis just before sex. These medications have made other treatments, such as penile implants, injections, and vacuum pumps, largely obsolete. They stimulate genital blood flow in women but have not proven to be very effective in improving the quality of arousal in women. In both men and women, however, they reverse the sexual side effects of antidepressant medications.

The side effects of the antidepressant medications that inhibit sexual arousal, such as the SSRIs and clomipramine, can be useful in the treatment of premature ejaculation. A low dose of the antidepressant, taken approximately thirty minutes prior to intercourse, can inhibit or delay orgasm and ejaculation. If one antidepressant does not work, another can be tried. Some physicians have also prescribed anesthetic creams to be spread on the head of the penis, to diminish sensation, but it is unclear whether this is effective. If these medication interventions are effective you may become increasingly confident in your ability to prolong arousal without ejaculation, and eventually medication will be unnecessary.

For many of us, condoms are an important tool for protecting ourselves and our partners from sexually transmitted diseases and for avoiding unwanted pregnancy. However, condoms can contribute to sexual performance problems. If you suffer from premature ejaculation you may have trouble slipping a condom on without triggering an orgasm. If you have erectile dysfunction you may have difficulty remaining rigid during placement. If you are already nervous about having sex the additional step of unwrapping and placing a condom on your penis, or on your partner's penis, may frustrate you further. The best solution is to practice placing a condom, either alone or with your partner, at a time when you are relaxed and not pressured to have sex. You may find that you are more comfortable with a particular style or size, and your partner may prefer the condom to be ridged or lubricated. With practice, a condom can become an enjoyable sexual tool and not just a frustrating requirement.

Sexual Preoccupations

You looked in a book at the library that said masturbation is normal. But you're not so sure. At least not like this. You've done it at least once a day ever since you discovered you could. When you got married, it didn't take long for your wife to figure out what was going on. She said she'd rather have you jerk off in the morning with a magazine than sleep around with someone else during the day. As long as you could still get it up when you were with her at night, things were fine.

Even when you have intercourse together your mind is elsewhere. You fantasize about doing it at work, on an airplane, and in the woods. Recently you've started getting excited about the idea of letting somebody else watch. You didn't think that would turn you on until you were interrupted once in a public restroom. You're not gay, but you've started slipping into porno theatres where guys can watch you while a video is playing. The only thing keeping you from pulling it out in front of a woman is that you might get arrested.

Sometimes you think it wouldn't be so bad if you got arrested. At least then you'd have to deal with the problem. You've tried unsuccessfully to stop on your own. All day long you're thinking about opportunities. You can't concentrate at work. Sometimes you slip out of meetings. At the end of the day you feel bad about having accomplished so little, and the only way to cheer yourself up is to waste another couple of hours looking for porno on the Internet. You wish you were like everyone else and could be satisfied with having sex with your wife a couple times a week.

Over the past two centuries doctors have tried to define certain sexual preoccupations, activities, frequencies, and propensities as deviant. But there has been little scientific basis for classifying some desires as normal and others as abnormal or excessive. Most people have sex for reasons other than procreation, which is perhaps the only biological justification for sex. All other sexual activity and fantasy is a matter of personal preference. Describing what is "sexy" is like describing what is "tasty": everyone has a different opinion.

Surveys have consistently shown that people experience more sex, and a greater variety of sexual behaviors and partners, than is commonly acknowledged. For example, most men and women have had sex as teenagers. Most unmarried young adults have sex at least once per week, and with a number of different partners by the time they marry. Most married couples are monogamous and have sex once or twice per week. But many report having sex daily. Among married men about one in five have never had sex with anyone other than his wife; a similar number admit to having had sex with someone else while married. Most women have engaged in anal intercourse, and about one in four continue to enjoy it. Many men have had sex with other men, though the vast majority have had sex with women as well.

Though there is a wide range of sexual practices, and an even wider range of sexual fantasies, some patterns of sexual desire can be problematic. In the past doctors used the terms satyriasis and nymphomania to refer to excessive sexual desires in men and women, respectively. Nowadays many therapists use the term sexual addiction, noting that sexual *cravings* have much in common with the urges to use drugs and alcohol. You may feel that you are constantly preoccupied with sex, that your sexual urges are out of your control, that sex interferes with other aspect of your life, and that the pursuit of sex is increasingly time-consuming and unfulfilling.

Like other addicting behaviors, sex is powerfully reinforcing. Sexual fantasy, sexual contact, and orgasm make you feel good. If you become addicted to sex you keep trying to recapture the excitement and arousal that sex has brought you in the past, even when it starts to become repetitive and disappointing. You plan your day around getting sex, and if you are unsuccessful you feel irritable. You find that you need sex more and more, and you may seek out more daring or extreme sexual venues, having become dissatisfied with the routine sex that you used to enjoy. You treat the people with whom you have sex as objects. They fulfill your immediate need for gratification, and then you move on.

You may cruise to meet strangers in bars, parks, saunas, and pornography stores. You may spend hours downloading pornography or trading photographs in chat rooms on the Web. I treated one married man who had sex with anyone he could find, male or female, including his mailman. Another kept a diary full of telephone numbers and would schedule several encounters each day. You may feel that you have no control over your desire to masturbate, whether you are unattached or in a monogamous relationship. You may spend large amounts of time and money buying pornographic magazines and videos, or you may pay for sex itself. You tell yourself that you have a problem, but you have trouble stopping. You are embarrassed by your behaviors, which you conceal from your loved ones.

It is hard to know how many people feel that their sex life is out of control. Psychiatrists have not systematically studied this question, in part because they have been more inclined to label only specific sexual interests as deviant, rather than viewing all sexual urges as potentially addicting. Psychiatrists who specialize in treating patients with sexual problems estimate that about one in ten adults are troubled by excessive sexual preoccupations and uncontrolled urges.

Paraphilias Refer to Distressing Sexual Preferences

Paraphilia is the term that psychiatrists use to refer to specific sexual tastes and practices that are distressing. I avoid referring to these sexual desires as deviant. Many of them, in fact, are quite common. Individuals or couples with a completely satisfactory sex life may find most of these practices titillating from time to time. There is nothing inherently unhealthy about most of them. What brings you to a therapist or psychiatrist is that you find your fantasies and practices upsetting, embarrassing, distracting, or overwhelming. You have difficulty controlling your urges, or you lose interest in more conventional sexual activities. You may have difficulty finding a partner who shares your tastes.

Fetishism involves being sexually aroused by objects, such as stiletto heels, underwear, or rubber clothing. Many of us may find these objects sexually exciting when they serve as accessories, for example when a loved one wears fancy underwear to bed. Or you may enjoy having sex on a bearskin rug, or using a dildo. This is a sign of creativity, not perversion. But if you have a fetish you are less interested in the person than in the underwear. You may masturbate alone with the object, and you may be unable to become aroused without it. Your sexual desire may lead you to engage in illegal behaviors, such as breaking into a woman's room to steal her lingerie.

Partialism refers to a sexual interest in specific body parts, such as feet or buttocks. I had one patient who was sexually aroused by the thought of licking the dirty toes of elderly ladies.

Transvestism involves a man being sexually excited by dressing in women's clothing and wearing make-up and wigs. Contrary to popular assumptions, men who find this sexually exciting are generally heterosexual, though gay men may cross-dress for other reasons (see "Identity Confusion"). If you find that you are aroused by the idea of wearing women's clothing, you probably find your desires confusing and embarrassing. You probably view yourself as very masculine in other capacities, and that is how others see you as well. You pursue your interest in secret, trying on your mother's or wife's clothing unbeknownst to either, or wearing women's panties underneath your regular clothes. The excitement you feel at getting dressed up is always in tension with your fear of being discovered and publicly humiliated. If your wife learns of your interest, you may have difficulty convincing her that your sexual interest is compatible with being masculine.

Sadism and masochism are terms named after the Marquis de Sade and Leopold von Sacher-Masoch, the novelists who wrote about these sexual tastes in great detail. Masochism involves the desire to be humiliated or controlled by another person during sex. This may include spanking or whipping, groveling, obeying commands, being tied up, or dressing in diapers. If you have masochistic interests, you may seek out prostitutes or join clubs or Web sites that bring masochists together with partners who enjoy playing the role of master or dominatrix. Interestingly your sexual interest in being humiliated or controlled probably does not extend to other areas. You may be an executive or commander with power over others during the workday. You probably enjoy losing control and sustaining pain only within certain limits. You may instruct your partner ahead of time on exactly how far to go.

Sadism involves the desire to inflict pain or humiliation on others. Some people find a little bit of sadistic role-playing sexually exciting. For example, you may imagine that your partner is helpless, or you may use a little bondage, hot wax, or spanking. In fact, you and your partner may exchange roles from time to time. If you have sadistic sexual interests, however, it is the genuine helplessness, vulnerability, pain, and fear of another person that you find sexually exciting. Sadistic interests are usually not confined to the sexual; if you have a sadistic personality style you probably lack empathy for others and are willing to exploit others for your own pleasure in a variety of situations (see "Antisocial Behavior"). If you have fantasies about harming or coercing another person, you may eventually want to carry out your fantasies and commit a sexual offense such as rape.

Some Paraphilias Can Lead to Sexual Offenses

Voyeurism, exhibitionism, and frottage are sexual behaviors that are considered deviant from a legal perspective because they involve nonconsenting victims. From a psychiatric standpoint, however, it must be acknowledged that many healthy people are sexually excited by these behaviors. Surveys have found that about one-third of college men admit to having taken advantage of a crowded situation to rub up against a stranger; nearly one-half report watching an unsuspecting person undress or have sex. Many couples have sex in semipublic places, or with their window shades open, where the chance of being discovered adds to the excitement.

Psychiatrists are more concerned if you are unable to control your urges to expose yourself, or to watch or grope others. If you have these urges you may engage in these acts on hundreds of occasions. You may spend hours planning your sexual behavior or looking for opportunities. You may take long subway rides in the hope of touching a stranger, or long walks looking for open windows. You may seek out secluded spots where you can surprise strangers with little risk of being caught. You run the risk of being arrested and of *traumatizing* others.

Most people who engage in one of these behaviors pursue the others as well. Some psychiatrists have begun to think of voyeurism, exhibitionism, frottage, and rape as disordered courtship behaviors, because they involve practices that are an instinctual part of seeking a sexual partner in nature. In human society, however, they are directed at strangers and do not lead to relationships or mutual sexual activity. For some people who have *antisocial* or sadistic personality traits, the element of forcing sexual attention on an unsuspecting victim may be particularly sexually arousing. Others may avoid dealing with the coercive nature of their behavior by fantasizing that the sexual attention is desired. If your victim is shocked, angry, afraid, or derisive, you may mistake her reaction for excitement.

Pedophilia is a persistent and intense sexual attraction to children who have not yet passed through puberty. Even though we may find the idea distasteful, it is not uncommon to have an occasional sexual thought about a child. For example, approximately one in five college men acknowledge finding adolescent girls sexually attractive. Approximately one in ten acknowledge fantasizing about children. However, if you find yourself fantasizing about children on a regular basis, or if you find that your urges are becoming hard to resist, or you begin to plan to approach children for sexual contact, then you should seek help. Even if you are not disturbed by your thoughts you should recognize that both you and a child could be harmed if you act on your urges.

Men are much more likely to have sex with children than women, but perhaps women are reported less often. Contrary to popular stereotypes, most men who suffer from pedophilia are heterosexual in their sexual interest and activity with adults, but their victims are at least as likely to be boys as girls. You may convince yourself that your victim was behaving in a sexually provocative way, or that you were helping children by teaching them about sex or by providing them love. It is unclear whether these distorted thoughts emerge to excuse behavior after the offense, or if the attitudes existed beforehand and set the stage for the offense to take place.

If you have pedophilic urges you will have fantasized about having sex with children long before you actually act on your urges. You may start to cultivate opportunities to work closely with children, by befriending neighbors or by working as a teacher, coach, or in daycare. In many cases a person who has sex with a child does not suffer from pedophilia. He may have been drunk, lonely, and curious, or he may have taken advantage of an unusual opportunity when left alone with a child. Outside of that incident, he may not have a tendency to fantasize about children.

Homosexual Desire Is Not a Sign of Mental Illness

Homosexuality is not an illness, but it bears discussion because it is misunderstood and still commonly thought of as deviant. The word homosexual can have two meanings. It can refer to a sexual act between two people of the same sex. It can also refer to a person's orientation, in which case the terms gay and lesbian are usually preferred (see "Identity Confusion"). The distinction is important because you may choose to have sex with someone of the same sex without ever considering yourself homosexual. In fact, that is usually the case. For example, many men who consider themselves straight can enjoy a sexual act with another man and not consider themselves gay, especially if they are the active (or penetrating) partner. As many as one in four men in America report having had a sexual experience to the point of orgasm with another man, though the practice is more common during teenage years. In contrast, fewer than one in twenty identifies himself as gay (exclusively homosexual). Rates of homosexual behavior and identification in women are reported to be about half those in men.

If you are exclusively attracted to people of the same sex, then you are probably gay. Your orientation is unlikely to change, though of course you can still choose what sexual behaviors you are willing to engage in. If you are attracted to both women and men, then you should not feel compelled to label yourself in any way, though some use the term "bisexual" to describe this pattern. Being attracted to both sexes is common. In fact, scientists wonder why so many people seem to be sexually attracted only to the opposite sex. Presumably society's expressed disapproval of homosexual behavior discourages many people from exploring their same-sex attractions.

How Do Atypical Sexual Interests and Behaviors Develop?

Sexual fantasies and behaviors are very difficult to study. For many reasons we may not be frank with scientific investigators. It is particularly difficult to obtain accurate information about behaviors that are illegal.

Most mental health workers presume that our sexual preferences are to some extent learned during childhood. Children experience pleasurable erotic sensations even before puberty and begin to associate them with specific activities, people, and objects. Your nanny's baby powder, father's facial hair, or mother's dresses may set the stage for sensations that you find arousing as an adult. Society also trains you to think of certain things as erotic and others as unappealing. There may be a genetic component to some sexual orientations. Some studies suggest that homosexuality may run in families. It is possible that some people may be predisposed to developing erotic interests in leather or rubber, for example, because of a unique sense of smell or touch.

Regardless of the cause, scientists have generally found that sexual orientations are established by the teenage years, whether your adult interest is in buttocks, women's clothing, strangers, or children. Fantasies that are sufficiently arousing may lead to exploratory acts. Even if you consider your sexual interest to be deviant and distressing, you may find yourself indulging it again and again, because it brings you more and more pleasure and relieves tension. Even if you are arrested for a sexual offense, the urges persist and you may resume the behaviors, though more cautiously at first.

Psychiatrists have found little in the way of personality features that distinguish people who have certain sexual preferences. Homosexuals are as well adjusted as heterosexuals, aside from having to cope with prejudice. Masochists, fetishists, and men who enjoy wearing women's clothing are otherwise indistinguishable from their friends and colleagues. People who commit sexual offenses against children or nonconsenting adults do not appear to have any particular personality style, aside from their willingness to break the law. They come from all walks of life, though they may seek jobs that provide them the opportunity to indulge their sexual interests. Rapists are no different on most psychological measures from other criminals.

Some conditions increase the likelihood that a person will engage in sexual behaviors that he would otherwise consider inappropriate. Alcohol *intoxication* and drug use reduces inhibitions. Though *depression* usually suppresses sexual drive, a minority of people with depression may engage in increased sexual behavior in an attempt to briefly dispel feelings of loneliness, boredom, and worthlessness. These sexual encounters bring only a brief period of relief, and they may ultimately lead you to feel more worthless and guilty. *Mania* causes an increase in sexual desire and a decrease in sexual inhibition, which psychiatrists refer to as hypersexuality. When you are manic you may engage in all sorts of sexual behaviors that you find embarrassing once you recover. Sexual behaviors may also be disinhibited during *psychosis,* when social judgment and communication skills can be severely impaired.

Some paranoid individuals are preoccupied with a delusional fear of being raped and may suspect malevolent sexual intentions from others. Sexual preoccupations are also seen in erotomanic and *jealous* delusions. If you suffer from *obsessive*-compulsive disorder (OCD) you may have recurrent intrusive thoughts and images of a sexual nature. In each of these conditions the disturbance is in thinking, not desire.

Some Treatments Exist for Sexual Preoccupations

It appears that most sexual preferences cannot be substantially redirected once they have developed. In the past century many tried to change their orientation from homosexual to heterosexual without significant success. Likewise, there is little evidence that heterosexual interest, or any of the paraphilias, are changeable. You may be encouraged, therefore, to come to terms with your sexual desires rather than wasting time trying to change them.

If you find your urges excessive or distracting, or if they pose a danger to you and others, you might find it helpful to adopt a relapse-prevention approach of the sort that has been employed in the management of other *cravings.* First you must recognize that you have a problem, that your sexual behavior is out of your control. You inform others about your preoccupations so that they can help support you in your efforts to avoid temptations. You work with your therapist to identify the feelings, such as loneliness, frustration, and anger, and the situations that lead you to fantasize. You learn to identify and change distorted thoughts that have facilitated your behaviors. Above all you must recognize that sexual urges are very compelling and that it will not be easy for you to avoid acting on them.

Some other behavioral techniques have been used, but without much long-term success. You can practice masturbating without allowing yourself to fantasize about the unwanted urges. If you do fantasize about them you can punish yourself by immediately thinking of humiliating consequences (such as being arrested or caught by your parents), or by exposing yourself to an electric shock (in a controlled fashion, with professional assistance) or noxious smell. You can masturbate to the point of exhaustion. You can keep a diary to monitor the extent of your urges and reward yourself in little ways each day that you manage to avoid acting on them.

Some medications may also be useful in inhibiting sexual desires. Most people complain about the sexual side effects of antidepressant medications (see "Depression"), but if you find yourself engaging in what you consider excessive and compulsive sexual behaviors, then the SSRI medications in particular may blunt your sexual drive. They may also help treat the anxiety and hopelessness that frequently accompany sexual addiction.

A more drastic approach is hormone therapy, sometimes unpleasantly referred to as chemical castration. Hormones that lower testosterone function can be administered as a daily pill or as a long-acting injection. You experience less sexual desire generally and have difficulty achieving an erection. This treatment is poorly studied and may not be effective or safe in all conditions.

Regardless of your approach to modifying your behavior you need to reduce your risk of contracting or spreading venereal diseases. Especially if you or your partner engage in sex with strangers, you must use a condom.

Sleep Problems

You lie in bed, afraid to open your eyes and check the clock. You must have fallen asleep sometime after midnight, but you have been waking up every hour since. You were exhausted when you went to bed, but as soon as you lay down you started thinking about your argument with your supervisor, your overdue project, and your credit card debt. Now all you can think about is how little sleep you are getting.

Even if you reset your alarm you won't get more than five hours of broken sleep before you have to get up. Then you will probably fall asleep in the office, like you did last week.

You put the pillow over your eyes and start chanting to yourself: "I must fall asleep, I must fall asleep, I must fall asleep."

Sleeping is like eating and drinking. Everyone has to sleep. If you do not get enough sleep your body will let you know. For the most part your body takes care of itself, and you get the right amount of sleep over time. That said, everyone has trouble sleeping now and then. Sometimes work and travel patterns interfere with your normal sleep cycle. Sometimes an underlying illness (medical or psychiatric) disrupts your sleep. And sometimes you have trouble sleeping for no obvious reason.

Normal patterns of sleep vary for each one of us. On average, eight hours of sleep is needed each night to feel rested. But some people do fine with six hours of sleep, while others need ten hours. (Babies sleep much more, and as we get advanced in age, we sleep a little less.) Some people are naturally alert in the morning and go to bed early. Others stay up late and sleep late. Some people feel best when they nap for an hour or two in the middle of the day. For others, a nap leads to grogginess later in the day and trouble sleeping at night. These variations are part of the body's circadian rhythms, daily patterns that are established through the release of hormones in the brain.

The quality of sleep varies throughout the night. During a typical night you will spend approximately two hours in deep sleep. Your body naturally slips into, and arises out of, deep sleep by passing through several other stages of lighter sleep. It is hard to wake up in the middle of deep sleep, and if someone wakes you up you feel sleepy and disoriented. You may say things that do not make sense, perhaps because you are confusing the real world with a dream you were experiencing. If you are allowed to fall back asleep, you may not remember having woken up. In deep sleep you can have very vivid and realistic dreams. However, you rarely remember them by the time you wake up in the morning. Even though you are asleep it is possible for you to move about or even speak without realizing it. For the most part, though, your body is in a resting state, with a lower pulse, lower blood pressure, slower respirations, and less muscle activity than if you were awake.

Scientists have identified another major phase of sleep which is called rapid eye movement (REM) sleep. You spend approximately two hours in REM sleep each night. REM sleep occurs during light sleep and, in some ways, is similar to being awake. Your brain remains very active, and your pulse, blood pressure, and breathing patterns are the same as when you are awake. You dream almost constantly during REM sleep, and the quality of the dreams tends to be stranger than during deep sleep. If you wake up during REM sleep, you may remember your dreams, though they may be difficult to understand or communicate to others.

During REM sleep the voluntary muscles that control the movements of your body are essentially paralyzed. Your eyes move back and forth behind their closed lids, but the rest of the body remains still. Also, the body does not sweat or shiver when the temperature in your bedroom rises or drops. As a result, you may wake up from REM sleep feeling chilled or hot. And men reliably develop an erection during REM sleep, regardless of the content of their dreams.

During a typical night's sleep you fall into deep sleep within an hour. The first period of deep sleep lasts for about half an hour, followed by your first, brief period of REM sleep. REM sleep may last only a few minutes at first, but episodes later in the night grow progressively longer.

You get all of your deep sleep in the first half of the night. When you wake up in the morning, you are likely to either be in light sleep or in the middle of a REM dream.

Trouble falling asleep, or remaining asleep, is called insomnia. About one-third of all Americans experience significant troubles with insomnia at some point. After a sleepless night you feel tired and irritable, you have trouble concentrating, and you find it difficult to stay awake (excessive sleepiness, or somnolence, in spite of adequate sleep occurs only rarely). When insomnia persists night after night you may also have *mood swings* during the day or become *depressed*.

What Causes Insomnia?

A common cause of trouble sleeping is a disruption in your daily sleep cycle. Your body expects you to fall asleep and wake up at generally the same time every day. For most of us sleep takes place when it is dark outside, and we wake up naturally to the sun. But if you travel across a few time zones your body's natural circadian rhythms will be out of phase. If you travel east, you find yourself wanting to stay up late and sleep late. If you travel west, you may fall asleep while others are still working or getting ready for dinner. Most people find it easier to travel west, since you can force yourself to stay up the first night and then have no difficulty falling asleep when you eventually make it to bed.

Working on night and evening shifts can also cause a disruption in your sleep patterns. Electric lighting and window shades can make up, somewhat, for being out of shift with the normal night and day. However, you have to carefully plan your schedule so that you can run errands, exercise, and spend time with family while sleeping through much of the day. You may find that you have difficulty winding down in the hours before you fall asleep, if these are the hours when your schedule overlaps with normal business or social time. But you can adapt to off-shift work and sleep patterns if your hours do not change from day to day. Unpredictable, or alternating, schedules are the most disruptive, since your body is constantly confused as to whether you should be awake or asleep.

In most cases trouble sleeping is a transient problem during times of moderate *stress*, excitement, or excessive work. You may not realize that you are particularly anxious or preoccupied, but once you lie down and turn off the lights you find that your thoughts will not be quiet. You replay conversations in your mind, or you plan dialog and encounters that you might have the next day. You think about the projects you are working on, the people you are working for, and all of the things that you have to take care of at home. You may worry about your children or other family members. When you are lying down with nothing to distract you, these ruminations seem to fill your head. It seems that the more you concentrate on ignoring your worries the more they remain on your mind. Falling asleep may, in itself, become a focus of your thoughts. You may worry more and more that you will be unable to fall asleep, and these worries take on a life of their own and keep you awake.

Everyone experiences trouble sleeping for a few days here and there as a result of commonplace worries. If your worries interfere frequently, or continuously, with your sleep, and if you are distracted by your worries during the day as well, you may be suffering from *anxiety*. It is important to recognize if you have anxiety, because your sleep will improve naturally once you receive appropriate treatment for your anxiety.

A number of other psychiatric conditions can predispose one to sleeping problems. In most cases, if you suffer from *depression* you will also have difficulty sleeping. Even if you fall asleep easily, you find yourself waking up frequently in the middle of the night. As a result, you may spend much of the night tossing in bed, feeling as sad and miserable as you did during the day. When you do manage to sleep you spend more time dreaming and less time in restful deep sleep. You do not feel refreshed when you wake up early in the morning. You feel exhausted throughout the day. Some people with depression sleep too much, often late into the morning.

Sleep problems are one of the earliest and most important signs of *mania*. As you become increasingly manic you find that you do not feel sleepy. You find it hard to sleep even if you know that sleep is important. I have treated several manic patients who were convinced that they no longer needed to sleep at all.

Trouble sleeping is also common during *psychosis*. Delusional fears may keep you awake, or you may be in such an agitated state that you cannot relax. Sleep is also disrupted in a number of conditions that cause *confusion,* such as dementia and delirium. Those who live or work with the elderly may have noticed that confusion and agitation sometimes increases after dark, a phenomenon referred to as sun-downing.

Drug or alcohol use can disrupt sleep in a number of ways (see "Intoxication"). Stimulants like cocaine, amphetamine, phencyclidine (PCP), ephedrine, and caffeine each interfere with normal sleep. When using these drugs, you do not feel like you need to sleep. In fact, amphetamine and ephedrine have both been used in the military to stimulate alertness and reduce the need for sleep. Many of us use caffeine for the same purpose. Sedating drugs, often referred to as downers, may induce sleep in the short term, but as your body gets used to them you will have difficulty falling asleep without them. Alcohol may also make you feel sleepy, but it interferes with the normal stages of sleep. If you go to bed drunk you will spend less time in deep sleep and not feel rested in the morning. During drug withdrawal the effects on sleep are usually reversed. Stimulant abusers will fall into a deep rebound sleep, while alcohol and sedative abusers will find it hard to fall asleep naturally for several days.

Prescription medications can also disturb normal sleep patterns. Stimulants like methylphenidate (Ritalin, used in the treatment of childhood *hyperactivity*) and theophyline (for asthma) can cause insomnia if they are taken too late in the day. Some antidepressant medications (see "Depression") can cause insomnia early in treatment, while others cause sedation. Many psychiatric medications, including the antipsychotics (see "Psychosis"), cause daytime sleepiness. In most cases the body adjusts, and the medications do not seem to be so sedating once a steady dose has been reached for a couple of weeks.

Many medical conditions can interfere with proper sleep, and if you have persistent insomnia or somnolence you should receive a thorough medical workup. Any medical condition can interfere with sleep indirectly. For example, if you are in pain or discomfort you may be unable to sustain sleep throughout the night. You may wake up, even briefly, every few minutes, with the result that you feel exhausted in the morning.

Sleep apnea is the most common medical cause of insomnia, accounting for nearly half of all cases referred to sleep laboratories. If you have sleep apnea your partner may have observed that you snore loudly and periodically gasp or stop breathing altogether for several seconds. Your sleep is restless, and you are exhausted during the day. Most people who suffer from sleep apnea are older, obese men. The condition can be dangerous but can be treated if you wear nasal tubes that provide pressurized air (keeping your airway open) throughout the night.

There Are Several Other Uncommon Sleep Disorders

Narcolepsy is an unusual condition characterized by sleep attacks. You experience the unexpected and sudden onset of REM sleep during waking hours and abruptly fall asleep. About half of the time you also lose muscle tone and collapse. You often experience *hallucinations* at the start of a sleep attack, when falling asleep, or when you awaken. Narcolepsy usually has its onset by young adulthood and tends to run in families. Narcolepsy is treated with stimulant medications taken during the day, or with modafinil (Provigil), which corrects an imbalance in a brain chemical called orexin.

Nightmares are frightening dreams and are experienced by everyone at some point, especially in early childhood. Nightmares occur during REM sleep, rather than in deep sleep. When you wake from a nightmare you are alert and can recall the vivid details of the dream. You may remain frightened, even after you realize it was just a dream. It may be difficult for you to fall back asleep. Nightmares tend to be more common during periods of *stress* or following *trauma,* but some people experience frequent nightmares and may benefit from treatment with antidepressant medications (see "Depression"), which suppress REM sleep.

Children not uncommonly experience night terrors and sleepwalking, both of which are disorders of deep sleep. If you have a night terror you wake up with a scream in a state of intense fear. Since you were deeply asleep you may be confused. You are not terrified of anything in particular, and you may fall back asleep and forget the episode when you wake up in the morning. Sleepwalking, which psychiatrists refer to as somnambulism, commonly accompanies night terrors. Children may appear to be awake as their eyes are open as they sit up, walk about, and engage in complex behaviors. However, they remain unconscious of what they are doing and do not remember any of it when they wake up. They typically return to sleep after a short time. Sleepwalking becomes less common during the teenage and adult years.

Bed-wetting, which doctors call nocturnal enuresis, is common in childhood but usually resolves in the preschool years. One in ten still wet the bed at age five, and one in twenty by age eight. Bed-wetting seems to have a large genetic component and is not an intentional behavior. It is best managed by rewarding your child when he does not wet the bed rather than blaming him when he does. You should limit how much he drinks before bedtime and consider purchasing a sensor alarm that is triggered when he wets himself. If he is motivated, and if you are patient, the alarm will train him to stop urinating within a couple of months. It is successful in most cases so long as your child is at least six years old. Medications can also be prescribed, but bed-wetting almost inevitably recurs when the medications are stopped.

Finally, a few disorders are characterized by abnormal muscular movements during sleep. About one in twenty individuals suffer from restless legs. When you lie down or sit you feel an uncomfortable sensation deep in your leg muscles. You feel you must keep your legs moving to avoid the crampy discomfort. When you are trying to fall asleep the continuous sensation and need to move your legs may make it difficult for you to fall asleep.

Nearly half of all elderly individuals experience nocturnal myoclonus, a condition in which the leg muscles contract abruptly and repetitively throughout the night, causing frequent awakenings. Approximately one in ten individuals grind their teeth, which doctors and dentists refer to as bruxism. Teeth grinding can damage teeth and may be loud enough to disrupt the sleep of others in the room. Finally, some men suffer from a rare condition in which muscles are not completely paralyzed during REM sleep (as they normally would be) and therefore respond to actions initiated while dreaming. You might be awakened, or even injured, by your partner as he kicks or reaches about in his sleep. Many of these movement disorders can be treated with medications (such as anticonvulsants or sedatives) after they are properly diagnosed.

How to Cope with Trouble Sleeping

Most common sleep difficulties can be cured with relatively simple adjustments in how you prepare to sleep. Psychiatrists refer to these simple lifestyle approaches as sleep hygiene. They are based on behavioral principles and on an understanding of how sleep works.

The first step, paradoxically, is to make sure that you are not getting too much sleep at the wrong time. If you sleep too late, go to bed too early, or take daytime naps, then your internal clock may become confused. When you try to make up for lost sleep you end up making the problem worse. You should decide what is the best time for you to wake up, and wake up at that time every day. If you can avoid sleeping late your body will make sure that you feel sleepy at the proper time, approximately eight hours before your wake-up time.

You should make bedtime a relaxed and pleasant time. Avoid strong physical exertion or large meals before bed. Consider taking a long, hot, soothing bath. You may find it useful to learn relaxation techniques (see "Anxiety") such as progressive muscular relaxation, which you can practice evenings in bed. Listen to quiet music or read a book until you are sleepy. Television may be too stimulating. Get a comfortable bed that is not too soft or too hard. Use curtains, air conditioners, or fans to create a comfortable temperature and minimize noise and light. Some people find it easier to sleep with some continuous, ambient noise in the background, but not loud and unpredictable noises. You should avoid using the bedroom for activities other than sleep, sex, and relaxation. If you eat, work, or entertain yourself in your bedroom, then your bed becomes a place you no longer find soothing.

Regular exercise causes both physical wellness and a sense of emotional wellbeing. It also tones muscles and relaxes your body, helping you to sleep more soundly. You should try to exercise several times a week, if not every day. But avoid exercising just before bedtime. Also avoid drinking alcohol or caffeine after dinner, since they can disrupt normal sleep.

If you find yourself lying awake in bed, get up, leave your bedroom, and pick up a book or listen to music until you are feeling sleepy again. If you stay in bed you become increasingly frustrated by, and anxious about, your inability to fall asleep. You do not want to waste more than a few minutes lying in bed thinking about not sleeping. Go do something. Eventually you will get sleepy again. When you return to bed you will probably fall asleep quickly, and you may stay asleep. Again, try to avoid oversleeping in the morning. If you wake up at your usual time you will be able to fall asleep more soundly the next evening and avoid a spiraling loss of control.

Hypnotic Medications

There are effective medications for inducing sleep (known as hypnotics), but none of them are recommended for continuous use. Many of them, like the benzodiazepine sedatives (see "Anxiety"), including temazepam (Restoril) and triazolam (Halcion), can be addicting if they are taken regularly and may cause rebound insomnia when they are stopped.

Nevertheless, sleep medications may help you to get through a temporary period of troubled sleep, especially when you are under stress or feeling sick. The antihistamine diphenhydramine (Benadryl) is a common ingredient in many over-the-counter medications taken for the common cold. It can also be taken on its own, whether or not you have a cold. Chloral hydrate is a sleep aide that was commonly prescribed in the past, especially for children, but it is no longer recommended since it can be dangerous even at relatively low doses. The newest and most effective medications for sleep, which appear not to be addicting or to have any significant side effects, are zolpidem (Ambien) and zaleplon (Sonata). As is the case with all hypnotic medications, you should not drive or engage in any tasks that require alertness after taking these medications.

A few botanical products may have sleep-inducing properties, but they are poorly studied and poorly regulated. Valerian and kava are both derived from plants that are reputed to cause sleepiness. Melatonin is a hormone that is released in the brain and that regulates circadian rhythms. Some people take melatonin before going to bed in an attempt to signal to the brain that it is time to sleep. But hormones have diverse effects on the body, and it is unwise to take them before their effects have been sufficiently studied. The chemical tryptophan (a naturally occurring amino acid) may also be helpful in inducing sleep. Though it had been sold as a nutritional supplement, manufacturing impurities have caused several deaths, and the product has been removed from the market. You may wish to have a glass of warm milk or chamomile tea (which has no caffeine) before bed, but these are probably more soothing than medicinal in their effects.

Sloppiness

Your mother has given up complaining. You used to be so neat, she would say. All of the newspapers are stacked chronologically, except for the clipped articles that are sorted by subject. You have piles for the FBI, the Mafia, and foreign affairs. Sometimes you sense a connection and start a new pile. She doesn't understand the connections.

The government has agents meddling everywhere. They are watching you as well, so you have to be careful what you throw away. You hide your trash in bags and boxes. You keep nail clippings and cut hair under the bed. Wrappers and junk mail go into the closet. You don't wash your clothes unless you have time to stand at the machine and make sure no one takes them. In the meantime you leave them on your bed or the floor, depending on how dirty they are. You started saving your urine in jars, in case you need to test it for drugs, but your mom threw a fit. Still, you piss into the sink, just in case they're monitoring the toilet bowl.

There are many advantages to cleanliness and organization. Germs, insects, and other pests thrive in dirty environments. You may be less efficient if your office and home are in a shambles. People may not want to associate with you if you smell like you have not washed, or if your clothing and hair are a mess. That said, sloppiness is usually not a sign of mental illness. We all have different temperaments, upbringings, and priorities that lead us to be more or less neat. You may be a sharp dresser and organized at work but have no interest in making your bed every day. Your office may be filled with seemingly random piles of memos and forms, but you know where everything is. You would be lost if your secretary were to put everything into files. You may be a high achiever in school though your room is a mess, with books, laundry, and sports equipment scattered about.

In fact, neatness is not always ideal. If you insist on making your bed, folding your clothes, washing the dishes, and filing your forms immediately, and if you scrub the tub, spray the counter, and wash the windows every day, then you may be too perfectionistic. Sometimes cleaning and organizing can take on a life of its own; you feel that you must clean and straighten up even when it serves no purpose. This can be a sign of *anxiety*, obsessions, or *compulsions*. Perfectionism, and an insistence on following rules for their own sake, is also typical of an *obsessive*-compulsive personality. If you think that someone you care about is being messy, you should consider whether you simply have different values about the importance of being neat in different settings, and whether you can both modify your expectations a little.

In some cases increasing sloppiness may be a sign of psychological difficulties. When we are under stress we tend to have less energy for routine tasks. You may be less inclined to straighten up or vacuum the house. You may let your mail and newspapers pile up. You may leave dirty dishes in the sink for days at a time. You may lose interest in your appearance, and you may postpone getting your hair cut or doing the laundry. These features become more pronounced in major *depression*. When you are depressed you feel worthless and hopeless, and you have little energy or motivation. You may stay in your house for a week at a time without washing or changing your clothes. If you spill trash or food you may be too exhausted to clean up. You may ignore deadlines and fail to return calls.

Sloppiness can also be seen in the other extreme of mood. When you experience *mania* you are too distracted to concentrate on such mundane matters as keeping a clean house. You have plenty of energy, but you have difficulty organizing yourself. You abandon one task after another as your thoughts race from topic to topic. You may go on a purchasing spree, buying groceries that will spoil and household items that you do not need. You may write hundreds of letters or jot down notes for brilliant ideas and then leave them lying about. In contrast to depression you are very concerned about your appearance, but your judgment is poor. You may wear garish make-up or adopt an outrageous hairstyle. You may wear shocking and mismatched clothing. As mania progresses you may stop sleeping, showering, and cleaning altogether.

Sloppiness is a common feature in schizophrenia (see "Psychosis"). If you have schizophrenia you may experience what psychiatrists refer to as negative symptoms. Unlike *delusions* and *hallucinations,* negative symptoms represent the absence of normal traits, and they tend to be seen between the acute episodes of psychosis that lead to hospitalization. During these periods of relative stability you may be unmotivated, unexcited, disinterested in spending time with others, and relatively lacking in emotional expressiveness. You may be unaware of these symptoms and how you come across to others. During these times it is also common to pay less attention to hygiene, and you may neglect to bathe unless someone reminds you. You may wear your clothing in multiple layers, creating an untidy appearance. I have treated patients who felt quite comfortable wearing three pairs of pants on top of each other, or a sweater and down jacket in the middle of summer. (This is not just a matter of sloppiness; some people with schizophrenia become cold easily.) You may not wash your clothing or realize when you begin to smell. The combination of unusual facial expressions, poor grooming, and atypical dress creates an appearance of *oddness* that many people associate with severe mental illness. Fortunately, the newer antipsychotic medications often treat the negative symptoms of schizophrenia, along with delusions and hallucinations.

During the active phases of schizophrenia, psychotic thinking may also lead to unusual grooming, hygiene, and household habits. For example, if you believe that someone is trying to follow you, you may wear frumpy clothing and a hood to try to disguise yourself. If you think that your family is casting spells or practicing voodoo on you, then you may save your nail clippings and stray hairs and dispose of them where they cannot be found. If you think that people are conspiring to kill you, you may be too distracted to clean up your room. In fact, you may draw the blinds, cover the television and radio, and barricade the doors and windows.

We might assume that the *compulsive* behavior seen in obsessive-compulsive disorder (OCD) would lead, if anything, to excessive cleanliness. If you have OCD you may have many rituals that involve washing and straightening up. You may do the laundry every day, clean countertops hourly, and wash your hands and face multiple times. However, these rituals are driven by illogical *obsessions* about germs, dirt, and symmetry. They are excessive and often counterproductive. If you wash your hands over and over again, they become chapped and vulnerable to rashes and infections. If you spend all of your time washing your clothes and endlessly straightening objects you have little time for more productive activities. Basic chores may be ignored.

If you have OCD you may have *compulsions* to hoard. You find it difficult to throw away or pack up objects that you no longer use. You may save old toothbrushes, clothes that you have outgrown, or receipts for minor purchases. You may worry that you will need these items in the future, even if you cannot think of a use for them at the moment. In some cases you may find yourself unable to throw away newspapers and magazines, keeping back issues that you will never again open. This behavior is often driven by a need for completeness. You cannot tolerate the idea of losing part of the collection that you have accumulated. In the most extreme cases I have seen patients who saved their own feces and urine in jars. They often could not explain why they saved these waste products. It seemed that they were unable to let any part of themselves go.

Sloppiness that emerges in childhood may be a sign of attention-deficit *hyperactivity* disorder (ADHD). When you are constantly running about and distracted you have difficulty being neat. You may start to make your bed or clean your room, only to abandon the task before it is completed. Since ADHD emerges in childhood, parents may suspect that the sloppiness is just a part of their child's personality. If it is due to ADHD, then trouble concentrating on tasks should be evident in other settings, such as in school and during extracurricular activities. Sloppiness should improve, along with other performance problems, during medication treatment. ADHD often persists into adulthood and can be a cause of sloppiness and disorganization.

Sloppiness can also emerge in old age as a sign of dementia. In dementia you may lose both your interest in and ability to keep yourself and your home clean. Because of *memory loss* you may forget to bathe or complete household chores. As the illness progresses you may be unable to perform simple tasks, such as turning on a faucet, without assistance. Sometimes a deterioration in hygiene is the first sign of dementia. I have treated several elderly patients who were brought into the hospital after they were found living alone in horrible conditions in their apartment, with trash, waste, and rotten food lying all around.

Poor hygiene can also be a sign of drug abuse or *intoxication*. When you are addicted you spend much of your time, energy, and money obtaining and using drugs. As you become increasingly dependent you may stop washing and changing your clothes. Your clothing may reek of marijuana smoke. Your breath may smell fruity during alcoholic binges. People who know you may think you look like a wreck and wonder what has happened to you.

There are no specific psychological methods for coping with sloppiness, aside from receiving treatment for the underlying illness. You should realize that both cleanliness and sloppiness tend to be reinforcing. The messier your home becomes, the harder it becomes to motivate yourself to clean. But once you have started to organize and clean, the task becomes easier to maintain. You may find it helpful to take on just one aspect of cleaning each day rather than postponing an overwhelming job day after day.

Speech Difficulties

Sh-sh-shoot! That girl noticed you checking her out. She turns to her girlfriend and giggles. But then she looks over at you again and smiles.

You hope she doesn't come over now. If you open your mouth, you'll make a fool of yourself. Once the game starts you can show off on the field. Maybe you could go for an ice cream afterwards. You're always more relaxed after the game. Maybe you won't trip all over your words.

Oh no, here she comes. You start to walk away, but it's too late. She says hello and asks you if you're on the team. "Bh-b-b-bh . . . hello! D-d-defense!" you sputter.

A variety of psychiatric conditions can affect the quality of speech. During *depression*, speech becomes quiet and slow. Speech becomes loud, rapid, and difficult to interrupt in *mania*. In psychosis and delirium speech reflects *nonsensical* or *confused* thinking. In each of these conditions alterations in speech may be an important sign of illness, but communication is not the primary problem, rather it is a disturbance in mood or thinking.

Primary problems with language development become apparent in childhood, when children are first learning to speak. Infants start to make rudimentary sounds (as opposed to noises like crying) at two months of age. You usually speak your first word around your first birthday. Over the next year you begin to use a number of basic words and put them together in simple phrases. By age three you are able to speak in sentences. Normally children make predictable errors in speaking during these early years. You may leave parts of words silent, such as final consonants (such as

"Da" instead of "Dad"). You master some consonants and diphthongs (like "r" and "th") later than others. Words may be repeated or left out of phrases.

This normal course of development assumes a nurturing home environment, average intellectual capacity, and normal hearing. If you have a hearing impairment you learn to speak more slowly and with greater difficulty, though hearing aids may help. Deaf children who are raised to communicate through sign language rather than speech may not show any delay in signing skills. Mental retardation and autism (see "Learning Difficulties") may first become apparent due to delays in speaking, even though the underlying problem is more pervasive. In Asperger's disorder, a higher functioning variety of autism, the quality of your speech may be quite *odd*.

Stuttering is perhaps the most recognizable communication disorder. At least one in one hundred children stutter at some time, especially during the preschool years. If you stutter you have disjointed speech characterized by repeating, extending, and getting stuck on sounds. Like the Looney Tunes cartoon character you sometimes give up and switch to a word that you can pronounce with less difficulty. The stutter comes and goes but is usually worse under stress. Speech may be completely normal when you speak to yourself or when you are alone in play. In many cases stuttering goes away during the adolescent years. If it persists a vicious cycle may develop in which your fear of stuttering in public makes you more likely to stutter. The cause of stuttering is unknown, but it tends to run in families. There is no evidence that it reflects internal psychological conflicts. Like other language and learning disorders, it is much more common in boys than girls.

Perhaps as many as one in ten children have disorders involving the proper articulation of sounds. Before starting kindergarten most children have learned to properly pronounce all of the sounds in words. If you have an articulation (or phonological) disorder, you continue to drop some sounds or mix up similar sounds, with the result that your speech sounds more childish. You may have a lisp, pronouncing "s" as if it were a soft "th." In mild cases only one or two sounds are affected. Most of the time, these difficulties with articulation resolve between kindergarten and third grade. The cause of articulation delays is not known, though they tend to run in families.

Some children have a more global language impairment, in spite of normal intelligence. You may not have uttered a single word or sound by the age of two. You understand what others say, but you respond with gesture and expressions. You begin to speak in your third or fourth year, but you have difficulty remembering words and pronouncing them correctly. By the time you enter school your use of grammar and your vocabulary are far behind your classmates. You may rush your words together in a confusing way. Psychiatrists refer to this as an expressive language disorder. In more severe cases you also have difficulty understanding language, which is referred to as a receptive language disorder. In addition to not speaking you are unable to understand even simple words and commands during your second year of life. You fail to communicate even with gestures. You are able to hear and respond to sounds other than speech. The cause of these language disorders, which affect up to three in one hundred children, is unknown. Children with the milder expressive disorder tend to recover almost completely, often without treatment. Children with the mixed disorder often develop multiple *learning problems* as well and continue to have language difficulties as they grow up.

Selective mutism is a rare condition in which a child who is able to speak fluently at home with family members refuses to speak with anyone else. Some may whisper to other children but not speak to adults. If you are selectively mute you may communicate in other ways, through gestures, expressions, and whispers. You may even write or draw or lead a person by the hand in order to express yourself. The condition is thought to be caused by shyness and nervousness (see "Avoidance") and often develops when a child reaches school age. The condition usually resolves spontaneously within a year or so.

Sometimes speech is disturbed because of a specific injury or abnormality of the brain, rather than because of a delay in language development. Dysarthria is a neurological term for difficulty articulating sounds with the tongue and mouth. If you suffer from dysarthria you may also have problems with swallowing and eating. Aphasia is a neurological term for problems comprehending or expressing language. Aphasia typically results from a stroke to the portions of the brain that process language, and the onset is usually rapid. Dysarthria and aphasia may be signs of a medical emergency and should be evaluated by a neurologist. They can also result from complications at birth.

Tourette's disorder is a tic disorder usually treated by neurologists (see "Movement Problems"). If you suffer from Tourette's disorder you experience both physical and vocal tics. Vocal tics are explosive utterances that come out of the blue, including throat clearing, curse words, and jingles. You may repeat the words that someone else has just spoken or a phrase you saw written down. You may find yourself shouting a thought that you had not intended to verbalize. These outbursts punctuate and interrupt your speech, though your articulation and use of language is otherwise normal. In many ways these tics are like *compulsions*. They may be resisted for a while, only to explode more dramatically.

How to Cope with Speech Problems

In many cases speech disorders are temporary conditions that delay or interfere with language processes during childhood but resolve prior to adulthood. Even so, an inability to articulate speech fluently may cause a child to feel immature, incompetent, or different from others. Classmates may assume that you are stupid, babyish, or disturbed and may tease or avoid you. You may learn to dread speaking at school and develop low *self-esteem,* especially in terms of academic performance. For this reason, learning about the illness and consulting a speech therapist may be helpful, even if the condition is likely to resolve spontaneously within a few years.

Speech therapy administered by a speech-language pathologist is the treatment of choice for most communication disorders. Speech therapists use a variety of behavioral techniques in individual or group tutoring to teach children proper language skills. Delays in language often lead to delays in learning, so additional educational interventions may also be needed. If you have a language problem you should undergo specific language testing as well as hearing testing to ensure that your language difficulty does not stem from trouble hearing.

If you suffer from stuttering you may wish to explore hypnosis or behavioral therapy, including relaxation techniques (see "Anxiety"). Unfortunately, these techniques have not been found to reduce stuttering in the long term, though they may bring some temporary relief. If stuttering persists you may find that both you and your listeners are more relaxed and less distracted if you inform them up front that you have a stutter.

Stress

Could things get any worse? Two months after you leave for college your girlfriend writes you a letter saying that she's splitting up with you. She had been visiting every weekend, and you were planning to get married in the spring. Now you don't know what to do. You've been crying every night, and you're not getting any work done. You keep calling her, and she just hangs up. You can't pay attention in class, and you had already fallen behind. Instead of doing your homework you keep writing to her but then tearing up the letter.

You're too embarrassed to tell your parents. They really like her. They're paying for school, and they might pull you out if you fail your upcoming midterms. You'd like to have someone to talk to, but you hardly know your roommates. You didn't see any reason to get to know them before, and now they do everything together, without you.

You know you should go and talk to your professors and explain the situation, but why should they care about your personal problems?

Stress and nervous breakdown are common and acceptable ways for most of us to refer to a temporary mental health problem. The terms are vague enough to protect our privacy. Breakdown implies that you had difficulty coping with a stressful situation, but that your health eventually recovered. It suggests a crisis and vulnerability overcome, rather than a chronic mental illness. You might use the term to refer to something as routine and surmountable as a period of loneliness and heartache following a romantic breakup, or to a more serious emotional crisis requiring a few days' stay in a hospital.

Psychiatrists prefer to use the term adjustment disorder to distinguish temporary maladjustments to stress from episodes of chronic mental illnesses like bipolar disorder and schizophrenia. An adjustment disorder is diagnosed if you experience emotional problems following a stressful life event. The most common stressful events include divorce of a spouse or parents, separation from a loved one, relocation, change in job duties, academic examinations and deadlines, financial losses, troubles with the law, serious illness, or the death (see "Grief") of someone close. Sometimes you find yourself facing several stresses at once. These are adjustments and crises that people normally encounter in life, but your usual resources and coping skills may break down.

Your underlying temperament may determine how you respond to bumps in the road of life. You may be naturally confident in your ability to handle new challenges. You may have faced, and successfully overcome, many crises in the past. Or you may be inclined to view setbacks as opportunities to grow and develop new experiences. On the other hand you may see each new crisis as another trick of fate, and you may feel that you are being worn down. It may seem that bad things happen only to you. You may live in the moment and view a temporary setback catastrophically. You may have poor *self-esteem* and underestimate your resiliency or blame yourself for an unavoidable situation.

Likewise, support from friends, family, colleagues, and organizations may help you get through a crisis without developing an adjustment disorder. You are more likely to be distressed following a romantic breakup if you are alone and struggling to make ends meet. Involved grandparents may help a child to feel secure and loved when his parents are divorcing. Unemployment checks, placement firms, and Internet job postings may provide a safety net that buoys your spirits when you lose your job. Lay counselors, religious ministers, and school guidance counselors may be able to provide reassurance and helpful suggestions that defuse the stress you would otherwise feel.

The symptoms that you experience during an adjustment disorder, or breakdown, are similar to the symptoms seen in *depression* and *anxiety*. You may become nervous, fidgety, and fearful. You constantly fret about your situation, replaying conversations in your mind. You worry about what will happen to you, and you *panic* as your mind keeps generating worst case scenarios. What if the check does not arrive tomorrow? What if she does not call back? What if I fail the test? You may have difficulty going to *sleep* as you lie in bed worrying. You may feel sad, lonely, and discouraged. You may cry and even have *suicidal thoughts,* wondering if you would be better off dead.

Some people respond to stress with *anger* and counterproductive behaviors. You may curse and throw things. You may take out your feelings on others, yelling at your wife, blaming your children, or refusing to tell anyone why you are upset. You may stay out late and get into fights and arguments. You may skip school or not show up for work. You may quietly fume while obstinately refusing to do anything productive.

Sometimes you may find that you handle a crisis well initially, but that the cumulative stress eventually gets to you. You may not realize that you are in distress until several weeks after the crisis peaks. Adjustment disorders may last for only a few days but still cause enough distress for you to seek help. The emotional disturbance can sometimes last for weeks or months. If symptoms are severe or last for several months after the crisis ends, you may be suffering from an episode of clinical *depression* or generalized *anxiety* that has taken on a life of its own and that might require treatment rather than just the passing of time.

Psychiatrists differentiate *grief* and *trauma* from adjustment disorders. When someone you love has died you may experience emotional disturbances similar to those described above. However, we expect people to become distressed and temporarily unable to function during bereavement, whereas adjustment disorders are unusually severe reactions to typical life stresses. Traumas are different from other stresses because they involve a serious threat of death or harm, rather than changes in circumstances. Acute trauma may induce sadness and anxiety but also fearfulness, a tendency to be easily startled, recurrent frightening memories, and *dissociative* feelings of being out of touch with reality.

How to Cope with Stress

Though it does not rise to the level of impairment that is seen in major depression, an adjustment disorder may be cause for seeking treatment. A session or two of therapy with a psychotherapist or counselor is often sufficient. Therapists refer to these short courses of treatment as crisis or time-limited therapy. Counseling usually involves a number of nonspecific techniques, some of which could be provided equally well by a wise friend or family member.

If you seek help a counselor will provide you information about typical responses to stress and will give you an opportunity to express feelings that you might find difficult to confide in others. You will make a list of your problems and create a plan for addressing them one by one. You will be able to bounce your ideas off the counselor with the aim of choosing strategies that are most likely to succeed and avoiding actions that will make the situation worse. The counselor will help you to uncover coping strategies that you may be neglecting. You will seek support from friends and family. You will be encouraged to advocate for yourself and to negotiate with or confront others. You will be encouraged to adopt a more positive attitude, to see opportunities that are latent in the crisis. You will be discouraged from viewing your situation as a catastrophe with no resolution in sight.

Most people feel better after sharing their feelings and developing some practical strategies for coping with the disturbance in their life. You may also want to learn some relaxation techniques (see "Anxiety") to reduce your nervousness generally and to help you to calm down and think clearly when under stress in the future. Medication might be prescribed for short-term relief of *anxiety* or for *sleeping problems,* if it is needed at all.

Suicidal Thoughts

When you bought the shotgun a week ago you told yourself that you would never use it. You wanted to have it "just in case" things didn't get better. You placed it in the garage, where your wife wouldn't see it.

But you've been thinking about it every day, nearly every hour. It is your little secret. You haven't told your doctor. He'd take it away or lock you up. Now, if the medication doesn't work, you still have a way out. The pain that you've been living with for so long would finally end. All you have to do is pull the trigger.

In the past decade, suicide was the eighth or ninth leading cause of death in the United States, accounting for more than thirty thousand deaths each year. Suicide is the third leading cause of death among teenagers and young adults. If you read about crime every day in the newspaper, you might be surprised to learn that rates of suicide are higher than rates of homicide.

Suicide is the intentional ending of your own life. Suicide is not necessarily a sign of mental illness, but it almost always is. It is a choice you make when you see no alternatives. Mental illness may cause a suicidal person to feel hopeless, to neglect other options, and to view suicide as a desirable escape.

People who succeed in committing suicide usually do so on their first or second attempt. Most people who commit suicide have given some prior warning that they are suicidal. For example, a person who is thinking of killing himself may say so directly, or he may speak about giving away his possessions and going to a better place. He may stop making plans for the future. He may say that nothing matters anymore. He may wrap up his professional and personal commitments and prepare letters to be opened at a future date. Only about six percent of suicide attempts are successful, but all suicidal statements and acts should serve as alarms. Most individuals who attempt suicide genuinely want to die at the time and are not simply looking for attention. Even if they are seeking attention, it is a dangerous and desperate way to do so, and it should be taken seriously.

Certain groups of people are particularly at risk of suicide. Rates of suicide are highest among the elderly, especially elderly white men. Women attempt suicide more frequently than men, but men are more often successful at killing themselves. In part, this is because men use more lethal methods. A majority of suicides are committed with a firearm. Women are more likely to attempt to overdose on medication. You are at greater risk if you are unmarried or live alone and if you are unemployed. You may be more likely to kill yourself if you are *depressed* with anxious, hopeless, and guilty feelings. A depressed person is also more likely to attempt suicide if he has recently lost a loved one, or if he suffers from a serious medical illness. Alcohol and drug use also greatly increase the risk of a suicide attempt.

Suicide Is Common in Major Depression

Approximately one out of every six individuals with untreated *depression* successfully commit suicide. This is a very high mortality rate, especially when you consider that five percent of individuals in the United States suffer from depression each year. If you have never experienced depression it is hard to imagine feeling so bad that you would be willing to kill yourself. Even if you have felt suicidal yourself, it is hard to comprehend later when you are feeling better and think back on those feelings. How could things have gotten so bad?

When you suffer from depression you are in pain and you cannot conceive of the possibility of ever feeling better. Death can seem an attractive option. At first you begin to wish that you were dead, but you are unwilling to consider taking the steps to kill yourself. Psychiatrists refer to this as passive suicidal ideation. This is a risky stage. A person who wishes his life would end might neglect to take care of his health or engage in careless behavior, not thinking about the future. For example, some people with passive suicidal ideation engage in unprotected sex, not caring if they contract AIDS. Others drink and drive recklessly.

Most people who begin to think about suicide are uncertain and wish that they could think of an alternative. You do not want to upset your family or others who depend on you. You may consider it a mortal sin or moral failing to take your own life. You may worry that a suicide attempt could be painful, or that you might make a mistake and fail to finish the job. But at some point many people suffering from depression give up and start to plan their own death. People who commit suicide have usually been planning to kill themselves for a long time, keeping a gun handy or stockpiling pills for an eventual overdose. Some individuals hold on to the possibility of committing suicide as their last hope when they have given up on everything else.

Unfortunately, family and psychiatrists are not always able to predict who will attempt suicide and who will not. The possibility of a suicide attempt needs to be considered whenever anyone is seriously depressed. Suicide is a taboo subject that most of us are afraid to discuss. It may even be difficult to read about. However, the depressed person who has been thinking about harming himself will usually be relieved that someone has asked. It can be a huge relief to learn that other people have such thoughts when depressed and yet survive them.

Paradoxically, the risk of suicide sometimes increases when an episode of depression is being properly treated. Usually you begin to recover energy before hopelessness and sadness have resolved. Suddenly, you find that you have the energy to carry out your intention. This is one of the reasons why suicide occurs more frequently immediately after discharge from a psychiatric hospital. The other reason is that people with depression are usually discharged from the hospital after only a few days, long before antidepressant medication has become fully effective. For these reasons, close outpatient follow-up and family supervision is very important.

Suicide Is Also Common in Other Serious Mental Illnesses

Though most people who kill themselves suffer from major depression, there are other mental illnesses that can lead to suicide. Suicide is the cause of death for twenty percent of individuals diagnosed with bipolar disorder (see "Mania"). As many as half of those with bipolar disorder attempt suicide, usually during an episode of depression, or during a severe manic episode in which mood becomes increasingly irritable, angry, and desperate. The rates of suicide may be higher in bipolar disorder in part because manic individuals are more energetic and *impulsive*. Individuals with depression are sometimes too fatigued and apathetic to make an attempt.

Approximately one out of every ten patients with schizophrenia (see "Psychosis") commit suicide, usually during the first ten years of illness. This is twenty times higher than the rate of suicide in the general population. In this sense schizophrenia is a potentially terminal illness. You may attempt suicide while you are psychotic, perhaps because you believe that the entire world is conspiring against you, or because you are terribly distraught and confused by your symptoms. Unfortunately, the risk of suicide in schizophrenia is even higher when these psychotic symptoms are resolving. The feeling of losing your mind, and the knowledge of having a serious illness, can be terrifying, even more so than the acute *delusions* and *hallucinations*. The good news is that some of the newer antipsychotic medications, especially clozapine, seem to reduce the risk of suicide.

Though people with depression usually plan their suicides, some who are not depressed attempt to kill themselves *impulsively* when they are extremely distraught. Breakup of a romance, job loss, death of a family member, criminal arrest, or other *stress* may precipitate dangerous behavior by someone who is not clinically depressed but who is unable to think of a better way to cope with the crisis. Adolescents are particularly vulnerable to impulsive suicide attempts. You may not intend to kill yourself so much as to express your distress and alert others to your need for help. But you may also be ambivalent and willing to die at the moment. If you survive an attempt to deliberately harm yourself your risks of successfully committing suicide in the next year are one hundred times higher than in the general population. In three out of one hundred cases you will go on to kill yourself. If you survive an impulsive attempt to kill yourself you may later refer to the episode as a nervous breakdown. Psychiatrists refer to these episodes of emotional and behavioral turmoil as adjustment disorders.

About half of those who have committed suicide had a personality disorder diagnosis. Borderline personality disorder is an illness that is characterized, in part, by repeated attempts to harm yourself, often in order to attract attention and avoid being abandoned (see "Self-Esteem Problems"). Some of these attempts are better understood as acts of *self-*

mutilation, rather than as suicidal acts, since they are not intended to cause death. Some are transparent gestures designed to attract attention or to manipulate others. Even so, the risk of genuine suicide, or of death occurring inadvertently during a gesture, is extremely high among those who suffer from borderline personality disorder. If you have this personality style, you are very sensitive to rejection, you feel terrible when you are slighted or abandoned by others, you act *impulsively,* and you may have a habit of harming yourself when you feel bad. A significant part of your therapy will involve learning safer methods of coping with unpleasant feelings. You may particularly benefit from a form of cognitive-behavioral therapy known as dialectical behavior therapy (DBT).

Rates of suicide are twenty times higher among drug and alcohol abusers than among nonabusers. Drug or alcohol abuse can cause a person to become suicidal in many ways. *Intoxication* or withdrawal from drugs may cause a short-lived but severe period of depression (often lasting only a few hours or days) during which you feel so bad that you may decide death would be better. You may feel so out of control and ashamed about your *cravings* for drugs or alcohol that suicide seems like the only way to stop using or to avoid embarrassment. You may feel especially hopeless after relapsing. Intoxication is also disinhibiting and dramatically increases the chance that you will attempt to kill yourself when upset. Most drugs exacerbate psychiatric symptoms, increase impulsiveness, and decrease judgment. If you are drunk or high a relatively minor difficulty may seem insurmountable. In the heat of the moment suicide may seem the easy way out.

How to Cope with Suicidal Thoughts

If you are having thoughts of harming yourself you need to tell your family and psychiatrist immediately so that they can help keep you safe until you are feeling better. If you do not have a psychiatrist you should call a suicide or crisis hotline or go to an emergency room. Though depression always feels as if it will last forever, it is highly likely to improve with time and treatment. After you are feeling better you will look back and be glad that you did not give up. Even when stresses seem overwhelming, you need to take the time to reflect and discuss them with others. You will see that you can tackle your problems one by one.

If someone you care about is depressed, one of your most important roles is to support your loved one when he thinks life is too much for him. It is okay for you to ask someone that you are close to if he has been thinking about death. Though these are questions which most of us are scared to ask, there is no evidence that asking about suicidal thoughts provokes a person to attempt suicide. Instead, most people feel some relief when they are asked about suicidal feelings. It is very frightening to contemplate killing yourself, not only because of the gruesome nature of the act itself, but because you are often alone with the thought. By asking your loved one about suicide you let him know that you care enough about him to discuss a difficult subject, that his suicidal thoughts are not uncommon in depression, and that, like many other people, he can get treatment that will help him survive.

You should take very seriously any comments by your loved one that he is feeling suicidal. A person who is thinking about killing himself may make only indirect statements about wrapping up his affairs or about not being around in the future. These comments provide an opportunity for you to ask whether he is making plans to kill himself. If someone tells you that he wants to kill himself, and particularly if he has a plan, then it is crucial to take whatever steps are needed to ensure his safety. It is best if you can encourage him to voluntarily seek help at a doctor's office or emergency room. You should also stress with him how important his life is to you and others. You should remove guns and extra pills from the house, along with any other tools he might use to attempt suicide.

If your loved one has children in his care, you should ensure that they are safe. I have treated several parents who had killed, or attempted to kill, their children before attempting suicide themselves. While depressed and out of touch with reality they hoped to spare their children the pain of living.

The responsibility of saving someone's life may be more than you want to shoulder on your own. You can call a suicide hotline, local mental health agency, or advocacy group. You can involve other family members and friends. Rarely, you may feel that you need to call the police when someone is determined to hurt himself. Fortunately, if you have to take this step, the person who feels suicidal most likely will thank you for intervening to save his life once he is no longer depressed.

If your loved one does kill himself, you are likely to experience *grief*. You may also become *angry* at your loved one and others who treated or cared for him. You may feel guilty for failing to prevent the suicide. You may be *traumatized* by the shock of finding your loved one dead. You may have to cope with the intrusion of the police and the media, the opinions of neighbors and, sometimes, religious complications. You should try to remind yourself that suicide is often not predictable, that it is the unfortunate result of serious illness and not a personal failing on your part or on the part of the victim. You may benefit from seeing a therapist yourself. The risk of suicide is almost twice as high among family members of a suicide victim, and you should take steps to reduce the chance that you or other surviving members of the family do not become hopeless and respond in the same way.

Trauma

What a terrible year it has been since your patrol partner died. You never go out, and you don't seem to enjoy things like you used to. No more parties with the other officers and their families. No more target practice. No more football games. All you do is sit at home and scream at the kids.

At least work has provided some relief. You haven't had as many spells since you requested a desk job. You have trouble concentrating sometimes, but at least you're not spacing out in the patrol car or shaking too badly to turn the steering wheel. Who can afford to have a partner like that on the streets?

It's bad enough what happened a year ago. You could hold a gun steady back then, but it didn't do much good. The killer shot first. You don't even remember what happened next. You found out later that when you returned fire you hit him square in the chest. At some point you called an ambulance. You can still picture your partner's glazed eyes and pale skin as they took him away. Sometimes those eyes wake you up in the middle of the night. His mouth moves, like he's trying to say something to you before he dies. Sometimes you think if you could just figure out what he was saying, these spells would go away.

Terrifying events can leave psychological scars that are as distressing and disabling as physical wounds. After experiencing a trauma you may develop symptoms of *anxiety, depression,* and *dissociation.* Psychiatrists have also come to recognize that many people, after the initial shock, develop a longer-lasting reaction to trauma that involves tense and fearful reliving and avoidance. Post-traumatic stress disorder (PTSD) is a syndrome that can be seen in response to traumas ranging from rape to combat. These are the two traumatic experiences that psychiatrists have studied most thoroughly, but other common traumas include injuries, accidents, natural disasters, and physical assaults, or any event in which you feel that your life or bodily integrity is seriously threatened. You may also find it traumatic to witness someone else being harmed or killed, or to unexpectedly learn of the death of someone very close to you.

When you are in a threatening situation, your body produces a variety of stress hormones (such as adrenaline, or norepinephrine) that prepare you to fight or to run away. Your pulse, blood pressure, and metabolism accelerate. You focus exclusively on the threat at hand. Smells, sounds, and bodily sensations are seared into your memory, presumably to help you recognize similar dangers in the future. You produce natural pain-killers that help you to ignore pain and keep fighting or running even after you have been injured. If the threat you face is overwhelming or out of your control, then you may shut down and become detached from the event, like an animal who freezes when caught. Cortisol, another stress hormone, is released by the brain and eventually brings your body back to its regular resting state. These chemical surges, or their failure to return to normal, are thought to underlie the symptoms seen in response to trauma.

Immediately after a trauma you may have difficulty shutting down your fear reaction. You remain tense, high-strung, and alert. You have trouble relaxing, sleeping, and concentrating on other matters. Not wanting to be taken by surprise again, you begin to expect danger at any moment, from any quarter. Unrelated noises or movements startle you. Anything that reminds you of the trauma can cause you to *panic*. Panic is a sign that your stress hormones remain high or are too easily triggered.

Stress hormones sensitize the parts of your brain that encode memories. During the traumatic event you may memorize portions of your experience in great detail. It is as if time has stopped, and the moment stays with you forever. You may have difficulty putting your recollections into words, because they are memorized as experiences rather than as thoughts. But the sensations can return to you vividly in the form of nightmares or *flash-backs* even in the first few days after the trauma.

On the other hand, you may have trouble remembering portions of the trauma. You may not recall the face of the person who assaulted you, only his smell and his voice. You may not remember being in any pain. You may recall arriving at a hospital or police station, but you have forgotten how you got there. You may not remember what you did to survive. This amnesia may result from the selective attention that you pay during a trauma to whatever is most important to your survival. You may ignore words, street signs, and pain while paying close attention to sounds and avenues of escape. Emotional feelings like disgust, terror, or humiliation may overwhelm your ability to pay attention to other thoughts.

The feeling of shock and numbness that occurs during trauma can persist in the days to come. You may feel detached from your life, and from things going on around you. You may feel that you are a different person, in a different world, or that you are not sure who you are. You may be waiting for the world to slow down and return to normal. You may feel like you are in a daze, that objects are seen through a fog. You may not know what to do next. You may appear apathetic and spacey to your loved ones. This *dissociation* from reality may be, along with panic attacks, a sign that the trauma has seriously affected you and that you are at risk for persistent symptoms of PTSD in the months to come. On the other hand, some degree of dissociation is commonly experienced even in those who do not go on to suffer from PTSD.

It is likely that you will experience a variety of emotions in the first days and weeks following a trauma. It is very common to feel sad, *angry,* anxious, ashamed, or guilty (especially if you survived an event in which others perished). You may feel that you have been treated unfairly. You may feel hopeless or helpless. You may feel that your life has been ruined, or that the world has become a dangerous place. You may be overwhelmed by losses of things that you valued, whether they be physical possessions, loved ones, or a sense of safety. You may be in physical pain as well.

About two-thirds of Americans have experienced at least one serious psychological trauma at some time during their life. Many experience the sorts of reactions described above. These reactions, which occur in the first few days to weeks following a trauma, are called acute stress reactions. In most cases, when you have been through a traumatic experience, these symptoms fade within a couple of days. You may still have an occasional nightmare, panic attack, or overreaction to a loud noise, but the symptoms do not disturb you in an ongoing fashion. Only one-fourth of those exposed to trauma go on to develop the persistent reaction that psychiatrists refer to as PTSD.

PTSD Involves Persistent Symptoms of Arousal, Reexperiencing, and Avoidance

Psychiatrists first identified the syndrome that we now know as PTSD from treating soldiers in wartime. Since ancient times it has been recognized that some soldiers go into a state of psychological shock following combat. In the past century therapists began to recognize that women who had been raped experienced the same cluster of signs and symptoms that had been described in combat reactions. The syndrome was then identified in victims of disasters, crime, and accidents. Most recently, following the terrorist attacks of September 11, it became clear that an entire population could be traumatized after witnessing the sudden destruction of large numbers of innocent people. To people around the country an entire way of life, and an assumption of safety, was under threat. Studies showed that vast numbers of Americans experienced *depression* or PTSD following the attacks, with rates as high as one in five for both illnesses among individuals living in lower Manhattan. Immediately following the attack therapists around the country mobilized to educate Americans about trauma and how to seek help.

The symptoms of PTSD are similar to the stress reactions that are normally seen immediately after a traumatic event. However, in PTSD the reaction persists for months or years and may get worse rather than fade away. The most obvious symptoms involve an increased level of nervous system arousal. If you have PTSD you startle easily. Loud noises or sudden movements may cause you to panic or enter a fighting stance. This can be seen among soldiers, police, and urban residents, who may hit the ground when a car backfires or a door is slammed. You are always scanning the environment for threat and are preoccupied with worries. You have trouble concentrating on mundane matters that you do not perceive as relevant to avoiding danger. You have *sleeping problems,* in part because of your nervous energy, and in part because of frequent nightmares. People you care about tell you that you have a short fuse, and you recognize that you lose your temper too easily, over minor matters. The trauma is past, but you act as if you are still under threat.

In PTSD, the trauma is endlessly relived. Years may have passed but it seems to you like only yesterday. The smells, tastes, sights, and pains remain vivid and easy to recall. The trauma seems to exist in a bubble, outside the normal passage of time, and you carry the bubble with you, slipping in and out of it, usually with little conscious control. Sometimes events around you bring the past into focus. For example, you see an Asian man on the street and suddenly feel like you are back in Vietnam, taking shelter from a grenade. These recollections can be much more powerful than simple memories. You may recall them as if they were actually happening to you again, as if you had stepped into your own past. These vivid recollections are called *flashbacks*. You may also experience nightmares in which the trauma is replayed. Your body is fooled by these intrusive recollections, releasing adrenaline as if you were genuinely in danger. Hours may pass before you are able to relax again.

The most frequently overlooked aspects of PTSD are the signs of emotional *avoidance*. You feel isolated from others. It seems that no one else understands what you have experienced, and what you are still going through. You may be embarrassed by your inability to leave the past behind. You may feel like this is your burden, that you cannot share it with anyone. You may be fearful of experiencing any emotions at all, because you lose control and scare those you love. You conclude that it would be better to just avoid emotions and relationships altogether. You especially try to avoid situations that take you back to the trauma. In therapy you may avoid discussing the very experiences that caused your symptoms.

Some of the symptoms of PTSD are similar to the symptoms of *depression* and *anxiety*. You no longer enjoy being around others or engaging in the activities that used to bring you pleasure. You appear emotionally constricted. You try to avoid public places for fear of having flashbacks or *panic* attacks. You are constantly worried, tense, or on the verge of losing your temper. You may drink or use drugs in an attempt to treat your nervous symptoms, but these only further erode your control, so that memories stream back and you become tearful or *angry* more easily. In fact, the rates of clinical depression and anxiety are both around fifty percent among those who have a diagnosis of PTSD. If you suffer from both PTSD and depression, you are more likely to have *suicidal thoughts* or to attempt suicide.

Who Is at Risk for PTSD?

Almost one in ten women, and one in twenty men, develop PTSD at some time during their lives. Half of the time, symptoms resolve in under a year. But symptoms may persist for years.

The chance of developing PTSD depends on the type of trauma you have experienced, the context in which the trauma occurs, and your vulnerability. Experiences are more traumatic if they are unexpected, life threatening, physically harmful, and intentional. For example, rape is one of the most potent causes of PTSD. Approximately two-thirds of women and men who have been raped develop PTSD. It is likely that a sexual assault is experienced as more humiliating and more personal than most other traumas, and it also usually involves physical penetration of the body and a threat of physical harm or death. The higher lifetime rate of PTSD among women reflects, in part, the much higher rates of rape and attempted sexual assault against women. Almost one-third of firefighters, and nearly half of battered women, develop PTSD. Rates are relatively low among combat veterans, with about one in ten developing PTSD. Even though combat almost universally involves the threat of death, and the witnessing of injury and death to others, these risks are understood as part of the job, are openly acknowledged, and are shared among your fellow combatants. The support of colleagues, family, and the home community probably protect against the development of combat PTSD.

Psychiatrists have tried to determine who may be most vulnerable to develop PTSD. Having experienced trauma in the past may make you more vulnerable to developing PTSD when you are traumatized again. Having another major mental illness, or having family members with mental illness, appears to raise your risk of PTSD. Children and the elderly are more likely to develop PTSD following similar traumas, perhaps because they have fewer coping skills or resources. If you lose your possessions or social supports around the time of the trauma, then you may be more vulnerable. This was seen following the World Trade Center disaster, when those who lost jobs, loved ones, or their homes were among the most likely to develop PTSD.

Repeated Childhood Abuse Can Cause More Varied Psychological Reactions

PTSD often occurs in an otherwise healthy adult following a single traumatic event. The situation can be much more complex when the trauma occurs repeatedly during the vulnerable periods of childhood and adolescence. According to surveys, many men and women report having been sexually or physically abused when growing up, though actual rates are difficult to determine. Studies have found that close to one in ten women report that they were molested or raped repeatedly before reaching adulthood. Reported rates among men are closer to one in forty. Approximately one in five adults report that their parents were physically aggressive. It is no surprise that your risk of PTSD, depression, anxiety, and *dissociation* are much higher if you have experienced repeated traumas, sometimes at the hands of your own parents or family members.

The sexual or physical abuse of children interferes with normal development. You learn to trust and love others through your relationship with your parents. When a mother or father seduces, beats, or fails to protect you, then you may grow up believing that no one can be trusted. You may confuse love and sex; and you may avoid sex altogether, or pursue sex in desperation. You may grow up without a clear image of yourself and your potential to form relationships with others. You may suffer from *self-esteem problems* and a feeling of being damaged. In many cases children are threatened to remain silent about abuse, or are too embarrassed to bring it to the attention of loved ones who might help them. This silence creates an environment where abuse can continue and where you feel that you have no support and must be to blame.

Many children run away from abusive homes, only to find themselves homeless or trapped in prostitution, reenacting the abuse that they were trying to escape. Approximately half the runaway population, and a greater number of prostitutes, report a childhood history of sexual abuse. If you were abused as a child, your risk of *self-mutilation, suicidal thinking,* suicide attempts, drug and alcohol abuse, and other *impulsive* behaviors is much higher. Your risk of having PTSD as an adult is about fifty percent if you were repeatedly abused. On the other hand, many who were sexually abused as children report that the abuse has had little or no effect on them as adults.

How to Cope with Trauma and Abuse

If you have recently experienced a significant trauma, you should recognize that it is quite common to have anxiety, sadness, trouble sleeping, and preoccupations for several weeks afterward. Unless these symptoms are consistently disturbing to you, there is probably no need for psychiatric treatment. Generally you can expect that your feelings about the trauma will fade over several weeks as your body and mind naturally heal. You will probably find it helpful to discuss your experience with your loved ones, so that they understand what you are going through and can provide support. You may find yourself avoiding the topic initially, only to burst into tears unexpectedly at a later date. You probably should not dwell on the trauma. Keep going to work, if you can, and try to make time to distract yourself with friends and loved ones. Spend some time relaxing and exercising. Trust yourself to figure out how much you need to process the trauma.

Many counselors are trained to administer trauma debriefing to victims immediately after a traumatic experience. In debriefing you are encouraged to describe what happened and to express your thoughts and feelings. The counselor educates you about typical reactions to stress and potential long-term symptoms, like those seen in PTSD. Unfortunately debriefing is widely used but poorly tested. Some studies have found that debriefing may increase the risk of becoming symptomatic. It may be healthier for you to avoid thinking about a trauma too much early on.

If your symptoms persist or worsen with time you may benefit from seeing a psychiatrist or therapist. The good news is that even PTSD can fade with time. About half of those who suffer from PTSD recover in about six months without any formal treatment. However, the illness can seriously impact your life in the meantime, and you should probably seek help rather than continue to suffer. If nothing else, you will learn about PTSD and feel less isolated and damaged. Sometimes PTSD emerges months or years after the trauma, often after another traumatic event has occurred.

The first challenge in the treatment of PTSD is to establish a relationship with your therapist in which you feel it is safe for you to talk about the trauma and your current symptoms. It may be difficult to trust that your therapist is strong enough to listen, or that he will not be judgmental or abandon you. You may be tempted to minimize your trauma, stating that it is no worse than what others experience. You may even blame yourself for the trauma, or for being unable to get on with life. Simply being able to speak openly of your experience can be extremely therapeutic, especially if others have encouraged you to remain silent. Sometimes group therapy can be helpful in providing you an opportunity to discuss your trauma with others who have had similar experiences (for example, as veterans or survivors of sexual assault).

Psychotherapy utilizes cognitive-behavioral techniques to treat the symptoms of PTSD. You learn relaxation skills for coping with *panic,* irritability, and chronic tenseness. You learn to recognize symptoms and identify and modify catastrophic thinking. For example, after a car accident therapy may help you to acknowledge that you are not placing your life in great danger every time you get back into a car. In fact, you may run greater risks by refusing to get into a car. You begin to realize that the trauma can be discussed in therapy without you losing control. You can think about the trauma without reliving it, and when you remember what happened you do not bring the threat back to life. You identify irrational thoughts you may have, such as feeling like you are to blame for what happened. As you become more comfortable you may expose yourself to triggers and situations that remind you of the trauma, to prove to yourself that the trauma is in the past and that you can manage your current reactions.

Anger management therapy may also be helpful if your PTSD leads you to lose your temper easily. Eye movement desensitization reprocessing (EMDR) is a type of therapy that has been touted for PTSD. In EMDR, the therapist moves his finger rapidly back and forth in front of your eyes while using other nonspecific psychotherapy techniques. However, there is no evidence that the finger movements that distinguish EMDR from other therapies serve any purpose. If you were sexually assaulted you may benefit from therapy that deals also with associated feelings, such as shame, self-blame, and poor *self-esteem,* that are commonly experienced. Nearly half of the victims of a sexual assault have *sexual performance problems* or decide not to have sex for months after the attack. You and your partner may find couple therapy useful.

Psychiatric medication may also be helpful for the treatment of PTSD symptoms. The SSRI antidepressant medications (see "Depression") have been proven effective in reducing arousal symptoms especially, though they may also be helpful in reducing flashbacks, nightmares, numbing, and social isolation. Antidepressants may also be effective for symptoms of *depression* and *anxiety* that commonly co-occur with PTSD.

If someone you care about has been recently traumatized you can help her by being supportive and by providing her with information about typical reactions to trauma. In providing support you want to communicate that the trauma was not her fault. Even if she made choices that you believe may have put her at risk, you can save that discussion until she is feeling stronger. You want to help her feel like life is returning to normal. Encourage her to join you in activities that she used to enjoy. Try not to dwell on the trauma if she feels uncomfortable and does not want to discuss it further. At the same time, never discourage her from bringing up the subject. After a terrible and frightening experience your loved one may feel like the world has been changed forever. She may feel alone in her experiences. The most important thing you can do is to communicate that you are still there for her.

If your loved one continues to have symptoms of PTSD long after the trauma has occurred, you should not give up hope. The symptoms of PTSD can fade with time, especially with treatment. Fortunately, most people who suffer from PTSD are nevertheless able to work and enjoy life with their families, even though they experience serious symptoms from time to time. You should continue to strike a balance between acknowledging the seriousness of the trauma and the current symptoms while seeking to preserve a normal life for your loved one and your family. There may be times when your loved one needs to have some space to be alone because the memories are too intrusive. There may be times when sleeping together or having sex may be difficult, because of nightmares or overwhelming emotions. You may have to recognize sometimes that you simply cannot fully appreciate what the trauma felt like to your loved one. But you want to always remain open for when she is ready to talk. Serving as a witness to your loved one's experience, and standing by her, is often the most important role you can play.

Recommended Resources

The following is a listing of contacts, books, and organizations that you may find helpful. Most of the organizations' Web sites provide information about diagnosis and treatment, suggestions for managing illness, and referrals to treatment and support groups. Many provide information in Spanish. You may also wish to refer to my Web site for any significant developments since this book was written: www.fiftysigns.com.

Hotlines

National Hopeline Network
201 North 23rd Street, Suite 100
Purcellville, VA 20132
Tel.: 800-SUICIDE (784-2433)
Web site: www.hopeline.com
Hopeline can connect you to a suicide crisis center in your area.

Covenant House Nineline
346 West 17th Street
New York, NY 10011-5020
Tel.: 800-999-9999
Assistance for children and adolescents in crisis.

Samaritans
Upper Mill, Kingston Road
Ewell, Surrey KT17 2AF
United Kingdom
Tel.: 08457-90-90-90 (England)
Web site: www.suicide-helplines.org
A hotline for individuals in emotional crisis. The Web site, which provides international contacts in multiple languages, was previously operated by Befrienders International.

Lifeline Australia
P.O. Box 173
Deakin ACT 2600
Australia
Tel.: 1300-13-11-14
Web site: www.lifeline.org.au
Suicide and crisis hotline.

LifeLine New Zealand
P.O. Box 74010, Market Road
Auckland 5
New Zealand
Tel.: 0800-LIFELINE (543-354)
Web site: www.lifeline.co.nz
Suicide and crisis hotline.

National Sex Assault Hotline
Rape, Abuse and Incest National Network (RAINN)
Tel.: 800-656-HOPE (4673)
Web site: www.rainn.org

National Domestic Violence Hotline
Tel.: 800-799-SAFE (7233)
Web site: www.ndvh.org

Health Hotlines
Web site: www.sis.nlm.nih.gov/hotlines
A listing of dozens of hotlines pertaining to a variety of medical and mental illnesses, sponsored by the National Library of Medicine.

Government Agencies that Promote Mental Health

Knowledge Exchange Network (KEN)
Center for Mental Health Services
Substance Abuse and Mental Health Services Administration (SAMHSA)
5600 Fishers Lane, Room 12-105
Rockville, MD 20857
Tel.: 301-443-2271
Web site: www.mentalhealth.org
KEN is packed with links to professional and consumer organizations and practical information, in English and Spanish. The Center will also link you to mental health resources in your state.

National Institute of Mental Health (NIMH)
6001 Executive Boulevard, Room 8184
MSC 9663, Bethesda, MD 20892-9663

Tel.: 866-615-6464
Web site: www.nimh.nih.gov
NIMH provides fact sheets on several illnesses in English and Spanish.

Canadian Health Network
Health Canada
A.L. 0900 C2
Ottawa, Canada K1A 0K9
Tel: 613-957-2991 (Canada)
Web site: www.canadian-health-network.ca

Mental Health and Wellbeing
Commonwealth of Australia Department of Health and Ageing
Mental Health Branch (MDP 37)
GPO Box 9848
Canberra ACT 2601
Australia
Tel.: 02-6289-1555
Web site: www.mentalhealth.gov.au

General Health Resources

Health Finder
Web site: www.healthfinder.gov
This Web site, developed by the U.S. Department of Health and Human Services,
will link you to information from other reliable professional and governmental organizations. You can browse through "mental disorders" and other medical topics
organized alphabetically in the "health library."

Medline Plus
Web site: www.medlineplus.gov
The National Library of Medicine provides this Web resource with information
about medications and illnesses. You can search the Medline database for abstracts
of published medical research.

National Center for Complementary and Alternative Medicine
Web site: www.nccam.nih.gov
A branch of the National Institutes of Health, NCCAM sponsors scientific trials of
alternative treatments, ranging from meditation to acupuncture and botanical remedies. NCCAM's Web site provides valuable information about the potential benefits and dangers of specific alternative treatments.

Mental Health Advocacy and Support

National Alliance for the Mentally Ill (NAMI)
Colonial Place Three

2107 Wilson Boulevard, Suite 300
Arlington, VA 22201
Tel.: 703-524-7600
Web site: www.nami.org
NAMI is the leading grassroots organization of family members and other supporters of people with severe mental illnesses. NAMI has branch offices throughout the United States.

National Mental Health Association (NMHA)
2001 North Beauregard Street, 12th Floor
Alexandria, VA 22311
Tel.: 703-684-7722; Mental Health Resource Center: 800-969-6642
Web site: www.nmha.org
NMHA is the oldest nonprofit U.S. organization in support of mental health. NMHA's Mental Health Resource Center provides referrals to mental health services and informative fact sheets about mental illness.

National Alliance for Research on Schizophrenia and Depression (NARSAD)
60 Cutter Mill Road, Suite 404
Great Neck, NY 11021
Tel.: 800-829-8289
Web site: www.narsad.org
NARSAD advocates for research and treatment of severe mental illnesses and provides informative brochures and listings of clinical research trials being conducted across the country.

Canadian Mental Health Association (CMHA)
8 King Street East, Suite 810
Toronto, Ontario M5C 1B5
Tel.: 416-484-7750 (Canada)
Web site: www.cmha.ca ·
The Web site is written in both English and French and provides numerous brochures about mental illness in languages not found on other sites.

Resource Center to Address Discrimination and Stigma
ADS Center
1211 Chestnut Street, 11th Floor
Philadelphia, PA 19107-4103
Tel.: 800-540-0320
Web site: www.adscenter.org
Provides resources for combating the stigma of mental illness. Sponsored by SAMHSA.

Books

Adamec, Christine A. *How to Live with a Mentally Ill Person: A Handbook of Mentally Ill Strategies.* New York: Wiley, 1996.

Amador, Xavier. *I Am Not Sick. I Don't Need Help! Helping the Seriously Mentally Ill Accept Treatment: A Practical Guide for Families and Therapists.* Cincinnati, OH: Vida, 2000.

Carter, Rosalynn, with Susan K. Golant. *Helping Someone with Mental Illness.* New York: Random House, 1999.

Stress and Anxiety

The Canadian Mental Health Association Web site (listed above) is an excellent resource for coping with stress.

Anxiety Disorder Association of America
8730 Georgia Avenue, Suite 600
Silver Spring, MD 20910
Tel.: 240-485-1001
Web site: www.adaa.org

Social Phobia/Social Anxiety Association
2058 E. Topeka Drive
Phoenix, AZ 85024
Web site: www.socialphobia.org

Books

Bourne, Edmund J. *Anxiety and Phobia Workbook,* 3rd edition. Oakland, CA: New Harbinger, 2001.

Butler, Gillian. *Overcoming Social Anxiety and Shyness.* New York: New York University Press, 2001.

Markway, Barbara G., Alec Pollard, Cheryl N. Carmin, and Teresa Flynn. *Dying of Embarrassment.* Oakland, CA: New Harbinger, 1992.

Wilson, Robert Reid. *Don't Panic: Taking Control of Anxiety Attacks.* New York: HarperCollins, 1996.

Depression and Mania

Depression and Bipolar Support Alliance
730 Franklin Street, Suite 501
Chicago, IL 60610
Tel.: 800-826-3632
Web site: www.dbsalliance.org
Formally known as the National Depressive and Manic Depressive Association (NDMDA).

Depression and Related Affective Disorders Association (DRADA)
2330 West Joppa Road, Suite 100
Lutherville, MD 21093
Tel.: 410-583-2929
Web site: www.drada.org

American Foundation for Suicide Prevention (AFSP)
120 Wall Street, 22nd Floor
New York, NY 10005
Tel.: 888-333-AFSP (2377)
Web site: www.afsp.org

American Association of Suicidology
4201 Connecticut Avenue, NW, Suite 408
Washington, DC 20008
Tel.: 202-237-2280
Web site: www.suicidology.org

Depression After Delivery (DAD)
91 East Somerset Street
Raritan, NJ 08869
Tel.: 800-944-4773
Web site: www.depressionafterdelivery.com
Resources and information about postpartum depression.

American Academy of Retired Persons Grief and Loss Programs
601 E Street, NW
Washington, DC 20049
Tel.: 888-687-2277
Web site: www.aarp.org/griefandloss
The AARP provides information, outreach services, and discussion forums.

Books

Berger, Diane, with Lisa Berger. *We Heard the Angels of Madness: A Family Guide to Coping with Manic Depression.* New York: HarperCollins, 1992

Cronkite, Kathy. *On the Edge of Darkness.* New York: Dell, 1994. Interviews with several celebrities who have experienced depression.

DePaolo, Jr., J. Raymond. *Understanding Depression: What We Know and What You Can Do About It.* New York: Wiley, 2003.

Dowling, Collette. *You Mean I Don't Have to Feel This Way? New Help for Depression, Anxiety and Addiction.* New York: Bantam Doubleday Dell, 1993.

Engram, Sara. *Mortal Matters: When a Loved One Dies.* Kansas City, MO: Andrews McMeel, 1990.

Fast, Julie A., and John D. Preston. *Loving Someone with Bipolar Disorder: Understanding and Helping Your Partner.* Oakland, CA: New Harbinger, 2004.

Golant, Mitch, and Susan K. Golant. *What to Do When Someone You Love Is Depressed.* New York: Henry Holt, 1998.

Greenberger, Dennis, and Christine A. Padesky. *Mind Over Mood: Change How You Feel by Changing the Way You Think.* New York: Guilford Press, 1995.

Jamison, Kay Redfield. *An Unquiet Mind: A Memoir of Moods and Madness*. New
    York: Random House, 1996.
    The author is a psychologist who writes of her experience with bipolar disorder.
Jamison, Kay Redfield. *Night Falls Fast: Understanding Suicide*. New York: Knopf,
    2000.
Papolos, Dimitri, and Janice Papolos. *Overcoming Depression: The Definitive Re-
    source for Patients and Families Who Live with Depression and Manic Depres-
    sion*, 3rd edition. New York: HarperCollins, 1997.
Quinnett, Paul G. *Suicide: The Forever Decision: For Those Thinking about Sui-
    cide, and for Those Who Know, Love and Counsel Them*. New York: Cross-
    road, 1987.
Sebastian, Linda. *Overcoming Postpartum Depression and Anxiety*. Omaha, NE:
    Addicus Books, 1998.
Solomon, Andrew. *The Noonday Demon: An Atlas of Depression*. New York:
    Simon & Schuster, 2002.
Styron, William. *Darkness Visible: A Memoir of Madness*. New York: Knopf,
    1991. A vivid account of the author's experience with depression and suicidal
    thoughts.

Schizophrenia and Psychosis

National Schizophrenia Foundation
403 Seymour Avenue, Suite 202
Lansing, MI 48933
Tel.: 800-482-9534
Web site: www.nsfoundation.org
A self-help organization founded by consumers recovering from schizophrenia and
other psychotic illnesses.

Schizophrenia.com
Web site: www.schizophrenia.com
A highly informative site put together by volunteers who have schizophrenia or
who have family members with schizophrenia.

Books

Backlar, Patricia. *The Family Face of Schizophrenia: True Stories of Mental Illness
    with Practical Advice from America's Leading Experts*. Los Angeles: Tarcher,
    1995.
Mueser, Kim T., and Susan Gingerich. *Coping with Schizophrenia: A Guide for
    Families*. Oakland, CA: New Harbinger, 1994.
Torrey, E. Fuller. *Surviving Schizophrenia: A Manual for Families, Consumers,
    and Providers*, 4th edition. New York: HarperCollins, 2001.

Obsessions and Compulsions

Obsessive-Compulsive Foundation
676 State Street
New Haven, CT 06511
Tel.: 203-401-2070
Web site: www.ocfoundation.org

Books

Baer, Lee, and Judith L. Rapoport. *Getting Control: Overcoming Your Obsession and Compulsions.* New York: Plume Books, 2000.

Foa, Edna B., and Reid Wilson. *Stop Obsessing! How to Overcome Your Obsessions and Compulsions.* New York: Bantam Books, 2001.

Grayson, Jonathan. *Freedom from Obsessive-Compulsive Disorder: A Personalized Program for Living with Uncertainty.* Los Angeles: Tarcher, 2003.

Haerle, Tracy, editor. *Children with Tourette's Syndrome: A Parent's Guide.* Bethesda, MD: Woodbine House, 1992

Neziroglu, Fugen A., and Jose A. Yaryura-Tobias. *Over and Over Again: Understanding Obsessive-Compulsive Disorder.* San Francisco: Jossey-Bass, 1997.

Osborne, Ian. *Tormenting Thoughts and Secret Rituals: The Hidden Epidemic of Obsessive-Compulsive Disorder.* New York: Random House, 1999.

Rapoport, Judith. *The Boy Who Couldn't Stop Washing: The Experience and Treatment of Obsessive-Compulsive Disorder.* New York: Signet, 1991.

Trauma

National Center for PTSD
U.S. Department of Veterans Affairs
Veterans Health Administration
1120 Vermont Avenue, NW
Washington, DC 20421
Tel.: 802-296-6300
Web site: www.ncptsd.org
The Center provides a Web site full of valuable information about post-traumatic stress disorder (PTSD), not limited to combat trauma.

Books

Herman, Judith Lewis. *Trauma and Recovery: The Aftermath of Violence — From Domestic Abuse to Political Terror.* New York: Basic Books, 1993.

Monahon, Cynthia. *Children and Trauma: A Guide for Parents and Professionals.* San Francisco: Jossey-Bass, 1997.

Shay, Jonathan. *Achilles in Vietnam: Combat Trauma and the Undoing of Character.* New York: Scribner, 1995.

Personality

Books

Bockian, Neil R., with Valerie Porr and Nora Elizabeth Villagram. *New Hope for People with Borderline Personality Disorder: Your Friendly, Authoritative Guide to the Latest in Traditional and Complementary Solutions.* New York: Crown, 2002.

Hare, Robert. *Without Conscience: The Disturbing World of the Psychopaths Among Us.* New York: Guilford Press, 1999. By the psychologist who reintroduced the concept of psychopathy, a variant of antisocial personality disorder.

Kreisman, Jerold J., and Hal Straus. *I Hate You, Don't Leave Me: Understanding the Borderline Personality.* New York: HarperCollins, 1991.

Drug and Alcohol Abuse

National Institute on Alcohol Abuse and Alcoholism (NIAAA)
5635 Fishers Lane, MSC 9304
Bethesda, MD 20892-9304
Web site: www.niaaa.nih.gov
A division of the National Institutes of Health.

National Institute on Drug Abuse (NIDA)
6001 Executive Boulevard, Room 5213
Bethesda, MD 20892-9561
Tel.: 301-443-1124
Web site: www.drugabuse.gov
Also a division of the National Institutes of Health, NIDA produces a number of pamphlets designed to inform teenagers and adults about the dangers of specific drugs.

Alcoholics Anonymous (AA)
AA World Services, Inc.
P.O. Box 459
New York, NY 10163
Tel.: 212-870-3400
Web site: www.alcoholics-anonymous.org
A worldwide organization of self-help groups for achieving and maintaining sobriety. Meetings take place at a variety of times and locations, and you can call the local hotline in your phonebook to find a convenient group.

Narcotics Anonymous (NA)
NA World Services
P.O. Box 9999
Van Nuys, CA 91409

Tel.: 818-773-9999
Web site: www.na.org
A similar organization of self-help groups, for those addicted to drugs. Local
groups can be found in your phonebook.

Al-Anon
Al-Anon Family Group Headquarters, Inc.
1600 Corporate Landing Parkway
Virginia Beach, VA 23454-5617
Tel.: 888-425-2666
Web site: www.al-anon.alateen.org
An organization of self-help groups that view alcoholism as a family problem to be
treated with the twelve-step principles. Alateen groups are for teenagers coping
with alcoholism in the family. Local Al-Anon and Alateen groups can be found in
your phonebook.

Books

Alcoholics Anonymous. *Alcoholics Anonymous,* 4th edition. New York: Alcoholics
Anonymous World Services, 2001.
Alcoholics Anonymous. *Twelve Steps and Twelve Traditions.* New York: Alcohol-
ics Anonymous World Services, 1993.
Brizer, David. *Quitting Smoking for Dummies.* New York: Wiley, 2003.
Kettelhack, Guy. *Sober and Free: Making Your Recovery Work for You.* New York:
Simon & Schuster, 1995.
Mooney, Al J., Arlene Eisenberg, and Howard Eisenberg. *The Recovery Book.*
New York: Workman, 1992.
Volpicelli, Joseph, and Mala Szalavitz. *Recovery Options: The Complete Guide:
How You and Your Loved Ones Can Understand and Treat Alcohol and Other
Drug Problems.* New York: Wiley, 2000.

Body Image and Eating Problems

National Association of Anorexia Nervosa and Associated Disorders (ANAD)
P.O. Box 7
Highland Park, IL 60035
Tel.: 847-831-3438
Web site: www.anad.org

Anorexia Nervosa and Related Eating Disorders (ANRED)
P.O. Box 5102
Eugene, OR 97405
Tel.: 541-344-1144
Web site: www.anred.com

National Eating Disorders Association
603 Stewart Street, Suite 803
Seattle, WA 98101
Tel.: 206-382-3587
Web site: www.nationaleatingdisorders.org

Books

Fairburn, Christopher. *Overcoming Binge Eating.* New York: Guilford Press, 1995.
Phillips, Katharine A. *The Broken Mirror: Understanding and Treating Body Dysmorphic Disorder.* New York: Oxford University Press, 1998.
Sacherm, Ira M., and Marc A. Zimmer: *Dying to Be Thin: Understanding and Defeating Anorexia Nervosa and Bulimia.* New York: Warner Books, 1987.

Sleep and Fatigue

National Sleep Foundation
1522 K Street, NW, Suite 500
Washington, DC 20055
Tel.: 202-347-3471
Web site: www.sleepfoundation.org
Provides information about trouble sleeping and helpful tips.

CFIDS Association of America
P.O. Box 220398
Charlotte, NC 28222-0398
Tel.: 704-365-2343
Web site: www.cfids.org
Self-help organization for chronic fatigue (and "immune dysfunction") syndrome and related conditions.

Books

Berne, Katrina. *Chronic Fatigue Syndrome, Fibromyalgia, and Other Invisible Illnesses.* Berkeley, CA: Publishers Group West, 2001.
Natelson, Benjamin H. *Facing and Fighting Fatigue: A Practical Approach.* New Haven, CT: Yale University Press, 1998.

Sexual Matters

The Sexual Dysfunction Association
Windmill Place Business Center
2-4 Windmill Lane
Southall, Middlesex UB2 4NJ
United Kingdom
Tel.: 0870-7743571 (England)
Web site: www.impotence.org.uk

Sex Addicts Anonymous
P.O. Box 70949
Houston, TX 77270
Tel.: 800-477-8191
Web site: www.sexaa.org
An organization of self-help groups founded on the twelve-step principles of Alco-
holics Anonymous. The Web site includes links to other sex addiction recovery
group organizations, such as Sexaholics Anonymous.

Books

Hazelden Foundation. *Hope and Recovery: A Twelve-Step Guide for Healing from
Compulsive Sexual Behavior.* Center City, MN: Hazelden, 1989.
Westheimer, Ruth K. *Sex for Dummies: A Reference Guide for the Rest of Us.*
New York: Wiley, 2001.

Children and Adolescents

American Association on Mental Retardation
444 North Capitol Street, NW, Suite 846
Washington, DC 20001-1512
Tel.: 800-424-3688
Web site: www.aamr.org

National Dissemination Center for Children with Disabilities
U.S. Department of Education
Office of Special Education Programs (OSEP)
P.O. Box 1492
Washington, DC 20013
Tel.: 800-695-0285
Web site: www.nichcy.org
Information about learning and language disorders, autism, attention-deficit hyper-
activity disorder, and other childhood disabilities, and resource listings by state.

Autism Society of America
7910 Woodmont Avenue, Suite 300
Bethesda, MD 20814-3067
Tel.: 800-328-8476
Web site: www.autism-society.org

Children and Adults with Attention Deficit Disorder (CHADD)
8181 Professional Place, Suite 150
Landover, MD 20785
Tel.: 800-233-4050
Web site: www.chadd.org

Attention Deficit Disorder Association
P.O. Box 543
Pottstown, PA 19464
Tel.: 484-945-2101
Web site: www.add.org
For adults with symptoms of attention-deficit hyperactivity disorder (ADHD).

Books

Barkley, Russell A. *Taking Charge of ADHD: The Complete Authoritative Guide for Parents*. New York: Guilford Press, 2000.

Fowler, Mary Cahill. *Maybe You Know My Kid: A Parents' Guide: Helping Your Child with Attention Deficit Hyperactivity Disorder*. New York: Kensington, 1998.

Hallowell, Edward M., and John J. Ratey. *Driven to Distraction: Recognizing and Coping with Attention Deficit Disorder from Childhood Through Adulthood*. New York: Simon & Schuster, 1995.

Harris, Scott O., and Edward N. Reynolds. *When Growing Up Hurts Too Much: A Parents' Guide to Knowing When and How to Choose a Therapist for Your Teenager*. Lanham, MD: Lexington Books, 1990.

Koplewicz, Harold S. *It's Nobody's Fault: New Hope and Help for Difficult Children and Their Parents*. New York: Random House, 1997.

Powers, Michael D., editor. *Children with Autism: A Parents' Guide*, 2nd edition. Bethesda, MD: Woodbine House, 2000.

Prince-Hughes, Dawn. *Songs of the Gorilla Nation: My Journey Through Autism*. New York: Crown, 2004.

Williams, Donna. *Nobody Nowhere: The Extraordinary Autobiography of an Autistic*. New York: HarperCollins, 1994.

Woodrich, David L. *Attention-Deficit/Hyperactivity Disorder: What Every Parent Wants to Know*, 2nd edition. Baltimore, MD: Brookes, 1999.

The Elderly

Alzheimer's Disease Education and Referral Center
P.O. Box 8250
Silver Spring, MD 20907-8250
Tel.: 800-438-4380
Web site: www.alzheimers.org
Sponsored by the National Institute of Aging, of the National Institutes of Health.

Alzheimer's Association
225 North Michigan Avenue, Floor 17
Chicago, IL 60601
Tel.: 800-272-3900
Web site: www.alz.org

Books

Dippel, Raye Lynne, and J. Thomas Hutton, editors. *Caring for the Alzheimer Patient: A Practical Guide,* 3rd edition. Amherst, NY: Prometheus Books, 1996.

Edwards, Allen Jack. *When Memory Fails: Helping the Alzheimer's and Dementia Patient.* New York: Da Capo Press, 1994.

Gretzner, Howard. *Alzheimer's: A Caregiver's Guide and Sourcebook,* 3rd edition. New York: Wiley, 2001.

Mace, Nancy L., and Peter V. Rabins. *The 36-Hour Day: A Family Guide to Caring for People with Alzheimer's Disease, Related Dementing Illnesses, and Memory Loss in Late Life,* 3rd edition. New York: Warner Books, 2001.

Other Special Interests

National Women's Health Resource Center
157 Broad Street, Suite 315
Red Bank, NJ 07701
Tel.: 877-986-9472
Web site: www.healthywomen.org
NWHRC is an information clearinghouse for topics related to women's health, including mental illnesses that disproportionately affect women.

The National Alliance for Hispanic Health
1501 Sixteenth Street, NW
Washington, DC 20036
Tel.: 866-SU-FAMILIA (783-2645)
Web site: www.hispanichealth.org
Bilingual information helpline (Su Familia) for medical information and referrals, including for mental health.

The National Medical Association
1012 Tenth Street, NW
Washington, DC 20001
Tel.: 202-347-1895
Web site: www.nmanet.org
Advocates for African-American patients and physicians. The Web site includes a physician locator tool for referrals to African-American physicians.

National Asian American Pacific Islanders Mental Health Association
1215 Nineteenth Street, Suite A
Denver, CO 80202
Tel.: 303-298-7910
Web site: www.naapimha.org
Provides fact sheets on several major mental illnesses in Chinese, Korean, Vietnamese, Khmer, and Hmong languages.

African and Caribbean Mental Health Services (ACMHS)
Zion Community Resource
339 Stretford Road
Hulme, Manchester M15 42Y
United Kingdom
Tel.: 0161-226-9562 (England)
Web site: www.comcarenet.co.uk/eise/uselinks/afrocar.htm
For individuals of African descent seeking assistance in the United Kingdom.

Pathways to Promise
5400 Arsenal Street
St. Louis, MO 63139
Web site: www.pathways2promise.org
An interfaith organization that provides information about ministering to the mentally ill.

Parents, Families and Friends of Lesbians and Gays (PFLAG)
1726 M Street, NW, Suite 400
Washington, DC 20036
Tel.: 202-467-8180
Web site: www.pflag.org
Promotes pride and acceptance of gay, lesbian, bisexual, and transgender individuals and their families. There are PFLAG chapters and support groups throughout the U.S.

Professional Organizations

American Psychiatric Association (APA)
1000 Wilson Boulevard, Suite 1825
Arlington, VA 22209-3901
Tel.: 703-907-7300
Web site: www.psych.org
The national organization of psychiatrists' Web site provides a directory of members, information on how to choose a psychiatrist, and summaries of books about mental illness.

American Psychological Association (also known as the APA)
750 First Street, NE
Washington, DC 20002-4242
Tel.: 800-374-2721
Web site: www.apa.org
The Web site for the national organization of psychologists provides helpful information about symptoms, the psychotherapies used to treat anxiety and mood disorders, and assistance in locating psychologists in your area.

American Academy of Child and Adolescent Psychiatry
3615 Wisconsin Avenue, NW
Washington, DC 20016-3007
Tel.: 202-966-7300
Web site: www.aacap.org
The national organization for psychiatrists who have specialized in treating children and adolescents. The Web site provides a referral directory and dozens of fact sheets on childhood and adolescent conditions, in both English and Spanish.

Royal College of Psychiatrists
17 Belgrave Square
London SW1X 8PG
United Kingdom
Tel.: 020-7235-2351 (England)
Web site: www.rcpsych.ac.uk
The Web site for this British professional organization provides several fact-sheets (some written in Chinese) as well as a useful glossary of psychiatric terms and links to other British and European organizations.

Irish College of Psychiatrists
121 St. Stephen's Green
Dublin, Ireland
Tel.: 353-1-402-2346 (Ireland)
Web site: www.irishpsychiatry.com

Canadian Psychiatric Association
260-441 MacLaren Street
Ottawa, Ontario K2P-2H3
Tel.: 613-234-2815 (Canada)
Web site: www.cpa-apc.org

Royal Australian and New Zealand College of Psychiatry
309 LaTrobe Street
Melbourne, VIC 3000
Australia
Tel.: 800-337-448 (Australia)
Web site: www.ranzcp.org

Caribbean Psychiatric Association (CARPA)
3rd Avenue, Belleville
St. Michael
Barbados, West Indies
Web site: www.caribpsych.org

Professional References

The American Psychiatric Association. *Diagnostic and Statistical Manual of Mental Disorders,* 4th edition, text revision. Washington, DC: APA Press, 2000.

The DSM presents the psychiatric consensus regarding common features and required criteria for diagnosing specific psychiatric illnesses.

The American Psychiatric Association. *Practice Guidelines for the Treatment of Psychiatric Disorders,* Compendium, 2004. Washington, DC: APA Press, 2004.

The APA periodically revises and publishes guidelines, and the evidence that supports them, for the treatment of several mental illnesses.

Gelder, Michael, Juan Jose Lopez-Ibor, and Nancy Andreasen, editors. *New Oxford Textbook of Psychiatry* (in two volumes). New York: Oxford University Press Inc., 2000.

Oxford also publishes the single volume *Shorter Oxford Textbook of Psychiatry,* 4th edition. New York: Oxford University Press Inc., 2001, edited by Michael Gelder, Richard Mayou, and Philip Cowen.

Sadock, Benjamin, and Virginia Sadock. *Kaplan and Sadock's Comprehensive Textbook of Psychiatry,* 7th edition (in two volumes). Baltimore: Williams & Wilkins, 1995.

The authors also provide a more condensed *Synopsis of Psychiatry,* 9th edition. Baltimore: Williams & Wilkins, 2002.

Index